Historical Viewpoints

Historical Viewpoints

Notable Articles from
American Heritage

FIFTH EDITION

Volume Two Since 1865

Editor

JOHN A. GARRATY

Columbia University

1817

HARPER & ROW, PUBLISHERS, New York
Cambridge, Philadelphia, San Francisco, Washington,
London, Mexico City, São Paulo, Sydney

Illustration and Article Acknowledgments can be found on page 461.

Sponsoring Editor: Robert Miller
Development Editor: Mary Lou Mosher
Project Editor: Ellen Meek Tweedy
Text Design: Joan Greenfield
Cover Design: Ron Gross
Cover Photo: Seattle-King County Convention and Visitors Bureau
Photo Research: Mira Schachne/Elsa Peterson
Production Manager: Willie Lane
Compositor: ComCom Division of Haddon Craftsmen, Inc.
Printer and Binder: R. R. Donnelley & Sons Company

All articles have appeared in *American Heritage, The Magazine of History,*
some under different titles.

Historical Viewpoints: Notable Articles from *American Heritage,*
Fifth Edition, Volume Two Since 1865

Library of Congress Cataloging in Publication Data

Historical Viewpoints

   Contents: v. 1. To 1877—v. 2. Since 1865.
   1. United States—History.   I. Garraty, John
Arthur, 1920–   .   II. American Heritage.
E178.6.H67   1987   973   86–22738
ISBN 0-06-042299-8 (v. 1)
ISBN 0-06-042301-3 (v. 2)

86 87 88 89 9 8 7 6 5 4 3 2 1

Contents

Introduction

This fifth edition has been inspired by the encouraging reception afforded the four earlier editions of *Historical Viewpoints* and by the fact that interesting new articles continue to appear in *American Heritage.* This edition contains six new essays. I have included these new selections because they seemed better suited to current historical interests and they present fresh points of view.

There are almost as many kinds of history as there are historians. In addition to the differences between political history and the social, economic, and cultural varieties, the discipline lends itself to such classifications as analytical, narrative, statistical, impressionistic, local, comparative, philosophical, and synthetic. Often the distinctions between one and another kind of history are overemphasized. No one can write good political history without some consideration of social, economic, and cultural questions; narrative history requires analysis to be meaningful; impressionistic treatments of past events are, in a way, statistical histories based on very tiny samples. Nevertheless, the different types exist and serve different purposes. Each focuses on part of the total human experience and sees it from a particular perspective; each, when well done, adds its own contribution to the total record.

It is therefore foolish to argue that any one historical approach is inherently better than all the others. Some are perhaps more generally useful (that is, more interesting to a wider segment of the population) or more suggestive at a particular time and place than others, but the distinctions are like those between a miniature and a mural, a sonnet and an epic poem. No one would suggest that "The Moonlight Sonata" was a waste of Beethoven's time because he was capable of producing the *Choral* symphony, or that Mozart should not have written "Eine Kleine Nachtmusik" because he had within him *Don Giovanni.* In the same way a monograph or an article of twenty pages can be as well worth doing and as satisfying to read as Edward Gibbon's *Decline and Fall of the Roman Empire.*

The most useless and confusing distinction commonly drawn between varieties of history is that separating "scholarly" from "popular" history. These terms came into existence during the latter half of the nineteenth century. Before that time, all history was popular in the sense that those who wrote it, viewing themselves as possessors of special information acquired through scholarship or through having observed firsthand the events they described, aimed to transmit that knowledge to anyone interested in the subject. But when history became "scientific" and professionalized, historians began to write primarily for other historians. They assumed that nonspecialists had no interest in their work or were incapable of understanding it, and even argued that to write history for the general reader was to prostitute one's talents. Therefore, although with many notable exceptions, the best-trained and most intelligent historians tended to forswear the task of transmitting their scholarly findings to ordinary readers.

Of course popular history continued to be written and read, but most of it was produced by amateurs. Its quality varied greatly. The scholarly prejudice against "popularizers" had a solid basis in fact. Too often popular history was—and still is—shallow, error-ridden, out of date before publication, a mere rehash of already written books, an exasperating mixture, as one critic has said, of "something we all knew before" and "something which is not so." Much of it was written by journalists and novelists who often lacked the patience, the professional skills, and the knowledge of sources that are as necessary for the writing of good history as narrative power, imagination, and lucidity of style.

It was chiefly with the hope of encouraging professional historians to broaden their perspectives that, beginning in the 1930s, a group of historians led by Professor Allan Nevins of Columbia University began to think of founding a general circulation magazine of American history. Their aim was a magazine in which solidly researched and significant articles would be presented in a way that would interest and educate readers who were not professional students of the past. Nevins himself, one of the great historians of the twentieth century, epitomized the combination they sought to produce. He was a prodigious scholar, author of dozens of learned volumes, and trainer of literally hundreds of graduate students, but he was also a fluent and graceful writer whose work was widely read and appreciated. Nevins's books won Pulitzer Prizes as well as academic renown.

The example provided by Nevins and a few other outstanding historians of his generation, such as Samuel Eliot Morison, undoubtedly influenced the gradual revival of concern for popular history that has occurred in recent times on the part of professional academic scholars. So did the increasing sophistication of the general reading public, which made it less difficult for these experts to write this type of history without sacrificing their intellectual standards. In any case, in 1954 the Nevins group—the Society of American Historians—

joined the American Association for State and Local History in sponsoring the hardcover magazine they had envisioned: *American Heritage.*

The success of *American Heritage* was rapid and substantial. It
achieved a wide circulation, and the best professional historians began
to publish in its pages. Its articles, at their best, have been authoritative, interesting, significant, and a pleasure to read. They have ranged
over the whole course of American history from the pre-colonial era
to the present, and have dealt with every aspect of American development from politics to painting and from economics to architecture.

The present selection from among the hundreds of essays and
book excerpts that have appeared in *American Heritage* since 1954 does
not pretend to offer "the best" of these articles, although any such
collection would undoubtedly include many of those I have chosen. It
seeks rather to provide a balanced assortment of articles to supple-
ment and enrich general college courses in American history. Keeping
in mind the structure of these courses and the topics they tend to
emphasize, I have reprinted here articles which, in my opinion, will add
depth and breadth to the student's understanding.

This is—by definition—popular history, but it is also history written
by experts. The articles differ in purpose and approach. Some present
new findings, some reexamine old questions from a fresh point of view,
others magisterially distill and synthesize masses of facts and ideas.
From the total, readers may extract, along with the specifics of the
individual essays, a sense of the variety and richness of historical literature. They will observe how forty-odd historians (and not all of them
academic scholars) have faced the task of presenting knowledge not to
other historians alone but to an audience of intelligent and interested
general readers.

Since most of the students enrolled in college history courses are
not specialists—even those who intend to become professional historians stand at the very beginning of their training—this approach seems
to me ideally adapted to their needs. Many, though by no means all,
of the subjects treated in these essays have also been covered in articles
in professional historical periodicals, often written by the same historians. But as here presented, without sacrifice of intellectual standards,
the material is not so much easier to grasp as it is more meaningful.
Details are clearly related to larger issues; historical characters are
delineated in the round, not presented as stick figures or automations;
too much previous knowledge is not assumed. I once read the draft of
an essay on the history of the Arabs which contained the sentence,
"The life and philosophy of Mohammed are well-known," and which
then went on to other less universally understood topics. Such essays
no doubt have their place, but that place is not in collections designed
for beginners, whatever the subject.

Finally, I believe that at least some of the essays I have included here illustrate the truth that history is, at its best, an art as well as a science. After all, the ancients gave history its own Muse, Clio. I hope and expect that students, from reading the following pages, will come to realize that history is a form of literature, that it can be *enjoyed,* not merely assimilated. Even those who see college history courses exclusively as training grounds for future professionals surely will not object if their students enjoy these readings while they learn.

Needless to say, I hope this book will serve even better than its predecessors the needs and interests of students of American history.

John A. Garraty

Historical Viewpoints

Part One

Reconstruction and Race Relations

In this 1897 photograph a black woman with her child and dog watches her husband, cane in hand, leave for work.

Why They Impeached
Andrew Johnson

DAVID HERBERT DONALD

The story of presidential Reconstruction after Lincoln is told in this essay by David Herbert Donald, Charles Warren Professor of American History at Harvard University. Lincoln's approach to restoring the Union was cautious, practical, thoughtful—humane in every sense of the word. Because of his assassination, however, the evaluation of his policy has to be a study in the might-have-beens of history. The Reconstruction policy of his successor, Andrew Johnson, superficially similar to Lincoln's, was reckless, impractical, emotional, and politically absurd. While historians have differed in evaluating his purposes, they have agreed unanimously that his management of the problem was inept and that his policy was a total failure.

Professor Donald's essay provides an extended character study of Johnson, and it is not an attractive portrait. Donald believes that Johnson "threw away a magnificent opportunity" to smoothly and speedily return the Confederate states to a harmonious place in the Union. But he also shows how difficult Johnson's task was and to how great an extent southern white opinion was set against the full acceptance of black equality. Donald is the author of many books, including a Pulitzer Prize-winning biography of the Massachusetts senator, Charles Sumner. ∎

Reconstruction after the Civil War posed some of the most discouraging problems that have ever faced American statesmen. The South was prostrate. Its defeated soldiers straggled homeward through a countryside desolated by war. Southern soil was untilled and exhausted; southern factories and railroads were worn out. The four billion dollars of southern capital invested in Negro slaves was wiped out by advancing Union armies, "the most stupendous act of sequestration in the history of Anglo-American jurisprudence." The white inhabitants of eleven states had somehow to be reclaimed from rebellion and restored to a firm loyalty to the United States. Their four million former slaves had simultaneously to be guided into a proper use of their new-found freedom.

For the victorious Union government there was no time for reflection. Immediate decisions had to be made. Thousands of destitute whites and Negroes had to be fed before long-range plans of rebuilding the southern economy could be drafted. Some kind of government had to be established in these former Confederate states, to preserve order and to direct the work of restoration.

A score of intricate questions must be answered: Should the defeated southerners be punished or pardoned? How should genuinely loyal southern Unionists be rewarded? What was to be the social, economic, and political status of the now free Negroes? What civil rights did they have? Ought they to have the ballot? Should they be given a freehold of property? Was Reconstruction to be controlled by the national government, or should the southern states work out their own salvation? If the federal government supervised the process, should the President or the Congress be in control?

Intricate as were the problems, in early April, 1865, they did not seem insuperable. President Abraham Lincoln was winning the peace as he had already won the war. He was careful to keep every detail of Reconstruction in his own hands; unwilling to be committed to any "exclusive, and inflexible plan," he was working out a pragmatic program of restoration not, perhaps, entirely satisfactory to any group, but reasonably acceptable to all sections. With his enormous prestige as commander of the victorious North and as victor in the 1864 election, he was able to promise freedom to the Negro, charity to the southern white, security to the North.

The blighting of these auspicious beginnings is one of the saddest stories in American history. The reconciliation of the sections, which seemed so imminent in 1865, was delayed for more than ten years. Northern magnanimity toward a fallen foe curdled into bitter distrust. Southern whites rejected moderate leaders, and inveterate racists spoke for the new South. The Negro, after serving as a political pawn

for a decade, was relegated to a second-class citizenship, from which
he is yet struggling to emerge. Rarely has democratic government so
completely failed as during the Reconstruction decade.

The responsibility for this collapse of American statesmanship is,
of course, complex. History is not a tale of deep-dyed villains or pure-
as-snow heroes. Part of the blame must fall upon ex-Confederates who
refused to recognize that the war was over; part upon freedmen who
confused liberty with license and the ballot box with the lunch pail;
part upon northern antislavery extremists who identified patriotism
with loyalty to the Republican party; part upon the land speculators,
treasury grafters, and railroad promoters who were unwilling to have
a genuine peace lest it end their looting of the public till.

Yet these divisive forces were not bound to triumph. Their success
was due to the failure of constructive statesmanship that could channel
the magnanimous feelings shared by most Americans into a positive
program of reconstruction. President Andrew Johnson was called
upon for positive leadership, and he did not meet the challenge.

Andrew Johnson's greatest weakness was his insensitivity to public
opinion. In contrast to Lincoln, who said, "Public opinion in this
country is everything," Johnson made a career of battling the popular
will. A poor white, a runaway tailor's apprentice, a self-educated
Tennessee politician, Johnson was a living defiance to the dominant
southern belief that leadership belonged to the plantation aristocracy.

As senator from Tennessee, he defied the sentiment of his section
in 1861 and refused to join the secessionist movement. When Lincoln
later appointed him military governor of occupied Tennessee, Johnson found Nashville "a furnace of treason," but he braved social ostra-
cism and threats of assassination and discharged his duties with boldness and efficiency.

Such a man was temperamentally unable to understand the northern mood in 1865, much less to yield to it. For four years the northern
people had been whipped into wartime frenzy by propaganda tales of
Confederate atrocities. The assassination of Lincoln by a southern
sympathizer confirmed their belief in southern brutality and heartless-
ness. Few northerners felt vindictive toward the South, but most felt
that the rebellion they had crushed must never rise again. Johnson
ignored this postwar psychosis gripping the North and plunged ahead
with his program of rapidly restoring the southern states to the Union.
In May, 1865, without any previous preparation of public opinion, he
issued a proclamation of amnesty, granting forgiveness to nearly all
the millions of former rebels and welcoming them back into peaceful
fraternity. Some few Confederate leaders were excluded from his general amnesty, but even they could secure pardon by special petition.
For weeks the White House corridors were thronged with ex-Confed-

erate statesmen and former southern generals who daily received presidential forgiveness.

Ignoring public opinion by pardoning the former Confederates, Johnson actually entrusted the formation of new governments in the South to them. The provisional governments established by the President proceeded, with a good deal of reluctance, to rescind their secession ordinances, to abolish slavery, and to repudiate the Confederate debt. Then, with far more enthusiasm, they turned to electing governors, representatives, and senators. By December, 1865, the southern states had their delegations in Washington waiting for admission by Congress. Alexander H. Stephens, once vice president of the Confederacy, was chosen senator from Georgia; not one of the North Carolina delegation could take a loyalty oath; and all of South Carolina's congressmen had "either held office under the Confederate States, or been in the army, or countenanced in some way the Rebellion."

Johnson himself was appalled, "There seems in many of the elections something like defiance, which is all out of place at this time." Yet on December 5 he strongly urged the Congress to seat these southern representatives "and thereby complete the work of reconstruction." But the southern states were omitted from the roll call.

Such open defiance of northern opinion was dangerous under the best of circumstances, but in Johnson's case it was little more than suicidal. The President seemed not to realize the weakness of his position. He was the representative of no major interest and had no genuine political following. He had been considered for the vice presidency in 1864 because, as a southerner and a former slaveholder, he could lend plausibility to the Republican pretension that the old parties were dead and that Lincoln was the nominee of a new, nonsectional National Union party.

A political accident, the new Vice President did little to endear himself to his countrymen. At Lincoln's second inauguration Johnson appeared before the Senate in an obviously inebriated state and made a long, intemperate harangue about his plebeian origins and his hard-won success. President, Cabinet, and senators were humiliated by the shameful display, and Charles Sumner felt that "the Senate should call upon him to resign." Historians now know that Andrew Johnson was not a heavy drinker. At the time of his inaugural display, he was just recovering from a severe attack of typhoid fever. Feeling ill just before he entered the Senate chamber, he asked for some liquor to steady his nerves, and either his weakened condition or abnormal sensitivity to alcohol betrayed him.

Lincoln reassured Republicans who were worried over the affair: "I have known Andy for many years; he made a bad slip the other day, but you need not be scared. Andy ain't a drunkard." Never again was

Andrew Johnson seen under the influence of alcohol, but his reformation came too late. His performance on March 4, 1865, seriously undermined his political usefulness and permitted his opponents to discredit him as a pothouse politician. Johnson was catapulted into the presidency by John Wilkes Booth's bullet. From the outset his position was weak, but it was not necessarily untenable. The President's chronic lack of discretion made it so. Where common sense dictated that a chief executive in so disadvantageous a position should act with great caution, Johnson proceeded to imitate Old Hickory, Andrew Jackson, his political idol. If Congress crossed his will, he did not hesitate to defy it. Was he not "the Tribune of the People"?

Sure of his rectitude, Johnson was indifferent to prudence. He never learned that the President of the United States cannot afford to be a quarreler. Apprenticed in the rough-and-tumble politics of frontier Tennessee, where orators exchanged violent personalities, crude humor, and bitter denunciations, Johnson continued to make stump speeches from the White House. All too often he spoke extemporaneously, and he permitted hecklers in his audience to draw from him angry charges against his critics.

On Washington's birthday in 1866, against the advice of his more sober advisers, the President made an impromptu address to justify his Reconstruction policy. "I fought traitors and treason in the South," he told the crowd; "now when I turn around, and at the other end of the line find men—I care not by what name you call them—who will stand opposed to the restoration of the Union of these States, I am free to say to you that I am still in the field."

During the "great applause" which followed, a nameless voice shouted, "Give us the names at the other end. . . . Who are they?"

"You ask me who they are," Johnson retorted. "I say Thaddeus Stevens of Pennsylvania is one; I say Mr. Sumner is another; and Wendell Phillips is another." Applause urged him to continue. "Are those who want to destroy our institutions . . . not satisfied with the blood that has been shed? . . . Does not the blood of Lincoln appease the vengeance and wrath of the opponents of this government?"

The President's remarks were as untrue as they were impolitic. Not only was it manifestly false to assert that the leading Republican in the House and the most conspicuous Republican in the Senate were opposed to "the fundamental principles of this government" or that they had been responsible for Lincoln's assassination; it was incredible political folly to impute such actions to men with whom the President had to work daily. But Andrew Johnson never learned that the President of the United States must function as a party leader.

There was a temperamental coldness about this plain-featured, grave man that kept him from easy, intimate relations with even his

A Harper's Weekly *cartoon depicts Johnson (left) and Thaddeus Stevens as engineers committed to a collision course.*

political supporters. His massive head, dark, luxuriant hair, deep-set and piercing eyes, and cleft square chin seemed to Charles Dickens to indicate "courage, watchfulness, and certainly strength of purpose," but his was a grim face, with "no genial sunlight in it." The coldness and reserve that marked Johnson's public associations doubtless stemmed from a deep-seated feeling of insecurity; this self-educated tailor whose wife had taught him how to write could never expose himself by letting down his guard and relaxing.

Johnson knew none of the arts of managing men, and he seemed unaware that face-saving is important for a politician. When he became President, Johnson was besieged by advisers of all political complexions. To each he listened gravely and non-committally, raising no questions and by his silence seeming to give consent. With Radical Senator Sumner, already intent upon giving the freedmen both homesteads and the ballot, he had repeated interviews during the first month of his presidency. "His manner has been excellent, & even sympathetic," Sumner reported triumphantly. With Chief Justice Salmon P. Chase, Sumner urged Johnson to support immediate Negro suffrage and found the President was "well-disposed, & sees the rights & necessities of the case." In the middle of May, 1865, Sumner reassured a Republican caucus that the President was a true Radical; he had listened repeatedly to the Senator and had told him "there is no difference between us." Before the end of the month the rug was

pulled from under Sumner's feet. Johnson issued his proclamation for
the reconstruction of North Carolina, making no provisions for Negro
suffrage. Sumner first learned about it through the newspapers.

While he was making up his mind, Johnson appeared silently receptive to all ideas; when he had made a decision, his mind was immovably
closed, and he defended his course with all the obstinacy of a weak
man. In December, alarmed by Johnson's Reconstruction proclama-
tions, Sumner again sought an interview with the President. "No
longer sympathetic, or even kindly," Sumner found, "he was harsh,
petulant, and unreasonable." The Senator was depressed by Johnson's
"prejudice, ignorance, and perversity" on the Negro suffrage issue.
Far from listening amiably to Sumner's argument that the South was
still torn by violence and not yet ready for readmission, Johnson attacked him with cheap analogies. "Are there no murders in Massachusetts?" the President asked.

"Unhappily yes," Sumner replied, "sometimes."

"Are there no assaults in Boston? Do not men there sometimes
knock each other down, so that the police is obliged to interfere?"

"Unhappily yes."

"Would you consent that Massachusetts, on this account, should be
excluded from Congress?" Johnson triumphantly queried. In the excitement the President unconsciously used Sumner's hat, which the
Senator had placed on the floor beside his chair, as a spittoon!

Had Johnson been as resolute in action as he was in argument, he
might conceivably have carried much of his party with him on his
Reconstruction program. Promptness, publicity, and persuasion could
have created a presidential following. Instead Johnson boggled.
Though he talked boastfully of "kicking out" officers who failed to
support his plan, he was slow to act. His own Cabinet, from the very
beginning, contained members who disagreed with him, and his secretary of war, Edwin M. Stanton, was openly in league with the Republican elements most hostile to the President. For more than two years
he impotently hoped that Stanton would resign; then in 1867, after
Congress had passed the Tenure of Office Act, he tried to oust the
Secretary. This belated firmness, against the letter of the law, led
directly to Johnson's impeachment trial.

Instead of working with his party leaders and building up political
support among Republicans, Johnson in 1866 undertook to organize
his friends into a new party. In August a convention of white southerners, northern Democrats, moderate Republicans, and presidential appointees assembled in Philadelphia to endorse Johnson's policy.
Union General Darius Couch of Massachusetts marched arm in arm
down the convention aisle with Governor James L. Orr of South Carolina, to symbolize the states reunited under Johnson's rule. The con-

JOHNSON'S LOVE FOR THE SOLDIER.

This cartoon is an example of the virulence of the attacks on Johnson by his enemies.

vention produced fervid oratory, a dignified statement of principles—but not much else. Like most third-party reformist movements it lacked local support and grass-roots organization.

Johnson himself was unable to breathe life into his stillborn third party. Deciding to take his case to the people, he accepted an invitation to speak at a great Chicago memorial honoring Stephen A. Douglas. When his special train left Washington on August 28 for a "swing around the circle," the President was accompanied by a few Cabinet members who shared his views and by the war heroes Grant and Farragut.

At first all went well. There were some calculated political snubs to the President, but he managed at Philadelphia, New York, and Albany to present his ideas soberly and cogently to the people. But Johnson's friends were worried lest his tongue again get out of control. "In all frankness," a senator wrote him, do not "allow the excitement of the moment to draw from you any *extemporaneous speeches.*"

At St. Louis, when a Radical voice shouted that Johnson was a "Judas," the President flamed up in rage. "There was a Judas and he was one of the twelve apostles," he retorted. ". . . The twelve apostles had a Christ. . . . If I have played the Judas, who has been my Christ that I have played the Judas with? Was it Thad Stevens? Was it Wendell Phillips? Was it Charles Sumner?" Over mingled hisses and applause, he shouted, "These are the men that stop and compare themselves with the Saviour; and everybody that differs with them . . . is to be denounced as a Judas."

Johnson had played into his enemies' hands. His Radical foes denounced him as a "trickster," a "culprit," a man "touched with insanity, corrupted with lust, stimulated with drink." More serious in consequence was the reaction of northern moderates, such as James Russell Lowell, who wrote, "What an anti-Johnson lecturer we have in Johnson! Sumner has been right about the *cuss* from the first. . . ." The fall elections were an overwhelming repudiation of the President and his Reconstruction policy.

Johnson's want of political sagacity strengthened the very elements in the Republican party which he most feared. In 1865 the Republicans had no clearly defined attitude toward Reconstruction. Moderates like Gideon Welles and Orville Browning wanted to see the southern states restored with a minimum of restrictions; Radicals like Sumner and Stevens demanded that the entire southern social system be revolutionized. Some Republicans were passionately concerned with the plight of the freedmen; others were more interested in maintaining the high tariff and land grant legislation enacted during the war. Many thought mostly of keeping themselves in office, and many genuinely believed, with Sumner, that "the Republican party, in its objects, is identical with country and with mankind." These diverse elements came slowly to adopt the idea of harsh Reconstruction, but Johnson's stubborn persistency in his policy left them no alternative. Every step the President took seemed to provide "a new encouragement to (1) the rebels at the South, (2) the Democrats at the North and (3) the discontented elements everywhere." Not many Republicans would agree with Sumner that Johnson's program was "a defiance to God and Truth," but there was genuine concern that the victory won by the war was being frittered away.

The provisional governments established by the President in the South seemed to be dubiously loyal. They were reluctant to rescind their secession ordinances and to repudiate the Confederate debt, and they chose high-ranking ex-Confederates to represent them in Congress. Northerners were even more alarmed when these southern governments began to legislate upon the Negro's civil rights. Some laws were necessary—in order to give former slaves the right to marry, to hold property, to sue and be sued, and the like—but the Johnson legislatures went far beyond these immediate needs. South Carolina, for example, enacted that no Negro could pursue the trade "of an artisan, mechanic, or shopkeeper, or any other trade or employment besides that of husbandry" without a special license. Alabama provided that "any stubborn or refractory servants" or "servants who loiter away their time" should be fined $50 and, if they could not pay, be hired out for six months' labor. Mississippi ordered that every Negro under eighteen years of age who was an orphan or not supported by his parents must be apprenticed to some white person, preferably the former owner of the slave. Such southern laws indicated a determination to keep the Negro in a state of peonage.

It was impossible to expect a newly emancipated race to be content with such a limping freedom. The thousands of Negroes who had served in the Union armies and had helped conquer their former Confederate masters were not willing to abandon their new-found liberty. In rural areas southern whites kept these Negroes under control through the Ku Klux Klan. But in southern cities white hegemony was less secure, and racial friction erupted in mob violence. In May, 1866, a quarrel between a Memphis Negro and a white teamster led to a riot in which the city police and the poor whites raided the Negro quarters and burned and killed promiscuously. Far more serious was the disturbance in New Orleans two months later. The Republican party in Louisiana was split into pro-Johnson conservatives and Negro suffrage advocates. The latter group determined to hold a constitutional convention, of dubious legality, in New Orleans, in order to secure the ballot for the freedmen and the offices for themselves. Through imbecility in the War Department, the Federal troops occupying the city were left without orders, and the mayor of New Orleans, strongly opposed to Negro equality, had the responsibility for preserving order. There were acts of provocation on both sides, and finally, on July 30, a procession of Negroes marching toward the convention hall was attacked.

"A shot was fired . . . by a policeman, or some colored man in the procession," General Philip Sheridan reported. "This led to other shots, and a rush after the procession. On arrival at the front of the Institute [where the convention met], there was some throwing of brick-bats by both sides. The police . . . were vigorously marched to the scene of disorder. The procession entered the Institute with the flag, about six or eight remaining outside. A row occurred between a policeman and one of these colored men, and a shot was again fired by one of the parties, which led to an indiscriminate firing on the building, through the windows, by the policemen.

"This had been going on for a short time, when a white flag was displayed from the windows of the Institute, whereupon the firing ceased and the police rushed into the building. . . . The policemen opened an indiscriminate fire upon the audience until they had emptied their revolvers, when they retired, and those inside barricaded the doors. The door was broken in, and the firing again commenced when many of the colored and white people either escaped out of the door, or were passed out by the policemen inside, but as they came out, the policemen who formed the circle nearest the building fired upon them, and they were again fired upon by the citizens that formed the outer circle."

Thirty-seven Negroes and three of their white friends were killed; 119 Negroes and seventeen of their white sympathizers were wounded. Of their assailants, ten were wounded and but one killed. President Johnson was, of course, horrified by these outbreaks, but the Memphis and New Orleans riots, together with the Black Codes, afforded a devastating illustration of how the President's policy actually operated. The southern states, it was clear, were not going to protect the Negroes' basic rights. They were only grudgingly going to accept the results of the war. Yet, with Johnson's blessing, these same states were expecting a stronger voice in Congress than ever. Before 1860, southern representation in Congress had been based upon the white population plus three fifths of the slaves; now the Negroes, though not permitted to vote, were to be counted like all other citizens, and southern states would be entitled to at least nine additional congressmen. Joining with the northern Copperheads, the southerners could easily regain at the next presidential election all that had been lost on the Civil War battlefield.

It was this political exigency, not misguided sentimentality nor vindictiveness, which united Republicans in opposition to the President.

Johnson's defenders have pictured Radical Reconstruction as the work of a fanatical minority, led by Sumner and Stevens, who drove their reluctant colleagues into adopting coercive measures against the South. In fact, every major piece of Radical legislation was adopted by the nearly unanimous vote of the entire Republican membership of Congress. Andrew Johnson had left them no other choice. Because he insisted upon rushing Confederate-dominated states back into the Union, Republicans moved to disqualify Confederate leaders under the Fourteenth Amendment. When, through Johnson's urging, the southern states rejected that amendment, the Republicans in Congress unwillingly came to see Negro suffrage as the only counterweight against Democratic majorities in the South. With the Reconstruction Acts of 1867 the way was open for a true Radical program toward the South, harsh and thorough.

Andrew Johnson became a cipher in the White House, futilely disapproving bills which were promptly passed over his veto. Through his failure to reckon with public opinion, his unwillingness to recognize his weak position, his inability to function as a party leader, he had sacrificed all influence with the party which had elected him and had turned over its control to Radicals vindictively opposed to his policies. In March, 1868, Andrew Johnson was summoned before the Senate of the United States to be tried on eleven accusations of high crimes and misdemeanors. By a narrow margin the Senate failed to convict him, and historians have dismissed the charges as flimsy and false. Yet perhaps before the bar of history itself Andrew Johnson must be impeached with an even graver charge—that through political ineptitude he threw away a magnificent opportunity.

Ride-in: A Century of Protest Begins

ALAN F. WESTIN

*The last quarter of the nineteenth century—after the federal govern-
ment relaxed its pressure on the southern states to deal fairly with their
black citizens—has been called "the nadir" of the history of black
Americans after emancipation. Some historians argue that the low
point came somewhat later, during the early twentieth century, but few
would disagree with the thesis that the period in question was indeed
disastrous for American blacks. Although never really treated decently
(in the North as well as in the South), they had made important gains
during Reconstruction; the Fourteenth and Fifteenth Amendments
"guaranteed" their political and civil rights, and Congress passed stiff
laws protecting these rights, including the Civil Rights Act of 1875,
which outlawed discrimination in places of public accommodation.*

*After the so-called Compromise of 1877, however, these gains were
gradually stripped away by a combination of southern pressure, northern indifference, and a series of crippling legal interpretations by the
Supreme Court. In this essay Professor Alan F. Westin of Columbia
University, an expert on constitutional history, describes one of the
first and most significant of the Supreme Court decisions of the era,
one which emasculated the Civil Rights Act of 1875. His story reads
in some ways like an account of the civil rights struggles of the 1950s
and 1960s, but with the terrible difference that freedom and justice
were in this instance the losers, not the winners of the fight.* ∎

It began one day early in January when a Negro named Robert Fox stepped aboard a streetcar in Louisville, Kentucky, dropped his coin into the fare box, and sat down in the white section of the car. Ordered to move, he refused, and the driver threw him off the car. Shortly after, Fox filed a charge of assault and battery against the streetcar company in the federal district court, claiming that separate seating policies were illegal and the driver's actions were therefore improper. The district judge instructed the jury that under federal law common carriers must serve all passengers equally without regard to race. So instructed, the jury found the company rules to be invalid and awarded damages of fifteen dollars (plus $72.80 in legal costs) to Mr. Fox.

Immediately there was sharp criticism of the Fox decision from the city and state administrations, both Democratic; the company defied the court's ruling and continued segregated seating. After several meetings with local federal officials and white attorneys co-operating with them, Louisville Negro leaders decided to launch a full-scale "ride-in." At 7 P.M. on May 12, a young Negro boy boarded a streetcar near the Willard Hotel, walked past the driver, and took a seat among the white passengers. The driver, under new company regulations, did not attempt to throw him off but simply stopped the car, lit a cigar, and refused to proceed until the Negro moved to "his place." While the governor, the Louisville chief of police, and other prominent citizens looked on from the sidewalks, a large crowd which included an increasingly noisy mob of jeering white teen-agers gathered around the streetcar.

Before long, there were shouts of "Put him out!" "Hit him!" "Kick him!" "Hang him!" Several white youths climbed into the car and began yelling insults in the face of the young Negro rider. He refused to answer—or to move. The youths dragged him from his seat, pulled him off the car, and began to beat him. Only when the Negro started to defend himself did the city police intervene: they arrested him for disturbing the peace and took him to jail.

This time the trial was held in Louisville city court, not the federal court. The magistrate ruled that streetcar companies were not under any obligation to treat Negroes exactly as they treated whites, and that any federal measures purporting to create such obligations would be "clearly invalid" under the constitutions of Kentucky and the United States. The defendant was fined, and the judge delivered a warning to Louisville Negroes that further ride-ins would be punished.

But the ride-in campaign was not halted that easily. In the following days, streetcar after streetcar was entered by Negroes who took seats in the white section. Now the drivers got off the cars entirely. On several occasions, the Negro riders drove the cars themselves, to the sound of cheers from Negro spectators. Then violence erupted. Bands of white youths and men began to throw Negro riders off the cars: windows were broken, cars were overturned, and for a time a general race riot threatened. Moderate Kentucky newspapers and many community leaders deplored the fighting; the Republican candidate for governor denounced the streetcar company's segregation policies and blamed the violence on Democratic encouragement of white extremists.

By this time, newspapers across the country were carrying reports of the conflict, and many editorials denounced the seating regulations. In Louisville, federal marshals and the United States attorney backed the rights of the Negro riders and stated that federal court action would be taken if necessary. There were even rumors that the President might send troops.

Under these threats, the streetcar company capitulated. Soon, all the city transit companies declared that "it was useless to try to resist or evade the enforcement by the United States authorities of the claim of Negroes to ride in the cars." To "avoid serious collisions," the company would thereafter allow all passengers to sit where they chose. Although a few disturbances took place in the following months, and some white intransigents boycotted the streetcars, mixed seating became a common practice. The Kentucky press soon pointed with pride to the spirit of conciliation and harmony which prevailed in travel facilities within the city, calling it a model for good race relations. Never again would Louisville streetcars be segregated.

The event may have a familiar ring, but it should not, for it occurred almost one hundred years ago, in 1871. The streetcars were horse-drawn. The President who considered ordering troops to Louisville was ex-General Grant, not ex-General Eisenhower. The Republican gubernatorial candidate who supported the Negro riders, John Marshall Harlan, was not a post-World War II leader of the G.O.P. but a former slaveholder from one of Kentucky's oldest and most famous political families. And the "new" Negroes who waged this ride-in were not members of the Congress of Racial Equality and the National Association for the Advancement of Colored People, or followers of Dr. Martin Luther King, but former slaves who were fighting for civil rights in their own time, and with widespread success.

And yet these dramatic sit-ins, ride-ins, and walk-ins of the 1870's are almost unknown to the American public today. The standard American histories do not mention them, providing only thumbnail references to "bayonet-enforced" racial contacts during Reconstruction. Most commentators view the Negro's resort to direct action as an invention of the last decade. Clearly, then, it is time that the civil-rights struggle of the 1870's and 1880's was rescued from newspaper files and court archives, not only because it is historically important but also because it has compelling relevance for our own era.

Contrary to common assumptions today, no state in the Union during the 1870's, including those south of the Mason-Dixon line, required separation of whites and Negroes in places of public accommodation. Admission and arrangement policies were up to individual owners. In the North and West, many theatres, hotels, restaurants, and public carriers served Negro patrons without hesitation or discrimination. Some accepted Negroes only in second-class accommodations, such as smoking cars on railroads or balconies in theatres, where they sat among whites who did not have first-class tickets. Other northern and western establishments, especially the more exclusive ones, refused Negro patronage entirely.

The situation was similar in the large cities of the southern and border states. Many establishments admitted Negroes to second-class facilities. Some gave first-class service to those of privileged social status—government officials, army officers, newspapermen, and clergymen. On the other hand, many places of public accommodation, particularly in the rural areas and smaller cities of the South, were closed to Negroes whatever their wealth or status.

From 1865 through the early 1880's, the general trend in the nation was toward wider acceptance of Negro patronage. The federal Civil Rights Act of 1866, with its guarantee to Negroes of "equal benefit of the laws," had set off a flurry of enforcement suits—for denying berths to Negroes on a Washington-New York train; for refusing to sell theatre tickets to Negroes in Boston; and for barring Negro women from the waiting rooms and parlor cars of railroads in Virginia, Illinois, and California. Ratification of the Fourteenth Amendment in 1868 had spurred more challenges. Three northern states, and two southern states under Reconstruction regimes, passed laws making it a crime for owners of public-accommodation businesses to discriminate. Most state and federal court rulings on these laws between 1865 and 1880 held in favor of Negro rights, and the rulings built up a steady pressure on owners to relax racial bars.

Nevertheless, instances of exclusion and segregation continued throughout the 1870's. To settle the issue once and for all (thereby reaping the lasting appreciation of the Negro voters), congressional Republicans led by Senator Charles Sumner pressed for a federal statute making discrimination in public accommodations a crime. Democrats and conservative Republicans warned in the congressional debates that such a law would trespass on the reserved powers of the

An 1875 Harper's Weekly *cartoon bore the caption, "Shall We Withdraw Our Troops?"*

states and reminded the Sumner supporters that recent Supreme Court decisions had taken a narrow view of federal power under the Civil War amendments.

After a series of legislative compromises, however, Sumner's forces were able to enact the statute; on March 1, 1875, "An Act to Protect all Citizens in their Civil and Legal Rights" went into effect. "It is essential to just government," the preamble stated, that the nation "recognize the equality of all men before the law, and . . . it is the duty of government in its dealings with the people to mete out equal and exact justice to all, of whatever nativity, race, color, or persuasion, religious or political . . ."

Section 1 of the act declared that "All persons within the jurisdiction of the United States shall be entitled to the full and equal enjoyment of the accommodations . . . of inns, public conveyances on land or water, theaters and other places of public amusement; subject only to the conditions and limitations established by law, and applicable alike to citizens of every race or color. . . ." Section 2 provided that any person violating the act could be sued in federal district court for a penalty of $500, could be fined $500 to $1,000, or could be imprisoned from thirty days to one year. (A separate section forbade racial discrimination in the selection of juries.)

Cartoonist Thomas Nast mocked the provision of the Civil Rights Act of 1875 that allowed blacks to collect $500 from those who barred them from places of public accommodation.

Reaction to the law was swift. Two Negro men were admitted to the dress circle of Macauley's Theatre in Louisville and sat through the performance without incident. In Washington, Negroes were served for the first time at the bar of the Willard Hotel, and a Negro broke the color line when he was seated at McVicker's Theatre in Chicago. But in other instances, Negroes were rejected despite "Sumner's law." Several hotels in Chattanooga turned in their licenses, became private boardinghouses, and accepted whites only. Restaurants and barber shops in Richmond turned away Negro customers.

Suits challenging refusals were filed en masse throughout the country. Perhaps a hundred were decided in the federal district courts during the late 1870's and early 1880's. Federal judges in Pennsylvania, Texas, Maryland, and Kentucky, among others, held the law to be constitutional and ruled in favor of Negro complainants. In North Carolina, New Jersey, and California, however, district judges held the law invalid. And when other courts in New York, Tennessee, Missouri, and Kansas put the issue to the federal circuit judges, the judges divided on the question, and the matter was certified to the United States Supreme Court.

But the Supreme Court did not exactly rush to make its ruling. Though two cases testing the 1875 act reached it in 1876 and a third in 1877, the Justices simply held them on their docket. In 1879, the Attorney General filed a brief defending the constitutionality of the law, but still the Court reached no decisions. In 1880, three additional cases were filed, but two years elapsed before the Solicitor General presented a fresh brief supporting the statute. It was not until late in 1883 that the Supreme Court passed upon the 1875 act, in what became famous as the *Civil Rights Cases* ruling. True, the Court was badly behind in its work in this period, but clearly the Justices chose to let the civil-rights cases "ripen" for almost eight years.

When they finally came to grips with the issue, six separate test suits were involved. The most celebrated had arisen in New York City in November of 1879. Edwin Booth, the famous tragedian and brother of John Wilkes Booth, had opened a special Thanksgiving week engagement at the Grand Opera House. After playing *Hamlet, Othello,* and *Richelieu* to packed houses, he was scheduled to perform Victor Hugo's *Ruy Blas* at the Saturday matinee on November 22.

One person who had decided to see Booth that Saturday was William R. Davis, Jr., who was later described in the press as a tall, handsome, and well-spoken Negro of twenty-six. He was the business agent of the *Progressive-American,* a Negro weekly published in New York City. At 10 o'clock Saturday morning, Davis' girl friend ("a bright octoroon, almost white," as the press put it), purchased two reserved seats at the box office of the Grand Opera House. At 1:30 P.M., Davis and his lady presented themselves at the theatre, only to be told by the doorkeeper, Samuel Singleton, that "these tickets are no good." If he would step out to the box office, Singleton told Davis, his money would be refunded.

It is unlikely that Davis was surprised by Singleton's action, for this was not the first time he had encountered such difficulties. Shortly after the passage of the 1875 act, Davis had been refused a ticket to the dress circle of Booth's Theatre in New York. He had sworn out a warrant against the ticket seller, but the failure of his witnesses to appear at the grand jury proceedings had led to a dismissal of the complaint. This earlier episode, as well as Davis' activity as a Negro journalist, made it probable that this appearance at the Opera House in 1879 was a deliberate test of the management's discriminatory policies.

Though Davis walked out of the lobby at Singleton's request, he did not turn in his tickets for a refund. Instead, he summoned a young white boy standing near the theatre, gave him a dollar (plus a dime for his trouble), and had him purchase two more tickets. When Davis and his companion presented these to Singleton, only the lady was allowed to pass. Again Davis was told that his ticket was "no good." When he now refused to move out of the doorway, Singleton called a policeman and asked that Davis be escorted off the theatre property. The officer told Davis that the Messrs. Poole and Donnelly, the managers of the Opera House, did not admit colored persons. "Perhaps the managers do not," Davis retorted, "but the laws of the country [do]."

The following Monday, November 24, Davis filed a criminal com-

TICKET OFFICE.

In this cartoon Leslie's Weekly *praised theatres that flaunted the 1875 law and refused to sell Negroes tickets.*

plaint; on December 9, this time with witnesses in abundance, Singleton was indicted in what the press described as the first criminal proceeding under the 1875 act to go to trial in New York. When the case opened on January 14, 1880, Singleton's counsel argued that the 1875 law was unconstitutional. "It interferes," he said, "with the right of the State of New York to provide the means under which citizens of the State have the power to control and protect their rights in respect to their private property." The assistant United States attorney replied that such a conception of states' rights had been "exploded and superseded long ago." It was unthinkable, he declared, that "the United States could not extend to one citizen of New York a right which the State itself gave to others of its citizens—the right of admission to places of public amusement."

The presiding judge decided to take the constitutional challenge under advisement and referred it to the circuit court, for consideration at its February term. This left the decision up to Justice Samuel Blatchford of the Supreme Court, who was assigned to the circuit court for New York, and District Judge William Choate. The two judges reached opposite conclusions and certified the question to the United States Supreme Court.

Davis' case, under the title of *United States v. Singleton,* reached the Supreme Court in 1880. Already lodged on the Court's docket were four similar criminal prosecutions under the act of 1875. *U.S. v. Stanley* involved the refusal of Murray Stanley in 1875 to serve a meal at his hotel in Topeka, Kansas, to a Negro, Bird Gee. *U.S. v. Nichols* presented the refusal in 1876 of Samuel Nichols, owner of the Nichols House in Jefferson City, Missouri, to accept a Negro named W. H. R. Agee as a guest. *U.S. v. Ryan* involved the conduct of Michael Ryan, doorkeeper of Maguire's Theatre in San Francisco, in denying a Negro named George M. Tyler entry to the dress circle on January 4, 1876. In *U.S. v. Hamilton,* James Hamilton, a conductor on the Nashville, Chattanooga, and St. Louis Railroad, had on April 21, 1879, denied a Negro woman with a first-class ticket access to the ladies' car.

There was a fifth case, with a somewhat different setting. On the evening of May 22, 1879, Mrs. Sallie J. Robinson, a twenty-eight-year-old Negro, purchased two first-class tickets at Grand Junction, Tennessee, for a trip to Lynchburg, Virginia, on the Memphis and Charleston Railroad. Shortly after midnight she and her nephew, Joseph C. Robinson, described as a young Negro "of light complexion, light hair, and light blue eyes," boarded the train and started into the parlor car. The conductor, C. W. Reagin, held Mrs. Robinson back ("bruising her arm and jerking her roughly around," she alleged) and pushed her into the smoker.

A few minutes later, when Joseph informed the conductor that he was Mrs. Robinson's nephew and was a Negro, the conductor looked surprised. In that case, he said, they could go into the parlor car at the next stop. The Robinsons finished the ride in the parlor car but filed complaints with the railroad about their treatment and then sued for $500 under the 1875 act. At the trial, Reagin testified that he had thought Joseph to be a white man with a colored woman, and his experience was that such associations were "for illicit purposes."

Counsel for the Robinsons objected to Reagin's testimony, on the ground that his actions were based on race and constituted no defense. Admitting the constitutionality of the 1875 law for purposes of the trial, the railroad contended that the action of its conductor did not fall within the statute. The district judge ruled that the motive for excluding persons was the decisive issue under the act: if the jury believed that the conductor had acted because he thought Mrs. Robinson "a prostitute travelling with her paramour," whether "well or ill-founded" in that assumption, the exclusion was not because of race and the railroad was not liable. The jury found for the railroad, and the Robinsons appealed.

These, with William Davis' suit against the doorkeeper of New York's Grand Opera House, were the six cases to which the Supreme Court finally turned in 1882. The Justices were presented with a learned and eloquent brief for the United States submitted by Solicitor

General Samuel F. Phillips, who reviewed the leading cases, described the history of the Civil War amendments to the Constitution, and stressed the importance to the rights of citizens of equal access to public accommodation. Four times since 1865, Phillips noted, civil-rights legislation had been enacted by a Congress filled with men who had fought in the Civil War and had written the war amendments. These men understood that "every rootlet of slavery has an individual vitality, and, to its minutest hair, should be anxiously followed and plucked up. . . ." They also knew that if the federal government allowed Negroes to be denied accommodation "by persons who notably were sensitive registers of local public opinion," then "what upon yesterday was only 'fact' will become 'doctrine' tomorrow."

The Supreme Court Justices who considered Phillips' brief and the six test cases were uncommonly talented, among them being Chief Justice Morrison R. Waite, a man underrated today; Joseph P. Bradley, that Court's most powerful intellect; and Stephen J. Field, a *laissez-faire* interpreter of American constitutional law. John Marshall Harlan, the youngest man on the Court, had already started on the course which was to mark him as the most frequent and passionate dissenter in the Gilded Age.

As a whole, the Court might have appeared to be one which would have looked favorably on the 1875 act. All were Republicans except Justice Field, and he was a Democrat appointed by Abraham Lincoln. All except Justice Harlan, who was the Court's only southerner, had made their careers primarily in the northern and western states. Without exception, all had supported the northern cause in the war, and none had any hostility toward Negroes as a class.

Yet on the afternoon of October 15, 1883, Justice Bradley announced that the Court found Sections 1 and 2 of the Civil Rights Act of 1875 to be unconstitutional. (This disposed of five of the cases; the sixth, *U.S. v. Hamilton,* was denied review on a procedural point.) There was added irony in the fact that Bradley delivered the majority opinion for eight of the Justices. A one-time Whig, Bradley had struggled for a North-South compromise in the darkening months of 1860–61, then had swung to a strong Unionist position after the firing on Fort Sumter. He had run for Congress on the Lincoln ticket in 1862 and in 1868 headed the New Jersey electors for Grant. When the Thirteenth and Fourteenth Amendments were adopted, he had given them firm support, and his appointment to the Supreme Court by Grant in 1870 had drawn no criticism from friends of the Negro, as had the appointment of John Marshall Harlan seven years later.

Bradley's opinion had a tightly reasoned simplicity. The Thirteenth Amendment forbade slavery and involuntary servitude, he noted, but

Justice John Marshall Harlan wrote the dissenting opinion on the Civil Rights Cases.

protection against the restoration of bondage could not be stretched to cover federal regulation of "social" discriminations such as those dealt with in the 1875 statute. As for the Fourteenth Amendment, that was addressed only to deprivations of rights by the *states;* it did not encompass *private* acts of discrimination. Thus there was no source of constitutional authority for "Sumner's law"; it had to be regarded as an unwarranted invasion of an area under state jurisdiction. Even as a matter of policy, Bradley argued, the intention of the war amendments to aid the newly freed Negro had to have some limits. At some point, the Negro must cease to be "the special favorite of the law" and take on "the rank of a mere citizen."

At the Atlanta Opera House on the evening of the Court's decision, the end man of Haverly's Minstrels interrupted the performance to announce the ruling. The entire orchestra and dress circle audience rose and cheered. Negroes sitting in the balcony kept their seats, "stunned," according to one newspaper account. A short time earlier, a Negro denied entrance to the dress circle had filed charges against the Opera House management under the 1875 act. Now his case—their case—was dead.

Of all the nine Justices, only John Marshall Harlan, a Kentuckian and a former slaveholder, announced that he dissented from the ruling. He promised to give a full opinion soon.

Justice Harlan's progress from a supporter of slavery to a civil-rights dissenter makes a fascinating chronicle. Like Bradley, he had entered politics as a Whig and had tried to find a middle road between secessionist Democrats and antislavery Republicans. Like Bradley, he became a Unionist after the firing on Fort Sumter. But there the parallels ended. Although Harlan entered the Union Army, he was totally opposed to freeing the slaves, and his distaste for Lincoln and the Radicals was complete. Between 1863 and 1868, he led the Conservative party in Kentucky, a third-party movement which supported the war but opposed pro-Negro and civil-rights measures as "flagrant invasions of property rights and local government."

By 1868, however, Harlan had become a Republican. The resounding defeat of the Conservatives in the 1867 state elections convinced him that a third party had no future in Kentucky. His antimonopoly views and his general ideas about economic progress conflicted directly with state Democratic policies, and when the Republicans nominated his former field commander, Ulysses S. Grant, for President, in 1868, Harlan was one of the substantial number of Conservatives who joined the G.O.P.

His views on Negro rights also changed at this time. The wave of vigilante activities against white Republicans and Negroes that swept Kentucky in 1868–70, with whippings and murders by the scores, convinced Harlan that federal guarantees were essential. He watched Negroes in Kentucky moving with dignity and skill toward useful citizenship, and his devout Presbyterianism led him to adopt a "brotherhood-of-man" outlook in keeping with his church's national position. Perhaps he may have been influenced by his wife, Mallie, whose parents were New England abolitionists. As a realistic Republican politician, he was also aware that 60,000 Kentucky Negroes would become voters in 1870.

Thus a "new" John Harlan took the stump as Republican gubernatorial candidate in 1871, the year of the Louisville streetcar ride-ins. He opened his rallies by confessing that he had formerly been anti-Negro. But "I have lived long enough," he said, "to feel that the most perfect despotism that ever existed on this earth was the institution of African slavery." The war amendments were necessary "to place it beyond the power of any State to interfere with . . . the results of the war. . . ." The South should stop agitating the race issue, and should turn to rebuilding itself on progressive lines. When the Democrats laughed at "Harlan the Chameleon" and read quotations from his earlier anti-Negro speeches, Harlan replied: "Let it be said that I am right rather than consistent."

Harlan soon became an influential figure in the Republican party and, when President Rutherford B. Hayes decided to appoint a southern Republican to the Supreme Court in 1877, he was a logical choice. Even then, the Negro issue rose to shake Harlan's life again. His confirmation was held up because of doubts by some senators as to his "real" civil-rights views. Only after Harlan produced his speeches between 1871 and 1877 and party leaders supported his firmness on the question was he approved.

Once on the Supreme Court, Harlan could have swung back to a conservative position on civil rights. Instead, he became one of his generation's most intense and uncompromising defenders of the Negro. Perhaps his was the psychology of the convert who defends his new faith more passionately, even more combatively, than the born believer. Harlan liked to think that he had changed because he knew the South and realized that any relaxation of federal protection of the rights of Negroes would encourage the "white irreconcilables" first to acts of discrimination and then to violence, which would destroy all hope of accommodation between the races.

When Harlan sat down in October of 1883 to write his dissent in the *Civil Rights Cases,* he hoped to set off a cannon of protest. But he simply could not get his thoughts on paper. He worked late into the night, and even rose from half-sleep to write down ideas that he was afraid would elude him in the morning. "It was a trying time for him," his wife observed. "In point of years, he was much the youngest man on the Bench; and standing alone, as he did in regard to a decision which the whole nation was anxiously awaiting, he felt that . . . he must speak not only forcibly but wisely." After weeks of drafting and discarding, Harlan seemed to reach a dead end. The dissent would not "write." It was at this point that Mrs. Harlan contributed a dramatic touch to the history of the *Civil Rights Cases.*

When the Harlans had moved to Washington in 1877, the Justice had acquired from a collector the inkstand which Chief Justice Roger Taney had used in writing all his opinions. Harlan was fond of showing this to guests and remarking that "it was the very inkstand from which the infamous *Dred Scott* opinion was written." Early in the 1880's, however, a niece of Taney's, who was engaged in collecting her uncle's effects, visited the Harlans. When she saw the inkstand she asked Harlan for it, and the Justice agreed. The next morning Mrs. Harlan, noting her husband's reluctance to part with his most prized possession, quietly arranged to have the inkstand "lost." She hid it away, and

Harlan was forced to make an embarrassed excuse to Taney's niece.

Now, on a Sunday morning, probably early in November of 1883, after Harlan had spent a sleepless night working on his dissent, Mallie Harlan remembered the inkstand. While the Justice was at church, she retrieved it from its hiding place, filled it with a fresh supply of ink and pen points, and placed it on the blotter of his desk. When her husband returned from church, she told him, with an air of mystery, that he would find something special in his study. Harlan was overjoyed to recover his symbolic antique. Mrs. Harlan's gesture was successful, for as she relates:

> The memory of the historic part that Taney's inkstand had played in the Dred Scott decision, in temporarily tightening the shackles of slavery upon the negro race in those ante-bellum days, seemed, that morning, to act like magic in clarifying my husband's thoughts in regard to the law . . . intended by Sumner to protect the recently emancipated slaves in the enjoyment of equal 'civil rights.' His pen fairly flew on that day and, with the running start he then got, he soon finished his dissent.

How directly the recollection of Dred Scott pervaded Harlan's dissent is apparent to anyone who reads the opinion. He began by noting that the pre-Civil War Supreme Court had upheld congressional laws forbidding individuals to interfere with recovery of fugitive slaves. To strike down the act of 1875 meant that "the rights of freedom and American citizenship cannot receive from the Nation that efficient protection which heretofore was unhesitatingly accorded to slavery and the rights of masters."

Harlan argued that the Civil Rights Act of 1875 was constitutional on any one of several grounds. The Thirteenth Amendment had already been held to guarantee "universal civil freedom"; Harlan stated that barring Negroes from facilities licensed by the state and under legal obligation to serve all persons without discrimination restored a major disability of slavery days and violated that civil freedom. As for the Fourteenth Amendment, its central purpose had been to extend national citizenship to the Negro, reversing the precedent upheld in the Dred Scott decision; its final section gave Congress power to pass appropriate legislation to enforce that affirmative grant as well as to enforce the section barring any state action which might deny liberty or equality. Now, the Supreme Court was deciding what legislation was appropriate and necessary for those purposes, although that decision properly belonged to Congress.

Even under the "State action" clause of the Fourteenth Amendment, Harlan continued, the 1875 act was constitutional; it was well established that "railroad corporations, keepers of inns and managers of places of public accommodation are agents or instrumentalities of the State." Finally, Harlan attacked the unwillingness of the Court's majority to uphold the public-carrier section of the act under Congress' power to regulate interstate trips. That was exactly what was involved in Mrs. Robinson's case against the Memphis and Charleston Railroad, he reminded his colleagues; it had not been true before that Congress had had to cite the section of the Constitution on which it relied.

In his peroration, Harlan replied to Bradley's comment that Negroes had been made "a special favorite of the law." The war amendments had been passed not to "favor" the Negro, he declared, but to include him as "part of the people for whose welfare and happiness government is ordained."

> Today, it is the colored race which is denied, by corporations and individuals wielding public authority, rights fundamental in their freedom and citizenship. At some future time, it may be that some other race will fall under the ban of race discrimination. If the constitutional amendments be enforced, according to the intent with which, as I conceive, they were adopted, there cannot be in this republic, any class of human beings in practical subjection to another class. . . .

The *Civil Rights Cases* ruling did two things. First, it destroyed the delicate balance of federal guarantee, Negro protest, and private enlightenment which was producing a steadily widening area of peacefully integrated public facilities in the North and South during the 1870's and early 1880's. Second, it had an immediate and profound effect on national and state politics as they related to the Negro. By denying Congress power to protect the Negro's rights to equal treatment, the Supreme Court wiped the issue of civil rights from the Republican party's agenda of national responsibility. At the same time, those southern political leaders who saw anti-Negro politics as the most promising avenue to power could now rally the "poor whites" to the banner of segregation.

If the Supreme Court had stopped with the *Civil Rights Cases* of 1883, the situation of Negroes would have been bad but not impossible. Even in the South, there was no immediate imposition of segregation in public facilities. During the late 1880's, Negroes could be found sharing places with whites in many southern restaurants, streetcars, and theatres. But increasingly, Democratic and Populist politicians found the Negro an irresistible target. As Solicitor General Phillips had warned the Supreme Court, what had been tolerated as the "fact" of discrimination was now being translated into "doctrine": between 1887 and 1891, eight southern states passed laws requiring railroads to separate all white and Negro passengers. The Supreme Court upheld these laws in the 1896 case of *Plessy v. Ferguson.* Then in the

Berea College case of 1906, it upheld laws forbidding private schools to educate Negro and white children together. Both decisions aroused Harlan's bitter dissent. In the next fifteen or twenty years, the chalk line of Jim Crow was drawn across virtually every area of public contact in the South.

Today, as this line is slowly and painfully being erased, we may do well to reflect on what might have been in the South if the Civil Rights Act of 1875 had been upheld, in whole or in part. Perhaps everything would have been the same. Perhaps forces at work between 1883 and 1940 were too powerful for a Supreme Court to hold in check. Perhaps "Sumner's law" was greatly premature. Yet it is difficult to believe that total, state-enforced segregation was inevitable in the South after the 1880's. If in these decades the Supreme Court had taken the same *laissez-faire* attitude toward race relations as it took toward economic affairs, voluntary integration would have survived as a countertradition to Jim Crow and might have made the transition of the 1950's less painful than it was. At the very least, one cannot help thinking that Harlan was a better sociologist than his colleagues and a better southerner than the "irreconcilables." American constitutional history has a richer ring to it because of the protest that John Marshall Harlan finally put down on paper from Roger Taney's inkwell in 1883.

Mississippi: The Past That Has Not Died

WALTER LORD

The situation that southern blacks and their white supporters had to contend with after the Civil War, a situation that had much to do with the frustration of President Johnson's policies and which helped to produce the Supreme Court decisions in the Civil Rights Cases and in Plessy v. Ferguson, *is described in the following essay by Walter Lord.*

This is a case study—a very useful historical approach that seeks, by examining one part of a subject, to throw light on the whole. The main advantages of the case study method are that it concentrates on a more easily mastered body of materials and permits the use of details and examples that in a broader treatment would have to be sacrificed to avoid excessive length. The disadvantages lie chiefly in the inevitable loss of perspective, and in the not always correct assumption that the case chosen is entirely typical. The effect is like looking at a distant landscape through a telescope or at a piece of tissue under a microscope. Elements that would be lost to the "normal" view are brought sharply into focus, but the image of the total object is lost or distorted.

Lord's essay on Mississippi after the Civil War is a fine example of the intelligent use of the case study. His selection of Mississippi, home of the most intransigent foes of Negro equality but also a region where blacks exercised considerable power during Reconstruction, undoubtedly produces a heightening effect that is somewhat at variance with the whole truth, but it brings out very clearly all the problems of the postwar South and the "solutions" found for them in the late nineteenth century. Mr. Lord is best known for his "you are there" style of history, first developed in his popular book, A Night to Remember, *the story of the sinking of the liner* Titanic. *However, he makes relatively little use of that technique in this essay, thus demonstrating that he is a sound analytical historian as well as a graphic storyteller.* ∎

Splinters flew in every direction as the northern troops hacked apart the chairs and tables of Edward McGehee, one of the wealthiest cotton planters in Wilkinson County, Mississippi. It was October 5, 1864, and Colonel E. D. Osband's men were simply acting on the philosophy expressed by General Sherman when he told a group of protesting Mississippians, "It is our duty to destroy, not build up; therefore do not look to us to help you."

Soon the work was done, the house in flames, and Edward McGehee left contemplating his only remaining possession—a gracefully carved grand piano. It was no comfort to Mr. McGehee, once the owner of hundreds of Negro slaves, that these deeds were done by a company of stern, efficient Negro soldiers.

Ruin upon ruin, the destruction continued for six more gruelling months of war. By the end, Mississippi seemed but a forest of chimneys. The whole town of Okolona could be bought for $5,000. There was not a fence left within miles of Corinth, not a clock running in Natchez. The capital, Jackson, was in ashes—the Confederate Hotel as complete a wreck as the cause it honored.

The first visitors from the North were stunned. Approaching old Charles Langworthy's home near Aberdeen, a man from Chicago recalled spending two pleasant weeks there back in 1855. Greeting the owner, the visitor quickly asked after Mr. Langworthy's five boys and two girls.

"Where is John, your oldest son?"

"Killed at Shiloh."

"Where is William?"

"Died of smallpox in the Army."

"And the other boys?"

"All were killed. . . ."

The Langworthy daughters came forward, dripping with mourning. Not only were their brothers gone; both also had lost their husbands in the service.

The incident was all too typical. Mississippi had sent 78,000 into the fight; only 28,000 came back. Whole companies were wiped out— the Vicksburg Cadets marched off 123 strong; only six returned. One legacy of this sacrifice was 10,000 orphans.

Nor were those who returned always able to play their full part. Surgery was not one of the happier aspects of the Civil War. Empty sleeves flapped everywhere. At a town meeting in Aberdeen a visitor noticed that one hundred of the three hundred men present had lost either an arm or a leg. It is not surprising that in the first year after the war Mississippi spent one fifth of its entire revenue for artificial limbs.

31

Painfully, the people of the state struggled to live again. Nearly everyone was wiped out. The greatest source of wealth—436,000 slaves worth over 218 million dollars—had vanished with Emancipation. The farm animals that meant so much to a rural people had been carried off—one out of every three mules gone. Most of the cotton was confiscated as Confederate property; any that escaped was mercilessly taxed by Washington. Land values crashed—on December 13, 1865, alone, the Vicksburg *Herald* advertised forty-eight plantations for sale or lease. After five years of war Mississippi tumbled from the nation's fifth state in per capita wealth to the very bottom of the list.

"My children, I am a ruined man," Thomas Dabney told his daughters one evening in November, 1866. In happier days Mr. Dabney had endorsed some notes. At the time there seemed little danger—the risk was good and Dabney was the wealthy owner of Burleigh, a fabulous plantation near the town of Raymond. But now times had changed, and the sheriff was downstairs.

Ultimately, Burleigh was auctioned off, and Dabney managed to buy it back only by consigning his cotton crop for years to come. Meanwhile, the family had nothing—even the "loyal" Negro servants had vanished. As the once pampered Dabney girls faced the novel prospect of housework, it looked like a major victory for General Sherman's perhaps apocryphal boast that he would force every southern woman to the washtub.

But this time the General had met his match. "He shall never bring my daughters to the washtub," Dabney thundered. "I'll do the washing myself!" And he did. Dabney was now seventy years old, but for the next two years he scrubbed away, grimly satisfied that here at least he was foiling the hated Yankee.

There were other consolations too, as the people of Mississippi struggled to recover. There was relief that the war was over—whatever their original feelings, most Mississippians were heartily sick of destruction. There was also hope that the state could get back into the Union rather painlessly; President Andrew Johnson had decided to carry on Lincoln's lenient plans for restoration. Best of all, there was the land. Mississippi's towns might lie in ruins, but her matchless asset was the soil itself. If only cotton could get going again . . .

But that was the problem. If the key to prosperity was cotton, the key to cotton had always been slaves—and there weren't any slaves any more. Over 380,000 freedmen aimlessly roamed the state, nearly all of them at loose ends, living where they chose, eating off the federal troops. The former owners had no influence. Most Negroes felt this was what freedom meant—no work. And there were plenty of people around the Union Army camps who advised them not to go back to their old masters. There were even rumors that Washington soon would be dividing up the plantations—forty acres and a mule for everyone.

Actually Washington was never more at cross-purposes. President Johnson suffered from being a states' rights Democrat from Tennessee, and as his prestige waned so did the chances for his lenient program. The Radical Republicans in Congress were winning control over national policy, but beyond a thirst for revenge, they had no clear-cut plans at all. As late as October, 1865, the Radical leader Thaddeus Stevens was asking his friend Charles Sumner if he knew of any good books on how the Russians freed their serfs.

The Negroes themselves could be of very little help in solving their problems. Over ninety-five per cent were illiterate. In the old days it had been illegal to teach the slaves to read or write, and now they were hopelessly ignorant. Few had any idea of citizenship, law, suffrage, or responsibility. Hauled before a court for stealing a bag of corn, one ex-slave happily camping on Jefferson Davis' plantation was asked if he wanted a jury trial.

"What's that?" was all he could say.

The whites felt cornered and helpless. For years they had done as they wanted with these people, and now the tables were turned. They were generally outnumbered, and in the rich cotton areas the margin seemed appalling—Bolivar County was eighty-seven per cent Negro; Issaquena County had 7,000 Negroes, only 600 whites.

But most frightening of all to white Mississippi residents were the Negro troops. When the United States Army's XVI Corps went home in August, 1865, 9,122 of the 10,193 Union soldiers still in the state were Negroes. Their mere presence seemed to invite the most hideous trouble. In Jackson, Major Barnes, commanding the 5th U.S. Colored Infantry, urged the local Negroes to defend their rights even to the "click of the pistol and at the point of the bayonet."

And incidents did happen. William Wilkinson was murdered at Lauderdale Springs by five of his former slaves for selling his plantation—they claimed it was rightfully theirs by Christmas. This sort of bloodshed was rare, but it was enough to set off the whites.

Terror bred fantastic rumors. The Natchez *Courier* warned that the county's Negroes were supposed to rise on New Year's Day. In Yazoo City the date was Christmas. The Brandon *Republican* set no date but reported, "They are evidently preparing something and it behooves us to be on the alert and prepare for the worst." There was nothing to any of these reports, but each rumor hardened the feelings of the whites.

They soon developed a fierce callousness toward the Negro, no matter how harmless he might be. On a quiet Sunday afternoon in Natchez an elderly freedman protested to a small white boy raiding his

D. H. Euyett painted this watercolor of the ruins of Jackson, Mississippi, in 1863, shortly after Sherman took the state's capital.

turnip patch. The boy shot him dead, and that was that. In Vicksburg the *Herald* complained that the town's children were hitting innocent bystanders when using their "nigger shooters."

Nor was it just the specter of Negro supremacy that aroused white Mississippians—Negro equality was just as bad. "God damn your soul, get off this boat!" raged the captain of the Memphis-Vicksburg packet on Christmas morning, 1865. The greeting was directed at a Negro couple who had dared ask for first-class passage. As their luggage was pitched ashore, the captain turned back to his work muttering, "They can't force their damned nigger equality on me."

Even when the principle of equality was acknowledged, the practice must have mystified the beneficiaries. "Take off your hat, you black scoundrel, or I'll cut your throat," a Mississippi state legislator yelled at his former slave; later he explained, "Sam, you've got just the same rights as a white man now, but not a bit better, and if you come into my room again without taking off your hat, I'll shoot you."

The case of Negro suffrage showed that even token equality was too much for whites to stomach. In 1865 President Johnson—already fearing for his generous Reconstruction program—urged William L. Sharkey, a former Mississippi Chief Justice whom the President had appointed as provisional governor, to make some gesture toward Negro enfranchisement. It might allay congressional doubts, for instance, if Mississippi gave the vote to those who could read the Constitution and write their names and who owned at least $250 in property—perhaps five per cent of the Negro population. Governor Sharkey couldn't have been less interested.

But the greatest anathema was Negro education. It was not so much a question of integrated schools; it was a question of any schools at all. At Oxford an angry band drove off the missionary assigned to the local freedmen's school, even though he was a southern man. At Okolona someone fired four shots at Dr. Lacy, the old Episcopal minister who was trying to teach the town's young Negroes.

"If any man from the North comes down here expecting to hold and maintain radical or abolitionist sentiments," warned the *Nation*'s correspondent, "let him expect to be shot down from *behind* the first time he leaves his home." Visitors were shocked by the sheer violence of the state's reaction. Lulled by a carefully cultivated tradition of moonlight and magnolias, they forgot that life in Mississippi had always been closer to the frontier than the Tidewater, indeed had been a true frontier as late as the 1830's.

Harder to explain was the stream of contradictory assurances that soon became so familiar. Negroes? "The southern people are really their best friends," a planter told author John T. Trowbridge in 1865. "We're the only ones that understand them," someone explained to Whitelaw Reid, another visitor. Just give the southerners time, begged the sympathetic editor of *DeBow's Review:* "If let alone to manage affairs in their own way, and with their intimate knowledge of Negro character, everything possible will be done in good time for the social, physical, and political advancement of the race."

There was also an odd element of fantasy in it all—almost as if the war hadn't been lost . . . in fact, as if Mississippi were dealing with Washington as an equal. When Whitelaw Reid doubted that Congress would seat the ex-Confederates who swept Mississippi's first postwar election of 1865, his listeners scoffed at the very thought. Of course they would be seated—"because of the tremendous pressure we can bring to bear." The Natchez *Courier* agreed: "The State of Mississippi still stands in all its grand individuality. Massachusetts has no more right to dictate to us now about our internal laws than she had five years ago—nor has she half the power. . . ."

Occasionally a voice of doubt was raised, but the moderates seemed, in the *Nation*'s words, "somewhat bewildered . . . bullied . . . humbugged." Usually they could be quickly silenced. When one Mississippi planter suggested in August, 1865, that the Negroes might be trained to use their rights, his companion shot back the clincher that was also getting familiar: "They'll be wanting to marry your daughters next."

And this was the heart of the matter. To the ordinary white Mississippian, political equality automatically led to social equality, which in turn automatically led to race-mixing. It was inevitable—and unthinkable. To a people brought up to believe that Negroes were genetically inferior—after all, that was why they were slaves—the mere hint of "mongrelization" was appalling. And all the more so in view of the homage paid the white southern woman. It was she who had sacrificed so much, whose purity, in fact, carried on the whole system. She was everything.

Of course there were other factors too. Cotton planters didn't want their field hands getting out of line; the red-neck farmers worried about Negroes taking their bread. Yet these were areas where something might be worked out; but there could be no compromise—not an inch—on anything that might open the door to race-mixing. Emancipation made absolutely no difference. "A monkey with his tail off," explained the Natchez *Courier,* "is a monkey still."

It didn't matter that the position was illogical. Northerners might snigger that if the Negro was so backward, why might he advance so far? Other visitors might wonder about the high percentage of Negroes with white blood—surely race-mixing must have once been all right with somebody. None of this made any difference. So in November, 1865, it was easy for the Jackson *Daily News* to lecture the state's first postwar government: "We must keep the ex-slave in a position of inferiority. We must pass such laws as will make him *feel* his inferiority."

Mississippi's new government understood. Under President Johnson's generous terms the state had freed the slaves but done little else. A new constitution had been drafted—but it seemed pretty much along prewar lines. A new state legislature had been chosen—but it featured many old leaders. A new governor had been elected—but he was Benjamin G. Humphreys, an outstanding Confederate general who hadn't even been pardoned yet. On November 20, 1865, Governor Humphreys set the tone of things in a message to the legislature: "Under the pressure of federal bayonets, urged on by the misdirected sympathies of the world, the people of Mississippi have abolished the institution of slavery. The Negro is free, whether we like it or not; we must realize that fact now and forever. To be free, however, does not make him a citizen, or entitle him to social or political equality with the white man."

A series of laws, later known as the Black Code, swiftly put the Negro in his place. He was allowed to marry, own property, sue and be sued, even testify if he was a party—but that was all. No Negro could vote, keep firearms, rent a home outside town, ride in a first-class railroad car with whites, or "make insulting gestures." Any unemployed Negro over eighteen was declared a vagrant, fined $50, and turned over to whoever paid up. Any unsupported Negro under eighteen could be apprenticed out. If he tried to run away, "the master or mistress" (the law easily slipped back into ante-bellum language) had the right to pursue and recapture.

Reaction was not long in coming. "We tell the white men of Mississippi," exploded the Chicago *Tribune* on December 1, "that the men of the North will convert the state of Mississippi into a frog pond before they will allow any such laws to disgrace one foot of soil in which the bones of our soldiers sleep and over which the flag of freedom waves."

Northern fury grew as other southern states followed Mississippi's lead with Black Codes of their own. Finally, in 1867 Congress threw out President Johnson's Reconstruction program and launched a far harsher one of its own. The Confederate-dominated state governments were scrapped, and the South was divided into five military districts, each under martial law. Negroes were given the vote, new constitutional conventions held. No state could get back into the Union until Congress approved its new government . . . until it granted Negro suffrage . . . until it ratified the Fourteenth Amendment, guaranteeing the people of every state (among other things) "equal protection of the laws."

Mississippi eventually knuckled under, but only after three more years of rear-guard defiance. By 1870, however, the state was "reconstructed," and by 1873 the local Radical Republicans were riding high. The electorate was fifty-seven per cent Negro—mostly illiterate and easily controlled. The legislature boasted sixty-four Negroes and twenty-four carpetbaggers. The Speaker of the House, the lieutenant governor, the superintendent of education were all Negroes. The new Reconstruction governor himself was an ex-Union officer—General Adelbert Ames, a remote, tactless New Englander who stayed away from Mississippi for protracted periods.

It would later be argued that this state government turned in an impressive performance, and indeed there were many bright spots. The Negro legislators included at least fifteen well-educated, conscientious clergymen. The carpetbaggers were often solid middle westerners who had come not to loot but to farm. The Negro troops had all been withdrawn, and only a token force of federals remained—for instance, 59 at Natchez, 129 at Vicksburg, about 700 men altogether. The state debt never got out of hand. There was little stealing—the only major case involved the carpetbag treasurer of the state hospital in Natchez who took $7,251.81. And all the while important things were being accomplished—war-damaged bridges repaired, northern innovations like free hospitals established, courts expanded to take care of freedmen, and a public-school system launched.

All this was done, but it would take the perspective of a century to

Entitled Reconstruction, *or "A White Man's
Government," this 1868 Currier and Ives cartoon summed
up northern liberals' simplistic view of the southern
dilemma.*

appreciate it. At the time the white people of Mississippi felt only
bitterness. They didn't care if most of the troops were gone; one blue
uniform was too many. They didn't know about worthy projects; they
only knew taxes on land had soared 1,300 per cent in five years. They
didn't notice that most key officials were honest; in their frayed poverty, they only saw any sign of waste: why, the state contingency fund
even paid for Governor Ames' bedpan. And perhaps most important,
they knew little about the conscientious work of many Negroes in
top-level positions; they only knew their own county, where they were
in daily contact, and that was often appalling.

Negro sheriffs, clerks, and magistrates thrashed about in confusion
and ignorance. In Warren County the sheriff couldn't write a simple
return. In Issaquena County not one member of the board of supervisors—responsible for handling the county's business—could read a
contract. There wasn't a justice of the peace in Madison County who
could write a summons.

Petty corruption spread everywhere, often induced by light-
fingered whites. Hinds County ran up a bigger printing bill in nine
months than the whole state paid in 1866–67. The Wilkinson County
board of supervisors shelled out $1,500 for three bridges—containing

four, eight, and twenty planks respectively. Vicksburg's Republican candidate for mayor staggered under twenty-three indictments. Nor were the dethroned Democrats entirely innocent. An officer in Vicksburg's clean-government group was caught charging the city $500 to move a safe from the river to the courthouse.

Little matter—it was all the same to most of white Mississippi. Reconstruction was to blame, and that meant the Negroes. Free voting and the shadow of federal bayonets might make them invulnerable to ordinary political tactics, but there were other ways. . . .

The shifting seasons merged into one long blur of desperate violence. There was the sunny October morning when Thomas Dabney's daughters heard a hail of shots and watched a Negro's riderless horse race across the Burleigh lawn . . . the starlit winter night in Monroe County when carpetbagger A. P. Huggins knelt on a lonely road as the K.K.K. delivered seventy-five lashes with a stirrup strap . . . the bright March day when the Meridian courthouse erupted in rifle fire and the Radical judge fell dead on his bench. . . .

"Life is not sacred as it is in the North," wrote correspondent Charles Nordhoff:

> Everybody goes armed, and every trifling dispute is ended with the pistol. The respectable people of the State do not discourage the practice of carrying arms as they should, they are astonishingly tolerant of acts which would arouse a Northern community to the utmost, and I believe that to this may be ascribed all that is bad in Mississippi—to an almost total lack of a right opinion; a willingness to see men take the law into their own hands; and, what is still worse, to let them openly defy the laws, without losing, apparently, the respect of the community.

In this atmosphere there was no hope for a man with the "wrong" attitude, whatever his credentials. At Aberdeen the town teacher, Dr. Ebart, had an impeccable southern background, but he favored Negro schools, and that was the end of his job. The pressure was too much. The white Republicans soon melted away. Many crossed over to the Democratic fold; others fled north; only a few stood by the helpless mass of Negroes. The moderates, who might have been a third force, seemed mesmerized by the fury of the blast. "The quiet, sensible and orderly people," mused Charles Nordhoff, "seem to have almost entirely resigned the power and supremacy which belong to them."

This was the picture by 1875, when, with state and local elections scheduled, the Democrats decided that the time had come formally to recapture control. A skillfully conceived strategy—to be known as the Mississippi Plan and later to be copied throughout the South—took care of the two chief obstacles: the Negro majority and federal bayonets.

"We are determined to have an honest election if we have to stuff the ballot box to get it," shouted one Democratic leader, and this was only a small part of the plan. Newspaper notices warned Negroes that they would be thrown off their land if they voted the Republican ticket. Democratic "rifle clubs," usually sporting conspicuous red shirts, drilled endlessly near Negro sections. In Hinds, Lowndes, and other counties, cannon appeared and "salutes" were fired near Republican rallies.

The Negro voters got the message, but the Democrats still faced the danger of federal intervention. The trick here was not to let things go too far, and the Democratic campaign chairman, General J. Z. George, proved a past master at the art of intimidation by indirection. Still, it was a delicate tightrope. The embattled Governor Ames was calling Washington for help, and the slightest slip might bring in the federals. . . .

A crash of rifle fire scattered the 1,200 Negroes swarming around the Republican barbecue at the little town of Clinton on September 4, 1875. Here and there men fell—not all of them black. Two young white hecklers were cut down by return fire as they scurried from the scene. It seemed that Negroes too could feel strongly about elections. Wholesale shooting began, and for days undeclared war raged around Clinton. On September 8 Governor Ames appealed to General Grant for troops to restore peace and supervise the coming elections. The whole future of Mississippi hung in the balance. A nod from the President, and all of General George's strategy would fall apart.

Grant looked the other way. "The whole public are tired out with these annual autumnal outbreaks in the South," the President sighed, "and the great majority are ready now to condemn any interference on the part of the government." Word was passed to Governor Ames through Attorney General Pierrepont to try harder, to exhaust his own resources before calling on Washington for aid.

It was really not Grant's fault. The country was indeed tired of Reconstruction, and the President was but echoing the national mood. Most people had never been for Negro civil rights in the first place. Freedom, yes; but that didn't necessarily mean all the privileges of citizenship. At the end of the war only six northern states let Negroes vote, and in 1867 the District of Columbia rejected Negro suffrage 7,337 to 36. Nor did anyone feel the Fourteenth Amendment had much to do with education. In fact, stalwart Union states like New York, Pennsylvania, and Ohio all had segregated schools. Congress itself set up a segregated school system in Washington only weeks after approving the Fourteenth Amendment.

These feelings were rising to the surface, now that the initial exhilaration of winning the war was over. Other forces were at work too: the implacable Thaddeus Stevens had died . . . anti-Grant liberals were happy to attack everything about the Administration, including Reconstruction . . . northern investors were anxious to resume "normal" relations with the South . . . the nation's eyes were turning to fresh, exciting visions in the Far West.

The new mood showed itself in various ways. Congress had indeed passed the Civil Rights Act of 1875 (protecting the Negro in public places like trains and restaurants), but it was the dying gasp of a lame-duck session. Besides, it was a shaky victory. A school integration provision had been defeated; also a "force bill" giving the measure teeth. Even more significant, the Supreme Court was now nibbling away at the earlier Reconstruction Acts. And in the background came a steady chorus from the press, "Let the South solve its own problems." The President understood and gave the nation its way.

The Silver Cornet Band led the Jackson victory parade to General George's house on election night, November 2, 1875. The returns were rolling in, and huge Democratic majorities were piling up: Morton, 233 to 17 . . . Deasonville, 181 to 0 . . . Yazoo County, 4,052 to 7. In the end the Democrats carried sixty-two of the state's seventy-four counties. In the time-honored fashion of all political leaders everywhere, General George gave full credit to the rank and file "for the redemption of our common mother, Mississippi." Governor Ames was a practical man. Exactly 146 days later, in exchange for the withdrawal by Democrats of a set of impeachment charges, he resigned his office, packed his bags, and left the state forever. In the word of the times, Mississippi had been "redeemed."

To Mississippi's Negroes redemption meant a loss of power but not the trappings. The men now running the state came from the old cotton-planting gentry, who got along well with their former slaves. Some of these leaders, like Lucius Quintus Cincinnatus Lamar, were far more interested in corporation law than in eight-cent cotton, but they still had a tradition of *noblesse oblige* and gave the Negroes considerable leeway—as long as they were "good."

This arrangement was further cemented by a sort of gentlemen's agreement with Washington after the presidential election of 1876. The South accepted Hayes' dubious claims to the Presidency, and in return the Republicans adopted Grant's hands-off attitude as the new administration line. The last troops were withdrawn, and the old Confederacy was left free to work out its own problems. But at the same time it was always understood that the Negroes would retain at least their surface gains. The redemption leaders happily agreed. In fact, the Jackson *Clarion* had accepted the obligation on the very morning after the great 1875 victory. Observing that Negroes had helped make the triumph possible, the paper declared that the state must now

"carry out in good faith the pledges of equal and even justice to them
and theirs in which they placed their confidence."

So the Negroes continued to vote and often held minor offices. Nor
were they barred from most public places. The two races drank at the
same bars and ate at the same restaurants, though at separate tables.
In Jackson, Angelo's Hall echoed with Negro laughter one week, white
the next. And when life was done, both races could rest together in
Greenwood Cemetery.

With the Negro's role settled, Mississippi's redemption government launched a massive economy wave. The conservative landowning
leaders had been hit hardest by the staggering taxes of Reconstruction,
and now they were determined to end all that. State expenditures were
slashed from $1,430,000 in 1875 to $518,000 in 1876. Teachers' sala-
ries alone fell from $55.47 a month in 1875 to $29.19 the following
year.

In a way it was all justifiable. Mississippi remained wretchedly poor.
In 1877 the state's per capita wealth was only $286, compared to a
$1,086 average in the northern states. Even as late as 1890 there were
only forty-six banks in the state, with combined cash assets of but
$635,000. The war had wiped out Mississippi, and there just seemed
no way to get going again. In those days the idea of federal recovery
aid was unknown—between 1865 and 1875 Washington spent 21 million dollars on public works in Massachusetts and New York, only
$185,000 in Mississippi and Arkansas.

Still, whatever the justification, Mississippi paid a high price for her
sweeping economies. Letting roads disintegrate meant even more
stagnant communities. Appropriating merely $5,392 a year for health
meant the end of nearly all services. Spending only $2 a head on
schoolchildren (against $20 in Massachusetts) meant mounting illiter-
acy and a new generation utterly untrained to advance in life.

Nor was cost-cutting a viable solution to the state's problems. Despite all the economies, conditions continued to slide. From the mid-
seventies to the early nineties cotton sagged from 11 cents to 5.8 cents
a pound. Field hands' pay fell from $15 to $12 a month . . . when there
was any cash at all. More often there was the sharecropping system,
which saw little money ever change hands. Yet the plantation owners
themselves were certainly not getting rich. Under a vicious system of
liens, they mortgaged their future crops for months or even years
ahead to get the tools and supplies needed for tomorrow.

Everything seemed to conspire against Mississippi. While crop
prices fell, the farmer's costs soared. Freight rates rigged in the East
increased his shipping charges. Combinations like the jute-bagging
trust raised the cost of his supplies. High tariffs added more to his
burden. Creditors insisted that he plant only cotton; shackled to a

one-crop system, his land quickly eroded. Even nature joined the conspiracy—a flood, freeze, or drought usually came along to spoil the few otherwise good years. Whether holding out in some paint-peeled mansion or hanging on in the squalor of a dog-trot cabin, most Mississippians knew only the bitterest poverty.

The state's landed leaders proved utterly unable to cope with the situation. They came from the lowlands—the cotton belt that had run everything in prewar days. They owed their authority to an odd combination of ante-bellum nostalgia and redemption heroics—certainly not new ideas. They easily took to the laissez-faire views of eastern business—tax concessions, hard money, railroad grabs like the Texas-Pacific. They shied away from new panaceas like government regulation and flexible currency. Their most lustrous figure, L. Q. C. Lamar, shuddered at the Greenback movement's "boundless, bottomless, and brainless schemes."

Such men neither understood nor even liked the up-country farmers who scratched away at the red clay hills to the east. Desperately these red-necks—along with a growing number of poor white tenants all over the state—turned to new and more radical sources of hope: the Farmers' Alliance and later the Populists.

And all the while they smouldered with growing hate—hatred for the Yankee banks and railroads that squeezed them so tightly . . . hatred for the Black Belt leaders who seemed to care so little . . . and, above all, hatred for the Negroes to whose level they were sinking so fast.

Jim Crow laws began to sprout . . . the first in twenty years. In 1888 Mississippi became the first state to have segregated waiting rooms. In 1890 Jackson extended the racial barrier beyond death by establishing a separate cemetery for Negroes. The rules grew ever more strict as the margin narrowed between white and colored living standards. If race was all the whites might have left, that was all the more reason to guard this sacred heritage. Woe to the Negro who flirted with crossing the line.

Lynchings multiplied at a fearful rate—nobody knows how many, for the press handled the incidents as casually as the weather. "Four Negroes were lynched at Grenada last week," remarked the Raymond *Gazette* on July 18, 1885, "also one at Oxford." That was the whole item.

With Mississippi in this mood, it certainly didn't help matters when the big landowners met the red-neck challenge with thousands of Negro votes from the black counties they controlled. A weird political duel, utterly lacking in logic or principle, developed as the eighties wore on. The old conservative leaders represented traditional white supremacy, yet relied on Negro votes to hold their power. The mass of poor whites had much in common with the Negro, yet fought him as a mortal enemy. The remaining Republicans in the state stood for the Negro's freedom, yet deserted him as a hopeless handicap. No wonder the Negro himself soon lost interest. Untrained in politics anyhow, he found Mississippi's brand far too confusing. Usually he just sold his vote to the highest bidder or was thrust aside while someone else cast it for him.

The situation proved too sordid to last. In 1890 a special convention assembled in Jackson to draw up a new state constitution. The solution, most people felt, was to take away the Negro's vote. Even the Black Belt leaders now agreed—the advantage Negro suffrage gave them was outweighed by the cost (usually a dollar a vote) and the ever-haunting possibility that the Negroes might some day decide to go back into politics for themselves. It was, of course, a little odd to keep Negroes from casting votes in order to stop white people from stealing them, but nobody worried too much about that. A far greater problem was how to do it. The Fifteenth Amendment specifically stated that the right to vote should not be abridged on account of color.

Clearly, the trick was to frame a set of qualifications that would technically apply to everybody but actually eliminate the Negro without touching the white. A poll tax alone was not enough—it might discourage more whites than Negroes. Nor would a literacy test do—there were thousands of good white voters who couldn't even write their names. In the end the convention came up with a series of devices which were, in the words of one delegate, "a monument to the resourcefulness of the human mind."

Most important were the new qualifications: all voters had to be able to read any section of the state constitution, or understand it when read to him, or give it a reasonable interpretation. This, of course, dumped the final decision into the lap of the examining registrar . . . who would know exactly what to do.

Reregistration began immediately. In 1885 over 1,600 Negroes had qualified in Panola County; by 1896 the figure stood at 114. The same thing happened everywhere: in Coahoma County only four per cent of its once-eligible Negroes now could vote; in De Soto, only five per cent; in Tunica, two per cent. Loyal Mississippians held their breath—how would the nation react to this giant wink at the Fifteenth Amendment?

They need not have worried. The White House was in friendly hands—first under the conservative Grover Cleveland, later under the benign William McKinley. Congress was no threat either—in 1894 it repealed most of the remaining civil rights laws. The western Populists were bitter at the Negroes for sticking by their old masters. The southern progressives felt that white solidarity would weld all classes more closely together. Eastern liberals recalled the reactionary leaders who had engineered Reconstruction—and found it easy to sympathize with Mississippi. And above all, there was the American mood—a moment of bursting national pride and pious imperialism. As the liberal *Atlantic Monthly* noted with gentle irony: "If the stronger and cleverer race is free to impose its will upon the 'new-caught sullen peoples' on the other side of the globe, why not in South Carolina and Mississippi?"

The Supreme Court added its blessing in 1898. In *Williams v. Mississippi* the justices solemnly declared there was no reason to suppose that the state's new voting qualifications were aimed especially at Negroes. . . .

As the new century dawned, it was clear that the Negro—stripped of his gains, abandoned by the courts, and rejected by the country—was in a highly vulnerable position. And for the Negro in Mississippi—the state which had invented the Black Code in 1865, pioneered the "Mississippi Plan" in 1875, and led the way to disenfranchisement in 1890—the future looked bleak indeed. . . .

Reluctant Conquerors: American Army Officers and the Plains Indians

THOMAS C. LEONARD

*The post-Civil War decades saw the tragic completion of the destruc-
tion of the cultures of the American Indian that began when Columbus
first set foot in the New World. Previously, at least some of the tribes
that inhabited what was to become the United States had been able to
maintain their cultural integrity more or less intact by falling back
before the white juggernaut into the western wilderness. After 1865
further retreat became impossible and in a few years the free Indians
were crushed and the survivors compelled to settle on reservations
where their conquerors expected them to become "civilized Americans."*

*The role of the Army in the destruction of the Indians has fre-
quently been described. What is unique about Thomas C. Leonard's
treatment of the subject is its focus on the thoughts and feelings of the
soldiers rather than on their deeds—on their appreciation of the Indians, not on their efforts to exterminate them. That professional soldiers should respect a foe so clever, so steadfast, so courageous, so
dignified in defeat is not difficult to understand. Yet Leonard does not
oversimplify or romanticize the reactions of the American military to
the Indians and their way of life. His essay presents a complex and
fascinating picture of a part of American history usually depicted in
grossly oversimplified terms. Professor Leonard, who teaches at the
University of California at Berkeley, is the author of* Above the Battle:
War-Making in America from Appomatox to Versailles. ∎

The white man's peace at Appomattox in 1865 meant war for the Plains Indians. In the next quarter century six and a half million settlers moved west of the Missouri River, upsetting a precarious balance that had existed between two million earlier pioneers and their hundred thousand "hostile" red neighbors. The industrial energy that had flowed into the Civil War now pushed rail lines across traditional hunting grounds. Some twenty-five thousand soldiers were sent west to meet insistent demands for protection coming from stockmen and miners spread out between the Staked Plains of Texas and the Montana lands watered by the Powder, Bighorn, and Yellowstone rivers.

It is ironic that the men who carried the wounds of the struggle to maintain the union of their own society now were ordered to dismember the culture of the native Americans. These Indian fighters today have been knocked out of that false gallery of heroes created by western novels and movies. On the centennial of the Battle of the Little Bighorn a granite mountain outside of Custer, South Dakota, is being carved into the shape of the Sioux warrior leader Crazy Horse. Times have changed, and a second look at the Army's Indian fighters is in order. They have a complex story to tell, one filled with an ambivalence about their enemy as well as about the civilians who sent them to fight.

The officer corps did not relish their double assignment of pushing Indians back from lands claimed by whites and, for good measure, "redeeming" native Americans from "barbarism"—for Christian civilization. In the letter books and official reports that these men kept so meticulously on the frontier there is a continual lament: civilian officials and opinion makers only cut budgets and issued contradictory directions. The rules of war demanded restraint and a fine regard for the enemy's rights, but it seemed as if the same civilians who interpreted these rules wanted quick work on the battlefield. The United States government itself broke the treaties that promised the Indians land, yet expected the Army to keep the peace through mutual trust.

At the same time that western settlers were clamoring for protection, their land grabs were provoking Indian retaliation. Not incidentally, army officers endured the torture of the annual congressional debate over how much their pay should be cut and seethed as western bankers charged 12 to 40 per cent to convert their government paper into the coin they needed on the frontier. "Friends" of the Indian—with their talk of a "conquest by kindness"—were a special annoyance. Eastern philanthropists like Edward A. Lawrence damned the officers when blood was shed and were among those who chillingly approved the "swift retribution" meted out to General Custer by the Sioux. Frontier forts rarely had the long, timbered stockades beloved by

Hollywood set designers—but perhaps many officers longed for a massive wall, high enough to repel civilians as well as Indians.

By 1870 General William T. Sherman doubted he could fight with honor on the plains; from the west and the east, he wrote, "we are placed between two fires." But Sherman may have been envied by another proud Civil War hero, General Philip H. Sheridan, who mused upon a shattered reputation as he watched whole frontier towns— wanting the extermination of Indians—turn out to hang him in effigy.

To officers so provoked, action seemed the thing to sweep away the complications of the Indian problem; to strike at the red man again and again appeared not only the quickest way to dry up civilian complaints but the just way to punish an incomprehensibly wild enemy. Sheridan pleaded with Sherman for authority to act upon the appalling reports that crossed his desk each week:

> Since 1862 at least 800 men, women, and children have been murdered within the limits of my present command, in the most fiendish manner; the men usually scalped and mutilated, their [he omits the word] cut off and placed in their mouth; women ravished sometimes fifty and sixty times in succession, then killed and scalped, sticks stuck in their persons, before and after death.

Sheridan said it was now a question of who was to remain alive in his district, red or white. As for himself: "I have made my choice." It was, in fact, Sheridan who first enunciated the judgment that would become the epitaph of so many native Americans: "The only good Indians I ever saw were dead."

Sheridan's choice, made in passion, proved extraordinarily complicated to carry out, for the fact is that the Indian fighters were troubled by various kinds of respect for their enemy. In the first place, no commander in the West could conceal his admiration for the red man's fighting skill. "Experience of late years," one reported to his colleagues, "has most conclusively shown that our cavalry cannot cope with the Indian man for man." Though these seasoned veterans and heroes reported a very favorable official casualty ratio, in more candid moments they pronounced that Indian fighting was the most difficult combat American soldiers had ever faced.

It followed that so high an estimate of the enemy's ability undermined the Army's pride in its own competence. Sheridan berated the inefficiency that made campaigns in the West "a series of forlorn hopes," and Sherman wrote in so many words to the Secretary of War what had silently haunted his fellow officers: ". . . it seems to be impossible to force Indians to fight at a disadvantage in their own country. Their sagacity and skill surpasses that of the white race." It

William Tecumseh Sherman, commander of the Army from 1869–1883.

further followed that victory against such valiant opponents was bitter-sweet. Both Sheridan and Sherman confessed to pity and compassion for the native Americans they had set out to destroy. As Sheridan wrote:

> We took away their country and their means of support, broke up their mode of living, their habits of life, introduced disease and decay among them and it was for this and against this they made war. Could anyone expect less?

Few officers escaped a sort of wistful appreciation of their primitive enemy in what they took to be his insatiable appetite for war—and not a few admired precisely this unrestrained aggressiveness. Indeed,

Starting in 1867, Philip Henry Sheridan was responsible for Indian campaigns in the West. In 1883, he succeeded Sherman as Army commander in chief.

peaceful assimilation seemed not good enough for the Indians. One of Sheridan's favorite generals sought a large audience to explain the temptations of the Indian culture:

> To me, Indian life, with its attendant ceremonies, mysteries, and forms, is a book of unceasing interest. Grant that some of its pages are frightful, and, if possible, to be avoided, yet the attraction is none the weaker. Study him, fight him, civilize him if you can, he remains still the object of your curiosity, a type of man peculiar and undefined, subjecting himself to no known law of civilization, contending determinedly against all efforts to win him from his chosen mode of life.
>
> If I were an Indian, I often think I would greatly prefer to cast my lot among those of my people who adhered to the free open plains rather than

submit to the confined limits of a reservation, there to be the recipient of the blessed benefits of civilization, with its vices thrown in without stint or measure.

Two years after he published this gratuitous advice, General George A. Custer met the object of his interest for the last time at the Little Bighorn.

General Nelson A. Miles, one of the officers who chased the Sioux after Custer's fall, had a personal reason for revenge: an Indian had taken a pointblank shot at him during an awkward moment in a peace parley. But Miles's reflections show the remarkable extent to which men like him overcame their anger with the enemy. The general spoke of the Indian's "courage, skill, sagacity, endurance, fortitude, and self-sacrifice of a high order" and of "the dignity, hospitality, and gentleness of his demeanor toward strangers and toward his fellow savages." Miles was inclined to think that lapses from this standard meant only that Indians had "degenerated through contact with the white man." Writing on this subject, he did not show the personal arrogance and pride that was the despair of his military superiors. Miles viewed Custer's fall in 1876 as a chastising message for the nation's centennial. He quoted Longfellow: ". . . say that our broken faith / wrought all this ruin and scathe, / In the Year of a Hundred Years."

Miles was not an eccentric in the sympathies he expressed. Colonel John Gibbon, for example, the man who discovered the mutilated bodies of the soldiers who had fallen with Custer at the Little Bighorn, seemed, during his subsequent chase of the Sioux, more angry at the "human ghouls" in the Army who had disturbed some Sioux graves than at the warriors who had killed his colleagues. Such desecrations, he thundered, "impress one with the conviction that in war barbarism stands upon a level only a little lower than our boasted civilization." By Gibbon's lights, the record of white hostility and treachery would force any man to fight: "Thus would the savage in us come to the surface under the oppression which we know the Indian suffers." Like so many Indian fighters who addressed the perennial "Indian question," Gibbon raised more questions about his own culture than he answered about his enemy's.

To these soldiers the courage and bearing of the red man suggested a purer way of life before the coming of the white man, and the military frequently searched for Greek and Roman analogies to suggest the virtues of its enemies. Heathens though they were, they had nobility. Even the Indians' faults might be excused by their manifestly lower stage of cultural evolution.

General George Crook was in a good position to speak of the red men's virtues, for as a fighting man he resembled them. In the field he

*A drawing of the Battle of Little Bighorn by Amos Bad
Heart Bull, an Oglala Sioux. Crazy Horse and Sitting Bull
are mounted before their warriors.*

dispensed with the army uniform and seemed only at ease when he was
free of all cumbersome marks of civilization. Crook left one post, he
tells us, "with one change of underclothes, toothbrush, etc., and went
to investigate matters, intending to be gone a week. But I got interested after the Indians and did not return there again for over two
years."

In the harsh campaigns in the Southwest, Crook taught his men to
move over the land like Apaches, and when white men failed him, he
was adept in recruiting Indians for army service. Frederic Remington
observed Crook's methods and saw they made officers less "Indian
fighters" than "Indian thinkers." "He's more of an Indian than I am,"
marveled one Apache. Crook repaid such compliments; back at West
Point to deliver a graduation address, he may have shocked many with
this observation:

With all his faults, and he has many, the American Indian is not half so
black as he has been painted. He is cruel in war, treacherous at times, and
not over cleanly. But so were our forefathers. His nature, however, is

responsive to treatment which assures him that it is based upon justice, truth, honesty, and common sense. . . .

Crook hesitated to condemn even the most ferocious Apaches, because he respected their spirit and believed that "we are too culpable as a nation, for the existing condition of affairs."

In the view of many officers the weaknesses of their own culture were more glaring than the faults of their enemy. "Barbarism torments the body; civilization torments the soul," one colonel concluded. "The savage remorselessly takes your scalp, your civilized friend as remorselessly swindles you out of your property." Indeed, many of the officers who led the fight for civilization seemed to accept Indian culture on its own terms. Colonel Henry B. Carrington—one of the field officers who supplied Sheridan with maddening accounts of Indian outrages—was an interesting case study. Carrington's official report of the eighty fallen soldiers under his command in the Fetterman fight in Wyoming in 1866 provided grisly reading:

> Eyes torn out and laid on the rocks; teeth chopped out; joints of fingers cut off; brains taken out and placed on rocks, with members of the body; entrails taken out and exposed; hands and feet cut off; arms taken out from sockets; eyes, ears, mouth, and arms penetrated with spearheads, sticks, and arrows; punctures upon every sensitive part of the body, even to the soles of the feet and the palms of the hand.

Yet Carrington's own response to this carnage was not vengeful but reflective, even scholarly. A year later Margaret Carrington, the colonel's wife, published *Ab-sa-ra-ka,* a study of the region the Army had fought to control. In her book she treated this Indian act of warfare with impressive open-mindedness, never directly condemning it. She did note that "the noblest traits of the soldiers were touchingly developed as they carefully handled the mutilated fragments" from the battlefield—but she also praised the Indian: "In ambush and decoy, *splendid.*" Close observers, she wrote, overcame anger to become reconciled, even sympathetic, to "the bold warrior in his great struggle."

As he took charge of enlarged sections of *Ab-sa-ra-ka* in the 1870's Colonel Carrington expanded on this theme of noble resistance. To him the barbarities of the *whites,* in their "irresponsible speculative emigration," overshadowed the red "massacre" of Fetterman's men. Carrington confessed, like Custer, "if I had been a red man as I was a white man, I should have fought as bitterly, if not as brutally, as the Indian fought." And standing before the American Association for the Advancement of Science in 1880 to read his official report of the Fetterman mutilations again, Carrington explained to the scientists that the Indian's disposition of enemies was intended to disable his foe in the afterlife, and so was quite understandable. Nor did he disparage the red man's values, but rather closed his address by suggesting some inadequacies on the other—his own—side: "From 1865 until the present time, there has not been a border campaign which did not have its impulse in the aggressions of a white man."

Few men in the West raised more unusual questions about both cultures than Captain John Bourke. He entered the campaigns, he wrote later, "with the sincere conviction that the only good Indian was a dead Indian, and that the only use to make of him was that of a fertilizer." But the notebooks of this odd, inquiring soul reveal a man haunted by the details of the enemy's life. Mastering several Indian languages, Bourke produced an impressive series of monographs on native religious ceremonies, and in 1895 he became president of the American Folklore Society. Learning proved corrosive to his early cultural pride, and at the end of his army service he was willing to admit that "the American aborigine is not indebted to his pale-faced brother, no matter what nation or race he may be, for lessons in tenderness and humanity."

Admittedly, Captain Bourke's appreciation of native culture was more complex than the respect paid by other Indian fighters. Acknowledging the red man's fighting prowess and noble character, Bourke was more deeply interested in Indian snake ceremonies and scatological rites—mysteries thoroughly repulsive to most white sensibilities. Indeed, his interest in these ceremonies was as intense and sustained as were his protestations of "horror" during each "filthy" and "disgusting" rite. He put all this scholarship and his rather prurient curiosity to work in *Scatologic Rites of All Nations,* where he observed such "orgies" throughout the development of Western civilization, even surviving in nations of what he called "high enlightenment." Here was no sentimental accommodation with Indian culture but a panoramic reminder to the white race of its own barbaric past. Thus the Indians' vices, no less than their virtues, set up a mirror before the advancing Christian whites.

It did not, of course, deter the whites. However noble their image of the savage may have been, it is important to recognize in all of these Indian fighters a fundamental conviction that the price of civilization was not too high. Aware as they were of the ambiguities of their mission, their sympathies and remorse never swayed them from their duty, and no officer of tender conscience was provoked to resign his commission.

How were such mixed emotions sustained? In point of fact, the military's apologia for the red man answered certain professional and psychological needs of the workaday Army. The Army, for both noble and ignoble reasons, wanted to assume control of the administration

Sioux chiefs at Pine Ridge, South Dakota, in 1891,
following the Battle of Wounded Knee.

of Indian affairs that had been held by civilians—a few good words for the long-suffering red man smoothed the way to this goal. Further, by praising the Plains Indians as relentless and efficient warriors the military justified its own ruthless strategy—and setbacks. Nor was frontier ethnology exactly disinterested; close study of the Indians often yielded military advantage for white men. And while empathy for the enemy clearly made the assignment to "redeem" the Indian more painful, there were some emotional satisfactions to be derived from even the most generous attitudes toward the Indians' way of life.

In some instances an officer's respect for the primitive's unfettered aggressiveness happily loosened his own. Thus General George Schofield, commander of the Department of the Missouri, could confess that "civilized man . . . never feels so happy as when he throws off a large part of his civilization and reverts to the life of a semi-savage." When Schofield acted on his own advice on a long hunting trip, he returned invigorated, recording that "I wanted no other occupation in life than to ward off the savage and kill off his food until there should no longer be an Indian frontier in our beautiful country." One of

Sherman's aides reached a similar ominous conclusion after saluting the red man's way of life. This officer was deeply impressed by his colleagues' glowing reports of the nobility of Indian religion, and, he mused,

> There is no doubt the Indians have, at times, been shamefully treated. . . . And there is no doubt a man of spirit would rebel. . . . However, it is useless to moralize about the Indians. Their fate is fixed, and we are so near their end, it is easy to see what that fate is to be. That the Indian might be collected, and put out of misery by being shot deliberately, (as it would be done to a disabled animal), would seem shocking, but something could be said in favor of such procedure.

This puzzling mixture of aggression and regret is less surprising if we take into account the ways, according to contemporary psychologists, that anger and frustration can give rise to these contrasting emotions. The officer corps was enraged by much of what it saw happening to America. The Indians' tactics seemed horrible yet ingenious. Their culture was repellent, but also alluring for its integrity. At the same time, evident in the reports and memoirs of these officers is a disturbing sense of having been abandoned by their own unworthy civilization. Army training and experience prevented these men from acting out their anger, and some anger was instead internalized and expressed in the mourning and guilt they exhibited so frequently. Their appreciation of the native Americans for what they had been was combined with a determination to punish a society for what it refused to become. Their fight for civilized settlement as it should be was troubled by their anger that some virtues, retained by the Indians, were slipping away from the white man.

If we appreciate the military's doubts—of its mandate, of its justice, of its ability, as well as of its commitments to civilization, duty, and progress—the tragedy of the West does not go away. It deepens. Was there an escape from the emotional trap in which the Army found itself? To refuse to win the West would have required a conversion to primitivism hard to imagine inside the ranks of army life and scarcely imaginable in ordinary men living ordinary lives outside of the Army. But the career of one lieutenant in the Nez Perce war illustrates that such a transformation was possible.

Charles Erskine Scott Wood (1852–1944) served on General O. O. Howard's staff, and it was he who took down the very moving speech of the defeated Chief Joseph. Wood's reflections on the Nez Perce campaign, published in the early 1880's, struck the conventional balance between remorse and pride. Surveying the shameful record of white treaty violations, he warned his army colleagues that retribution

might follow. Yet there seemed to be no other possible outcome—
"forces" were "silently at work, beyond all human control," against
the red man's survival. Wood, a gifted literary man, proceeded to join
the somewhat crowded celebration of the culture he had worked to
destroy, hymning the vividness and nobility of the Indian, qualities
that seemed poignant by their passing. But in all this he declined to
attack directly the civilization that had corrupted and supplanted the
Indians', and his fashionable sympathy sounded much like General
Custer's.

But Wood was, in time, to change greatly. He quit the Army, entered the Columbia Law School, and began to cause trouble. Not
satisfied with the state of letters or the law in his time, Wood allied
himself with the radical Industrial Workers of the World and searched
for a literary form to express his increasingly anarchistic temperament.
The fruit of this veteran's singular rehabilitation was a long experimental poem, *The Poet in the Desert,* an affecting personal renunciation
of "civilization" and a call for the revolt of the masses against privilege.
Wood, with booming voice and flowing white beard, was in the twentieth century rather like Father Time—reminding Americans of sins
against the Indians. He knew:

> *I have lain out with the brown men*
> *And know they are favored.*
> *Nature whispered to them her secrets,*
> *But passed me by.*
>
> *I sprawled flat in the bunch-grass, a target*
> *For the just bullets of my brown brothers betrayed.*
> *I was a soldier, and, at command,*
> *Had gone out to kill and be killed.*
>
> *We swept like fire over the smoke-browned tee-pees;*
> *Their conical tops peering above the willows.*
> *We frightened the air with crackle of rifles,*
> *Women's shrieks, children's screams,*
> *Shrill yells of savages;*
> *Curses of Christians.*
> *The rifles chuckled continually.*
> *A poor people who asked nothing but freedom,*
> *Butchered in the dark.*

Wood's polemic is more straightforward than many that are asserted today on behalf of the native Americans. He learned—and his
colleagues in the Army demonstrated—that respect and compassion
for another culture are very unsure checks on violence. And Wood's
life points out one of the costs of war that Americans have generally

been spared: in a prolonged campaign the victor can emerge attracted to his enemy's faith. Our frontier officers had put a civil war behind them and were not ready to turn against their society to save the red man. But their thoughtfully expressed ambivalence toward their task of winning the West throws a revealing light on a history that is still too often falsified with glib stereotypes.

Part Two

Impact of Industrialism

Pennsylvania coal miners, their gas lamps burning, before descending into the pit.

John D. Rockefeller: America's First Billionaire

ROBERT L. HEILBRONER

The driving force behind late nineteenth-century economic growth, social change, and the thousand new developments that heralded the birth of modern America was the rapid expansion of industry. Industrialization made the United States the richest nation in the world and placed some of its citizens among the world's richest men. At one and the same time it fostered the belief that individuals could rise from rags to riches in a generation and the fear that great extremes between the wealthy and the poor would destroy opportunity, even democracy. It lent credence to the idea that Americans were gross materialists, but it also produced a philanthropic outpouring of unprecedented dimensions.

If any one person epitomized the industrialization of the United States to the average late nineteenth-century citizen it was certainly John D. Rockefeller, the master of Standard Oil. To critics, Rockefeller was the robber baron par excellence, the greedy monopolist who crushed competitors ruthlessly and ruled the oil refining business like an oriental monarch. Yet to others he typified the perfect industrial statesman, the efficient, imaginative organizer who provided cheaper and better products than his competitors and who, having amassed a great fortune as a result of his ability, devoted his mature years to equally beneficial philanthropic activities.

Professor Robert L. Heilbroner, an economist at the New School for Social Research, the author of this essay, has written extensively in the field of economic history and thought. In works such as The Worldly Philosophers, The Great Ascent, *and* The Limits of American Capitalism *he has repeatedly demonstrated that it is possible to write history that is at once popular and scholarly even when dealing with highly technical material.* ■

The incredibly shrunken face of an animate mummy, grotesque behind enormous black-rimmed glasses; the old boy tottering around the golf course, benign and imperturbable, distributing his famous dimes; the huge foundation with its medical triumphs; the lingering memory of the great trust and the awed contemplation of the even greater company; and over all, the smell of oil, endlessly pumping out of the earth, each drop adding its bit to the largest exaction ever levied on any society by a private individual—with such associations it is no wonder that the name has sunk into the American mind to an extraordinary degree. From his earliest days the spendthrift schoolboy is brought to his senses with: "Who do you think you are, John D. Rockefeller?"

Yet for all the vivid associations, the man himself remains a shadowy presence. Carnegie, Morgan, or Ford may not have entered so decisively into the American parlance, but they are full-blooded figures in our memory: Carnegie, brash, bustling, proselytizing; Morgan, imperious, choleric, aloof; Ford, shrewd, small-town, thing-minded. But what is John D. Rockefeller, aside from the paper silhouettes of very old age and the aura of immense wealth?

Even his contemporaries did not seem to have a very clear impression of Rockefeller as a human being. For forty years of his active career, he was commonly regarded as an arch economic malefactor—La Follette called him the greatest criminal of the age—and for twenty years, as a great benefactor—John Singer Sargent, painting his portrait, declared himself in the presence of a medieval saint—but neither judgment tells us much about the man. Nor do Ida Tarbell or Henry Demarest Lloyd, both so skillful in portraying the company, succeed in bringing to life its central figure; he lurks in the background, the Captain Nemo of Standard Oil. Similarly, in the reminiscences of his associates we catch only the glimmer of a person—a polite, reserved man, mild in manner, a bit of a stickler for exactitude, totally unremarkable for anything he says or for any particular style of saying it. Surely there must be more to John D. than this! What sort of man was this greatest of all acquisitors? What was the secret of his incredible success?

His mother came of a prosperous Scottish farming family, devout, strait-laced, uncompromising. She springs out at us from her photographs: a tired, plain face, deep-set eyes, and a straight, severe mouth announce Eliza Davison Rockefeller's tired, straight, severe personality. Rockefeller later recalled an instance when he was being whipped by her and finally managed to convince her that he was innocent of a supposed misdemeanor. "Never mind," she said, "we have started in on this whipping and it will do for the next time." Her approach to life made an indelible impression—even in his old age Rockefeller could hear her voice enjoining: "Willful waste makes woeful want."

His father, William Avery Rockefeller, was cut from a different bolt of cloth. Big, robust, and roistering, he treated his sons with a curious mixture of affection and contempt. "I trade with the boys," he boasted to a neighbor, "and skin 'em and I just beat 'em every time I can. I want to make 'em sharp." Sharp himself, he was in and out of a dozen businesses in John's youth and, we have reason to suspect, as many beds. Later, when his son was already a prominent businessman, we can still follow his father's erratic career, now as "Doctor" William A. Rockefeller, "the Celebrated Cancer Specialist," peddling his cures on the circuit. Still later, when John D. had become a great eminence in New York, the father drops into obscurity—only to materialize from time to time in the city, where he is shown around by an embarrassed Standard Oil underling. At the very end he simply disappears. Joseph Pulitzer at one time offered a prize of $8,000 for news of his whereabouts, and the rumor spread that for thirty-five years old William had led a double life, with a second wife in Illinois. No one knows.

It was an unpleasantly polarized family situation, and it helps us understand the quiet, sober-sided boy who emerged. His schoolmates called John "Old pleased-because-I'm-sad," from the title of a school declamation that fitted him to perfection; typically, when the boys played baseball, he kept score. Yet, if it was subdued, it was not an unhappy boyhood. At home he milked the cow and drove the horse and did the household chores that were expected of a boy in upstate New York, but after hours he indulged with his brothers, William and Frank, in the usual boyhood escapades and adventures. A favorite pastime, especially savored since it was forbidden, was to go skating at night on the Susquehanna. On one occasion William and John saved a neighbor's boy from drowning, whereupon their evening's sally had to be admitted. Eliza Rockefeller praised their courage—and whipped them soundly for their disobedience.

Always in the Rockefeller home there was the stress on gainful work. Their father may have worked to make them sharp, but their mother worked to make them industrious. John was encouraged to raise turkeys, and he kept the money from their sale in a little box on the mantel until he had accumulated the sum of $50. A neighboring farmer asked to borrow the amount at seven per cent for a year, and his mother approved. During that summer John dug potatoes at thirty-seven and a half cents a day. When the farmer repaid the loan with $3.50 in interest, the lesson was not lost on John: the earning power of capital was much to be preferred to that of labor.

He was then only in his teens—he was born in 1839—but already, frugal ways, a deliberate manner, and a strong sense of planning and

Three faces of John D. Rockefeller: (top) the earnest young man at 18, a clerk to become partner in his own firm; (bottom left) at 35, the commanding businessman; (bottom right) at 91, the "shrunken face of an animate mummy" still active in retirement.

purposefulness were in evidence. As his sister Lucy said: "When it's raining porridge, you'll find John's dish right side up." But now the time for summer jobs was coming to an end. The family had moved from Moravia and Oswego, where John had grown up, to Cleveland, where he went to the local high school in his fifteenth and sixteenth years. For a few months he attended Folsom's Commercial College, where he learned the elements of bookkeeping—and then began the all-important search for the first real job.

That search was performed with a methodical thoroughness that became a hallmark of the Rockefeller style. A list of promising establishments was drawn up—nothing second-rate would do—and each firm was hopefully visited. Rebuffed on the first go-round, John went the rounds again undaunted, and then a third time. Eventually his perseverance was rewarded. He became a clerk in the office of Hewitt & Tuttle, commission merchants and produce shippers. Typically, he took the job without inquiring about salary, hung his coat on a peg, climbed onto the high bookkeeper's stool, and set to work. It was a red-letter day in his life; later, when he was a millionaire many times over, the flag was regularly hoisted before his house to commemorate September 26, 1855.

Work came naturally, even pleasurably to John Rockefeller. He was precise, punctual, diligent. "I had trained myself," he wrote in his memoirs, ". . . that my check on a bill was the executive act which released my employer's money from the till and was attended with more responsibility than the spending of my own funds."

With such model attitudes, Rockefeller quickly advanced. By 1858 his salary (which turned out to be $3.50 a week) had more than tripled, but when Hewitt & Tuttle were unable to meet a request for a further raise, he began to look elsewhere. A young English acquaintance named Maurice Clark, also a clerk, was similarly unhappy with his prospects, and the two decided to form a produce-shipping firm of their own. Clark had saved up $2,000, and John Rockefeller had saved $900; the question was, where to get the last necessary $1,000. John knew that at age twenty-one he was entitled to a patrimony of this amount under his father's will, and he turned to William Rockefeller for an advance. His father listened with mingled approval and suspicion, and finally consented to lend his son the money if John would pay interest until he was twenty-one. "And John," he added, "the rate is ten."

Rockefeller accepted the proposition, and Clark & Rockefeller opened its doors in 1859. The Cleveland *Leader* recommended the principals to its readers as "experienced, responsible, and prompt," and the venture succeeded from the start. In its first year the firm made a profit of $4,400; in the second year, $17,000; and when the Civil War began, profits soared. Rockefeller became known as an up-and-coming young businessman, a man to be watched. Even his father agreed. From time to time he would come around and ask for his loan back, just to be sure the money was really there, but then, unable to resist ten per cent interest, he would lend it back again.

Meanwhile an adult personality begins to emerge. A picture taken just before he married Laura Spelman in 1864 shows a handsome man of twenty-five with a long, slightly mournful visage, a fine straight nose, a rather humorless mouth. Everyone who knew him testified to his virtues. He was industrious, even-tempered, generous, kind; and if it was not a sparkling personality, it was not a dour one. Yet there is something not quite attractive about the picture as a whole. Charitable from his earliest days, he itemized each contribution—even the tiniest—in his famous Ledger A, with the result that his generosity, of which there was never any doubt, is stained with self-observance and an over-nice persnicketiness. Extremely self-critical, he was given to intimate "pillow talks" at night in which he took himself to task for various faults, but the words he recalled and later repeated—"Now a little success, soon you will fall down, soon you will be overthrown . . ." smack not so much of honest self-search as of the exorcising of admonitory parental voices. He was above all orderly and forethoughted, but there is a compulsive, and sometimes a faintly repellent quality about his self-control. He recounts that when he was travelling as a commission merchant, he would never grab a bite in the station and wolf it down, like the others on the train, but "if I could not finish eating properly, I filled my mouth with as much as it would hold, then went leisurely to the train and chewed it slowly before swallowing it."

Yet the faults, far from constituting major traits in themselves, were minor flaws in an essentially excellent character. Rockefeller forged ahead by his merits, not by meanness—and among his merits was a well-developed capacity to size up a business situation coolly and rationally. Living in Cleveland, he could scarcely fail to think about one such situation virtually under his nose. Less than a day's journey by train were the Oil Regions of Pennsylvania, one of the most fantastic locales in America. A shambles of mud, dying horses (their skins denuded by petroleum), derricks, walking beams, chugging donkey engines, and jerry-built towns, the Regions oozed oil, money, and dreams. Bits of land the size of a blanket sold on occasion for three and four hundred dollars, pastures jumped overnight into fortunes (one pasture rose from $25,000 to $1,600,000 in three months), whole villages bloomed into existence in a matter of months. Pithole, Pennsylvania, an aptly named pinprick on the map, became the third largest center for mail in Pennsylvania and boasted a $65,000 luxury hotel. Within a few years it was again a pinprick, and the hotel was sold for $50.

It is uncertain whether Rockefeller himself visited the Oil Regions in the halcyon early 1860's. What is certain is that he sniffed oil in Cleveland itself, where the crude product was transported by barge and barrel for distillation and refining. In any event, the hurly-burly, the disorganization, and above all the extreme riskiness of the Oil Regions would never have appealed to Rockefeller's temperament. Let someone else make a million or lose it by blindly drilling for an invisi-

ble reservoir—a surer and far steadier route to wealth was available to
the refiner who bought the crude oil at thirty-one or thirty-two cents
a gallon and then sold the refined product at eighty to eighty-five cents.

The chance to enter the refining business came to Clark and Rockefeller in the person of an enterprising and ingenious young engineer
named Sam Andrews. Andrews, recently come from England (by coin-
cidence, he was born in the same town as Clark), was restive in his job
in a land refinery and eager to try his hand at oil refining. He talked
with his fellow townsman and through Clark met Rockefeller. The
three agreed to take a fling at the business. Andrews, together with
Clark's brothers, took on the production side, and Maurice Clark and
Rockefeller the financial side. Thus in 1863 Andrews, Clark & Company was born. Rockefeller, content behind the anonymity of the
"Company," had contributed, together with his partner, half the total
capital, but he retained his interest in the produce business. The investment in oil was meant to be no more than a side venture.

But the side venture prospered beyond all expectation. The demand for refined oil increased by leaps and bounds. As Allan Nevins
has written: "A commodity that had been a curiosity when Lincoln was
nominated, had become a necessity of civilization, the staple of a vast
commerce, before he was murdered." And the supply of oil, despite
a thousand warnings, auguries, and dire prophecies that the mysteri-
ous underground springs would dry up, always matched and over-
matched demand.

As the business boomed, so did the number of refineries. One
could go into the refinery business for no more capital than it took to
open a well-equipped hardware store, and Cleveland's location with its
favoring rivers and fortunately placed rail lines made it a natural center
for the shipment of crude oil. Hence by 1866, only two years after
Andrews, Clark & Company had opened its doors, there were over
thirty refineries along the Cleveland Flats, and twenty more would be
added before the year was out.

The Rockefeller refinery was among the largest of these. In Sam
Andrews had been found the perfect plant superintendent; in Clark
and Rockefeller, the perfect business management. From half-past six
in the morning, when Andrews and Clark would burst in on their
partner at breakfast, until they parted company just before supper, the
three talked oil, oil, oil. Slowly, however, Andrews and Rockefeller
found themselves at odds with Clark. They had become convinced that
oil was to be a tremendous and permanent business enterprise; Clark
was more cautious and less willing to borrow to expand facilities.
Finally, in 1865, it was decided to put the firm up for auction among
themselves, the seller to retain the produce business. "It was the day
that determined my career," Rockefeller recalled long afterward. "I

felt the bigness of it, but I was as calm as I am talking to you now."
When at last Maurice Clark bid $72,000, Rockefeller topped him by
$500. Clark threw up his hands. "The business is yours," he declared.

From the beginning Rockefeller & Andrews, as the new firm was
called, was a model of efficiency. Even before acquiring the firm, Rockefeller had become interested in the economies of plant operation.
When he found that plumbers were expensive by the hour, he and Sam
Andrews hired one by the month, bought their own pipes and joints,
and cut plumbing costs in half. When cooperage grew into a formidable item, they built their own shop where barrels cost them only forty
per cent of the market price, and soon costs were cut further by the
acquisition of a stand of white oak, a kiln, and their own teams and
wagons to haul the wood from kiln to plant. The emphasis on cost
never ceased; when Rockefeller & Andrews had long since metamor-
phosed into the Standard Oil Company and profits had grown into the
millions, cost figures were still carried to three decimal places. One day
Rockefeller was watching the production line in one of his plants,
where cans of finished oil were being soldered shut. "How many drops
of solder do you use on each can?" he inquired. The answer was forty.
"Have you ever tried thirty-eight? No? Would you mind having some
sealed with thirty-eight and let me know?" A few cans leaked with
thirty-eight, but with thirty-nine all were perfect. A couple of thousand
dollars a year were saved.

The zeal for perfection of detail was from the beginning a factor
in the growth of Rockefeller's firm. More important was his meeting
in 1866 with Henry M. Flagler, the first of a half-dozen associates who
would bring to the enterprise the vital impetus of talent, enthusiasm,
and a hard determination to succeed. Flagler, a quick, ebullient, bold
businessman who had fought his way up from the poverty of a small-
town parsonage, was a commission merchant of considerable prominence when Rockefeller met him. The two quickly took a liking to one
another, and Rockefeller soon induced Flagler to join the fast-expand-
ing business. Flagler brought along his own funds and those of his
father-in-law, Stephen Harkness, and this fresh influx of capital made
possible even further expansion. Rockefeller, Andrews & Flagler—
soon incorporated as the Standard Oil Company—rapidly became the
biggest single refinery in Cleveland.

Flagler brought to the enterprise an immense energy and a playful-
ness that Rockefeller so egregiously lacked. The two main partners
now had a code word in their telegrams—AMELIA—which meant
"Everything is lovely and the goose hangs high." And everything *was*
lovely. One of Flagler's first jobs was to turn his considerable bargaining skills to a crucial link in the chain of oil-processing costs. All the
major refineries bought in the same market—the Oil Regions—and all

Henry M. Flagler.

sold in the same markets—the great cities—so that their costs of purchase and their prices at the point of sale were much alike. In between purchase and sale, however, lay two steps: the costs of refining and the costs of transportation. In the end it was the latter that was to prove decisive in the dog-eat-dog struggle among the refineries.

For the railroads needed a steady flow of shipments to make money, and they were willing to grant rebates to the refiners if they would level out their orders. Since there were a number of routes by which to ship oil, each refiner was in a position to play one road against another, and the Standard, as the biggest and strongest refiner in Cleveland, was naturally able to gain the biggest and most lucrative discounts on its freight. This was a game that Flagler played with consummate skill. Advantageous rebates soon became an important means by which the Standard pushed ahead of its competitors—and in later years, when there were no more competitors, an important source of revenue in themselves. By 1879, when the Rockefeller concern had become a giant, a government investigatory agency estimated that in a period of five months the firm had shipped some eighteen million barrels of oil, on which rebates ran from eleven per cent on the B&O to *forty-seven* per cent on the Pennsylvania Railroad. For the five months, rebates totalled over ten million dollars.

This is looking too far ahead, however. By 1869, a scant three years after Flagler had joined it, the company was worth about a million dollars, but it was very far from being an industrial giant or a monopoly. Indeed, the problem which constantly plagued Rockefeller and his associates was the extreme competition in the oil business. As soon as business took a downturn—as it did in 1871—the worst kind of cutthroat competition broke out; prices dropped until the Titusville *Herald* estimated that the overage refiner lost seventy-five cents on each barrel he sold.

As the biggest refiner, Rockefeller naturally had the greatest stake in establishing some kind of stability in the industry. Hence he set about to devise a scheme—the so-called South Improvement Company—which would break the feast-and-famine pattern that threatened to overwhelm the industry. In its essence the South Improvement Company was a kind of cartel aimed at holding up oil prices—by arranging "reasonable" freight rates for its own members while levying far higher ones on "outsiders." Since the scheme was open to all, presumably there would soon be no outsiders, and once all were within the fold, the refiners could operate a single, powerful economic unit.

The plan might have worked but for the inability of such headstrong and individualistic groups as the railroads and the producers to cooperate for more than a passing moment. When the producers in the Oil Regions rose in wrath against a plan which they (quite rightly) saw as a powerful buying combination against them, the scheme simply collapsed.

The idea of eliminating competition did not, however, collapse with it. Instead, Rockefeller turned to a plan at once much simpler and much more audacious. If he could not eliminate competition, then perhaps he could eliminate his competitors by buying them up one by one—and this he set out to do. The plan was set in motion by a meeting with Colonel Oliver Payne, the chief stockholder in Rockefeller's biggest competitor. Briefly Rockefeller outlined the ruinous situation which impended if competition were permitted to continue unbridled; equally briefly, he proposed a solution. The Standard would increase its capitalization, the Payne plant would be appraised by impartial judges, and its owners would be given stock in proportion to their equity. As for Payne himself, Rockefeller suggested he should take an active part in the management of the new, bigger Standard Oil.

Payne quickly assented; so did Jabez Bostwick, the biggest refiner in New York, and one after another the remaining refiners sold out. According to Rockefeller, they were only too glad to rid themselves of their burdensome businesses at fair prices; according to many of the refiners, it was a question of taking Rockefeller's offer or facing sure ruin. We need not debate the point here; what is certain is that by the end of 1872 the Standard was the colossus of Cleveland. There remained only the United States to conquer.

Rockefeller himself was in his mid-thirties. The slightly melancholy visage of the younger man had altered; a thick mustache trimmed straight across the bottom hid his lips and gave to his face a commanding, even stern, aspect. In a family portrait we see him standing rather stiffly, carefully dressed as befits a man in his station. For he was already rich—even his non-oil investments, as he wrote to his wife, were enough to give him independence, and his style of life had changed as his fortune had grown. He and his wife now lived in Forest Hill, a large, gaunt house on eighty acres just east of Cleveland. He had begun to indulge himself with snappy trotters, and on a small scale commenced what was to become in time a Brobdingnagian pastime—moving landscape around.

In town, in his business pursuits, he was already the reserved, colorless, almost inscrutable personality who baffled his business contemporaries; at home, he came as close as he could to a goal he sought assiduously—relaxation. His children were his great delight: he taught them to swim and invented strange and wonderful contraptions to keep them afloat; he bicycled with them; he played daring games of blindman's buff—so daring in fact that he once had to have stitches taken in his head after running full tilt into a doorpost.

It was, in a word, the very model of a Victorian home, affectionate, dutiful, and, of course, rich. An air of rectitude hung over the establishment, not so much as to smother it, but enough to give it a distinctive flavor. Concerts (aside from the performances of their children), literature, art, or theatre were not Rockefeller amusements; in entertaining, their tastes ran to Baptist ministers and business associates. An unpretentious and earnest atmosphere hid—or at least disguised—the wealth; until they were nearly grown up the children had no idea of "who they were."

And of course the beneficences continued and grew: $23,000 for various charities in 1878, nearly $33,000 in 1880, over $100,000 in 1884. But the nice preciseness of giving was maintained; a pledge card signed in 1883 for the Euclid Avenue Baptist Church reads:

Mrs. Rockefeller	$10.00 each week
Self	30.00 each week
Each of our four children	00.20 each week

How rich was Rockefeller by 1873, a mere ten years after Andrews, Clark & Company had opened its doors? We cannot make an accurate estimate, but it is certain that he was a millionaire several times over.

In another ten years his Standard Oil holdings alone would be worth a phenomenal twenty million dollars—enough, with his other investments, to make him one of the half-dozen richest men in the country.

But now a legal problem began to obtrude. The Standard Oil Company was legally chartered in Ohio, and it had no right to own plants in other states. Not until 1889 would New Jersey amend its incorporation laws to allow a corporation chartered within the state to hold the stock of corporations chartered elsewhere. Hence the question: how was the Standard legally to control its expanding acquisitions in other states?

The problem was solved by one of Rockefeller's most astute lieutenants—Samuel Dodd, a round little butterball of a man with an extraordinarily clear-sighted legal mind and an unusually high and strict sense of personal integrity. Because he believed that he could render the best advice to the Standard if he was above any suspicion of personal aggrandizement, he repeatedly refused Rockefeller's offers to make him a director or to buy for him stock which would have made him a multimillionaire.

The sword which Dodd applied to the Gordian knot of interstate control was the device of the trust. In brief, he proposed a single group of nine trustees, with headquarters in New York, who would hold "in trust" the certificates of all Standard's operating companies, including the major company in Ohio itself. In 1882 the Standard Oil Trust was formally established, with John and his brother William Rockefeller, Flagler, Payne, Bostwick, John D. Archbold, Charles Pratt, William G. Warden, and Benjamin Brewster as trustees. (Sam Andrews had sold the last of his stock to Rockefeller four years before, saying the business had grown too big.) In fact, though not in law, one enormous interstate corporation had been created.

Few people even at this time appreciated quite how great the company was. By the 1880's the Standard was the largest and richest of all American manufacturing organizations. It had eighty-five per cent of a business which took the output of 20,000 wells and which employed 100,000 people. And all this before the advent of the automobile. The colossus of the Standard was built not on the internal combustion engine but on the kerosene lamp.

With the creation of the Trust the center of gravity of the concern moved to New York. Rockefeller himself bought a $600,000 brownstone on West Fifty-fourth Street, where the round of teas and dinners for temperance workers, church people, and Standard executives soon went on. The Trust itself occupied No. 26 Broadway, an eleven-story "skyscraper" with gay striped awnings shading its large windows. It was soon known as the most famous business address in the world. There Rockefeller appeared daily, usually in high silk hat, long coat, and gloves—the accepted costume for the big business executive of the time.

At 26 Broadway Rockefeller was the commanding figure. But his exercise of command, like his personality, was notable for its lack of color, dash, and verve. Inquiring now of this one, now of that, what he thought of such and such a situation, putting his questions methodically and politely in carefully chosen words, never arguing, never raising his voice, Rockefeller seemed to govern his empire like a disembodied intelligence. He could be, as always, a stickler for detail; an accountant recalls him suddenly materializing one day, and with a polite "Permit me," turning over the ledger sheets, all the while murmuring, "Very well kept, very indeed," until he stopped at one page: "A little error here; will you correct it?" But he could also be decisive and absolutely determined. "He saw strategic points like a Napoleon, and he swooped down on them with the suddenness of a Napoleon," wrote Ida Tarbell. Yet even that gives too much of the impression of dash and daring. She was closer to the mark when she wrote: "If one attempts to analyse what may be called the legitimate greatness of Mr. Rockefeller's creation in distinction to its illegitimate greatness, he will find at the foundation the fact that it is as perfectly centralized as the Catholic Church or the Napoleonic government." It was true. By 1886 the Standard had evolved a system of committees, acting in advisory roles to the active management, which permitted an incalculably complex system to function with extraordinary ease. It is virtually the same system that is used today. Rockefeller had created the great Trust on which the eyes of the whole world were fastened, but behind the Trust, sustaining it, operating it, maintaining it, he had created an even greater Organization.

"It's many a day since I troubled you with a letter," wrote William Warden, a onetime independent Cleveland refiner who had been bought out and was now a trustee and major official in the Standard, "and I would not do so now could I justify myself in being silent. . . . We have met with a success unparalleled in commercial history, our name is known all over the world, and our public character is not one to be envied. We are quoted as representative of all that is evil, hard hearted, oppressive, cruel (we think unjustly), but men look askance at us, we are pointed at with contempt, and while some good men flatter us, it's only for our money . . . This is not pleasant to write, for I had longed for an honored position in commercial life. None of us would choose such a reputation; we all desire a place in the honor & affection of honorable men."

It was a cry of anguish, but it was amply justified. By the 1880's the Standard was not only widely known—it was notorious. In part its increasingly bad business reputation originated in the business community itself. Stories began to circulate of the unfair advantage taken by the colossus when it bid for smaller properties: the case of the Widow Backus, whose deceased husband's refinery was supposedly bought for a pittance, was much talked about. Many of these tales— the Backus case in particular—were simply untrue. But as the Standard grew in size and visibility, other business practices came to light which *were* true, and which were hardly calculated to gain friends for the company.

Foremost among these practices was an evil device called the drawback. Not content with enjoying a large competitive advantage through its special rebates, Standard also forced the railroads to pay it a portion of the freight charges paid by non-Standard refiners! Thus Daniel O'Day, a particularly ruthless Standard official, used his local economic leverage to get a small railroad to carry Standard's oil at ten cents a barrel, to charge all independents thirty-five cents, *and to turn over the twenty-five cent differential to a Standard subsidiary.* Another Standard agent, finding that a competitor's car had slipped through without paying the Standard exaction, wrote the road to collect the amount owing, adding: "Please turn another screw."

Such incidents and practices—always denied by the company and never admitted by Rockefeller—plagued the Standard for years. And the impression of highhandedness was not much improved by the behavior of the Standard's officials when they went on public view. John D. Archbold, a key executive called to testify before New York State's Hepburn Committee in 1879, was a typical bland witness. When pressed hard, he finally admitted he was a stockholder of the Standard. What was his function there? "I am a clamorer for dividends. That is the only function I have in connection with the Standard Oil Company." Chairman Alonzo Hepburn asked how large dividends were. "I have no trouble transporting my share," answered Archbold. On matters of rebates he declined to answer. Finally Hepburn asked him to return for further questioning the next day. "I have given today to the matter," replied Archbold politely. "It will be impossible for me to be with you again."

Not least, there was the rising tide of public protest against the monopoly itself. In 1881 Henry Demarest Lloyd, a journalist of passionate reformist sentiments, wrote for the *Atlantic Monthly* an article called "The Story of a Great Monopoly." Editor William Dean Howells gave it the lead in the magazine, and overnight it was a sensation (that issue of the *Atlantic* went through seven printings). "The family that uses a gallon of kerosene a day pays a yearly tribute to the Standard of $32 . . . ," wrote Lloyd. "America has the proud satisfaction of having furnished the world with the greatest, wisest, and meanest monopoly known to history."

Standard's profits were nothing so great as described by Lloyd, but that hardly mattered. If the article was imprecise or even downright wrong in detail, it was right in its general thrust. What counted was Lloyd's incontrovertible demonstration that an individual concern had grown to a position of virtual impregnability, a position which made it in fact no longer subordinate to the states from which it drew its legal privilege of existence, but their very peer or better in financial strength and even political power. Before Lloyd wrote his article, the Standard was the source of rage or loss to scattered groups of producers, businessmen, or consumers. When he was through with his indictment, it was a national scandal.

That it should be a scandal was totally incomprehensible to John D. The mounting wave of protest and obloquy perplexed him more than it irritated him. Ida Tarbell's famous—and generally accurate— *History of the Standard Oil Company* he dismissed as "without foundation." The arrogance of an Archbold he merely chuckled at, recounting the Hepburn testimony in his *Random Reminiscences of Men and Events* with the comment that Archbold had a "well-developed sense of humor." With his own passion for order, he understood not a whit the passions of those whose demise was required that order might prevail. On one occasion when he was testifying in court, he spied in the courtroom George Rice, an old adversary (against whom, as a matter of fact, the famous screw had been turned, and whom Rockefeller had once offered to buy out). As he left the witness stand, Rockefeller walked over to Rice and, putting out his hand, said: "How do you do, Mr. Rice? You and I are getting to be old men, are we not?"

Rice ignored the hand. "Don't you think, Mr. Rice," pursued Rockefeller, "it might have been better if you had taken my advice years ago?"

"Perhaps it would," said Rice angrily. "You said you would ruin my business and you have done so."

"Pshaw! Pshaw!" rejoined Rockefeller.

"Don't you pooh-pooh me," said Rice in a fury. "I say that by the power of your great wealth you have ruined me."

"Not a word of truth in it," Rockefeller answered, turning and making his way through the crowd. "Not a word of truth in it."

He could not in fact bring himself to believe that there was a word of truth in any of it. There was nothing to argue about concerning the need for giant enterprise, or "industrial combinations" as they were called. They were simply a necessity, a potentially dangerous necessity admittedly, but a necessity nonetheless. All the rest was ignorance or willful misunderstanding. "You know," he wrote to a university president who offered to prepare a scholarly defense of Standard's policies, "that great prejudice exists against all successful business enterprise—the more successful, the greater the prejudice."

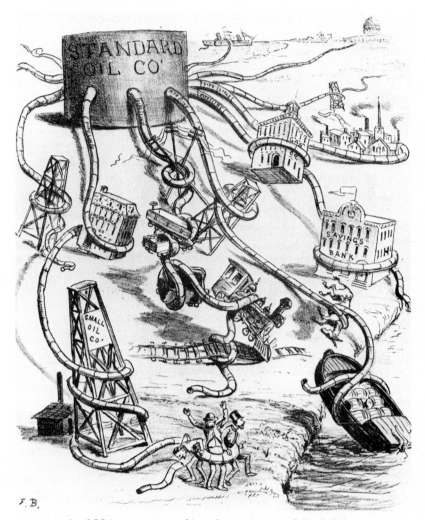

*An 1884 cartoon attacking the "octopus" of Rockefeller's
Standard Oil Company. The creature's tentacles reach
everywhere from the small oil company to the nation's
capitol dome.*

It was common, during the early 1900's, to read thunderous accusations against the Standard Oil Company and its sinister captain, but
the fact was that John D. Rockefeller had severed all connection with
the business as early as 1897. When news came to him, ten years later,
that the great Trust had been heavily fined by the government, he read
the telegram and without comment went on with his game of golf. At
the actual dissolution of the Trust in 1911, he was equally uncon-

cerned. For already his interests were turning away from business management toward another absorbing role—the disposition of the wealth which was now beginning to accumulate in truly awesome amounts.

Here enters the last of those indispensable subordinates through whom Rockefeller operated so effectively. Frederick T. Gates, onetime minister, now a kind of Baptist minister-executive, met Rockefeller when Gates played a crucial role in the studies that established the need for a great new university in Chicago. Shortly he became the catalytic figure in instituting the university with a Rockefeller gift of $600,000. (Before he was done, Rockefeller would give it 80 million dollars.) Then one morning in 1889, when the two were chatting, Rockefeller suddenly said: "I am in trouble, Mr. Gates." He told him of the flood of appeals which now came by the sackful, and of his inability to give away money with any satisfaction until he had made the most thorough investigation into the cause. Rockefeller continued: "I want you to come to New York and open an office here. You can aid me in my benefactions by taking interviews and inquiries and reporting the results for action. What do you say?"

Gates said yes, and it was under his guidance, together with that of Rockefeller's son, John D., Jr., that the great philanthropies took root: the General Education Board, which pioneered in the educational, social, and medical development of our own South; the Rockefeller Institute for Medical Research, quickly famous for its campaign against yellow fever; the Rockefeller Foundation with its far-ranging interests in the promotion of research. Not that the giving was done hastily. Gates had a meticulousness of approach which suited his employer perfectly. It was not until 1900 that more than 2 million dollars was given away, not until 1905 that the total of annual giving exceeded 10 million dollars, not until 1913 that the great climactic disbursements began to be made: 45 million dollars that year and 65 million the next, to establish the Rockefeller Foundation; finally 138 million dollars in 1919 to support the philanthropies already endowed.

Gates took his philanthropic duties with ministerial zeal and profound seriousness. Raymond Fosdick, president of the Rockefeller Foundation, recalls Gates' last meeting as a trustee. Shaking his fist at the startled board, he boomed: "When you die and come to approach the judgment of Almighty God, what do you think He will demand of you? Do you for an instant presume to believe He will inquire into your petty failures or your trivial virtues? No! He will ask just one question: 'What did you do as a Trustee of the Rockefeller Foundation?' "

Gates was more than just a philanthropic guide. Rapidly he became a prime business agent for Rockefeller in the large business deals which inevitably continued to arise. When Rockefeller came into immense iron properties along the Mesabi Range, it was Gates who superintended their development and the creation of a giant fleet of ore carriers, and it was Gates who carried through their eventual sale to Morgan and Frick at the huge price of 88.5 million dollars. It was the only time in Gates' long association with John D. that he indicated the slightest desire to make money for himself. When the immense iron deal was complete and Gates had made his final report, Rockefeller, as usual, had no words of praise, but listened attentively and without objection and then said, with more emphasis than usual, "Thank you, Mr. Gates!" Gates looked at him with an unaccustomed glint in his eye. "Thank you is not enough, Mr. Rockefeller," he replied. Rockefeller understood and promptly saw to it that Gates was remunerated handsomely.

John D. was becoming an old man now. His face, sharper with age, took on a crinkled, masklike appearance, in the midst of which his small eyes twinkled. Golf had become a great passion and was performed in the deliberate Rockefeller manner. A boy was hired to chant: "Keep your head down," useless steps were saved by bicycling between shots, and even when he was playing alone, every stroke was remorselessly counted. (John D. was once asked to what he owed the secret of the success of Standard Oil; he answered: "To the fact that we never deceived ourselves.")

To the outside world the old man more and more presented a quaint and benevolent image. By the 1920's the antitrust passions of the 1890's and early 1900's had been transmuted into sycophancy of big business; there were no more cries of "tainted money," but only a hopeful queuing up at the portals of the great foundations. The man who had once been denounced by Theodore Roosevelt and Tolstoy and William Jennings Bryan was now voted, in a popular poll, one of the Greatest Americans. Cartoonists and feature writers made the most of his pith helmet and his paper vest, his monkishly plain food, his beaming, almost childlike expression. To the outside world he seemed to live in a serene and admirable simplicity, which indeed he did, in a purely personal sense. But the reporters who told of his afternoon drives did not report that the seventy miles of road over his estate at Pocantico Hills were built by himself, that the views he liked so well were arranged by moving hills around as an interior decorator moves chairs. The perfection of Pocantico became an obsession: some railway tracks that were in the way were relocated at the cost of $700,000, a small college that spoiled a view was induced to move for $1,500,000, a distant smokestack was camouflaged. It was, to repeat George Kaufman's famous line, an example of what God could have done if He'd only had the money.

In the midst of it all was the never-failingly polite, always slightly disengaged old man, somehow disappointing in close view, somehow smaller than we expect. There are mannerisms and eccentricities, of course, which, when viewed under the magnification of 900 million dollars, take on a certain prominence, but they are peccadilloes rather than great flaws. There is the enormous industrial generalship, to be sure, but it is a generalship of logic and plan, not of dash and daring. There is the generosity on a monumental scale, but then again, not on such a scale as to cut the Rockefeller fortune by ninety per cent, as was the case with Carnegie. Rockefeller gave away over half a billion, but probably he kept at least that much for his family.

In short, the more we look into the life of John D. Rockefeller, the more we look into the life of an incredibly successful—and withal, very unremarkable—man. It is a curious verdict to pass on the greatest acquisitor of all time, and yet it is difficult to avoid the conclusion that John Flynn has perfectly phrased: "Rockefeller in his soul was a bookkeeper." We can see the bookkeeperishness in unexpected but telling places, such as in his *Random Reminiscences,* where he dilates on the importance of friendship, but cites as a dubious friend the man who protests, "I can't indorse your note, because I have an agreement with my partners not to . . ."; or again, when he expands on the nonmaterial pleasures of life, such as gardening, but adds as a clincher: "We make a small fortune out of ourselves, selling to our New Jersey place at $1.50 and $2.00 each, trees which originally cost us only five or ten cents at Pocantico." Whether he turns to friendship or to nature, money is the measure.

These are surely not the sentiments of greatness—but then John D. was not a great man. Neither was he, needless to say, a bad man. In most ways he was the very paragon of the business virtues of his day, and at the same time the perfect exemplar of the unvirtues as well. It is likely that he would have made his mark in any field, but unlikely that any commodity other than oil would have offered such staggering possibilities for industrial growth and personal aggrandizement. He personified in ideas the typical business thought of his day—very Christian, very conventional, very comfortable.

Yet as the image of John D. recedes, we realize the pointlessness of such personal appraisals. We study Rockefeller not so much as a person but as an agent—an agent for better and worse in the immense industrial transformation of America. Viewed against this stupendous process of change, even the largest lives take on a subordinate quality, and personal praise and blame seem almost irrelevant. And Rockefeller was not one of the largest lives—only one of the luckiest.

In the end there was only the frail ghost of a man, stubbornly resisting the inevitable. His son, John D., Jr., whom he had fondly called "my greatest fortune," had long since taken over the reins of the great foundations and had begun to refashion the Rockefeller image in his own way: Rockefeller Center, The Cloisters, the restoration of Williamsburg. His grandsons, among them one who would one day aspire to the Presidency of the United States, were already young men, carefully imbued with the family style: determination, modesty on the grand scale, a prudent balance between self-interest and altruism. And the Standard itself, now split and resplit into a handful of carefully noncollusive (and equally carefully noncompetitive) companies, was bigger and more powerful than ever. All in all, it was an extraordinary achievement, and the old man must have   joyed it to the hilt. For it had indeed rained porridge, and his dish had surely been kept right side up.

The Immigrant: White and Black

BERNARD A. WEISBERGER

Coexistent with the flood of "new" immigrants that poured into American cities from eastern and southern Europe beginning in the 1880s was a similar migration of American blacks from the South. Like so many of the Europeans, they were from rural backgrounds and essentially peasants. These black "immigrants" had the advantage of being American citizens and of speaking English from the start, but besides lacking in experience in city ways, they labored under the handicap of racial prejudice, less rigid than in the South but nevertheless stultifying in its effects. Thus, as Bernard Weisberger shows in this discussion of their fate before the Great Depression of the 1930s, they endured all the burdens of their European fellows and then some, although, again like the Europeans, they also profited from the opportunities that city life provided.

Dr. Weisberger, formerly a professor of history at Chicago, Rochester, and other universities, is currently devoting himself full time to historical research and writing. Among his books are The American Newspaperman, The New Industrial Society, *and other works.* ∎

As any really thoughtful statesman knows, it is one of the ironies of history that great decisions often have entirely unexpected consequences. Until men are given the gift of prophecy, "Forgive them; for they know not what they do" is an appropriate motto for those who judge political performances. But in some cases, "Congratulate them; for they know not what they do" might be as apt.

It is hard to say which version applies to the congressmen who passed the Johnson-Reed immigration restriction act of 1924. In that year they heeded a warning sounded by a New England poet some twenty years earlier. "Wide open and unguarded stand our gates," Thomas Bailey Aldrich intoned, and through them, he warned, poured a "motley throng" of immigrants. If not checked, they would soon tear the clustered stars from Liberty's brow and trample them in the dust.

By passing an immigration act that sharply limited the number of admissible newcomers, particularly those of Southern and Eastern European origin, the lawmakers appeared to answer the cry of Aldrich and others like him. They shut the gate on further "unassimilable" additions to the American "melting pot." Yet at the very time of this action another wave of immigration into the great cities was gathering momentum. No restrictive laws could bar it, for it was made up of freeborn American citizens. They were black men and women, moving from a poverty-stricken South to the urban frontier.

That was the first paradox. And there was a second. The children of the "motley throng," who presumably could not be Americanized, became, in the forty years after the gates were slammed shut, largely absorbed into the major currents of American life. But, for complex reasons, the children of the "immigrant within," the northward-moving black, still remained unmelted.

To understand these ironies is to learn much about the meaning of success and its connection with race and nationality in the United States.

The reaction against unlimited immigration arose in part from the sheer volume of the influx after 1900. Where some fourteen million newcomers had arrived in the forty years between 1860 and 1900, thirteen million more poured in during the fifteen years that followed. Such a torrent of immigrants was bound to disturb even a relatively tolerant society, with plenty of land and jobs for all. Americans of the pre-World War I era watched the frontier's free land disappear and wondered anxiously if the bull market for labor might not, in due course, dry up as well. Nor were they quite as tolerant as their grandfathers had been. Doubts about the economics of immigration were supplemented by unhappiness with its changing sources after 1900. Post-1900 immigrants were no longer mainly from Germany, England,

Ireland, or Scandinavia. They came instead from Italy and from the undigested religious and national minorities within the sprawling Hohenzollern, Ottoman, Hapsburg, and Romanov empires. They were Jews, Catholics, and followers of Eastern Orthodox rites.

The palpable "differentness" of the newcomers disturbed a basically Protestant population of Northern European origin. This disturbance resulted in a series of charges against them. They undermined American standards of living by working for a pittance. They were milking the United States of dollars to send home but returning nothing to their communities. They voted docilely at the summons of the ward leaders for a dollar or two a head. They were radical agitators. They crammed the jails and charity hospitals. They helplessly, hopelessly, lacked the Anglo-Saxon genius for self-improvement and self-rule.

It was under the sway of such arguments that Congress passed not one, but a series of restrictive acts, beginning in 1917 and climaxing in 1924. But hardly was the ink dry on the lawbooks before the children of the fearfully regarded "new" immigrants began to make the grade in America, despite all the gloomy predictions. Except in the Depression era they found plenty of jobs. In the needle trades, in construction gangs, in steel mills and railroads, the Italians, Poles, Bohemians, Hungarians, Greeks, and other "ethnics" furnished muscle for growing industries. Others set up grocery stores, bars, barbershops, drugstores, laundries, or restaurants to serve the urban neighborhoods into which they moved. Still others made their way to farms, which provided food for the multiplying mouths of urban regions.

Economic success fuelled physical mobility. There were still unsettled areas around the cities that beckoned to those who disliked the crowded streets of the Promised Land. Around New York an Italian family could easily find, in Queens or Staten Island, a reasonably priced house with land enough for gardening. Or a Jewish storekeeper could escape the Lower East Side, if he had a good year or two, and find ocean breezes in Brooklyn.

Jobs and housing were two rungs of the ladder that led up from steerage. Then there were the schools. Urban classrooms were crowded, but not to the breaking point. In them, thousands of immigrant children learned the rules of civic behavior by which all Americans supposedly lived. More significantly, they acquired the skills that spelled job advancement. High-school training in basic English and mathematics equipped young new Americans for sales and secretarial work or minor civil-service posts. It was more than adequate for a skilled or semiskilled worker—a painter, plumber, or electrician. And with a little post-high-school training, say two years of night college, doors were opened to nursing, pharmacy, accounting, and even law and medicine.

Finally, the traditionally hospitable political machine embraced the immigrants and their children, especially as the latter reached voting age. At first given only minor slots on the tickets, Italians, Poles, and Jews gradually turned up as mayors, governors, senators, and Cabinet members. . . .

Meanwhile, what of the blacks? As European immigrants moved upward, the wave of Negro arrivals from the South flowed into the jobs and neighborhoods, at the bottom levels of desirability, that had just been vacated. From the start, as always, the blacks marched a hard road to a different drum. The journey of black families to a Promised Land under the North Star was, in one sense, part of a universal movement. They were rural people, and everywhere in developing nations rural people pricked up their ears at the sound of the factory whistle. And the nearly nine million American Negroes who lived in the South in 1910 (and made up 90 per cent of the nation's total black population) were predominantly a peasantry, living on farms, confronting permanent tenantry, poverty, ignorance, and disease. A government commission studying farm labor crisply summarized their plight that year: "There is absolutely nothing before them on the farm . . . no prospect . . . but to continue until they die." From this desperation they began to flee, in a movement that still continues in the 1970's. By 1970 about half of black America lived outside what might well be called their "old country."

They came to the cities by train in the early days, pouring onto the platforms with their bundles and their boxes, looking around, filling their eyes with the sights of Mecca. They came in response to letters and messages from relatives—or sometimes in response to nothing more than ads clipped from the Pittsburgh *Courier,* the *Amsterdam News,* the Baltimore *Afro-American,* or the Chicago *Defender* that said things like "3000 laborers to work on railroad. Factory hires all race help. More positions open than men for them." It was very encouraging. True, the unions would not easily accept black men, so the factory jobs turned out many times to be the hardest, the dirtiest, the ones offering the smallest promise of advancement. Or else they were jobs for strike-breakers, which was a dangerous way to earn a living. Even a scab's work was not always available, so black men (and women) had to do the traditional chores of their people in America: cooking, cleaning, fetching, and grooming for white men.

Still, it was the North. Schools were better than those open to Negroes in the South. The coarser humiliations of legalized segregation were somewhat muted. Voting was possible, and there might be

a future for the young. There was an air of promise. Many black men
in the city, members of Booker T. Washington's National Negro Business League, were making money as owners of their own barbershops,
funeral parlors, and livery stables. Washington's well-known antagonist, W. E. B. DuBois, was talking about a "talented tenth" of the
Negro race, which would save its future. In 1909 DuBois and other
Negro leaders had helped to found the National Association for the
Advancement of Colored People, then a "radical" force fighting courtroom battles for black rights. At their side were sympathetic and brilliant whites like Mary White Ovington, Joel Spingarn, Oswald Garrison Villard, and Moorefield Storey. In 1910 the National Urban
League was founded to set about opening job opportunities for blacks.
A new day did seem on the way.

There were drawbacks, of course. Living quarters were scarce.
Northern whites would seldom accept black neighbors except perhaps
along the alleys behind their houses; so old Negro districts, cramped
for expansion, grew desperately crowded. The poet Langston Hughes,
born in 1902, lived with his family in Cleveland in 1916 and remembered that they always seemed to inhabit attics or basements and to pay
a lot for them. When white people did finally rent to Negroes, they
would cut up their houses into five or six apartments and charge
goldrush prices for each—and for garages and sheds, too.

But a northern city offered a little acceptance to Negroes when they
were still definitely a minority. Hughes went to Central High School.
Once it had taught the children of proper Clevelanders; by 1916 it was
full of the children of the foreign-born, divided mainly between mutually suspicious Jews and Catholics. When elections were held for class
officers, Hughes often won as the "compromise candidate," having
apparently the advantage of being considered neither Jew nor Gentile.
On a summer vacation he visited Chicago, which was also exciting.
South State Street was "in its glory" in 1918, "a teeming Negro street
with crowded theaters, restaurants, and cabarets. And excitement from
noon to noon. Midnight was like day. The street was full of workers
and gamblers, prostitutes and pimps, church folks and sinners. The
tenements on either side were very congested. For neither love nor
money could you find a decent place to live."

Even more attractive than Chicago for many a bright young Negro
was a place that had once been a quiet Manhattan suburb, "the rural
retreat of the aristocratic New Yorker"—a place called Harlem. After
1900, Negro real-estate operators began to buy buildings there, hoping to open the ownership of tidy homes to worthy blacks. They undoubtedly had profits in mind, but they also hoped to avoid the creation in New York of a "Niggertown," a "Buzzard's Alley," a
"Bronzeville," as Negro slums were already called in other cities. And

Recently there has been a renewed interest in the paintings
of the black artist Jacob Lawrence. In the late 1930s he
painted a series of sixty panels as a record of the black
exodus from the South. Shown here are two powerful visual
statements of some of the reasons for the mass migration:
(above) a lynching and (below) the white planter who often
gave short weight or otherwise managed to cheat his
sharecropping tenants.

Harlem in 1927.

though New York's Negro population began to increase markedly after 1910, they seemed for a while to be succeeding. White residents, unsurprisingly, fled before the migrants, who were described by one newspaper as "black hordes . . . eating through the very heart of Harlem." But they left behind a Harlem that suddenly became a magnet for black artists and intellectuals, who made it their cultural capital.

While young whites revelled in Mencken, Hemingway, Eliot, Pound, Stravinsky, cubism, and Dada, black poets and writers like James Weldon Johnson and Claude McKay and Countee Cullen, black scholars like Carter G. Woodson, Alain Locke, and E. Franklin Frazier, and black musicians like Bessie Smith and Duke Ellington sang their various lyrics of emancipation. Not all of them lived in Harlem, but for most it was at least their spiritual home. Langston Hughes spoke for a whole black generation when he described how it was to come up from the subway under Harlem after a long absence. "I stood there, dropped my bags, took a deep breath and felt happy again."

And yet there was another side to Harlem in the 1920's. It might float the mirage of a "new Negro" before the eyes of intellectuals, but they quickly perceived that New York was a place where good jobs for blacks were scarce and pay was skimpy. And when, between 1920 and

1930, the city's black population rose by another 115 per cent, good will and hope collapsed. Black and white slumlords found that milking decayed buildings for a few years was more profitable than long-time investments in repairs, and so black Harlemites endured falling plaster, exposed wiring, malfunctioning plumbing and heating systems, and rats and roaches. Disease flourished in Harlem; Negro death rates climbed.

From this squalor Negroes sought everywhere for escape. A few turned to political radicalism; more to red-hot religion—Christianity melted in the crucible of memory and pain. Sometimes they pursued the anodyne of hope by gambling on a "hit" in the numbers game. Sometimes they clutched the transient solace of liquor or drugs. Each night the squeals and swoops of jazz mingled with the exhortations of preachers in storefront churches, while the pushers and whores and gamblers—black themselves—separated other blacks from what cash the grocer and landlord had left them.

And, slowly, many of the children whose parents had moved north to give them a second chance died spiritually. Small dark wraiths wandered the streets with keys on strings around their necks, while fathers who had given up the fight drifted, somewhere, and mothers scrubbed kitchens in white people's homes. Those black youngsters who made it to school were bowed by psychological burdens that few white teachers understood. Not only were they recent "immigrants," but they also suffered from the peculiar inadequacy of their southern background.

Despite the glamour of the "Harlem Renaissance," the nation's best-known black community had become by 1930 what it would remain for forty years at least—a place of enmity between policeman and community, where many local businessmen were outsiders and enemies. It was a pit of dilapidation and of fury often turned inward by blacks to become self-destruction, a center of narcotics traffic and crime. . . .

The Diaspora in America: A Study of Jewish Immigration

DAVID BOROFF

Because except for Indians all Americans are themselves at least the descendants of immigrants, it is perhaps not surprising that "native born" citizens have often displayed a kind of love-hate attitude toward newcomers. They recognize in these newcomers their own successes and failures, their pride in what they have forgotten or rejected in their heritage. This ambivalence has been exacerbated by the very real conflicts that immigration has caused. On the one hand, the immigrant has always been a national asset—his labor and intelligence add to the productivity and wealth of society; his culture enriches and diversifies American civilization. On the other hand, the immigrant has represented competition, strangeness, unsettling change. Most immigrants have been poor and many upon arrival have been ill-adjusted to American values and habits. Social and economic problems have frequently resulted, especially when large numbers have flooded into the country in relatively short periods of time. This last point explains why the late nineteenth and early twentieth centuries produced the movement to restrict immigration, for the influx was greater then than at any other time.

In this essay the late David Boroff of New York University discusses the impact of Jewish immigrants on the United States and the impact of the nation on these immigrants. He focuses chiefly on the period after 1880, when Jewish immigration was heaviest. His account provides a vivid picture of the life of these people, and helps explain both why they, as well as other immigrants, were sometimes disliked and why they were themselves at times ambivalent in their reactions to America. ∎

It started with a tiny trickle and ended in a roaring flood. The first to come were just twenty-three Jews from Brazil who landed in New Amsterdam in 1654, in flight from a country no longer hospitable to them. They were, in origin, Spanish and Portuguese Jews (many with grandiloquent Iberian names) whose families had been wandering for a century and a half. New Amsterdam provided a chilly reception. Governor Peter Stuyvesant at first asked them to leave, but kinder hearts in the Dutch West India Company granted them the right to stay, "provided the poor among them . . . be supported by their own nation." By the end of the century, there were perhaps one hundred Jews; by the middle of the eighteenth century, there were about three hundred in New York, and smaller communities in Newport, Philadelphia, and Charleston.

Because of their literacy, zeal, and overseas connections, colonial Jews prospered as merchants, though there were artisans and laborers among them. The Jewish community was tightly knit, but there was a serious shortage of trained religious functionaries. There wasn't a single American rabbi, for example, until the nineteenth century. Jews were well regarded, particularly in New England. Puritan culture leaned heavily on the Old Testament, and Harvard students learned Hebrew; indeed, during the American Revolution, the suggestion was advanced that Hebrew replace English as the official language of the new country. The absence of an established national religion made it possible for Judaism to be regarded as merely another religion in a pluralistic society. The early days of the new republic were thus a happy time for Jews. Prosperous and productive, they were admitted to American communal life with few restrictions. It is little wonder that a Jewish spokesman asked rhetorically in 1820: "On what spot in this habitable Globe does an Israelite enjoy more blessings, more privileges?"

The second wave of immigration during the nineteenth century is often described as German, but that is misleading. Actually, there were many East European Jews among the immigrants who came in the half century before 1870. However, the German influence was strong, and there was a powerful undercurrent of Western enlightenment at work. These Jews came because economic depression and the Industrial Revolution had made their lot as artisans and small merchants intolerable. For some there was also the threatening backwash of the failure of the Revolution of 1848. Moreover, in Germany at this time Jews were largely disfranchised and discriminated against. During this period, between 200,000 and 400,000 Jews emigrated to this country, and the Jewish population had risen to about half a million by 1870.

This was the colorful era of the peddler and his pack. Peddling was an easy way to get started—it required little capital—and it often rewarded enterprise and daring. Jewish peddlers fanned out through the young country into farmland and mining camp, frontier and Indian territory. The more successful peddlers ultimately settled in one place as storekeepers. (Some proud businesses—including that of Senator Goldwater's family—made their start this way.) Feeling somewhat alienated from the older, settled Jews, who had a reputation for declining piety, the new immigrants organized their own synagogues and community facilities, such as cemeteries and hospitals. In general, these immigrants were amiably received by native Americans, who, unsophisticated about differences that were crucial to the immigrants themselves, regarded all Central Europeans as "Germans."

Essentially, the emigration route was the same between 1820 and 1870 as it would be in the post-1880 exodus. The travellers stayed in emigration inns while awaiting their ship, and since they had all their resources with them, they were in danger of being robbed. The journey itself was hazardous and, in the days of the sailing vessels when a good wind was indispensable, almost interminable. Nor were the appointments very comfortable even for the relatively well to do. A German Jew who made the journey in 1856 reported that his cabin, little more than six feet by six feet, housed six passengers in triple-decker bunks. When a storm raged, the passengers had to retire to their cabins lest they be washed off the deck by waves. "Deprived of air," he wrote, "it soon became unbearable in the cabins in which six sea-sick persons breathed." On this particular journey, sea water began to trickle into the cabins, and the planks had to be retarred.

Still, the emigration experience was a good deal easier than it would be later. For one thing, the immigrants were better educated and better acquainted with modern political and social attitudes than the oppressed and bewildered East European multitudes who came after 1880. Fewer in number, they were treated courteously by ships' captains. (On a journey in 1839, described by David Mayer, the ship's captain turned over his own cabin to the Jewish passengers for their prayers and regularly visited those Jews who were ill.) Moreover, there was still the bloom of adventure about the overseas voyage. Ships left Europe amid the booming of cannon, while on shore ladies enthusiastically waved their handkerchiefs. On the way over, there was a holiday atmosphere despite the hazards, and there was great jubilation when land was sighted.

There were, however, rude shocks when the voyagers arrived in this country. The anguish of Castle Garden and Ellis Island was well in the future when immigration first began to swell. But New York seemed inhospitable, its pace frantic, the outlook not entirely hopeful. Isaac M. Wise, a distinguished rabbi who made the journey in 1846, was appalled. "The whole city appeared to me like a large shop," he wrote, "where everyone buys or sells, cheats or is cheated. I had never before seen a city so bare of all art and of every trace of good taste; likewise I had never witnessed anywhere such rushing, hurrying, chasing, running . . . Everything seemed so pitifully small and paltry; and I had had so exalted an idea of the land of freedom." Moreover, he no sooner landed in New York than he was abused by a German drayman whose services he had declined. "Aha! thought I," he later wrote, "you have left home and kindred in order to get away from the disgusting Judaeophobia and here the first German greeting that sounds in your ears is hep! hep!" (The expletive was a Central European equivalent of "Kike.") Another German Jew who worked as a clothing salesman was affronted by the way customers were to be "lured" into buying ("I did not think this occupation corresponded in any way to my views of a merchant's dignity").

After 1880, Jewish immigration into the United States was in flood tide. And the source was principally East Europe, where by 1880 three quarters of the world's 7.7 million Jews were living. In all, over two million Jews came to these shores in little more than three decades—about one third of Europe's Jewry. Some of them came, as their predecessors had come, because of shrinking economic opportunities. In Russia and in the Austro-Hungarian empire, the growth of large-scale agriculture squeezed out Jewish middlemen as it destroyed the independent peasantry, while in the cities the development of manufacturing reduced the need for Jewish artisans. Vast numbers of Jews became petty tradesmen or even *luftmenschen* (men without visible means of support who drifted from one thing to another). In Galicia, around 1900, there was a Jewish trader for every ten peasants, and the average value of his stock came to only twenty dollars.

Savage discrimination and pogroms also incited Jews to emigrate. The Barefoot Brigades—bands of marauding Russian peasants—brought devastation and bloodshed to Jewish towns and cities. On a higher social level, there was the "cold pogrom," a government policy calculated to destroy Jewish life. The official hope was that one third of Russia's Jews would die out, one third would emigrate, and one third would be converted to the Orthodox Church. Crushing restrictions were imposed. Jews were required to live within the Pale of Settlement in western Russia, they could not Russify their names, and they were subjected to rigorous quotas for schooling and professional training. Nor could general studies be included in the curriculum of Jewish religious schools. It was a life of poverty and fear.

Nevertheless, the *shtetl,* the typical small Jewish town, was a triumph of endurance and spiritual integrity. It was a place where degradation and squalor could not wipe out dignity, where learning flourished in the face of hopelessness, and where a tough, sardonic humor

provided catharsis for the tribulations of an existence that was barely
endurable. The abrasions and humiliations of everyday life were
healed by a rich heritage of custom and ceremony. And there was
always Sabbath—"The Bride of the Sabbath," as the Jews called the
day of rest—to bring repose and exaltation to a life always sorely tried.

To be sure, even this world showed signs of disintegration. Secular
learning, long resisted by East European Jews and officially denied to
them, began to make inroads. Piety gave way to revolutionary fervor,
and Jews began to play a heroic role in Czarist Russia's bloody history
of insurrection and suppression.

This was the bleak, airless milieu from which the emigrants came.
A typical expression of the Jewish attitude toward emigration from
Russia—both its hopefulness and the absence of remorse—was provided by Dr. George Price, who had come to this country in one of the
waves of East European emigration:

> Should this Jewish emigrant regret his leave-taking of his native land which
> fails to appreciate him? No! A thousand times no! He must not regret
> fleeing the clutches of the blood-thirsty crocodile. Sympathy for this coun-
> try? How ironical it sounds! Am I not despised? Am I not urged to leave?
> Do I not hear the word *Zhid* constantly? . . . Be thou cursed forever my
> wicked homeland, because you remind me of the Inquisition . . . May you
> rue the day when you exiled the people who worked for your welfare.

After 1880, going to America—no other country really lured—
became the great drama of redemption for the masses of East European Jews. (For some, of course, Palestine had that role even in the late
nineteenth century, but these were an undaunted Zionist cadre prepared to endure the severest hardships.) The assassination of Czar
Alexander II in 1881, and the subsequent pogrom, marked the beginning of the new influx. By the end of the century, 700,000 Jews had
arrived, about one quarter of them totally illiterate, almost all of them
impoverished. Throughout East Europe, Jews talked longingly about
America as the "goldene medinah" (the golden province), and biblical
imagery—"the land of milk and honey"—came easily to their lips.
Those who could write were kept busy composing letters to distant
kin—or even to husbands—in America. (Much of the time, the husband went first, and by abstemious living saved enough to fetch wife
and children from the old country.) Children played at "emigrating
games," and for the entire *shtetl* it was an exciting moment when the
mail-carrier announced how many letters had arrived from America.

German steamship companies assiduously advertised the glories of
the new land and provided a one-price rate from *shtetl* to New York.
Emigration inns were established in Brody (in the Ukraine) and in the
port cities of Bremen and Hamburg, where emigrants would gather for

the trip. There were rumors that groups of prosperous German Jews would underwrite their migration to America; and in fact such people often did help their co-religionists when they were stranded without funds in the port cities of Germany. Within Russia itself, the government after 1880 more or less acquiesced in the emigration of Jews, and connived in the vast business of "stealing the border" (smuggling emigrants across). After 1892, emigration was legal—except for those of draft age—but large numbers left with forged papers, because that proved to be far easier than getting tangled in the red tape of the Czarist bureaucracy. Forged documents, to be sure, were expensive— they cost twenty-five rubles, for many Jews the equivalent of five weeks' wages. Nor was the departure from home entirely a happy event. There were the uncertainties of the new life, the fear that in America "one became a gentile." Given the Jewish aptitude for lugubriousness, a family's departure was often like a funeral, lachrymose and anguished, with the neighbors carting off the furniture that would no longer be needed.

For people who had rarely ventured beyond the boundaries of their own village, going to America was an epic adventure. They travelled with pitifully little money; the average immigrant arrived in New York with only about twenty dollars. With their domestic impedimenta— bedding, brass candlesticks, samovars—they would proceed to the port cities by rail, cart, and even on foot. At the emigration inns, they had to wait their turn. Thousands milled around, entreating officials for departure cards. There were scenes of near chaos—mothers shrieking, children crying; battered wicker trunks, bedding, utensils in wild disarray. At Hamburg, arriving emigrants were put in the "unclean" section of the *Auswandererhallen* until examined by physicians who decided whether their clothing and baggage had to be disinfected. After examination, Jews could not leave the center; other emigrants could.

The ocean voyage provided little respite. (Some elected to sail by way of Liverpool at a reduction of nine dollars from the usual rate of thirty-four dollars.) Immigrants long remembered the "smell of ship," a distillation of many putrescences. Those who went in steerage slept on mattresses filled with straw and kept their clothes on to keep warm. The berth itself was generally six feet long, two feet wide, and two and a half feet high, and it had to accommodate the passenger's luggage. Food was another problem. Many Orthodox Jews subsisted on herring, black bread, and tea which they brought because they did not trust the dietary purity of the ship's food. Some ships actually maintained a separate galley for kosher food, which was coveted by non-Jewish passengers because it was allegedly better.

Unsophisticated about travel and faced by genuine dangers, Jewish emigrants found the overseas trip a long and terrifying experience. But

Her decks jammed with hopeful immigrants, the S.S.
Patricia *arrives at Ellis Island in 1906.*

when land was finally sighted, the passengers often began to cheer and
shout. "I looked up at the sky," an immigrant wrote years later. "It
seemed much bluer and the sun much brighter than in the old country.
It reminded me on [sic] the Garden of Eden."

Unhappily, the friendly reception that most immigrants envisioned
in the new land rarely materialized. Castle Garden in the Battery, at
the foot of Manhattan—and later Ellis Island in New York Harbor—
proved to be almost as traumatic as the journey itself. "Castle Garden," an immigrant wrote, "is a large building, a Gehenna, through
which all Jewish arrivals must pass to be cleansed before they are
considered worthy of breathing freely the air of the land of the almighty dollar. . . . If in Brody, thousands crowded about, here tens of
thousands thronged about; if there they were starving, here they were
dying; if there they were crushed, here they were simply beaten."

One must make allowances for the impassioned hyperbole of the
suffering immigrant, but there is little doubt that the immigration

officials were harassed, overworked, and often unsympathetic. Authorized to pass on the admissibility of the newcomers, immigration officers struck terror into their hearts by asking questions designed to
reveal their literacy and social attitudes. "How much is six times six?"
an inspector asked a woman in the grip of nervousness, then casually
asked the next man, "Have you ever been in jail?"

There were, of course, representatives of Jewish defense groups
present, especially from the Hebrew Immigrant Aid Society. But by
this time, the immigrants, out of patience and exhausted, tended to
view them balefully. The Jewish officials tended to be highhanded, and
the temporary barracks which they administered on Ward's Island for
those not yet settled became notorious. Discontent culminated in a riot
over food; one day the director—called The Father—had to swim
ashore for his life, and the police were hastily summoned.

Most immigrants went directly from Castle Garden or Ellis Island
to the teeming streets of Manhattan, where they sought relatives or
landsleit (fellow townsmen) who had gone before them. Easy marks for
hucksters and swindlers, they were overcharged by draymen for carrying their paltry possessions, engaged as strikebreakers, or hired at
shamelessly low wages.

"Greenhorn" or "greener" was their common name. A term of
vilification, the source of a thousand cruel jokes, it was their shame and
their destiny. On top of everything else, the immigrants had to abide
the contempt of their co-religionists who had preceded them to America by forty or fifty years. By the time the heavy East European immigration set in, German Jews had achieved high mercantile status and
an uneasy integration into American society. They did not want to be
reminded of their kinship with these uncouth and impoverished Jews
who were regarded vaguely as a kind of Oriental influx. There was a
good deal of sentiment against "aiding such paupers to emigrate to
these shores." One charitable organization declared: "Organized immigration from Russia, Roumania, and other semi-barbarous countries is a mistake and has proved to be a failure. It is no relief to the
Jews of Russia, Poland, etc., and it jeopardizes the well-being of the
American Jews."

A genuine uptown-downtown split soon developed, with condescension on one side and resentment on the other. The German Jews
objected as bitterly to the rigid, old-world Orthodoxy of the immigrants as they did to their new involvement in trade unions. They were
fearful, too, of the competition they would offer in the needle trades.
(Indeed, the East Europeans ultimately forced the uptown Jews out of
the industry.) On the other side of the barricades, Russian Jews complained that at the hands of their uptown brethren, "every man is
questioned like a criminal, is looked down upon . . . just as if he were

Immigrant women and children at Ellis Island eating their
first American meal (1906).

standing before a Russian official." Nevertheless, many German Jews
responded to the call of conscience by providing funds for needy
immigrants and setting up preparatory schools for immigrant children
for whom no room was yet available in the hopelessly overcrowded
public schools.

Many comfortably settled German Jews saw dispersion as the answer to the problem. Efforts were made to divert immigrants to small
towns in other parts of the country, but these were largely ineffective.
There were also some gallant adventures with farming in such remote
places as South Dakota, Oregon, and Louisiana. Though the Jewish
pioneers were brave and idealistic, drought, disease, and ineptitude
conspired against them. (In Oregon, for example, they tried to raise
corn in cattle country, while in Louisiana they found themselves in
malarial terrain.) Only chicken farming in New Jersey proved to be
successful to any great degree. Farm jobs for Jews were available, but
as one immigrant said: "I have no desire to be a farm hand to an
ignorant Yankee at the end of the world. I would rather work here at
half the price in a factory; for then I would at least be able to spend
my free evenings with my friends."

It was in New York, then, that the bulk of the immigrants settled—
in the swarming, tumultuous Lower East Side—with smaller concen-

trations in Boston, Philadelphia, and Chicago. Far less adaptable than
the German Jews who were now lording it over them, disoriented and
frightened, the East European immigrants constituted a vast and exploited proletariat. According to a survey in 1890, sixty per cent of all
immigrant Jews worked in the needle trades. This industry had gone
through a process of decentralization in which contractors carried out
the bulk of production, receiving merely the cut goods from the manufacturer. Contracting establishments were everywhere in the Lower
East Side, including the contractors' homes, where pressers warmed
their irons on the very stove on which the boss's wife was preparing
supper. The contractors also gave out "section" work to families and
landsleit who would struggle to meet the quotas at home. The bondage
of the sewing machine was therefore extended into the tenements,
with entire families enslaved by the machine's voracious demands. The
Hester Street "pig market," where one could buy anything, became
the labor exchange; there tailors, operators, finishers, basters, and
pressers would congregate on Saturday in the hope of being hired by
contractors.

Life in the sweatshops of the Lower East Side was hard, but it made
immigrants employable from the start, and a weekly wage of five dollars—the equivalent of ten rubles—looked good in immigrant eyes.
Moreover, they were among their own kin and kind, and the sweatshops, noisome as they were, were still the scene of lively political and
even literary discussions. (In some cigar-making shops, in fact, the
bosses hired "readers" to keep the minds of the workers occupied with
classic and Yiddish literature as they performed their repetitive
chores.) East European Jews, near the end of the century, made up a
large part of the skilled labor force in New York, ranking first in
twenty-six out of forty-seven trades, and serving, for example, as bak-
ers, building-trade workers, painters, furriers, jewellers, and tinsmiths.

Almost one quarter of all the immigrants tried their hands as
tradesmen—largely as peddlers or as pushcart vendors in the mad-
house bazaar of the Lower East Side. For some it was an apprentice-
ship in low-toned commerce that would lead to more elegant careers.
For others it was merely a martyrdom that enabled them to subsist. It
was a modest enough investment—five dollars for a license, one dollar
for a basket, and four dollars for wares. They stocked up on pins and
needles, shoe laces, polish, and handkerchiefs, learned some basic
expressions ("You wanna buy somethin'?"), and were on their hapless
way.

It was the professions, of course, that exerted the keenest attraction
to Jews, with their reverence for learning. For most of them it was too
late; they had to reconcile themselves to more humble callings. But it
was not too late for their children, and between 1897 and 1907, the

*A New York sweatshop,
photographed about
1910.*

number of Jewish physicians in Manhattan rose from 450 to 1,000. Of
all the professions it was medicine that excited the greatest veneration.
(Some of this veneration spilled over into pharmacy, and "druggists"
were highly respected figures who were called upon to prescribe for
minor—and even major—ills, and to serve as scribes for the letters that
the immigrants were unable to read and write themselves.) There were
Jewish lawyers on the Lower East Side and by 1901 over 140 Jewish
policemen, recruited in part by Theodore Roosevelt, who, as police
commissioner, had issued a call for "the Maccabee or fighting Jewish
type."

The Lower East Side was the American counterpart of the ghetto
for Jewish immigrants, as well as their glittering capital. At its peak,
around 1910, it packed over 350,000 people into a comparatively small
area—roughly from Canal Street to Fourteenth Street—with as many
as 523 people per acre, so that Arnold Bennett was moved to remark
that "the architecture seemed to sweat humanity at every window and
door." The most densely populated part of the city, it held one sixth
of Manhattan's population and most of New York's office buildings
and factories. "Uptowners" used to delight in visiting it (as a later
generation would visit Harlem) to taste its exotic flavor. But the great

mass of Jews lived there because the living was cheap, and there was a vital Jewish community that gave solace to the lonely and comfort to the pious.

A single man could find lodgings of a sort, including coffee morning and night, for three dollars a month. For a family, rent was about ten dollars a month, milk was four cents a quart, kosher meat twelve cents a pound, bread two cents a pound, herring a penny or two. A kitchen table could be bought for a dollar, chairs at thirty-five cents each. One managed, but the life was oppressive. Most families lived in the notorious "dumbbell" flats of old-law tenements (built prior to 1901). Congested, often dirty and unsanitary, these tenements were six or seven stories high and had four apartments on each floor. Only one room in each three or four room apartment received direct air and sunlight, and the families on each floor shared a toilet in the hall.

Many families not only used their flats as workshops but also took in boarders to make ends meet. Jacob Riis tells of a two-room apartment on Allen Street which housed parents, six children, and six boarders. "Two daughters sewed clothes at home. The elevator railway passed by the window. The cantor rehearses, a train passes, the shoemaker bangs, ten brats run around like goats, the wife putters. . . . At night we all try to get some sleep in the stifling, roach-infested two rooms." In the summer, the tenants spilled out into fire escapes and rooftops, which were converted into bedrooms.

Nevertheless, life on the Lower East Side had surprising vitality. Despite the highest population density in the city, the Tenth Ward had one of the lowest death rates. In part, this was because of the strenuous personal cleanliness of Jews, dictated by their religion. Though only eight per cent of the East European Jews had baths, bathhouses and steam rooms on the Lower East Side did a booming business. There was, of course, a heavy incidence of tuberculosis—"the white plague." Those who were afflicted could be heard crying out, *"Luft! Gib mir luft!"* ("Air! Give me air!"). It was, in fact, this terror of "consumption" that impelled some East Side Jews to become farmers in the Catskills at the turn of the century, thus forerunning the gaudy career of the Catskill Borscht Belt resort hotels. The same fear impelled Jews on the Lower East Side to move to Washington Heights and the Bronx, where the altitude was higher, the air presumably purer.

Alcoholism, a prime affliction of most immigrant groups, was almost unknown among Jews. They drank ritualistically on holidays but almost never to excess. They were, instead, addicted to seltzer or soda water—Harry Golden's "2¢ plain"—which they viewed as "the worker's champagne." The suicide rate was relatively low, though higher than in the *shtetl,* and there was always a shudder of sympathy when the Yiddish press announced that someone had *genumen di ges* (taken gas).

The Lower East Side was from the start the scene of considerable crime. But its inhabitants became concerned when the crime rate among the young people seemed to rise steeply around 1910. There was a good deal of prostitution. The dancing academies, which achieved popularity early in this century, became recruiting centers for prostitutes. In 1908–9, of 581 foreign women arrested for prostitution, 225 were Jewish. There was the notorious Max Hochstim Association, which actively recruited girls, while the New York Independent Benevolent Association—an organization of pimps—provided sick benefits, burial privileges, bail, and protection money for prostitutes. The membership was even summoned to funerals with a two-dollar fine imposed on those who did not attend. Prostitution was so taken for granted that Canal Street had stores on one side featuring sacerdotal articles, while brothels were housed on the other.

Family life on the Lower East Side was cohesive and warm, though there was an edge of shrillness and hysteria to it. Marriages were not always happy, but if wives were viewed as an affliction, children were regarded as a blessing. The kitchen was the center of the household, and food was almost always being served to either family or visitors. No matter how poor they were, Jewish families ate well—even to excess—and mothers considered their children woefully underweight unless they were well cushioned with fat.

It was a life with few conventional graces. Handkerchiefs were barely known, and the Yiddish newspapers had to propagandize for their use. Old men smelled of snuff, and in spite of bathing, children often had lice in their hair and were sent home from school by the visiting nurse for a kerosene bath. Bedbugs were considered an inevitability, and pajamas were viewed as an upper-class affectation. Parents quarrelled bitterly—with passionate and resourceful invective—in the presence of their children. Telephones were virtually unknown, and a telegram surely meant disaster from afar.

The zeal of the immigrants on behalf of their children was no less than awe-inspiring. Parents yearned for lofty careers for their offspring, with medicine at the pinnacle. In better-off homes, there was always a piano ("solid mahogany"), and parents often spent their precious reserves to arrange a "concert" for their precocious youngsters, followed by a ball in one of the Lower East Side's many halls.

To be sure, the children inspired a full measure of anxiety in their parents. "Amerikane kinder" was the rueful plaint of the elders, who could not fathom the baffling new ways of the young. Parents were nervous about their daughters' chastity, and younger brothers—often six or seven years old—would be dispatched as chaperones when the

*The immigrants' new home: a crowded, noisy, but friendly
street on New York's Lower East Side.*

girls met their boy friends. There was uneasiness about Jewish street
gangs and the growing problem of delinquency. The old folks were
vexed by the new tides of secularism and political radicalism that were
weaning their children from traditional pieties. But most of all, they
feared that their sons would not achieve the success that would redeem
their own efforts, humiliations, and failures in the harsh new land.
Pressure on their children was relentless. But on the whole the children did well, astonishingly well. "The ease and rapidity with which
they learn," Jacob Riis wrote, "is equalled only by their good behavior
and close attention while in school. There is no whispering and no
rioting at these desks." Samuel Chotzinoff, the music critic, tells a story

which reveals the attitude of the Jewish schoolboy. When an alterca-
tion threatened between Chotzinoff and a classmate, his antagonist's
reaction was to challenge him to spell "combustible."

The Lower East Side was a striking demonstration that financial
want does not necessarily mean cultural poverty. The immigrant Jews
were nearly always poor and often illiterate, but they were not cultur-
ally deprived. In fact, between 1890 and World War I, the Jewish
community provides a remarkable chapter in American cultural history. Liberated from the constrictions of European captivity, immigrant Jews experienced a great surge of intellectual vitality. Yiddish,
the Hebrew-German dialect which some people had casually dismissed
as a barbarous "jargon," became the vehicle of this cultural renas-
cence. Between 1885 and 1914, over 150 publications of all kinds
made their appearance. But the new Yiddish journalism reached its
apogee with the *Jewish Daily Forward* under the long editorial reign of
Abraham Cahan. The *Forword* was humanitarian, pro-labor, and social-
istic. But it was also an instrument for acclimatizing immigrants in the
new environment. It provided practical hints on how to deal with the
new world, letters from the troubled *(Bintel Brief),* and even, at one
time, a primer on baseball ("explained to non-sports"). The *Forward*
also published and fostered an enormous amount of literature in Yiddish—both original works by writers of considerable talent, and translations of classic writers.

In this cultural ferment, immigrants studied English in dozens of
night schools and ransacked the resources of the Aguilar Free Library
on East Broadway. "When I had [a] book in my hand," an immigrant
wrote, "I pressed it to my heart and wanted to kiss it." The Educational
Alliance, also on East Broadway, had a rich program designed to make
immigrant Jews more American and their sons more Jewish. And there
were scores of settlement houses, debating clubs, ethical societies, and
literary circles which attracted the young. In fact, courtships were
carried on in a rarefied atmosphere full of lofty talk about art, politics,
and philosophy. And though there was much venturesome palaver
about sexual freedom, actual behavior tended to be quite strait-laced.

But the most popular cultural institution was the café or coffee
house, which served as the Jewish saloon. There were about 250 of
them, each with its own following. Here the litterateurs sat for hours
over steaming glasses of tea; revolutionaries and Bohemians gathered
to make their pronouncements or raise money for causes; actors and
playwrights came to hold court. For immigrant Jews, talk was the
breath of life itself. The passion for music and theatre knew no bounds.
When Beethoven's Ninth Symphony was performed one summer night
in 1915, mounted police had to be summoned to keep order outside
Lewisohn Stadium, so heavy was the press of crowds eager for the

twenty-five-cent stone seats. Theatre (in Yiddish) was to the Jewish immigrants what Shakespeare and Marlowe had been to the groundlings in Elizabethan England. Tickets were cheap—twenty-five cents to one dollar—and theatregoing was universal. It was a raucous, robust, and communal experience. Mothers brought their babies (except in some of the "swellest" theatres, which forbade it), and peddlers hawked their wares between the acts. There were theatre parties for trade unions and *landsmanschaften* (societies of fellow townsmen), and the audience milled around and renewed old friendships or argued the merits of the play. The stage curtain had bold advertisements of stores or blown-up portraits of stars.

There was an intense cult of personality in the Yiddish theatre and a system of claques not unlike that which exists in grand opera today. The undisputed monarch was Boris Thomashefsky, and a theatre program of his day offered this panegyric:

> *Thomashefsky! Artist great!*
> *No praise is good enough for you!*
> *Of all the stars you remain the king*
> *You seek no tricks, no false quibbles;*
> *One sees truth itself playing.*
> *Your appearance is godly to us*
> *Every movement is full of grace*
> *Pleasing is your every gesture*
> *Sugar sweet your every turn*
> *You remain the king of the stage*
> *Everything falls to your feet.*

Many of the plays were sentimental trash—heroic "operas" on historical themes, "greenhorn" melodramas full of cruel abandonments and tearful reunions, romantic musicals, and even topical dramas dealing with such immediate events as the Homestead Strike, the Johnstown Flood, and the Kishinev Pogrom of 1903. Adaptability and a talent for facile plagiarism were the essence of the playwright's art in those days, and "Professor" Moses Horwitz wrote 167 plays, most of them adaptations of old operas and melodramas. The plays were so predictable that an actor once admitted he didn't even have to learn his lines; he merely had to have a sense of the general situation and then adapt lines from other plays.

There was, of course, a serious Yiddish drama, introduced principally by Jacob Gordin, who adapted classical and modernist drama to the Yiddish stage. Jewish intellectuals were jubilant at this development. But the process of acculturation had its amusing and grotesque aspects. Shakespeare was a great favorite but *"verbessert and vergrossert"* (improved and enlarged). There was the Jewish *King Lear* in which

Cordelia becomes Goldele. (The theme of filial ingratitude was a "natural" on the Lower East Side, where parents constantly made heroic sacrifices.) *Hamlet* was also given a Jewish coloration, the prince becoming a rabbinical student who returns from the seminary to discover treachery at home. And *A Doll's House* by Ibsen was transformed into *Minna,* in which a sensitive and intelligent young woman, married to an ignorant laborer, falls in love with her boarder and ultimately commits suicide.

Related to the Jewish love of theatre was the immigrant's adoration of the cantor, a profession which evoked as much flamboyance and egotistical preening as acting did. (In fact, actors would sometimes grow beards before the high holy-days and find jobs as cantors.) Synagogues vied with each other for celebrated cantors, sometimes as a way of getting out of debt, since tickets were sold for the high-holy-day services.

The Lower East Side was a vibrant community, full of color and gusto, in which the Jewish immigrant felt marvelously at home, safe from the terrors of the alien city. But it was a setting too for fierce conflict and enervating strain. There were three major influences at work, each pulling in a separate direction: Jewish Orthodoxy, assimilationism, and the new socialist gospel. The immigrants were Orthodox, but their children tended to break away. *Cheders* (Hebrew schools) were everywhere, in basements and stores and tenements, and the old custom of giving a child a taste of honey when he was beginning to learn to read—as symbolic of the sweetness of study—persisted. But the young, eager to be accepted into American society, despised the old ways and their "greenhorn" teachers. Fathers began to view their sons as "freethinkers," a term that was anathema to them. Observance of the Law declined, and the Saturday Sabbath was ignored by many Jews. A virulent antireligious tendency developed among many "enlightened" Jews, who would hold profane balls on the most sacred evening of the year—Yom Kippur—at which they would dance and eat non-kosher food. (Yom Kippur is a fast day.) And the trade-union movement also generated uneasiness among the pious elders of the Lower East Side. "Do you want us to bow down to your archaic God?" a radical newspaper asked. "Each era has its new Torah. Ours is one of freedom and justice."

But for many immigrants the basic discontent was with their American experience itself. The golden province turned out to be a place of tenements and sweatshops. A familiar cry was *"a klug af Columbus!"* ("a curse on Columbus") or, "Who ever asked him, Columbus, to discover America?" Ellis Island was called *Trernindzl* (Island of Tears), and Abraham Cahan, in his initial reaction to the horrors of immigration, thundered: "Be cursed, immigration! Cursed by those conditions which have brought you into being. How many souls have you broken, how many courageous and mighty souls have you shattered." The fact remains that most Jewish immigrants, in the long run, made a happy adjustment to their new land.

After 1910, the Lower East Side went into a decline. Its strange glory was over. New areas of Jewish settlement opened up in Brooklyn, the Bronx, and in upper Manhattan. By the mid-twenties, less than ten per cent of New York's Jews lived on the Lower East Side, although it still remained the heartland to which one returned to shop, to see Yiddish theatre, and to renew old ties. By 1924 Jewish immigration into the United States was severely reduced by new immigration laws, and the saga of mass immigration was done. But the intensities of the Jewish immigrant experience had already made an indelible mark on American culture and history that would endure for many years.

The Age of the Bosses

WILLIAM V. SHANNON

The rapid industrialization of the United States after the Civil War, which produced great tycoons like Andrew Carnegie and encouraged millions of work-hungry Europeans to migrate, changed the shape of society in a variety of ways. One of the most obvious and important of these was industrialization's effect on where and how people lived. Huge industrial concerns brought together masses of workers in one place; commercial and service enterprises sprang up alongside the factories; in short, great cities rapidly developed and America was on its way to becoming an urban nation.

The advantages of urbanization were great—new wealth, better educational opportunities, a wide range of amusements; soon a more refined and complex culture emerged. But great problems also appeared—crowded, unhealthy living conditions, crime and vice, and countless others. Not the least of these was the problem of how to govern these gigantic agglomerations. More government was essential to run a city, yet the nation had lived for the better part of a century by the motto: "that government is best which governs least." New kinds of government were necessary—building and sanitary codes, social services, a system of representation suited to a mass but atomized society—for which no precedents existed.

It was this situation, as William V. Shannon explains, that produced the big-city political machines and the bosses who ran them. Shannon shows that the bosses served a function; they filled a gap in the political system created by the changes resulting from swift industrialization and urban growth. Eventually better machinery than the "machine" was devised to perform that function, although the proper government of cities still eludes us today. As a former editor of the New York Times, *Mr. Shannon brings to this subject a thorough knowledge of modern urban politics and, as the author of* The American Irish, *an equally solid understanding of the old boss system.* ∎

The big cities and the political bosses grew up together in America. Bossism, with all its color and corruption and human drama, was a natural, perhaps even a necessary accompaniment to the rapid development of cities. The new urban communities did not grow slowly and according to plan; on the contrary, huge conglomerations of people from all over the world and from widely varying backgrounds came together suddenly, and in an unplanned, unorganized fashion fumbled their way toward communal relationships and a common identity. The political bosses emerged to cope with this chaotic change and growth. Acting out of greed, a ruthless will for mastery, and an imperfect understanding of what they were about, the bosses imposed upon these conglomerations called cities a certain feudal order and direction.

By 1890 virtually every sizable city had a political boss or was in the process of developing one. By 1950, sixty years later, almost every urban political machine was in an advanced state of obsolescence and its boss in trouble. The reason is not hard to find. Some of the cities kept growing and all of them kept changing, but the bosses, natural products of a specific era, could not grow or change beyond a certain point. The cities became essentially different, and as they did, the old-style organizations, like all organisms which cannot adapt, began to die. The dates vary from city to city. The system began earlier and died sooner in New York. Here or there, an old-timer made one last comeback. In Chicago, the organization and its boss still survive. But exceptions aside, the late nineteenth century saw the beginning, and the middle twentieth, the end, of the Age of the Bosses. What follows is a brief history of how it began, flourished, and passed away.

Soft-spoken Irish farmers from County Mayo and bearded Jews from Poland, country boys from Ohio and sturdy peasants from Calabria, gangling Swedes from near the Arctic Circle and Chinese from Canton, laconic Yankees from Vermont villages and Negro freedmen putting distance between themselves and the old plantation—all these and many other varieties of human beings from every national and religious and cultural tradition poured into America's cities in the decades after the Civil War.

Rome and Alexandria in the ancient world had probably been as polyglot, but in modern times the diversity of American cities was unique. Everywhere in the Western world, cities were growing rapidly in the late nineteenth century; but the Germans from the countryside who migrated to Hamburg and Berlin, the English who moved to Birmingham and London, and the French who flocked to Paris stayed among fellow nationals. They might be mocked as country bumpkins and their clothes might be unfashionable, but everyone they met spoke the same language as themselves, observed the same religious and secular holidays, ate the same kind of food, voted—if they had the franchise at all—in the same elections, and shared the same sentiments and expectations. To move from farm or village to a big European city was an adventure, but one still remained within the reassuring circle of the known and the familiar.

In American cities, however, the newcomers had nothing in common with one another except their poverty and their hopes. They were truly "the up-rooted." The foreign-born, unless they came from the British Isles, could not speak the language of their new homeland. The food, the customs, the holidays, the politics, were alien. Native Americans migrating to the cities from the countryside experienced their own kind of cultural shock: they found themselves competing not with other Americans but with recently arrived foreigners, so that despite their native birth they, too, felt displaced, strangers in their own country.

It was natural for members of each group to come together to try to find human warmth and protection in Little Italy or Cork Hill or Chinatown or Harlem. These feelings of clannish solidarity were one basis of strength for the political bosses. A man will more readily give his vote to a candidate because he is a neighbor from the old country or has some easily identifiable relationship, if only a similar name or the same religion, than because of agreement on some impersonal issue. Voters can take vicarious satisfaction from his success: "One of our boys is making good."

With so many different races and nationalities living together, however, mutual antagonisms were present, and the opportunity for hostility to flare into open violence was never far away. Ambitious, unscrupulous politicians could have exploited these antagonisms for their own political advantage, but the bosses and the political organizations which they developed did not function that way. If a man could vote and would "vote right," he was accepted, and that was the end of the matter. What lasting profit was there in attacking his religion or deriding his background?

Tammany early set the pattern of cultivating every bloc and faction and making an appeal as broad-based as possible. Of one precinct captain on the Lower East Side it was said: "He eats corned beef and kosher meat with equal nonchalance, and it's all the same to him whether he takes off his hat in the church or pulls it down over his ears in the synagogue."

Bosses elsewhere instinctively followed the same practice. George B. Cox, the turn-of-the-century Republican boss of Cincinnati, pasted together a coalition of Germans, Negroes, and old families like the Tafts and the Longworths. James M. Curley, who was mayor of Boston on and off for thirty-six years and was its closest approximation to a political boss, ran as well in the Lithuanian neighborhood of South Boston and the Italian section of East Boston as he did in the working-class Irish wards. In his last term in City Hall, he conferred minor patronage on the growing Negro community and joined the N.A.A.C.P.

The bosses organized neighborhoods, smoothed out antagonisms, arranged ethnically balanced tickets, and distributed patronage in accordance with voting strength as part of their effort to win and hold power. They blurred divisive issues and buried racial and religious hostility with blarney and buncombe. They were not aware that they were actually performing a mediating, pacifying function. They did not realize that by trying to please as many people as possible they were helping to hold raw new cities together, providing for inexperienced citizens a common meeting ground in politics and an experience in working together that would not have been available if the cities had been governed by apolitical bureaucracies. Bossism was usually corrupt and was decidedly inefficient, but in the 1960's, when antipoverty planners try to stimulate "community action organizations" to break through the apathy and disorganization of the slums, we can appreciate that the old-style machines had their usefulness.

When William Marcy Tweed, the first and most famous of the big-city bosses, died in jail in 1878, several hundred workingmen showed up for his funeral. The *Nation* wrote the following week:

> Let us remember that he fell without loss of reputation among the bulk of his supporters. The bulk of the poorer voters of this city today revere his memory, and look on him as the victim of rich men's malice; as, in short, a friend of the needy who applied the public funds, with as little waste as was possible under the circumstances, to the purposes to which they ought to be applied—and that is to the making of work for the working man. The odium heaped on him in the pulpits last Sunday does not exist in the lower stratum of New York society.

This split in attitude toward political bosses between the impoverished many and the prosperous middle classes lingers today and still colors historical writing. To respectable people, the boss was an exotic, even grotesque figure. They found it hard to understand why anyone would vote for him or what the sources of his popularity were. To the urban poor, those sources were self-evident. The boss ran a kind of ramshackle welfare state. He helped the unemployed find jobs, interceded in court for boys in trouble, wrote letters home to the old country for the illiterate; he provided free coal and baskets of food to tide a widow over an emergency, and organized parades, excursions to the beach, and other forms of free entertainment. Some bosses, such as Frank Hague in Jersey City and Curley in Boston, were ener-

*Two of the most memorable
and politically long-lived of
the bosses were Jersey City's
Frank Hague (this page) and
Boston's James M. Curley
(right).*

getic patrons of their respective city hospitals, spending public funds
lavishly on new construction, providing maternity and children's clin-
ics, and arranging medical care for the indigent. In an era when social
security, Blue Cross, unemployment compensation, and other public
and private arrangements to cushion life's shocks did not exist, these
benefactions from a political boss were important.

In every city, the boss had his base in the poorer, older, shabbier
section of town. Historians have dubbed this section the "walking city"
because it developed in the eighteenth and early nineteenth centuries,
when houses and businesses were jumbled together, usually near the
waterfront, and businessmen and laborers alike had to live within
walking distance of their work. As transportation improved, people
were able to live farther and farther from their place of work. Population dispersed in rough concentric circles: the financially most successful lived in the outer ring, where land was plentiful and the air was
clean; the middle classes lived in intermediate neighborhoods; and the
poorest and the latest arrivals from Europe crowded into the now-
rundown neighborhoods in the center, where rents were lowest. Politics in most cities reflected a struggle between the old, boss-run wards
downtown and the more prosperous neighborhoods farther out, which
did not need a boss's services and which championed reform. The
more skilled workingmen and the white-collar workers who lived in the

intermediate neighborhoods generally held the balance of power between the machine and the reformers. A skillful boss could hold
enough of these swing voters on the basis of ethnic loyalty or shared
support of a particular issue. At times, he might work out alliances with
business leaders who found that an understanding with a boss was
literally more businesslike than dependence upon the vagaries of reform.

But always it was the poorest and most insecure who provided the
boss with the base of his political power. Their only strength, as Professor Richard C. Wade of the University of Chicago has observed, was
in their numbers.

> These numbers were in most cases a curse; housing never caught up with
> demand, the job market was always flooded, the breadwinner had too
> many mouths to feed. Yet in politics such a liability could be turned into
> an asset. If the residents could be mobilized, their combined strength
> would be able to do what none could do alone. Soon the "boss" and the
> "machine" arose to organize this potential. The boss system was simply
> the political expression of inner city life.

At a time when many newcomers to the city were seeking unskilled
work, and when many families had a precarious economic footing, the
ability to dispense jobs was crucial to the bosses. First, there were jobs

to be filled on the city payroll. Just as vital, and far more numerous, were jobs on municipal construction projects. When the machine controlled a city, public funds were always being spent for more schools, hospitals, libraries, courthouses, and orphanages. The growing cities had to have more sewer lines, gas lines, and waterworks, more paved streets and trolley tracks. Even if these utilities were privately owned, the managers needed the goodwill of city hall and were responsive to suggestions about whom to hire.

The payrolls of these public works projects were often padded, but to those seeking a job, it was better to be on a padded payroll than on no payroll. By contrast, the municipal reformers usually cut back on public spending, stopped projects to investigate for graft, and pruned payrolls. Middle- and upper-income taxpayers welcomed these reforms, but they were distinctly unpopular in working-class wards.

Another issue that strengthened the bosses was the regulation of the sale of liquor. Most women in the nineteenth century did not drink, and with their backing, the movement to ban entirely the manufacture and sale of liquor grew steadily stronger. It had its greatest support among Protestants with a rural or small-town background. To them the cities, with their saloons, dance halls, cheap theatres, and red-light districts, were becoming latter-day versions of Sodom and Gomorrah.

Many of the European immigrants in the cities, however, had entirely different values. Quite respectable Germans took their wives to beer gardens on Sundays. In the eyes of the Irish, keeping a "public house" was an honorable occupation. Some Irish women drank beer and saw no harm in going to the saloon or sending an older child for a bucketful—"rushing the growler," they called it. Poles, Czechs, Italians, and others also failed to share the rage of the Prohibitionists against saloons. Unable to entertain in their cramped tenements, they liked to congregate in neighborhood bars.

The machine also appealed successfully on the liquor issue to many middle-class ethnic voters who had no need of the machine's economic assistance. Thus, in New York in 1897, Tammany scored a sweeping victory over an incumbent reform administration that had tried to enforce a state law permitting only hotels to sell liquor on Sundays. As one of the city's three police commissioners, Theodore Roosevelt became famous prowling the tougher neighborhoods on the hunt for saloon violations, but on the vaudeville stage the singers were giving forth with the hit song, "I Want What I Want When I Want It!" As a character in Alfred Henry Lewis' novel *The Boss* explained it, the reformers had made a serious mistake: "They got between the people and its beer!"

In 1902, Lincoln Steffens, the muckraker who made a name for himself writing about political bossism, visited St. Louis to interview

Joseph W. Folk, a crusading district attorney. "It is good businessmen that are corrupting our bad politicians," Folk told him. "It is good business that causes bad government in St. Louis." Thirty-five years later, Boss Tom Pendergast was running the entire state of Missouri on that same reciprocal relationship.

Although many factory owners could be indifferent to politics, other businessmen were dependent upon the goodwill and the efficiency of the municipal government. The railroads that wanted to build their freight terminals and extend their lines into the cities, the contractors who erected the office buildings, the banks that held mortgages on the land and loaned money for the construction, the utility and transit companies, and the department stores were all in need of licenses, franchises, rights of way, or favorable rulings from city inspectors and agencies. These were the businesses that made the big pay-offs to political bosses in cash, blocks of stock, or tips on land about to be developed.

In another sense, profound, impersonal, and not corrupt, the business community needed the boss. Because the Industrial Revolution hit this country when it was still thinly populated and most of its cities were overgrown towns, American cities expanded with astonishing speed. For example, in the single decade from 1880 to 1890, Chicago's population more than doubled, from a half million to over a million. Minneapolis and St. Paul tripled in size. New York City increased from a million to a million and a half; Detroit, Milwaukee, Columbus, and Cleveland grew by sixty to eighty per cent.

Municipal governments, however, were unprepared for this astonishing growth. Planning and budgeting were unknown arts. City charters had restrictive provisions envisaged for much smaller, simpler communities. The mayor and the important commissioners were usually amateurs serving a term or two as a civic duty. Authority was dispersed among numerous boards and special agencies. A typical city would have a board of police commissioners, a board of health, a board of tax assessors, a water board, and many others. The ostensible governing body was a city council or board of aldermen which might have thirty, fifty, or even a hundred members. Under these circumstances, it was difficult to get a prompt decision, harder still to coordinate decisions taken by different bodies acting on different premises, and easy for delays and anomalies to develop.

In theory, the cities could have met their need for increased services by municipal socialism, but the conventional wisdom condemned that as too radical, although here and there a city did experiment with publicly owned utilities. In theory also, the cities could have financed public buildings and huge projects such as water and sewer systems by frankly raising taxes or floating bonds. But both taxes and debt were

*A famous political cartoon by Thomas Nast shows the
Tammany tiger (the symbol of the Tammany Hall machine)
in a Roman arena attacking the republic. The tiger snarls:
"What are you going to do about it?"*

no more popular then than they are now. Moreover, the laissez-faire
doctrine which holds that "that government is best which governs
least" was enshrined orthodoxy in America from the 1870's down to
the 1930's.

As men clung to such orthodox philosophies, the structures of
government became obsolete; they strained to meet unexpected demands as a swelling number of citizens in every class clamored for
more services. In this climate the bosses emerged. They had no scru-
ples about taking shortcuts through old procedures or manipulating
independent boards and agencies in ways that the original city fathers had never intended. They had no inhibiting commitment to any
theory of limited government. They were willing to spend, tax, and
build—and to take the opprobrium along with the graft. Sometimes,
like Hague in Jersey City, Curley in Boston, and Big Bill Thompson
in Chicago, they got themselves elected mayor and openly assumed
responsibility. More often, like Pendergast in Kansas City, Cox in
Cincinnati, the leaders of Tammany, and the successive Republican
bosses of Philadelphia, they held minor offices or none, stayed out of
the limelight, and ran city government through their iron control of
the party organization. In ruling Memphis for forty years, Ed Crump

In this contemporary cartoon Michael Ramus has pictured Mayor Daley of Chicago as "The Last Leaf" on the blasted tree of old-style urban bossism.

followed one pattern and then the other. Impeached on a technicality after being elected three times as mayor, Crump retreated to the back rooms and became even more powerful as the city's political boss.

What manner of men became political bosses? They were men of little education and no social background, often of immigrant parentage. A college-educated boss like Edward Flynn of The Bronx was a rarity. Bosses often began as saloonkeepers, because the saloon was a natural meeting place in poorer neighborhoods in the days before Prohibition. They were physically strong and no strangers to violence. Seventy-five years ago, most men made their living with brawn rather than brain, and a man who expected to be a leader of men had to be tough as well as shrewd. Open violence used to be common at polling places on Election Day, and gangs of repeaters roamed from one precinct to another. Although the typical boss made his way up through that roughneck system, the logic of his career led him to suppress violence. Bloody heads make bad publicity, and it is hard for any political organization to maintain a monopoly on violence. Bosses grew to prefer quieter, more lawful, less dangerous methods of control. Ballot-box stuffing and overt intimidation never disappeared entirely, but gradually they receded to weapons of last resort.

Political bosses varied in their idiosyncrasies and styles. A few, like Curley, became polished orators; others, like the legendary Charles Murphy of Tammany Hall, never made speeches. They were temperate, businesslike types; among them a drunk was as rare as a Phi Beta Kappa. If they had a generic failing it was for horses and gambling. Essentially they were hardheaded men of executive temper and genuine organizing talents; many, in other circumstances and with more education, might have become successful businessmen.

They have disappeared now, most of them. Education has produced a more sophisticated electorate; it has also encouraged potential bosses to turn away from politics toward more secure, prestigious, and profitable careers. A young man who had the energy, persistence, and skill in 1899 to become a successful political boss would in 1969 go to college and end up in an executive suite.

The urban population has also changed. The great flood of bewildered foreigners has dwindled to a trickle. In place of the European immigrants of the past, today's cities receive an influx of Negroes from the rural South, Puerto Ricans, Mexicans, and the white poor from Appalachia. As they overcome the language barrier and widen their experience, the Puerto Ricans are making themselves felt in urban politics. New York City, where they are most heavily concentrated, may have a Puerto Rican mayor in the not too distant future.

But the other groups are too isolated from the rest of the community to put together a winning political coalition of have-nots. The Mexicans and the ex-hillbillies from Appalachia are isolated by their unique cultural backgrounds, the Negroes by the giant fact of their race. Inasmuch as they make up a quarter to a third of the population in many cities, are a cohesive group, and still have a high proportion of poor who have to look to government for direct help, the Negroes might have produced several bosses and functioning political machines had they been of white European ancestry. But until Negroes attain a clear numerical majority, they find it difficult to take political power in any city because various white factions are reluctant to coalesce with them.

Regardless of the race or background of the voters, however, there are factors which work against the old-style machines. Civil service regulations make it harder to create a job or pad a payroll. Federal income taxes and federal accounting requirements make it more difficult to hide the rewards of graft. Television, public relations, and polling have created a whole new set of political techniques and undermined the personal ties and neighborhood loyalties on which the old organizations depended.

The new political style has brought an increase in municipal government efficiency and probably some decline in political corruption and misrule. But the politics of the television age puts a premium on hypocrisy. Candor has gone out the window with the spoils system. There is still a lot of self-seeking in politics and always will be. But gone are the days of Tammany's Boss Richard Croker, who when asked by an investigating committee if he was "working for his own pocket," shot back: "All the time—same as you." Today's politicians are so busy tending their images that they have become incapable of even a mildly derogatory remark such as Jim Curley's: "The term 'codfish aristocracy' is a reflection on the fish."

Curley entitled his memoirs *I'd Do It Again*. But the rough-and-tumble days when two-fisted, rough-tongued politicians came roaring out of the slums to take charge of America's young cities are not to come again.

Hail Liberty!

DAVID G. McCULLOUGH
FREDERICK ALLEN

This selection is made up of excerpts from two American Heritage *articles, articles that were written more than eight years apart. The sections describing the events that occurred in 1886 when the Statute of Liberty was formally unveiled were written by David G. McCullough, author of* The Path Between the Seas, *an account of the construction of the Panama Canal;* The Great Bridge, *which describes the building of the Brooklyn Bridge; and* Mornings on Horseback, *a moving account of the early life of Theodore Roosevelt. The material dealing with the construction of the statue and its transportation to New York comes from an article by Frederick Allen, senior editor of* American Heritage, *that is primarily concerned with the renovation of "Miss Liberty" that was completed in time for the celebration of her hundredth birthday on July 4, 1986, a celebration that in so many ways resembled the one that McCullough describes.* ∎

October 28, 1886, was a day unique in the history of New York City: a day of lofty speeches and colorful heroes on parade, of boisterous crowds—the biggest since Grant's funeral the year before—and miserable weather and the noisiest, most chaotic water pageant ever put on in New York Harbor. It was, in the words of the *New York Times*, the day "a hundred Fourths of July broke loose." It was the day they unveiled *Liberty Enlightening the World,* a gigantic statue, a gift from the people of France to the people of the United States in honor of the hundredth anniversary of the signing of the Declaration of Independence.

The statue had been built in Paris during the late eighteen seventies and early eighties, from a model by the French sculptor Auguste Bartholdi. . . .

The statue's genesis began, according to Bartholdi, at a dinner party in 1865 at the home of Edouard de Laboulaye, a prominent French historian, admirer of America, and leader of the Republican opposition under Napoleon III. De Laboulaye suggested the erection of a colossal monument to Independence, to be organized jointly by France and America, and the concept immediately caught the imagination of the young Alsatian sculptor, who liked the idea both politically and artistically—he had traveled to Egypt in the 1850s and been deeply impressed by the colossal sculptures there.

No immediate action was taken on de Laboulaye's proposal, however. In the meantime Bartholdi met Ismail Pasha, the khedive of Egypt, and in 1867 proposed the construction of an enormous lighthouse to stand at the entrance to the Suez Canal, which would be completed two years later. Bartholdi did sketches for the lighthouse that gave it the form of an enormous human figure with a torch in its upraised hand. But Ismail Pasha was never won over, and by 1869 the idea was dropped.

In 1871, Bartholdi set sail for America armed with letters of introduction from de Laboulaye, hoping to stimulate interest in a great statue to be erected during the centennial, 1876, in honor of the "ancient friendship of France and the United States." He wrote to de Laboulaye before he left: "I will try to glorify the Republic and Liberty over there, in the hope that someday I will find it again here. . . ." His proposal was well received, and he found an ideal site for the statue: Bedloe's Island, in New York Harbor, formerly a quarantine station, a refuge for Tories, an ordnance depot, a garrison, a recruiting post, and today renamed Liberty Island.

In 1875, with moderate Republicans triumphant in France, the project was publically announced, and the Union Franco-Americaine was formed to raise funds. It soon became clear, however, that the statue would not be ready in time for the centennial.

Bartholdi sketched this rough design of the statue in watercolors. The drawing is small, only 3 1/4 by 4 3/4 inches.

The statue first took shape as a clay miniature four feet tall. The model for the body may have been Bartholdi's future wife; the face, he admitted, was his mother's. Mme Bartholdi, a strong-willed widow, had raised her sons alone in Paris but had returned to the family's hometown of Colmar by the 1870s. Colmar and the rest of Alsace had been ceded to the Germans at the end of the Franco-Prussian War, in 1871, and Bartholdi was undoubtedly moved by the irony of using the face of his mother, whose homeland had been usurped, on his statue of Liberty.

Starting with the four-foot-tall model, the statue was enlarged several times, first to a plaster model 9.4 feet tall—one-sixteenth of the final size of the statue—then to one-quarter size, and finally to full-size pieces. Each time, as many as nine thousand measurements had to be made to proportionately increase the statue's dimensions. And each time, Bartholdi made changes in the finished plaster model to adjust to the new scale. This work was done at the Parisian firm of Gaget, Gauthier & Cie, and according to a dubious popular etymology to which every member of the restoration team seems to subscribe, miniatures of the statue sold to raise money became known as *Gagets* and, in this country, gave birth to the word "gadget."

Next the plaster form was reproduced as a skin of copper sheets.

Hammered copper had become popular in the nineteenth century as a material for large-scale art and architectural works. It was at once light, workable, and relatively inexpensive—hammering made it both thinner and more rigid than any cast metal. In the Gaget, Gauthier studios, latticed wooden molds were built to conform to each full-scale plaster piece. On these molds, over three hundred sheets of copper $3/32$ inch thick were hammered into shape, and further hammering was done afterward to achieve the correct detailing.

How was this copper shell 151 feet tall and barely $1/10$ inch thick to stand up to the winds of New York Harbor? Liberty's first engineer, Eugène Emmanuel Viollet-le-Duc, . . . died in 1879 before his system could be implemented, and he was replaced by Gustave Eiffel, who at forty-seven had made a name for himself as the developer of numerous technological innovations that allowed him to build spectacularly long, high railroad bridges using great, sweeping arches and tall iron pylons. His plan for the statue was the antithesis of Viollet-le-Duc's.

The statue's weight is borne by a central pylon based on a typical Eiffel bridge pylon, consisting of four iron piers rising ninety-seven feet and held together by nine levels of horizontal struts and diagonal cross-bracing. . . . Marvin Trachtenberg describes Eiffel's structural system in his study of the monument, *The Statute of Liberty*, as an "uncanny prophecy of stressed-skin construction that would become crucial in twentieth-century aeronautic engineering (in airplane wings, for example)."

The statue was erected in Paris in 1884 and officially presented to the U.S. ambassador there on the Fourth of July. In 1885 it arrived in New York packed in 214 crates. The pedestal, America's responsibility, was embarrassingly far from completion—fund-raising had been inadequate and money had run out. But Joseph Pulitzer, a Hungarian immigrant, mounted a front-page campaign in his New York *World* excoriating the American rich for failing to come through and calling on the paper's readers to help. He listed the name of every donor inside the paper, and the *World* quickly raised $100,000 from 121,000 readers. . . .

Bedloe's Island . . . had been the site of, among other things, a pesthouse, a gallows, a military prison, a dump, and a hospital. By October of the following year the statue was all but finished, and, understandably, it was the talk of the town. From crown to toe the Goddess measured 151 feet, a good 50 feet more than the Colossus of Rhodes. Her waist was 35 feet thick, her head 10 feet thick, big enough to hold thirty people. Counting the pedestal, the statute stood over 305 feet, or about 20 feet taller than the steeple on old Trinity Church, then the highest structure on the Manhattan skyline. But above all, seen from the Battery or from Brooklyn Heights, from the

The hand, with torch, of the Statue of Liberty was on display in Madison Square Park, New York City, from 1876 to 1884.

flats of New Jersey or from the rail of a Staten Island ferry, *Liberty* seemed big enough in size and in concept to do what its creator and its donors had intended: it seemed to give both scale and meaning to the vast open space of the harbor. It seemed to say: This is indeed the Gateway to the New World. And that, it seemed to all New York, was reason enough for more than the usual sort of celebration.

Preparations for the event had been front-page news for several days before October 28. There was to be a mammoth parade from Central Park down Fifth Avenue to Broadway and on to the Battery; an unveiling ceremony of a dignity to suit the statue's size was planned; and the day was to end gloriously with a spectacular display of fireworks in the harbor. The visiting French dignitaries and the receptions in their honor, the military units scheduled to march in the parade, the arrival of the President from Washington, were items of the highest interest and were described in effusive detail. So was the other major topic of the week—the weather. For two days a fine, steady drizzle had been falling, soaking the city, choking the harbor with fog, and giving editorial writers, bandmasters, politicians, and families as far out as

Connecticut considerable cause for concern. But the long-awaited day dawned rainless. It was raw and sullen, to be sure. Buildings and streets had a somber look. Along the parade route the red, white, and blue of the Stars and Stripes and the Tricolor hung damp and limp. In the harbor, visibility was limited to a few hundred feet. But, for the moment, there was no rain.

By nine o'clock the crowds filled the sidewalks up and down Fifth Avenue and Broadway. At the side streets enterprising draymen had their wagons fitted up with seats renting for as much as fifty cents. Steps, stoops, roof tops, the best windows, were thick with spectators. Schools were closed. Business, except for restaurants and saloons, was suspended, though a few large stores had taken the trouble to clear their windows of goods and had set up chairs for special friends and visitors. Venders were doing a brisk trade in penny apples, umbrellas, and commemorative medals showing the statue on one side, Bartholdi's head on the other. Cheap prints of the Brooklyn Bridge, hawked as authentic works by Bartholdi, were also selling well, especially among the recent immigrants. And more than one lithograph of General Grant, left over from the occasion of the previous year, was purchased as a faithful likeness of the great French sculptor.

It was almost 10 A.M. At the far end of Fifth Avenue, up past Fifty-ninth Street, beside the dripping autumn foliage of Central Park, the marchers tuned their instruments, checked over bridles and buttons, and readied themselves for the moment when President Cleveland would start his ride to the reviewing stand at Madison Square.

The President had come up from Washington by special train the evening before, and had spent the night at the home of Secretary of the Navy William C. Whitney at Fifth Avenue and Fifty-seventh Street. At exactly ten o'clock his party came out of the Whitney front door. Cleveland tipped his black silk hat to the applauding crowd. The scarlet-coated Marine band, with John Philip Sousa conducting, struck up a march, and the presidential procession moved off behind General Charles P. Stone, the white-bearded marshal of "Liberty Day." The official ceremonies had begun, right on time. The streets resounded with a hearty roar; and a thin, chill rain that would last the rest of the day began to fall noiselessly.

In the next three and a half hours row on row of tossing manes, waving plumes, and slanting bayonets, and more than 20,000 men, followed the President down Fifth Avenue, then moved on down Broadway all the way to the Battery. At the reviewing stand, near City Hall, they passed before an imposing group including Cleveland, Bartholdi, Viscount Ferdinand de Lesseps (the builder of the Suez Canal), and General Phil Sheridan. President Cleveland stood beaming in spite of the drizzle, returning the salutes of each unit that passed, obviously pleased by the warm reception he had received. The first band to go by broke out with the "Marseillaise," in honor of the French luminaries on the stand. And none thereafter dared break the precedent if they could possibly manage it. There were bands of seventy pieces and bands of seven, bands from Hoboken and Poughkeepsie, Philadelphia, Boston, and Buffalo, bands from most of the city's armories, theatres, and dance halls—over a hundred in all. Some of their regalia, as one reporter felt obliged to point out, was "somewhat moldy and careworn and a little moth-eaten." Still the music was "amazingly enthusiastic and discordant."

Formations of mounted Army Regulars pranced by, followed by four battalions of bluejackets from the *Tennessee,* the *Alliance,* and the *Yantic,* of the North Atlantic Squadron, which had steamed in for the occasion and now lay anchored in the harbor. There were also Rochambeau Grenadiers, Italian volunteers in magnificent gold-trimmed uniforms and feathered shakos, a battalion of fiercely mustached Philadelphia policemen, a carriage with a few ancient veterans of the War of 1812, another full of Mexican War veterans. A division of Grand Army veterans marched by, some in the colorful garb of the Zouaves, some hobbling on wooden legs. There were Elks, Masons, state governors, cane-swinging students from Columbia who gave the President a rousing college cheer, and a red-shirted volunteer fire brigade led by a limping, indestructible local hero named Harry Howard, who got the biggest cheer of anyone. And finally a venerable carriage that had belonged to George Washington went rolling by, pulled by eight dapple-grey Normans.

Sweeping past the President's stand, the marchers went on down Broadway to Wall Street, where, according to one witness, the ticker-tape reception was so enthusiastic that "every window appeared to be a paper mill," then on to the Battery and the rain-soaked crowd that swarmed about the sea wall, hoping for a glimpse of the main attraction of the day, the unveiling. Their hopes, however, were futile. The thick, salt-smelling mist that had enshrouded the city for days shut off all view of the statue, and hid most of the spectacle that was taking place just offshore.

By now the harbor was a honking, tooting, whistling carnival of ships of every imaginable shape and size. There were yachts, ferries, barges, a dozen kinds of launches, shrill-shrieking tugs on a day off, French and American men-of-war, all bunting-bedecked; steamboats, river boats, police boats, sailboats, rowboats, boats big, small, old, new, the decks of some of them so black with sight-seers that they listed almost to the point of toppling into the choppy waters. One big excursion boat, the *Grand Republic,* had over 3,000 people on board.

Tickets to witness the unveiling and the "grand naval parade" had been on sale for weeks. For fifty or seventy-five cents, thousands clambered aboard steamers with names like *Sylvan Dell, Cephus,* and *Magnolia* to enjoy a box-lunch outing that began about eleven and was meant to finish with the evening fireworks. Quite a few of the city's more popular clubs and fraternal orders had chartered their own boats and fitted them out with brass bands and champagne. The Union League Club had its own steamer, as did the Woman Suffrage Association, the New York Society of Amateur Photographers, the Grand Army veterans, the aldermen, and the Brotherhood of Locomotive Engineers. A few more adventurous souls chartered their own rowboats and bobbed about through the foul afternoon, narrowly missing the huge throbbing paddle wheels of the steamers and evoking extraordinary remarks from many a frenzied pilot.

The number of ships officially designated to take part in the pageant came to just over 300. Shortly after noon they had started forming two lines in the Hudson, waiting for the President and his party to depart for the unveiling from the foot of West Twenty-third Street. Then, at two forty-five, the *Tennessee* fired a broadside and every ship with cannon or deck gun, steam whistle or foghorn, joined in as the President's boat, the *Dispatch,* covered from prow to stern with flags of all nations, came through at full speed. At Bedloe's Island the official party was greeted by a twenty-one-gun salute, then quickly ushered to the flag-draped platform at the base of the statue, which, looming above, glistened with rain, its upraised arm hazy in the mist and smoke, its face covered with the French ensign.

After the appropriate introductions had been made, Gilmore's 22nd Regiment Band played "Hail to the Chief" just loud enough to be heard above the continuing din. After about fifteen minutes, when things had quieted down somewhat, Dr. Richard Storrs, a noted Brooklyn clergyman, began a prayer in the midst of which one tugboat captain let loose a whistle that was quickly answered in kind by his colleagues in the flotilla. "The prayer," as the *Herald* commented the following morning, "was conducted under disadvantages such as never before beset a minister of God."

Next came the doughty de Lesseps, who, dressed in evening clothes, gave his speech bareheaded in the rain; though he spoke in French he managed to still the whistles and impress his audience enormously.

Senator William Evarts of New York followed, and did very well for the first few minutes. But by this time Bartholdi and a few companions had climbed up inside the statue to the torch some 300 feet above; and, on a mistaken signal, he pulled the cord that unveiled the face. The flag fell, and a great cheer went up: "Hail, Liberty!" Everyone was on his feet, every ship responded with a deafening crescendo of whistles

*One hundred years after the first installation, a rebuilt
"Lady Liberty" was rededicated in a blaze of fireworks on
July 3, 1986.*

and horns, another broadside exploded from the *Tennessee,* bells rang on the mainland, Gilmore's band launched into "America"—and Evarts sat down. About twenty minutes after that, the President made a brief acceptance speech in which he called the statue a "token of the affection and consideration of the people of France" and vowed that "we will not forget that Liberty has here made her home; nor shall her chosen altar be neglected. Willing votaries shall keep its fires alive, and they shall gleam upon the shores of our sister Republic in the East. [Great applause.] Reflected thence and joined with answering rays, a stream of light shall pierce the darkness of ignorance and man's oppression until liberty shall enlighten the world. [An overwhelming roar of approval.]"

A few closing remarks were made by Chauncey M. Depew, the railroad magnate; Bishop Henry C. Potter said a benediction; and, at twenty minutes to five, the President, amid still another twenty-one-gun salute, left for Jersey City and his train back to Washington. The sunset gun went off on Governor's Island.

The fireworks had to be postponed a few nights because of the weather. But the Goddess of Liberty had officially taken her stand at the entrance of America's great harbor, where she would beckon millions from the Old World in the years to come.

The Myth of the Happy Yeoman

RICHARD HOFSTADTER

The following essay, like Oliver La Farge's essay on the American Indian in Volume One, is a study in the differences between reality and people's view of reality. Usually the historian seeks only for the reality and discards the myths that surround it in the records of the past. But in some contexts the myths themselves are vitally important and thus the proper subject of historical analysis.

The concept of the yeoman farmer had, as the late Professor Richard Hofstadter of Columbia University demonstrates, a solid basis in fact in early America. Farming was for many a way of life, not primarily a way of making a living. But national growth and development changed this steadily, and after the rapid expansion of industrialization the true yeoman practically disappeared. Why the myth persisted is the subject of Hofstadter's inquiry. The tale is part of the larger story of the impact of the Industrial Revolution on American thought, a subject which Hofstadter developed at greater length in his Pulitzer Prize history, The Age of Reform. ∎

The United States was born in the country and has moved to the city. From the beginning its political values as well as ideas were of necessity shaped by country life. The early American politician, the country editor, who wished to address himself to the common man, had to draw upon a rhetoric that would touch the tillers of the soil; and even the spokesman of city people knew that his audience had been in very large part reared upon the farm.

But what the articulate people who talked and wrote about farmers and farming—the preachers, poets, philosophers, writers, and statesmen—liked about American farming was not, in every respect, what the typical working farmer liked. For the articulate people were drawn irresistibly to the noncommercial, non-pecuniary, self-sufficient aspect of American farm life. To them it was an ideal.

Writers like Thomas Jefferson and Hector St. John de Crèvecœur admired the yeoman farmer not for his capacity to exploit opportunities and make money but for his honest industry, his independence, his frank spirit of equality, his ability to produce and enjoy a simple abundance. The farmer himself, in most cases, was in fact inspired to make money, and such self-sufficiency as he actually had was usually forced upon him by a lack of transportation or markets, or by the necessity to save cash to expand his operations.

For while early American society was an agrarian society, it was fast becoming more commercial, and commercial goals made their way among its agricultural classes almost as rapidly as elsewhere. The more commercial this society became, however, the more reason it found to cling in imagination to the noncommercial agrarian values. The more farming as a self-sufficient way of life was abandoned for farming as a business, the more merit men found in what was being left behind. And the more rapidly the farmers' sons moved into the towns, the more nostalgic the whole culture became about its rural past. Throughout the nineteenth and even in the twentieth century, the American was taught that rural life and farming as a vocation were something sacred.

This sentimental attachment to the rural way of life is a kind of homage that Americans have paid to the fancied innocence of their origins. To call it a "myth" is not to imply that the idea is simply false. Rather the "myth" so effectively embodies men's values that it profoundly influences their way of perceiving reality and hence their behavior.

Like any complex of ideas, the agrarian myth cannot be defined in a phrase, but its component themes form a clear pattern. Its hero was the yeoman farmer, its central conception the notion that he is the ideal man and the ideal citizen. Unstinted praise of the special virtues of the farmer and the special values of rural life was coupled with the assertion that agriculture, as a calling uniquely productive and uniquely important to society, had a special right to the concern and protection of government. The yeoman, who owned a small farm and worked it with the aid of his family, was the incarnation of the simple, honest, independent, healthy, happy human being. Because he lived in close communion with beneficent nature, his life was believed to have a wholesomeness and integrity impossible for the depraved populations of cities.

His well-being was not merely physical, it was moral: it was not merely personal, it was the central source of civic virtue; it was not merely secular but religious, for God had made the land and called man to cultivate it. Since the yeoman was believed to be both happy and honest, and since he had a secure propertied stake in society in the form of his own land, he was held to be the best and most reliable sort of citizen. To this conviction Jefferson appealed when he wrote: "The small land holders are the most precious part of a state."

In origin the agrarian myth was not a popular but a literary idea, a preoccupation of the upper classes, of those who enjoyed a classical education, read pastoral poetry, experimented with breeding stock, and owned plantations or country estates. It was clearly formulated and almost universally accepted in America during the last half of the eighteenth century. As it took shape both in Europe and America, its promulgators drew heavily upon the authority and the rhetoric of classical writers—Hesiod, Xenophon, Cato, Cicero, Virgil, Horace, and others—whose works were the staples of a good education. A learned agricultural gentry, coming into conflict with the industrial classes, welcomed the moral strength that a rich classical ancestry brought to the praise of husbandry.

Chiefly through English experience, and from English and classical writers, the agrarian myth came to America, where, like so many other cultural importations, it eventually took on altogether new dimensions in its new setting. So appealing were the symbols of the myth that even an arch-opponent of the agrarian interest like Alexander Hamilton found it politic to concede in his *Report on Manufactures* that "the cultivation of the earth, as the primary and most certain source of national supply . . . has intrinsically a strong claim to pre-eminence over every other kind of industry." And Benjamin Franklin, urban cosmopolite though he was, once said that agriculture was "the only *honest way*" for a nation to acquire wealth, "wherein man receives a real increase of the seed thrown into the ground, a kind of continuous miracle, wrought by the hand of God in his favour, as a reward for his innocent life and virtuous industry."

Among the intellectual classes in the eighteenth century the agrarian myth had virtually universal appeal. Some writers used it to give simple, direct, and emotional expression to their feelings about life and nature; others linked agrarianism with a formal philosophy of natural rights. The application of the natural rights philosophy to land tenure became especially popular in America. Since the time of Locke it had been a standard argument that the land is the common stock of society to which every man has a right—what Jefferson called "the fundamental right to labour the earth"; that since the occupancy and use of land are the true criteria of valid ownership, labor expended in cultivating the earth confers title to it; that since government was created to protect property, the property of working landholders has a special claim to be fostered and protected by the state.

At first the agrarian myth was a notion of the educated classes, but by the early nineteenth century it had become a mass creed, a part of the country's political folklore and its nationalist ideology. The roots of this change may be found as far back as the American Revolution, which, appearing to many Americans as the victory of a band of embattled farmers over an empire, seemed to confirm the moral and civic superiority of the yeoman, made the farmer a symbol of the new nation, and wove the agrarian myth into his patriotic sentiments and idealism.

Still more important, the myth played a role in the first party battles under the Constitution. The Jeffersonians appealed again and again to the moral primacy of the yeoman farmer in their attacks on the Federalists. The family farm and American democracy became indissolubly connected in Jeffersonian thought, and by 1840 even the more conservative party, the Whigs, took over the rhetorical appeal to the common man, and elected a President in good part on the strength of the fiction that he lived in a log cabin.

The Jeffersonians, moreover, made the agrarian myth the basis of a strategy of continental development. Many of them expected that the great empty inland regions would guarantee the preponderance of the yeoman—and therefore the dominance of Jeffersonianism and the health of the state—for an unlimited future. The opening of the trans-Allegheny region, its protection from slavery, and the purchase of the Louisiana Territory were the first great steps in a continental strategy designed to establish an internal empire of small farms. Much later the Homestead Act was meant to carry to its completion the process of continental settlement by small homeowners. The failure of the Homestead Act "to enact by statute the fee-simple empire" was one of the original sources of Populist grievances, and one of the central points at which the agrarian myth was overrun by the commercial realities.

Above all, however, the myth was powerful because the United States in the first half of the nineteenth century consisted predominantly of literate and politically enfranchised farmers. Offering what seemed harmless flattery to this numerically dominant class, the myth suggested a standard vocabulary to rural editors and politicians. Although farmers may not have been much impressed by what was said about the merits of a noncommercial way of life, they could only enjoy learning about their special virtues and their unique services to the nation. Moreover, the editors and politicians who so flattered them need not in most cases have been insincere. More often than not they too were likely to have begun life in little villages or on farms, and what they had to say stirred in their own breasts, as it did in the breasts of a great many townspeople, nostalgia for their early years and perhaps relieved some residual feelings of guilt at having deserted parental homes and childhood attachments. They also had the satisfaction in the early days of knowing that in so far as it was based upon the life of the largely self-sufficient yeoman the agrarian myth was a depiction of reality as well as the assertion of an ideal.

Oddly enough, the agrarian myth came to be believed more widely and tenaciously as it became more fictional. At first it was propagated with a kind of genial candor, and only later did it acquire overtones of insincerity. There survives from the Jackson era a painting that shows Governor Joseph Ritner of Pennsylvania standing by a primitive plow at the end of a furrow. There is no pretense that the Governor has actually been plowing—he wears broadcloth pants and a silk vest, and his tall black beaver hat has been carefully laid in the grass beside him—but the picture is meant as a reminder of both his rustic origin 'and his present high station in life. By contrast, Calvin Coolidge posed almost a century later for a series of photographs that represented him as haying in Vermont. In one of them the President sits on the edge of a hay ring in a white shirt, collar detached, wearing highly polished black shoes and a fresh pair of overalls; in the background stands his Pierce Arrow, a secret service man on the running board, plainly waiting to hurry the President away from his bogus rural labors. That the second picture is so much more pretentious and disingenuous than the first is a measure of the increasing hollowness of the myth as it became more and more remote from the realities of agriculture.

Throughout the nineteenth century hundreds upon hundreds of thousands of farm-born youths sought their careers in the towns and cities. Particularly after 1840, which marked the beginning of a long cycle of heavy country-to-city migration, farm children repudiated their parents' way of life and took off for the cities where, in agrarian theory if not in fact, they were sure to succumb to vice and poverty.

When a correspondent of the *Prairie Farmer* in 1849 made the mistake of praising the luxuries, the "polished society," and the economic opportunities of the city, he was rebuked for overlooking the fact that city life *"crushes, enslaves,* and *ruins so many thousands of our young men* who are insensibly made the victims of *dissipation,* of *reckless speculation,* and of *ultimate crime."* Such warnings, of course, were futile. "Thousands of young men," wrote the New York agriculturist Jesse Buel, "who annually forsake the plough, and the honest profession of their fathers, if not to win the fair, at least form an opinion, too often confirmed by mistaken parents, that agriculture is not the road to wealth, to honor, nor to happiness. And such will continue to be the case, until our agriculturists become qualified to assume that rank in society to which the importance of their calling, and their numbers, entitle them, and which intelligence and self-respect can alone give them."

Rank in society! That was close to the heart of the matter, for the farmer was beginning to realize acutely not merely that the best of the world's goods were to be had in the cities and that the urban middle and upper classes had much more of them than he did but also that he was losing in status and respect as compared with them. He became aware that the official respect paid to the farmer masked a certain disdain felt by many city people. "There has . . . a certain class of individuals grown up in our land," complained a farm writer in 1835, "who treat the cultivators of the soil as an inferior caste . . . whose utmost abilities are confined to the merit of being able to discuss a boiled potato and a rasher of bacon." The city was symbolized as the home of loan sharks, dandies, fops, and aristocrats with European ideas who despised farmers as hayseeds.

The growth of the urban market intensified this antagonism. In areas like colonial New England, where an intimate connection had existed between the small town and the adjacent countryside, where a community of interests and even of occupations cut across the town line, the rural-urban hostility had not developed so sharply as in the newer areas where the township plan was never instituted and where isolated farmsteads were more common. As settlement moved west, as urban markets grew, as self-sufficient farmers became rarer, as farmers pushed into commercial production for the cities they feared and distrusted, they quite correctly thought of themselves as a vocational and economic group rather than as members of a neighborhood. In the Populist era the city was totally alien territory to many farmers, and the primacy of agriculture as a source of wealth was reasserted with much bitterness. "The great cities rest upon our broad and fertile prairies," declared Bryan in his "Cross of Gold" speech. "Burn down your cities and leave our farms, and your cities will spring up again as if by magic; but destroy our farms, and the grass will grow in the streets of every city in the country." Out of the beliefs nourished by the agrarian myth there had arisen the notion that the city was a parasitical

According to this 1869 engraving from The Prairie Farmer, *each occupation has its uses, but the farmer alone foots all the bills.*

growth on the country. Bryan spoke for a people raised for generations on the idea that the farmer was a very special creature, blessed by God, and that in a country consisting largely of farmers the voice of the farmer was the voice of democracy and of virtue itself.

The agrarian myth encouraged farmers to believe that they were not themselves an organic part of the whole order of business enterprise and speculation that flourished in the city, partaking of its character and sharing in its risks, but rather the innocent pastoral victims of a conspiracy hatched in the distance. The notion of an innocent and victimized populace colors the whole history of agrarian controversy.

For the farmer it was bewildering, and irritating too, to think of the great contrast between the verbal deference paid him by almost everyone and the real economic position in which he found himself. Improving his economic position was always possible, though this was often done too little and too late; but it was not within anyone's power to stem the decline in the rural values and pieties, the gradual rejection of the moral commitments that had been expressed in the early exaltations of agrarianism.

It was the fate of the farmer himself to contribute to this decline. Like almost all good Americans he had innocently sought progress from the very beginning, and thus hastened the decline of many of his own values. Elsewhere the rural classes had usually looked to the past, had been bearers of tradition and upholders of stability. The American farmer looked to the future alone, and the story of the American land became a study in futures.

In the very hours of its birth as a nation Crèvecœur had congratulated America for having, in effect, no feudal past and no industrial present, for having no royal, aristocratic, ecclesiastical, or monarchial power, and no manufacturing class, and had rapturously concluded: "We are the most perfect society now existing in the world." Here was the irony from which the farmer suffered above all others: the United States was the only country in the world that began with perfection and aspired to progress.

To what extent was the agrarian myth actually false? During the colonial period, and even well down into the nineteenth century, there were in fact large numbers of farmers who were very much like the yeomen idealized in the myth. They were independent and self-sufficient, and they bequeathed to their children a strong love of craftsmanlike improvisation and a firm tradition of household industry. These yeomen were all too often yeomen by force of circumstance. They could not become commercial farmers because they were too far from the rivers or the towns, because the roads were too poor for bulky traffic, because the domestic market for agricultural produce was too small and the overseas markets were out of reach. At the beginning of the nineteenth century, when the American population was still living largely in the forests and most of it was east of the Appalachians, the yeoman farmer did exist in large numbers, living much as the theorists of the agrarian myth portrayed him.

But when the yeoman practiced the self-sufficient economy that was expected of him, he usually did so not because he wanted to stay out of the market but because he wanted to get into it. "My farm," said a farmer of Jefferson's time, "gave me and my family a good living on the produce of it; and left me, one year with another, one hundred and fifty dollars, for I have never spent more than ten dollars a year, which was for salt, nails, and the like. Nothing to wear, eat, or drink was purchased, as my farm provided all. With this saving, I put money to interest, bought cattle, fatted and sold them, and made great profit." Great profit! Here was the significance of self-sufficiency for the characteristic family farmer. Commercialism had already begun to enter the American Arcadia.

For, whatever the spokesman of the agrarian myth might have told him, the farmer almost anywhere in early America knew that all around him there were examples of commercial success in agriculture—the tobacco, rice, and indigo, and later the cotton planters of the South, the grain, meat, and cattle exporters of the middle states.

The farmer knew that without cash he could never rise above the hardships and squalor of pioneering and log-cabin life. So the savings from his self-sufficiency went into improvements—into the purchase of more land, of herds and flocks, of better tools; they went into the building of barns and silos and better dwellings. Self-sufficiency, in short, was adopted for a time in order that it would eventually be unnecessary.

Between 1815 and 1860 the character of American agriculture was transformed. The rise of native industry created a home market for agriculture, while demands arose abroad for American cotton and foodstuffs, and a great network of turnpikes, canals, and railroads helped link the planter and the advancing western farmer to the new markets. As the farmer moved out of the forests onto the flat, rich prairies, he found possibilities for machinery that did not exist in the forest. Before long he was cultivating the prairies with horse-drawn mechanical reapers, steel plows, wheat and corn drills, and threshers.

The farmer was still a hardworking man, and he still owned his own land in the old tradition. But no longer did he grow or manufacture almost everything he needed. He concentrated on the cash crop, bought more and more of his supplies from the country store. To take full advantage of the possibilities of mechanization, he engrossed as much land as he could and borrowed money for his land and machinery. The shift from self-sufficient to commercial farming varied in time throughout the West and cannot be dated with precision, but it was complete in Ohio by about 1830 and twenty years later in Indiana, Illinois, and Michigan. All through the great Northwest, farmers whose fathers might have lived in isolation and self-sufficiency were surrounded by jobbers, banks, stores, middlemen, horses, and machinery.

This transformation affected not only what the farmer did but how he felt. The ideals of the agrarian myth were competing in his breast, and gradually losing ground, to another, even stronger ideal, the notion of opportunity, of career, of the self-made man. Agrarian sentiment sanctified labor in the soil and the simple life; but the prevailing Calvinist atmosphere of rural life implied that virtue was rewarded with success and material goods. Even farm boys were taught to strive for achievement in one form or another, and when this did not take them away from the farms altogether, it impelled them to follow farming not as a way of life but as a *career*—that is, as a way of achieving substantial success.

The sheer abundance of the land—that very internal empire that had been expected to insure the predominance of the yeoman in American life for centuries—gave the *coup de grâce* to the yeomanlike way of life. For it made of the farmer a speculator. Cheap land invited extensive and careless cultivation. Rising land values in areas of new settlement tempted early liquidation and frequent moves. Frequent and sensational rises in land values bred a boom psychology in the American farmer and caused him to rely for his margin of profit more on the appreciation in the value of his land than on the sale of crops. It took a strong man to resist the temptation to ride skyward on lands that might easily triple or quadruple their value in one decade and then double in the next.

What developed in America, then, was an agricultural society whose real attachment was not, like the yeoman's, to the land but to land values. The characteristic product of American rural society, as it developed on the prairies and the plains, was not a yeoman or a villager, but a harassed little country businessman who worked very hard, moved all too often, gambled with his land, and made his way alone.

While the farmer had long since ceased to act like a yeoman, he was somewhat slower in ceasing to think like one. He became a businessman in fact long before he began to regard himself in this light. As the nineteenth century drew to a close, however, various things were changing him. He was becoming increasingly an employer of labor, and though he still worked with his hands, he began to look with suspicion upon the working classes of the cities, especially those organized in trade unions, as he had once done upon the urban fops and aristocrats. Moreover, when good times returned after the Populist revolt of the 1890's, businessmen and bankers and the agricultural colleges began to woo the farmer, to make efforts to persuade him to take the businesslike view of himself that was warranted by the nature of his farm operations. "The object of farming," declared a writer in the *Cornell Countryman* in 1904, "is not primarily to make a living, but it is to make money. To this end it is to be conducted on the same business basis as any other producing industry."

The final change, which came only with a succession of changes in the twentieth century, wiped out the last traces of the yeoman of old, as the coming first of good roads and rural free delivery, and mail order catalogues, then the telephone, the automobile, and the tractor, and at length radio, movies, and television largely eliminated the difference between urban and rural experience in so many important areas of life. The city luxuries, once so derided by farmers, are now what they aspire to give to their wives and daughters.

In 1860 a farm journal satirized the imagined refinements and affectations of a city girl in the following picture:

> Slowly she rises from her couch. . . . Languidly she gains her feet, and oh! what vision of human perfection appears before us: Skinny, bony, sickly, hipless, thighless, formless, hairless, teethless. What a radiant belle! . . . The ceremony of enrobing commences. In goes the dentist's naturalization efforts; next the witching curls are fashioned to her "classically molded head." Then the womanly proportions are properly adjusted; hoops, bustles, and so forth, follow in succession, then a profuse quantity of whitewash, together with a "permanent rose tint" is applied to a sallow complexion; and lastly the "killing" wrapper is arranged on her systematical and matchless form.

But compare this with these beauty hints for farmers' wives from the *Idaho Farmer*, April, 1935:

> Hands should be soft enough to flatter the most delicate of the new fabrics. They must be carefully manicured, with none of the hot, brilliant shades of nail polish. The lighter and more delicate tones are in keeping with the spirit of freshness. Keep the tint of your fingertips friendly to the red of your lips, and check both your powder and your rouge to see that they best suit the tone of your skin in the bold light of summer.

Nothing can tell us with greater finality of the passing of the yeoman ideal than these light and delicate tones of nail polish.

Part Three

Age of Reform

Unemployed white and black workers parade in New York City in 1909 to protest discriminatory hiring practices.

Was Bryan a Reformer?

JOHN A. GARRATY

The leading figures of the Progressive Era have suffered considerably at the hands of historians in recent years. Their insensitivity to the fate of black citizens becomes ever more apparent as scholars study their attitudes toward racial minorities. Their middle-class orientation stands in stark contrast to their radical rhetoric. Their inconsistent record on such questions as immigration and labor legislation, as well as their widespread support of imperialistic ventures, appears less than liberal from a contemporary point of view. Indeed, one historian, Gabriel Kolko, has titled his study of the Progressive Era The Triumph of Conservatism.*

The following essay criticizes one leading Progressive from a different perspective and is in part an attempt to cast certain doubts on the character of most American reform movements and their leaders. The subject examined here—William Jennings Bryan—was certainly a prominent Progressive. He, most of his contemporaries, and most historians have considered him a reformer. Yet as I have tried to show, his personal inadequacies raise serious questions about his liberalism, as well as about his judgment. ■

"The President of the United States may be an ass," wrote H. L. Mencken during the reign of Calvin Coolidge, "but he at least doesn't believe that the earth is square, and that witches should be put to death, and that Jonah swallowed the whale." The man to whom the vitriolic Mencken was comparing President Coolidge was William Jennings Bryan of Nebraska, one of the dominant figures in the Progressive movement. According to Mencken, Bryan was a "peasant," a "zany without sense or dignity," a "poor clod," and, in addition, an utter fraud. "If the fellow was sincere, then so was P. T. Barnum," he sneered.

It was certainly easy enough, and tempting, for sophisticates to come to the conclusion that Bryan was a buffoon and a fake. His undignified association in his declining years with the promotion of Florida real estate and his naïve and bigoted religious views, so pitilessly exposed by Clarence Darrow during the famous "Monkey Trial" in Dayton, Tennessee, lent substance to the Mencken view of his character. So did Bryan's smug refusal, while Secretary of State under Woodrow Wilson, to serve alcoholic beverages at Department receptions and dinners because of his personal disapproval of drinking, and his objection to the appointment of ex-President Charles W. Eliot of Harvard as Ambassador to China on the ground that Eliot was a Unitarian, and therefore not a real Christian. "The new Chinese civilization," said Bryan, "was founded upon the Christian movement." Eliot's appointment might undermine the work of generations of pious missionaries, he implied. Bryan's unabashed partisanship—he talked frankly after Wilson's election of filling government positions with "deserving Democrats"—did not seem to jibe with his pretensions as a reformer. And his oratorical style, magnificent but generally more emotional than logical, was disappointing to thinking people. John Hay called him a "Baby Demosthenes" and David Houston, one of his colleagues in Wilson's Cabinet, stated that "one could drive a prairie schooner through any part of his argument and never scrape against a fact." Being largely a creature of impulse, Bryan was, Houston added, "constantly on the alert to get something which has been represented to him as a fact to support or sustain his impulses."

But these flaws and blind spots were not fundamental weaknesses; they should never be allowed to overshadow Bryan's long years of devoted service to the cause of reform. If there were large areas about which he knew almost nothing, there were others where he was alert, sensible, and well-informed; certainly he was not a stupid man, nor was he easily duped or misled. Although a professional politician, as his remark about "deserving Democrats" makes clear, he was utterly honest personally and devoted to the cause of the people, as he understood it.

He was perfectly attuned to the needs and aspirations of rural America. In the early nineties he was in the forefront of the fight against high tariffs on manufactured goods. Later in the decade he battled for currency reform. At the turn of the century he was leading the assault against imperialism. During Theodore Roosevelt's primacy he was often far ahead of the intrepid Teddy, advocating a federal income tax, the eight-hour day, the control of monopoly and the strict regulation of public utilities, woman suffrage, and a large number of other startling innovations. Under Wilson he played a major part in marshaling support in Congress for the Federal Reserve Act and other New Freedom measures. Whatever his limitations, his faults, or his motives, few public men of his era left records as consistently "progressive" as Bryan's.

For years he led the Democratic party without the advantage of holding office. Three times he was a presidential candidate; although never elected, he commanded the unswerving loyalty of millions of his fellow citizens for nearly thirty years. He depended more on his intuition than on careful analysis in forming his opinions, but his intuition was usually sound; he was more a man of heart than of brain, but his heart was great.

Bryan was known as the Great Commoner, and the title was apt. He was a man of the people in origin and by instinct. He was typical of his age in rendering great respect to public opinion, whether it was informed or not. To Bryan the voice of the people was truly the voice of God. "I don't know anything about free silver," he announced while running for Congress early in the nineties. "The people of Nebraska are for free silver and I am for free silver. I will look up the arguments later." (It should be added that he did indeed "look up the arguments later." Less than a year after making this promise he arose in the House to deliver without notes a brilliant three-hour speech on the money question, a speech of great emotional power, but also fact-laden, sensible, and full of shrewd political arguments. When he sat down, the cheers rang out from both sides of the aisle.)

Bryan was born in Salem, Illinois, in 1860, a child of the great Middle West. Growing up in the heart of the valley of democracy, he absorbed its spirit and its sense of protest from his earliest years. After being graduated from Illinois College in 1881, he studied law in Chicago and for a time practiced his profession in Jacksonville, Illinois. But in 1887, stimulated by a talk with a law-school classmate from that city, he moved west to Lincoln, Nebraska. He quickly made his way in this new locale. Within a year he was active in the local Democratic organization, and in 1890, a month before his thirtieth birthday, he won his party's nomination for congressman.

Nebraska was traditionally a Republican state, its loyalty to the party of Lincoln forged in the heat of the Civil War. But by 1890 tradition was rapidly losing its hold on voters all over the Middle West. For the farmers of the American heartland were in deep trouble, and the Republican party seemed unwilling to do much to help them.

Tumultuous social and economic changes shaped the nation in the years after Appomattox. Within a single generation the United States was transformed from what was essentially a land of farmers into a modern industrial society, and in the process the Middle West was caught in a relentless economic vise. During the flush times of the sixties, when the Union Army was buying enormous amounts of food and fodder, and foreign demand was unusually high, the farmers of the region had gone into debt in order to buy more land and machinery. In the seventies and eighties, however, agricultural prices, especially those of such major staple crops as wheat and cotton, fell steeply. Wheat, which had sold as high as $2.50 a bushel in wartime, was down to fifty cents by the early nineties.

The impact of this economic decline was intensified by the changing social status of the farmer. Agriculture was losing its predominant place in American life. In the days of the Founding Fathers, about ninety per cent of the population was engaged in working the soil, and the farmer was everywhere portrayed as the symbol of American self-reliance and civic virtue. "Those who labor in the earth," Jefferson said, "are the chosen people of God." But as the factory began to outstrip the farm, the farmer lost much of his standing. While the old symbol remained—it was especially in evidence around election time—a new and disturbing image of the farmer as a hick, a rube, a hayseed—a comic mixture of cocky ignorance, shrewd self-interest, and monumental provincialism—began to challenge it.

Naturally the farmers resented their loss of both income and prestige, but there was little they could do about either. Price declines were largely a response to worldwide overproduction, resulting from improvements in transportation and the opening up of new farmlands in Australia, Argentina, Canada, Russia, and elsewhere. Nor did the farmers, who desired manufactured goods as much as everyone else, really want to reverse the trend that was making them a minority group in a great industrial nation. But as they cast about for some way out of their plight, they were profoundly disturbed by certain results of the new development which did seem amenable to reform.

Industrial growth meant the mushrooming of great cities. These gave birth to noxious slums where every kind of vice flourished, where corrupt political organizations like the venal Tweed Ring in New York were forged, and where radical political concepts like socialism and anarchism sought to undermine "the American way of life." In the words of Jefferson, the farmers' hero, cities were "ulcers on the body politic."

Giant industries also attracted hordes of immigrants; these seemed to threaten the Middle West both by their mere numbers and by their "un-American" customs and points of view. Could the American melting pot absorb such strange ingredients without losing much of its own character?

Furthermore, to the citizens of Nebraska and other agricultural states, the new industrial barons appeared bent on making vassals of every farmer in America. The evidence seemed overwhelming: Huge impersonal corporations had neither souls nor consciences; profit was their god, materialism their only creed. The "interests," a tiny group of powerful tycoons in great eastern centers like Boston, New York, and Philadelphia, were out to enslave the rest of the country. Farmers worked and sweated only to see the "interests" make off with most of the fruit of their toil. Too many useless middlemen grew fat off the mere "handling" of wheat and cotton. Monopolistic railroads over-charged for carrying crops to market, unscrupulous operators of grain elevators falsely downgraded prime crops and charged exorbitant fees. Cynical speculators drove the price of staples up and down, sometimes making and losing millions in a matter of minutes, without the slightest regard for the effect of their operations on the producers whose sweat made their deadly game possible.

Conspiring with bankers and mortgage holders, all these groups combined to dictate the federal government's money policy. Population and production were surging forward; more money was needed simply to keep up with economic growth. Yet the government was deliberately cutting down on the amount of money in circulation by retiring Civil War greenbacks. On debt-ridden farmers plagued by overproduction, the effect of this deflation was catastrophic. Or so it seemed from the perspective of rural America.

While undoubtedly exaggerated, this indictment of the "interests" was taken as gospel throughout large sectors of the South and West. As a result, demands for "reform" quickly arose. The leading reformers were for the most part sincere, but few of them were entirely altruistic and many were decidedly eccentric. Participating in the movement for a variety of motives but without coming to grips with the main problem of American agriculture—overproduction—were coarse demagogues like Senator "Pitchfork Ben" Tillman of South Carolina, and unwashed characters like the wise-cracking congressman from Kansas, "Sockless Jerry" Simpson. There were professional orators like the angry Mary Ellen Lease (her detractors called her "Mary Yellin' "), and homespun economic theorists like "Coin" Harvey and

"General" Jacob Coxey, who believed so strongly in paper money that he named his son Legal Tender. The excesses of such people frightened off many Americans who might otherwise have lent a sympathetic ear to the farmers' complaints; others who might have been friendly observed the antics of the reformers with contempt and wrote off the whole movement as a joke.

Since neither of the major parties espoused the farmers' cause wholeheartedly, much of the protest found its way into various third-party organizations. At first, discontented elements concentrated on opposing the government's policy of retiring the paper money put in circulation during the Civil War. To save these greenbacks from extinction a Greenback (later Greenback-Labor) party sprang up. In 1878 its candidates polled a million votes, but decline followed as currency reformers turned to other methods of inflation.

Meanwhile the Patrons of Husbandry, better known as the Grange, originally a social organization for farm families, had begun to agitate in local politics against the middlemen who were draining off such a large percentage of the farmers' profits. In the seventies the Grangers became a power in the Middle West; in state after state they obtained the passage of laws setting maximum rates for railroads and prohibiting various forms of discrimination. The operations of grain elevators were also subjected to state regulation by "Granger Laws" in states such as Illinois, Iowa, Wisconsin, and Minnesota. The Grange abandoned political activity in the eighties, but other farm organizations quickly took its place. These coalesced first into the Northern Alliance and the Southern Alliance, and around 1890 the two Alliances joined with one another to become the Populist party.

Although William Jennings Bryan was a Democrat, he had grown up amid the agitations of the Granger movement. His father had even run for Congress in the seventies with Greenback party support. The aspirations and the general point of view of the midwestern farmers were young Bryan's own. Public men, he admitted late in life to the journalist Mark Sullivan, are "the creatures of their age. . . . I lived in the very center of the country out of which the reforms grew, and was quite naturally drawn to the people's side."

And they to his, one must add. Discontented farmers in his district were on the lookout for men who understood them and their problems. In 1888 the Republicans had carried the seat by 3,000 votes; now, in 1890, Bryan swept in with a lead of 6,713.

Bryan made an excellent record in his first Congress. He was a hardworking member, studying the technicalities of the tariff question for months before making his first important speech. But he saw that the tariff was rapidly being replaced by the money question as the crucial issue of the day. When he yielded the floor after completing his

A wood engraving from a newspaper in 1873 showing a gathering of Grangers.

tariff speech, he collared a young Texas congressman named Joseph W. Bailey, who posed as a financial expert. Sitting on a sofa in the rear of the House chamber, he quizzed Bailey about the problem of falling prices. Bailey told him the tariff had little or no effect on the plight of the farmer; the whole difficulty arose from "an appreciation in value of gold." Interested, Bryan demanded a list of books on the subject and was soon deep in a study of the money question.

To a man like Bryan, studying the money question meant searching for some means of checking the deflationary trend that was so injurious to his farmer constituents. He quickly discovered that most farm-belt financial authorities felt this could best be done by providing for the free coinage of silver. In 1873 the United States had gone on the gold standard, which meant that only gold was accepted for coinage at the mint. By going back to bimetallism, the amount of bullion being coined would be increased, and if the favorable ratio of sixteen to one between silver and gold were established, the production of silver for coinage would be greatly stimulated.

To press for the free coinage of silver at a ratio of sixteen to one with gold seemed less radical or dangerous than to demand direct inflation of the currency through the printing of greenbacks. Silver, after all, was a precious metal; coining it could not possibly lead to the sort of "runaway" inflation that had helped ruin the South during the Civil War. Debtors and other friends of inflation could also count on the powerful support of silver-mine interests. The free-coinage issue thus had a powerful political appeal. Despite the opposition of most conservative businessmen, the silverites were able, in 1878 and again in 1890, to obtain legislation providing for the coinage of *some* silver, although not enough to check the downward trend of prices.

Within a month after his tariff speech Bryan was calling for free coinage, and he stressed the issue in his successful campaign for re-election in 1892. But the new President, Democrat Grover Cleveland, was an ardent gold-standard man, and when a severe depression struck the country early in 1893, he demanded that the Silver Purchase Act of 1890, which had raised the specter of inflation in the minds of many businessmen, be repealed by Congress at once. In this way he committed his party to the resumption of the single gold standard.

Bryan refused to go along with this policy. Threatening to "serve my country and my God under some other name" than "Democrat" unless the Administration changed its mind, he resisted the repeal of the silver act in a brilliant extemporaneous speech. Cleveland carried the day for repeal, but Bryan emerged as a potential leader of the silver wing of the Democrats.

In 1894 he sought a wider influence by running for the United States Senate. In those days senators were still chosen by the state legislatures; to be elected Bryan would need the support of Nebraska's Populists as well as of his own party. He worked hard for fusion, but Populist support was not forthcoming. Though the Democrats backed Populist candidate Silas A. Holcomb for the governorship, the Populists refused to reciprocate and ran their own man for the Senate seat. The Republican candidate therefore won easily.

At this stage the Populists were trying hard to become a truly national party. Their program, besides demanding the free coinage of silver and various land reforms desired by farmers, called for government ownership of railroads, a graduated income tax, the direct election of U.S. senators, the eight-hour day, and a number of additional reforms designed to appeal to eastern workingmen and other dissatisfied groups. As early as 1892 their presidential candidate, James B. Weaver, had polled over a million votes; in 1894 the party won six seats in the Senate and seven in the House of Representatives. At least in Nebraska, the Populists were not yet ready to merge with the "conservative" Democratic organization.

Defeat for the Senate did not harm Bryan politically. He was still in his early thirties; to one so young, merely having run for the Senate brought considerable prestige. Also, he had conducted an intelligent and forceful campaign. Even so it was a defeat, certainly not calculated to lead him to the remarkable decision that he made after the Nebraska legislature had turned him down. This decision was to seek nomination for the Presidency of the United States itself!

The young man's "superlative self-assurance" (one might call it effrontery but for the fact that his daring plan succeeded) staggers the imagination. Many men within his party were far better known than he, and his state, Nebraska, was without major influence in Democratic affairs. With Cleveland and the national organization dead-set against free coinage and other inflationary schemes, Bryan's chances of capturing the nomination seemed infinitesimal. But if bold, his action was by no means foolish. Democratic voters were becoming more and more restive under Cleveland's conservative leadership. At least in Bryan's part of the nation, many thoughtful members of the party were beginning to feel that they must look in new directions and find new leaders if they were not to be replaced by the Populists as the country's second major party. Recognizing this situation before most politicians did, Bryan proceeded to act upon his insight with determination and dispatch.

First of all, he set out to make himself known beyond his own locality. Accepting the editorship of the Omaha *World-Herald* at a tiny salary in order to obtain a forum, he turned out a stream of editorials on the silver question, which he sent to influential politicians all over the country. He toured the South and West with his message, speaking everywhere and under all sorts of conditions: to close-packed, cheering throngs and to tiny groups of quiet listeners. His argument was simple but forceful, his oratory magnetic and compelling. Always he made sure to meet local leaders and to subject them to his genial smile, his youthful vigor, his charm, his sincerity. He did not push himself forward; indeed, he claimed to be ready to support any honest man whose program was sound. But he lost no chance to point out to all concerned his own availability. "I don't suppose your delegation is committed to any candidate," he wrote to a prominent Colorado Democrat in April of 1896. "Our delegation may present my name." When the Democratic convention finally met in Chicago, Bryan believed that he was known personally to more of the delegates than any other candidate.

Few delegates took his campaign seriously, however. At the convention, one senator asked Bryan who he thought would win out. Bryan replied characteristically that he believed he himself "had as good a chance to be nominated as anyone," and proceeded to tick off the sources of his strength: Nebraska, "half of the Indian Territory, . . ." but before Bryan could mention his other backers the senator lost interest and walked off with some of his cronies. The candidate, amiable and serene, took no offense. A majority of the delegates favored his position on silver. No one had a clear lead in the race. All he needed was a chance to plead his case.

The opportunity—Bryan called it an "unexpected stroke of luck," although he planned for it brilliantly—came when he was asked to close the debate on the platform's silver plank. When he came forward to address the jam-packed mob in the Chicago auditorium he was tense, but there was a smile on his face, and to observers he seemed the picture of calm self-confidence. He began quietly, but his voice resounded in the farthest corners of the great hall and commanded the attention of every delegate. He was conscious of his own humble position, he told the throng, but he was "clad in the armor of a righteous cause" and this entitled him to speak. As he went on, his tension evaporated and his voice rose. When he recounted the recent history of the struggle between the forces of gold and silver, the audience responded eagerly. "At the close of a sentence," he wrote later, "it would rise and shout, and when I began upon another sentence, the room was still as a church."

He spoke for silver as against gold, for the West over the East, for "the hardy pioneers who have braved all the dangers of the wilderness" as against "the few financial magnates who, in a back room, corner the money of the world."

> We have petitioned, and our petitions have been scorned; we have entreated, and our entreaties have been disregarded; we have begged, and they have mocked when our calamity came. We beg no longer; we entreat no more; we petition no more. *We defy them!*

The crowd thundered its agreement. Bryan proceeded. One after another he met the arguments of the party's Cleveland wing head on. Free silver would disturb the business interests? "Gold bugs" were defining the term too narrowly. Remember that wage earners, crossroads merchants, and farmers were also businessmen. The cities favored the gold standard? Their prosperity really depended upon the prosperity of the great agricultural regions of the land, which favored bimetallism. "Burn down your cities and leave our farms," he said, "and your cities will spring up again as if by magic; but destroy our farms and the grass will grow in the streets of every city in the country."

Now Bryan was absolute master of the delegates. "I thought of a choir," he recalled afterward, "as I noted how instantaneously and in unison they responded to each point made." The crowd cheered because he was reflecting its sentiments, but also because it recognized,

This 1896 cartoon entitled "The Sacrilegious Candidate"
implies that Bryan used religious metaphors for
opportunistic purposes.

suddenly, its leader—handsome, confident, righteously indignant, yet
also calm, restrained, and ready for responsibility. His mission accomplished, it was time to close, and Bryan had saved a marvelous figure
of speech, tested in many an earlier oration, for his climax. "You shall
not press down upon the brow of labor this crown of thorns," he
warned, bringing his hands down suggestively to his temples; "you
shall not crucify mankind upon a cross of gold." Dramatically he extended his arms to the side, the very figure of the crucified Christ.

Amid the hysterical demonstration that followed, it was clear that
Bryan had accomplished his miracle. The next day, July 9, he was
nominated for the Presidency on the fifth ballot.

The issue was clear-cut, for the Republicans had already declared for the gold standard and nominated the handsome, genial, and thoroughly conservative William McKinley. As a result, the Populists were under great pressure to go along with Bryan. While the Democrats had not adopted all the radical Populist demands, their platform contained a number of liberal planks in addition to that on free silver, including one calling for a federal income tax and another for stiffer controls of the railroad network. For the Populists to insist on nominating a third candidate would simply insure the election of the "gold bug" McKinley. Not every important Populist favored fusion; some were ready to concede defeat in 1896 and build their party for the future on broadly radical lines. "The Democratic idea of fusion," said Tom Watson of Georgia angrily, is "that we play Jonah while they play whale." But the rich scent of victory in the air was too much for the majority to resist. "I care not for party names," said "Sockless Jerry" Simpson bluntly; "it is the substance we are after, and we have it in William J. Bryan." Indeed, Bryan's friendly association with the Populists in earlier campaigns and his essentially Populistic views on most questions made it difficult for the party to oppose him. "We put him to school," one anti-Bryan Populist later remarked, "and he wound up by stealing the school-books." In any case, the Populist convention endorsed him; thus the silver forces united to do battle with the Republicans.

Both Bryan and McKinley men realized at once that this was to be a close and crucial contest. Seldom have the two great parties divided so clearly on fundamental issues; a showdown was inevitable; a major turning point in American history had been reached. Silver against gold was but the surface manifestation of the struggle. City against countryside, industry against agriculture, East against South and West, the nineteenth century against the twentieth—these were the real contestants in 1896.

After Bryan's nomination McKinley's manager, Mark Hanna, abandoned plans for a vacation cruise in New England waters and plunged into the work of the campaign. The situation was "alarming," he told McKinley. A "communistic spirit" was abroad, business was "all going to pieces." A mighty effort was called for. Hanna raised huge sums by "assessing" the great bankers, oil refiners, insurance men, and meat packers, using the threat of impending business chaos and wild inflation to loosen the purse strings of the tycoons. While McKinley, "the advance agent of prosperity," conducted a dignified and carefully organized campaign from his front porch in Canton, Ohio, 1,400 paid speakers beat the bushes for votes in every doubtful district. The Republican campaign committee distributed more than 120,000,000 pieces of literature printed in ten languages to carry its message to the voters. Boiler-plate editorials and other releases were sent free to hundreds of small-town newspapers. Hanna, Theodore Roosevelt said, "has advertised McKinley as if he were a patent medicine!" The Republican organization reached a peak of efficiency and thoroughness never before approached in a political contest; the campaign marked a methodological revolution that has profoundly affected every presidential contest since.

Bryan had little money, and no organizational genius like Hanna to direct his drive. But he too effected a revolution that has left its mark on modern campaigning. McKinley's front porch technique was novel only in the huge number of visiting delegations that Hanna paraded across his man's lawn and the exaggerated care that the candidate took to avoid saying anything impolitic. It had always been considered undignified for a presidential nominee to go out and hunt for votes on his own. Bryan cast off this essentially hypocritical tradition at the very start. He realized that the concerted power of business and the press were aligned against him, and that his own greatest assets were his magnificent ability as a political orator and his personal sincerity and charm. His opponent could afford to sit tight; *he* must seek out the people everywhere if they were to receive his message. Between summer and November he traveled a precedent-shattering 18,000 miles, making more than 600 speeches and addressing directly an estimated 5,000,000 Americans. His secretary estimated that he uttered between 60,000 and 100,000 words every day during the campaign.

On the stump he was superb. Without straining his voice he could make himself heard to a restless open-air throng numbered in the tens of thousands. He was equally effective at the whistle stops, outlining his case from the rear platform of his train while a handful of country people gazed earnestly upward from the roadbed. He was unfailingly pleasant and unpretentious. At one stop, while he was shaving in his compartment, a small group outside the train began clamoring for a glimpse of him. Flinging open the window and beaming through the lather, he cheerfully shook hands with each of these admirers. Neither he nor they, according to the recorder of this incident, saw anything unusual or undignified in the performance. Thousands of well-wishers sent him good luck charms and messages of encouragement. "If the people who have given me rabbits' feet in this campaign will vote for me, there is no possible doubt of my election," he said in one speech. It was because of this simple friendliness that he became known as "the Great Commoner."

Bryan was also unfailingly interesting. Even his most unsympathetic biographer admits that he spoke so well that at every stop the baggagemen from the campaign train would run back to listen to his talk—and this despite a schedule that called for as many as thirty speeches a day.

Bryan's presidential campaign opponent in 1896, William McKinley, making his nomination acceptance speech in the manner in which he conducted his campaign: on the front porch of his house in Canton, Ohio.

Such a campaign is an effective means of projecting an image of a candidate and his general point of view. It is not well suited for the making of complicated arguments and finely drawn distinctions; for that the McKinley approach was far superior. Wisely, for it was clearly the issue uppermost in the minds of most voters, Bryan hammered repeatedly at the currency question. He did not avoid talking about other matters: he attacked the railroads and the great business monopolists and the "tyranny" of the eastern bankers. He deplored the use of militia in labor disputes and of the injunction as a means of breaking strikes. He spoke in favor of income taxes, higher wages, and relief for hard-pressed mortgagees. But the silver issue was symbolic, and the Democratic position sound. There *was* a currency shortage; deflation *was* injuring millions of debtors and pouring a rich unearned increment into the pockets of bondholders. To say, as Henry Demarest Lloyd did at the time and as many liberal historians have since, that Bryan made free silver the "cowbird" of the reform movement, pushing out all other issues from the reform nest and thus destroying them, is an exaggeration and a distortion. All effective politicians stick to a small number of simple issues while on the stump; otherwise, in the hectic conflict of a hot campaign, they project no message at all. There is no reason to suspect that, if elected, Bryan would have forgotten about other reform measures and concentrated only on the currency.

For a time Bryan's gallant, singlehanded battle seemed to be having an effect on public opinion, and Republican leaders became thoroughly frightened. In addition to money, threats and imprecations now became weapons in the campaign. A rumor was circulated that Bryan was insane. The *New York Times* devoted columns to the possibility, and printed a letter from a supposed psychologist charging that he was suffering from "paranoia querulenta," "graphomania," and "oratorical monomania." "Men," one manufacturer told his workers, "vote as you please, but if Bryan is elected . . . the whistle will not blow Wednesday morning." According to the *Nation,* which was supporting McKinley, many companies placed orders with their suppliers "to be executed in case Mr. Bryan is defeated, and not otherwise." A Chicago company that held thousands of farm mortgages politely asked all its "customers" to indicate their presidential preferences—a not very subtle form of coercion but probably an effective one. In some cases men were actually fired because of their political opinions.

By the time election day arrived the McKinley managers were so confident of victory that Hanna began returning new contributions as no longer necessary. Nevertheless, a final monumental effort was made to get out the vote. Free transportation was provided to carry citizens to and from the polls, men were paid for time lost in voting, and in doubtful districts floaters and other disreputables were rounded up

An 1896 Bryan campaign poster bearing the full text of his "Cross of Gold" speech.

and paraded to the ballot boxes. Everywhere in the crucial North Central states the Hanna machine expended enormous efforts, and in these states the decision was made. McKinley carried them all and with them the nation. In the electoral college McKinley won by 271 to 176, but the popular vote was close—7,036,000 to 6,468,000. The change of a relative handful of votes in half a dozen key states would have swung the election to Bryan.

The victory, however, was McKinley's, and conservatives all over America—and the world—echoed the sentiment of Hanna's happy telegram to the President-elect: GOD'S IN HIS HEAVEN, ALL'S RIGHT WITH THE WORLD! A watershed in the economic and social history of the United States had been crossed. The rural America of the nineteenth century was making way for the industrial America of the twentieth. Soon business conditions began to improve, agricultural prices inched upward, new discoveries of gold relieved the pressure on the money supply. While McKinley and Hanna (now senator from Ohio) ruled in Washington, the era of complacent materialism and easy political virtue that had entered American politics on the coattails of General Grant seemed destined to continue indefinitely. Reform, it appeared, was dead.

That these appearances were deceiving was due in considerable measure to William Jennings Bryan. Unchastened by defeat and always cheerful ("It is better to have run and lost than never to have run at all," he said), he maintained the leadership of his party. Consistently he took the liberal position on important issues. Despite his strong pacifism he approved of fighting Spain in 1898 in order to free Cuba. "Humanity demands that we should act," he said simply. He enlisted in the Army and rose to be a colonel, although he saw no action during the brief conflict. The sincerity of his motives was proved when the war ended, for he then fought against the plan to annex former Spanish colonies. Running for President a second time in 1900, he made resistance to imperialism an issue in the campaign along with free silver. If both of these were poorly calculated to win votes in 1900, they were nonetheless solidly in the liberal tradition. Bryan lost to McKinley again, this time by 861,459 votes, and leadership of the reform movement passed, after McKinley's assassination, to Theodore Roosevelt. But Bryan continued the fight. In 1904, battling almost alone against conservatives in his own party, he forced the adoption of a fairly liberal platform (including strong antitrust, pro-labor, and antitariff planks), and when the conservative Judge Alton B. Parker was nonetheless nominated for President, Bryan kept up his outspoken criticism. While remaining loyal to the Democratic party he announced boldly: "The fight on economic questions . . . is not abandoned. As soon as the election is over I shall . . . organize for the campaign of 1908."

In that campaign Bryan, once more the Democratic nominee, was once more defeated in his personal quest of the Presidency, this time by Roosevelt's handpicked successor, William Howard Taft. Immediately he announced that he would not seek the office again, thus throwing the field open to other liberals.

Although he thus abandoned formal leadership of the Democrats, Bryan continued to advocate reform. Throughout the Taft administration he campaigned up and down the country to bolster the liberal wing of his party. When the 1912 nominating convention met in Baltimore, he introduced and won approval of a highly controversial resolution denouncing Wall Street influence, and he stated repeatedly that he would not support any candidate who was under the slightest obligation to Tammany Hall. The platform, as one historian says, "was a progressive document, in the best Bryan tradition." In the end Bryan threw his support to Woodrow Wilson. While this alone did not account for Wilson's nomination, it was very important in his election, for it assured him the enthusiastic backing of millions of loyal Bryanites.

Nothing reveals Bryan's fine personal qualities better than his support of Wilson, for the former Princeton professor had opposed the Great Commoner since 1896, when he had called the Cross of Gold speech "ridiculous." In 1904 he had publicly demanded that the Bryan wing be "utterly and once and for all driven from Democratic counsels." As late as 1908 he had refused to appear on the same platform with Bryan. Mr. Bryan, he said, "is the most charming and lovable of men personally, but foolish and dangerous in his theoretical beliefs." During the campaign of that year he refused to allow Bryan to deliver a campaign speech on the Princeton campus.

By 1912 Wilson had become far more liberal and no longer opposed most of Bryan's policies; even so, had Bryan been a lesser man he would not have forgiven these repeated criticisms. But he was more concerned with Wilson's 1912 liberalism than with personal matters, despite the publication of an old letter in which Wilson had expressed the wish to "knock Mr. Bryan once and for all into a cocked hat!" He shrugged off the "cocked hat" letter, and when Wilson paid him a handsome public tribute they became good friends. Furthermore, during the 1912 campaign, Bryan campaigned vigorously for Wilson, making well over four hundred speeches within a period of seven weeks. When Wilson won an easy victory in November, Bryan reacted without a trace of envy or bitterness. "It is a great triumph," he declared, "Let every Democratic heart rejoice." A few months later he said in a speech in Chicago:

> Sometimes I have had over-sanguine friends express regret that I did not reach the presidency. . . . But I have an answer ready for them. I have told

them that they need not weep for me. . . . I have been so much more
interested in the securing of the things for which we have been fighting
than I have been in the name of the man who held the office, that I am
happy in the thought that this government, through these reforms, will be
made so good that a citizen will not miss a little thing like the presidency.

Wilson made Bryan Secretary of State. He was needed in the administration to help manage his many friends in Congress. The strategy worked well, for Bryan used his influence effectively. His role was
particularly crucial in the hard fight over the Federal Reserve bill, but
his loyal aid was also important in passing income tax legislation and
a new antitrust law and in other matters as well.

In managing foreign affairs Bryan was less successful, for in this
field he was ill-prepared. Because of his frank belief in the spoils
system, he dismissed dozens of key professional diplomats, replacing
them with untrained political hacks. Naturally the Foreign Service was
badly injured. His policy of not serving alcoholic beverages at official
functions because of his personal convictions caused much criticism at
home and abroad. "W. J. Bryan not only suffers for his principles and
mortifies his flesh, as he has every right to do," the London *Daily
Express* complained, "but he insists that others should suffer and be
mortified." The Secretary's continuing Chautauqua lectures, at which
he sometimes appeared on the same platform with vaudeville enter-
tainers and freaks, were attacked by many as undignified for one who
occupied such a high official position.

Bryan had answers to all these criticisms: the State Department had
been overly snobbish and undemocratic; Wilson had agreed to his
"grape juice" policy before appointing him; no one should be
ashamed of speaking to the American people. He could also point to
his "cooling-off treaties" with some twenty nations, which provided
machinery for avoiding blow-ups over minor diplomatic imbroglios.

Unfortunately Bryan had but a dim understanding of Latin American problems and unwittingly fostered American imperialism on many
occasions. His narrow-minded belief that he knew better than local
leaders what was "good" for these small countries showed that he had
no comprehension of cultural and nationalistic elements in other
lands. Although well intended, his policies produced much bad feeling
in South and Central America. Bryan did suggest lending Latin American nations money "for education, sanitation and internal development," a policy that anticipated our modern Point Four approach to
underdeveloped areas. Wilson, however, dismissed the idea because
he thought it "would strike the whole country . . . as a novel and radical
proposal."

When the World War broke out in 1914, Bryan, like his chief, adopted a policy of strict neutrality. America, he said, should attempt to mediate between the belligerents by suggesting "a more rational basis of peace." Bryan believed in real neutrality far more deeply than Wilson, who was not ready to face the possibility of a German victory. "We cannot have in mind the wishes of one side more than the wishes of the other side," Bryan warned the President after the latter had prepared a stiff note of protest against German submarine warfare. And when, after the sinking of the *Lusitania,* Wilson sent a series of threatening messages to Germany, Bryan resigned as Secretary of State. He never again held public office.

It would have been better for Bryan's reputation if he had died in 1915; instead he lived on for another decade, as amiable and well-intentioned as ever but increasingly out of touch with the rapidly changing times. He made no effort to keep up with the abrupt intellectual developments of the twentieth century, yet he was accustomed to speak his mind on current issues and continued to do so. There had always been those who had considered his uncomplicated faith in time-tested moral principles and in popular rule rather naïve; in the cynical, scientific, and amoral twenties only a relative handful of rural oldtimers saw much virtue in his homilies on the people's unfailing instinct to do always what was "right" and "good." In the world of Calvin Coolidge the old Populist fires no longer burned very brightly, and Bryan's anti-business bias seemed terribly old-fashioned. Many had considered him an anachronism even in Wilson's day; by Harding's he had simply ceased to count in politics. More and more he confined himself to religious questions. His ardent piety was heart-warming, but he was a smug and intolerant Fundamentalist whose ignorance of modern science and ethics did not prevent him from expounding his "views" on these subjects at length. The honest opinions of "the people," he believed, could "settle" scientific and philosophical questions as easily as political ones.

Advancing age, as well as increasing preoccupation with revealed religion, was making Bryan less tolerant. Never one to give much thought to reasoned counterarguments, he became, in the twenties, an outspoken foe of many aspects of human freedom. He defended prohibition, refused to condemn the Ku Klux Klan, and participated eagerly in the notorious Scopes anti-evolution trial in Dayton, Tennessee, with all its overtones of censorship and self-satisfied ignorance. The final great drama of Bryan's life occurred when Clarence Darrow mercilessly exposed his simple prejudices on the witness stand. Bryan complacently maintained, among other things, that Eve was actually made from Adam's rib and that Jonah had really been swallowed by the whale. The rural audience cheered, but educated men all over the world were appalled.

Bryan (right) at the end of his career, with Clarence Darrow during the Scopes trial.

Throughout his lifetime, Bryan was subject to harsh and almost continual criticism, and at least superficially he failed in nearly everything he attempted. But he was too secure in his faith to be injured by criticism, and he knew that for over two decades his influence was greater than any of his contemporaries save Theodore Roosevelt and Wilson. His life was useful and happy, for he rightly believed that he had made a lasting contribution to his country's development. Nor is it fair to condemn him for his limited intelligence and superficial understanding of his times. Other political leaders of at best ordinary intellect have done great deeds, sometimes without appreciating the meaning of events they have helped to shape. Still, there was tragedy in Bryan's career—he was unable to grow.

In 1896 he was indeed the peerless leader, vital, energetic, dedicated, and, in a measure, imaginative. He saw the problems of Nebraska farmers, realized their wider implications, and outlined a reasonable program designed to deal with them. He was almost elected

President as a result, despite his youth and inexperience. Suddenly he was a celebrity; thereafter he moved into a wider world and lived there at his ease. He did not abandon his principles, and he helped achieve many important reforms, for which we must always honor him, but he soon ceased to feed upon new ideas. In a sense, despite the defeats, life's rewards came to him too easily. His magnetic voice, his charm, his patent sincerity, the memory of the heroic fight of '96—these things secured his place and relieved him of the need to grapple with new concepts.

Although he was a man of courage, strength, and endurance, Bryan was essentially lax and complacent. He preferred baggy clothes, a full stomach, the easy, undemanding companionship of small minds. For years the momentum of 1896 carried him on, but eventually the speeding world left him far behind. Fortunately for his inner well-being, he never realized what had happened. A few days after Darrow had exposed his shallowness before the world, he died peacefully in his sleep, as serene and unruffled by events as ever.

Jane Addams: Urban Crusader

ANNE FIROR SCOTT

As the reputations of Progressive political leaders have declined, those of some of the social reformers of the era have risen. This is particularly true of social workers like Jane Addams and other founders of the settlement-house movement, who in modern eyes seem to have had a more profound grasp of the true character of the problems of their age and to have worked more effectively and with greater dedication in trying to solve those problems than did any of the politicians.

These social workers were quite different from those of today— they were more personally involved and far less professionally oriented. Many were also, it is true, somewhat patronizing in their approach to those they sought to help and they took a rather romantic and thus unrealistic view of the potentialities both of the poor and of their own capacity to help the poor. This essay by Professor Anne Firor Scott of Duke University makes clear, however, that Jane Addams of Chicago's Hull-House was neither patronizing nor a romantic. Professor Scott is the author of The Southern Lady: From Pedestal to Politics *and* The American Woman: Who Was She? ∎

If Alderman Johnny Powers of Chicago's teeming nineteenth ward had only been prescient, he might have foreseen trouble when two young ladies not very long out of a female seminary in Rockford, Illinois, moved into a dilapidated old house on Halsted Street in September, 1889, and announced themselves "at home" to the neighbors. The ladies, however, were not very noisy about it, and it is doubtful if Powers was aware of their existence. The nineteenth ward was well supplied with people already—growing numbers of Italians, Poles, Russians, Irish, and other immigrants—and two more would hardly be noticed.

Johnny Powers was the prototype of the ward boss who was coming to be an increasingly decisive figure on the American political scene. In the first place, he was Irish. In the second, he was, in the parlance of the time, a "boodler": his vote and influence in the Chicago Common Council were far from being beyond price. As chairman of the council's finance committee and boss of the Cook County Democratic party he occupied a strategic position. Those who understood the inner workings of Chicago politics thought that Powers had some hand in nearly every corrupt ordinance passed by the council during his years in office. In a single year, 1895, he was to help to sell six important city franchises. When the mayor vetoed Powers' measures, a silent but significant two-thirds vote appeared to override the veto.

Ray Stannard Baker, who chanced to observe Powers in the late nineties, recorded that he was shrewd and silent, letting other men make the speeches and bring upon their heads the abuse of the public. Powers was a short, stocky man, Baker said, "with a flaring gray pompadour, a smooth-shaven face [sic], rather heavy features, and a restless eye." One observer remarked that "the shadow of sympathetic gloom is always about him. He never jokes; he has forgotten how to smile . . ." Starting life as a grocery clerk, Powers had run for the city council in 1888 and joined the boodle ring headed by Alderman Billy Whalen. When Whalen died in an accident two years later, Powers moved swiftly to establish himself as successor. A few weeks before his death Whalen had collected some thirty thousand dollars—derived from the sale of a city franchise—to be divided among the party faithful. Powers alone knew that the money was in a safe in Whalen's saloon, so he promptly offered a high price for the furnishings of the saloon, retrieved the money, and divided it among the gang—at one stroke establishing himself as a shrewd operator and as one who would play the racket fairly.

From this point on he was the acknowledged head of the gang. Charles Yerkes, the Chicago traction tycoon, found in Powers an ideal tool for the purchase of city franchises. On his aldermanic salary of three dollars a week, Powers managed to acquire two large saloons of

his own, a gambling establishment, a fine house, and a conspicuous collection of diamonds. When he was indicted along with two other corrupt aldermen for running a slot machine and keeping a "common gambling house," Powers was unperturbed. The three appeared before a police judge, paid each other's bonds, and that was the end of that. Proof of their guilt was positive, but convictions were never obtained.

On the same day the Municipal Voters League published a report for the voters on the records of the members of the city council. John Powers was described as "recognized leader of the worst element in the council . . . [who] has voted uniformly for bad ordinances." The League report went on to say that he had always opposed securing any return to the city for valuable franchises, and proceeded to document the charge in detail.

To his constituents in the nineteenth ward, most of whom were getting their first initiation into American politics, Powers turned a

The antagonists: Jane Addams (left) in London in 1888 just prior to taking on Johnny Powers, Democratic ward boss, seen here (right) in a photograph taken about 1910.

different face. To them, he was first and last a friend. When there were celebrations, he always showed up: if the celebration happened to be a bazaar, he bought freely, murmuring piously that it would all go to the poor. In times of tragedy he was literally Johnny on the spot. If the family was too poor to provide the necessary carriage for a respectable funeral, it appeared at the doorstep—courtesy of Johnny Powers and charged to his standing account with the local undertaker. If the need was not so drastic, Powers made his presence felt with an imposing bouquet or wreath. "He has," said the Chicago *Times-Herald*, "bowed with aldermanic grief at thousands of biers."

Christmas meant literally tons of turkeys, geese, and ducks—each one handed out personally by a member of the Powers family, with good wishes and no questions asked. Johnny provided more fundamental aid, too, when a breadwinner was out of work. At one time he is said to have boasted that 2,600 men from his ward (about one third of the registered voters) were working in one way or another for the city of Chicago. This did not take into account those for whom the grateful holders of traction franchises had found a place. When election day rolled around, the returns reflected the appreciation of job-holders and their relatives.

The two young ladies on Halsted Street, Jane Addams and Ellen

Starr, were prototypes too, but of a very different kind of figure: they were the pioneers of the social settlement, the original "social workers." They opposed everything Johnny Powers stood for.

Jane Addams' own background could hardly have been more different from that of John Powers. The treasured daughter of a well-to-do small-town businessman from Illinois, she had been raised in an atmosphere of sturdy Christian principles.

From an early age she had been an introspective child concerned with justifying her existence. Once in a childhood nightmare she had dreamed of being the only remaining person in a world desolated by some disaster, facing the responsibility for rediscovering the principle of the wheel! At Rockford she shared with some of her classmates a determination to live to "high purpose," and decided that she would become a doctor in order to "help the poor."

After graduation she went to the Woman's Medical College of Philadelphia, but her health failed and she embarked on the grand tour of Europe customary among the wealthy. During a subsequent trip to Europe in 1888, in the unlikely setting of a Spanish bull ring, an idea that had long been growing in her mind suddenly crystallized: she would rent a house "in a part of the city where many primitive and actual needs are found, in which young women who had been given over too exclusively to study, might restore a balance of activity along traditional lines and learn something of life from life itself . . ." So the American settlement-house idea was born. She and Ellen Starr, a former classmate at the Rockford seminary who had been with her in Europe, went back to Chicago to find a house among the victims of the nineteenth century's fast-growing industrial society.

The young women—Jane was twenty-nine and Ellen thirty in 1889—had no blueprint to guide them when they decided to take up residence in Mr. Hull's decayed mansion and begin helping "the neighbors" to help themselves. No school of social work had trained them for this enterprise: Latin and Greek, art, music, and "moral philosophy" at the seminary constituted their academic preparation. Toynbee Hall in England—the world's first settlement house, founded in 1884 by Samuel A. Barnett—had inspired them. Having found the Hull house at the corner of Polk and Halsted—in what was by common consent one of Chicago's worst wards—they leased it, moved in, and began doing what came naturally.

Miss Starr, who had taught in an exclusive girls' preparatory school, inaugurated a reading party for young Italian women with George Eliot's *Romola* as the first book. Miss Addams, becoming aware of the desperate problem of working mothers, began at once to organize a kindergarten. They tried Russian parties for the Russian neighbors, organized boys' clubs for the gangs on the street, and offered to bathe all babies. The neighbors were baffled, but impressed. Very soon children and grownups of all sorts and conditions were finding their way to Hull-House—to read Shakespeare or to ask for a volunteer midwife; to learn sewing or discuss socialism; to study art or to fill an empty stomach. There were few formalities and no red tape, and the young ladies found themselves every day called upon to deal with some of the multitude of personal tragedies against which the conditions of life in the nineteenth ward offered so thin a cushion.

Before long, other young people feeling twinges of social conscience and seeking a tangible way to make their convictions count in the world of the 1890's came to live at Hull-House. These "residents," as they were called, became increasingly interested in the personal histories of the endless stream of neighbors who came to the House each week. They began to find out about the little children sewing all day long in the "sweated" garment trade, and about others who worked long hours in a candy factory. They began to ask why there were three thousand more children in the ward than there were seats in its schoolrooms, and why the death rate was higher there than in almost any other part of Chicago. They worried about youngsters whose only playground was a garbage-spattered alley that threatened the whole population with disease. (Once they traced a typhoid epidemic to its source and found the sewer line merging with the water line.) In the early days Hull-House offered bathtubs and showers, which proved so popular a form of hospitality that the residents became relentless lobbyists for municipal baths.

Hull-House was not the only American settlement house—indeed, Jane Addams liked to emphasize the validity of the idea by pointing out that it had developed simultaneously in several different places. But Hull-House set the pace, and in an astonishingly short time its founder began to acquire a national reputation. As early as 1893 Jane Addams wrote to a friend: "I find I am considered the grandmother of social settlements." She was being asked to speak to gatherings of learned gentlemen, sociologists and philosophers, on such subjects as "The Subjective Necessity for Social Settlements." When the Columbian Exposition attracted thousands of visitors to Chicago in 1893, Hull-House became—along with the lake front and the stockyards—one of the things a guest was advised not to miss. By the mid-nineties, distinguished Europeans were turning up regularly to visit the House and examine its workings. W. T. Stead, editor of the English *Review of Reviews,* spent much time there while he gathered material for his sensational book, *If Christ Came to Chicago.* By that time two thousand people a week were coming to Hull-House to participate in some of its multifarious activities, which ranged from philosophy classes to the Nineteenth Ward Improvement Association.

Neither her growing reputation nor the increasing demand for speeches and articles, however, distracted Jane Addams from what was to be for forty years the main focus of a many-sided life: Hull-House and the nineteenth ward. Much of her early writing was an attempt to portray the real inner lives of America's proliferating immigrants, and much of her early activity, an effort to give them a voice to speak out against injustice.

The Hull-House residents were becoming pioneers in many ways, not least in the techniques of social research. In the *Hull-House Maps and Papers,* published in 1895, they prepared some of the first careful studies of life in an urban slum, examining the details of the "home-work" system of garment making and describing tumble-down houses, overtaxed schools, rising crime rates, and other sociological problems. The book remains today an indispensable source for the social historian of Chicago in the nineties.

Jane Addams' own interest in these matters was far from academic. Her concern for the uncollected garbage led her to apply for—and receive—an appointment as garbage inspector. She rose at six every morning and in a horse-drawn buggy followed the infuriated garbage contractor on his appointed rounds, making sure that every receptacle was emptied. Such badgering incensed Alderman Powers, in whose hierarchy of values cleanliness, though next to godliness, was a good bit below patronage—and he looked upon garbage inspection as a job for one of his henchmen. By now John Powers was becoming aware of his new neighbors; they were increasingly inquisitive about things close to Johnny Powers' source of power. By implication they were raising a troublesome question: Was Johnny Powers really "taking care of the poor"?

For a while, as one resident noted, the inhabitants of the House were "passive though interested observers of their representative, declining his offers of help and co-operation, refusing politely to distribute his Christmas turkeys, but feeling too keenly the smallness of their numbers to work against him." They were learning, though, and the time for passivity would end.

In company with many other American cities, Chicago after 1895 was taking a critical look at its political life and at the close connections that had grown up between politics and big business during the explosive era of industrial expansion following the Civil War. "The sovereign people may govern Chicago in theory," Stead wrote; "as a matter of fact King Boodle is monarch of all he surveys. His domination is practically undisputed."

The Municipal Voters League, a reform organization that included many of Jane Addams' close friends, was founded in 1896 in an effort to clean up the Common Council, of whose sixty-eight aldermen fifty-

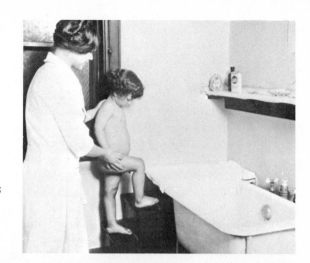

Children were Hull-House's
first concern. Infants were
bathed (right) and moppets
put into nursery school
(below).

Older boys (right) took shop
lessons to prepare them to
become successful artisans.

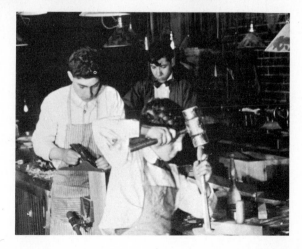

eight were estimated to be corrupt. The League aimed to replace as many of the fifty-eight as possible with honest men. But it was not easy: in 1896, as part of this campaign, a member of the Hull-House Men's Club ran for the second aldermanic position in the ward and against all expectations was elected. Too late, his idealistic backers found that their hero had his price: Johnny Powers promptly bought him out.

Jane Addams was chagrined but undiscouraged. By the time Powers came up for re-election in 1898, she had had time to observe him more closely and plan her attack. Her opening gun was a speech—delivered, improbably enough, to the Society for Ethical Culture—with the ponderous and apparently harmless title, "Some Ethical Survivals in Municipal Corruption." But appearances were deceptive: once under way, she took the hide off Powers and was scarcely easier on his opponents among the so-called "better elements."

She began by pointing out that for the immigrants, who were getting their first initiation in self-government, ethics was largely a matter of example: the officeholder was apt to set the standard and exercise a permanent influence upon their views. An engaging politician whose standards were low and "impressed by the cynical stamp of the corporations" could debauch the political ideals of ignorant men and women, with consequences that might, she felt, take years to erase.

Ethical issues were further complicated, she said, by habits of thought brought to the New World from the Old. Many Italians and Germans had left their respective fatherlands to escape military service; the Polish and Russian Jews, to escape government persecution. In all these cases, the government had been cast in the role of oppressor. The Irish, in particular, had been conditioned by years of resentment over English rule to regard any successful effort to feed at the public crib as entirely legitimate, because it represented getting the better of their bitterest enemies.

On the other hand, Miss Addams continued, there was nothing the immigrants admired more than simple goodness. They were accustomed to helping each other out in times of trouble, sharing from their own meager store with neighbors who were even more destitute. When Alderman Powers performed on a large scale the same good deeds which they themselves were able to do only on a small scale, was it any wonder that they admired him?

Given this admiration, and their Old World resentments toward government, the immigrants' developing standards of political morality suffered when Powers made it clear that he could "fix" courts or find jobs for his friends on the city payroll. It cheapened their image of American politics when they began to suspect that the source of their benefactor's largess might be a corrupt bargain with a traction tycoon, or with others who wanted something from the city of Chicago and were willing to pay for it.

Hull-House residents, Miss Addams said, very early found evidence of the influence of the boss's standards. When the news spread around the neighborhood that the House was a source of help in time of trouble, more and more neighbors came to appeal for aid when a boy was sent to jail or reform school, and it was impossible to explain to them why Hull-House, so ready to help in other ways, was not willing to get around the law as the Alderman did.

Removing Alderman Powers from office, Jane Addams told the sober gentlemen of the Society for Ethical Culture, would be no simple task. It would require a fundamental change in the ethical standards of the community, as well as the development of a deeper insight on the part of the reformers. These latter, she pointed out, with all their zeal for well-ordered, honest politics, were not eager to undertake the responsibilities of self-government 365 days a year. They were quite willing to come into the nineteenth ward at election time to exhort the citizenry, but were they willing to make a real effort to achieve personal relationships of the kind that stood Johnny Powers in such good stead?

On this last point, Hull-House itself had some experience. As Florence Kelley—a Hull-House resident who was to become a pioneer in the Illinois social reform movement—subsequently wrote:

> The question is often asked whether all that the House undertakes could not be accomplished without the wear and tear of living on the spot. The answer, that it could not, grows more assured as time goes on. You must suffer from the dirty streets, the universal ugliness, the lack of oxygen in the air you daily breathe, the endless struggle with soot and dust and insufficient water supply, the hanging from a strap of the overcrowded street car at the end of your day's work; you must send your children to the nearest wretchedly crowded school, and see them suffer the consequences, if you are to speak as one having authority and not as the scribes . . .

By 1898, after nine years of working with their neighbors, the Hull-House residents were ready to pit their influence against that of Powers. Jane Addams' philosophical address to the Ethical Culture society was followed by others in which she explained more concretely the relationships between Yerkes, Chicago's traction czar, and the city council, relationships in which Johnny Powers played a key role. With several important deals in the making, 1898 would be a bad year for Yerkes to lose his key man in the seats of power.

The election was scheduled for April. The reformers—led by Hull-House and supported by independent Democrats, the Cook County

Republicans, and the Municipal Voters League—put up a candidate of their own, Simeon Armstrong, to oppose Powers, and undertook to organize and underwrite Armstrong's campaign. By the end of January, the usually imperturbable Powers suddenly began paying attention to his political fences. The newspapers noted with some surprise that it was the first time he had felt it necessary to lift a finger more than two weeks in advance of election day.

His first move was an attack on Amanda Johnson, a Hull-House resident who had succeeded Miss Addams as garbage inspector. A graduate of the University of Wisconsin and described by the papers as blond, blue-eyed, and beautiful, she had taken the civil service examination and duly qualified for the position. Alderman Powers announced to the world that Miss Johnson, shielded by her civil service status, was telling his constituents not to vote for him. The Chicago *Record* dropped a crocodile tear at the sad picture of the martyred alderman:

> General sympathy should go out to Mr. Powers in this, his latest affliction. Heretofore he has been persecuted often by people opposed to bad franchise ordinances. He has been hounded by the upholders of civil service reform. He has suffered the shafts of criticism directed at his career by disinterested citizens. A grand jury has been cruel to him. Invidious comments have been made in his hearing as to the ethical impropriety of gambling institutions. . . . It is even believed that Miss Johnson in her relentless cruelty may go so far as to insinuate that Mr. Powers' electioneering methods are no better than those attributed to her—that, indeed, when he has votes to win, the distinctions of the civil service law do not deter him from going after those votes in many ways.

Powers' next move was to attempt a redistricting that would cut off the eastern, or Italian, end of his ward, which he took to be most seriously under Hull-House influence. It was reported that he also felt this area had been a "large source of expense to him through the necessity of assisting the poor that are crowded into that district." "These people," the Chicago *Record* reported, "formerly tied to him by his charities are said to be turning toward Hull-House and will vote solidly against him next spring."

Neither of Powers' first efforts was notably successful. A few days after his attack on Miss Johnson the *Tribune* reported:

> Trouble sizzled and boiled for Alderman John Powers in his own bailiwick last night. The Nineteenth Ward Independent club raked over the Alderman's sins . . . and . . . much indignation was occasioned by Alderman Powers' opposition to Miss Amanda Johnson. One Irish speaker says Johnny is a disgrace to the Irish race now that he has descended to fighting "poor working girls."

Meantime, Powers' colleagues on the council redistricting committee had no intention of saving his skin at the expense of their own, and stood solidly against his gerrymandering effort. Now the shaken boss began to show signs of losing his temper. He told reporters that if Miss Addams didn't like the nineteenth ward she should move out. Later, still more infuriated, he announced that Hull-House should be driven out. "A year from now there will be no such institution," he said flatly, adding that the women at Hull-House were obviously jealous of his charities. The *Record* published a cartoon showing Powers pushing vainly against the wall of a very substantial house.

The news of the campaign soon spread beyond the bounds of Chicago. The New York *Tribune* commented that Powers

> wouldn't mind Miss Addams saying all those things about him if he didn't begin to fear that she may succeed in making some of his well-meaning but misled constituents believe them. She is a very practical person, and has behind her a large volunteer staff of other practical persons who do not confine their efforts to "gassin' in the parlors," but are going about to prove to the plain people of the nineteenth ward that a corrupt and dishonest man does not necessarily become a saint by giving a moiety of his ill-gotten gains to the poor.

By March the campaign was waxing warm, and Powers resorted to an attempt to stir up the Catholic clergy against Miss Addams and the reform candidate. One of the Hull-House residents, a deputy factory inspector and a Catholic herself, went directly to the priests to find out why they were supporting Powers. When she reported, Jane Addams wrote to a friend:

> As nearly as I can make out, the opposition comes from the Jesuits, headed by Father Lambert, and the parish priests are not in it, and do not like it. Mary talked for a long time to Father Lambert and is sure it is jealousy of Hull-House and money obligations to Powers, that he does not believe the charges himself. She cried when she came back.

In another letter written about the same time, Miss Addams said that Powers had given a thousand dollars to the Jesuit "temperance cadets," who had returned the favor with a fine procession supporting Powers' candidacy. "There was a picture of your humble servant on a transparency and others such as 'No petticoat government for us . . .' We all went out on the corner to see it, Mr. Hinsdale carefully shielding me from the public view."

By now the battle between Hull-House and Johnny Powers was sharing headlines in Chicago newspapers with the blowing up of the *Maine* in Havana's harbor and the approach of the war with Spain. "Throughout the nineteenth ward," said the *Tribune,* "the one absorbing topic of conversation wherever men are gathered is the fight being made against Alderman Powers." It was rumored that Powers had offered a year's free rent to one of the opposition leaders if he would move out of the ward before election day, and the Hull-House group let it be known that the Alderman was spending money freely in the ward, giving his lieutenants far more cash to spread around than was his custom. "Where does the money come from?" Jane Addams asked, and answered her own question: "From Mr. Yerkes." Powers was stung, and challenged her to prove that he had ever received one dollar from any corporation.

"Driven to desperation," said the *Tribune,* "Ald. Powers has at last called to his aid the wives and daughters of his political allies." Determined to fight fire with fire, he dropped his opposition to "petticoat politicians" and gave his blessing to a Ladies Auxiliary which was instructed to counteract the work of the women of Hull-House. An enterprising reporter discovered that few of the ladies had ever seen Miss Addams or been to Hull-House, but all were obediently repeating the charge that she had "blackened and maligned the whole ward" by saying that its people were ignorant, criminal, and poor.

As the campaign became more intense, Jane Addams received numbers of violent letters, nearly all of them anonymous, from Powers' partisans, as well as various communications from lodginghouse keepers quoting prices for votes they were ready to deliver! When the Hull-House residents discovered evidence of ties between banking, ecclesiastical, and journalistic interests, with Powers at the center, they proceeded to publicize all they knew. This brought upon their heads a violent attack by the Chicago *Chronicle,* the organ of the Democratic ring.

Suddenly a number of nineteenth-ward businessmen who had signed petitions for the reform candidate came out for Powers. They were poor and in debt; Powers gave the word to a landlord here, a coal dealer there, and they were beaten. The small peddlers and fruit dealers were subjected to similar pressure, for each needed a license to ply his trade, and the mere hint of a revocation was enough to create another Powers man.

When Alderman John M. Harlan, one of the stalwarts of the Municipal Voters League, came into the ward to speak, Powers supplied a few toughs to stir up a riot. Fortunately Harlan was a sturdy character, and offered so forcefully to take on all comers in fisticuffs that no volunteers appeared. Allowed to proceed, he posed some embarrassing questions: Why did nineteenth-ward residents have to pay ten-cent trolley fares when most of the city paid five? Why, when Powers was head of the city council's free-spending committee on street paving, were the streets of the ward in execrable condition? Why were the

Chicago's old Hull mansion, refurbished and renamed Hull-House, about 1910.

public schools so crowded, and why had Powers suppressed a petition, circulated by Hull-House, to build more of them?

Freely admitting Powers' reputation for charity, Harlan made the interesting suggestion that the councilman's motives be put to the test: Would he be so generous as a private citizen? "Let us retire him to private life and see."

Powers was pictured by the papers as being nearly apoplectic at this attack from Miss Addams' friend. He announced that he would not be responsible for Harlan's safety if he returned to the nineteenth ward. (Since no one had asked him to assume any such responsibility, this was presumed to be an open threat.) Harlan returned at once, telling a crowd well-laced with Powers supporters that he would "rather die in my tracks than acknowledge the right of John Powers to say who should and who should not talk in this ward." Summoning up the memory of Garibaldi, he urged the Italians to live up to their tradition of freedom and not allow their votes to be "delivered."

In a quieter vein, Miss Addams too spoke at a public meeting of Italians, where, it was reported, she received profound and respectful attention. "Show that you do not intend to be governed by a boss," she told them. "It is important not only for yourselves but for your children. These things must be made plain to them."

As the campaign progressed, the reformers began to feel they had a real chance of defeating Powers. Jane Addams was persuaded to go in search of funds with which to carry out the grand finale. "I sallied forth today and got $100," she wrote, and "will have to keep it up all week; charming prospect, isn't it?" But on about the twentieth of March she began to have serious hopes, too, and redoubled her efforts.

As election day, April 6, approached, the Chicago *Tribune* and the Chicago *Record* covered the campaign daily, freely predicting a victory for the reformers. Alas for all predictions. When election day came, Powers' assets, which Jane Addams had so cogently analyzed in that faraway speech to the Society for Ethical Culture, paid off handsomely. It was a rough day in the nineteenth ward, with ten saloons open, one man arrested for drawing a gun, and everything, as Miss Addams wrote despondently when the count began to come in, "as bad as bad can be." Too many election judges were under Powers' thumb. The reform candidate was roundly defeated. Hull-House went to court to challenge the conduct of the election, but in the halls of justice Powers also had friends. It was no use.

Even in victory, however, Powers was a bit shaken. Hull-House had forced him, for the first time, to put out a great effort for re-election. It was obviously *not* going to move out of the nineteenth ward; indeed, if the past was any portent, its influence with his constituents would increase.

Powers decided to follow an ancient maxim, "If you can't lick 'em, join 'em." Early in the 1900 aldermanic campaign, several Chicago papers carried a straight news story to the effect that Hull-House and Johnny Powers had signed a truce, and quoted various paternally benevolent statements on the Alderman's part. In the *Chronicle,* for example, he was reported to have said: "I am not an Indian when it comes to hate . . . let bygones be bygones." A day or two later another rash of stories detailed a number of favors the Alderman was supposed to have done for Hull-House.

Jane Addams was furious, and after considerable deliberation she decided to reply. It was one of the few times in her long public career when she bothered to answer anything the newspapers said about her. She knew that with his eye on the campaign, the master politician was trying to give the appearance of having taken his most vigorous enemy into camp. She had been observing him too long not to realize what he was up to, and she could not possibly let him get away with it.

On February 20, 1900, a vigorous letter from Miss Addams appeared in nearly all the Chicago papers, reaffirming the attitude of Hull-House toward Mr. Powers. "It is needless to state," she concluded, "that the protest of Hull-House against a man who continually disregards the most fundamental rights of his constituents must be permanent."

Permanent protest, yes, but as a practical matter there was no use waging another opposition campaign. Powers held too many of the cards. When all was said and done, he had proved too tough a nut to crack, though Hull-House could—and did—continue to harass him. An observer of the Municipal Voters League, celebrating its success in the *Outlook* in June, 1902, described the vast improvement in the Common Council, but was forced to admit that a few wards were "well-nigh hopeless." He cited three: those of "Blind Billy" Kent, "Bathhouse John" Coughlin, and Johnny Powers.

From a larger standpoint, however, the battle between "Saint Jane" (as the neighbors called Jane Addams when she was not around) and the Ward Boss was not without significance. It was one of numerous similar battles that would characterize the progressive era the country over, and many of them the reformers would win. Because of her firsthand experience, because she lived *with* the immigrants instead of coming into their neighborhood occasionally to tell them what to do, Jane Addams was perhaps the first of the urban reformers to grasp the real pattern of bossism, its logic, the functions it performed, and the reason it was so hard to dislodge. Years later political scientists, beginning to analyze the pattern, would add almost nothing to her speech of 1898. If copies of *The Last Hurrah* have reached the Elysian fields, Jane Addams has spent an amused evening seeing her ideas developed so well in fictional form.

The campaign of 1898 throws considerable light on Jane Addams' intensely practical approach to politics, and upon a little-known aspect of the settlement-house movement. If anyone had told her and Ellen Starr in 1889 that the logic of what they were trying to do would inevitably force them into politics, they would have hooted. But in due time politics, in many forms, became central to Hull-House activity. For Jane Addams herself, the campaign against Powers was the first in a long series of political forays, all essentially based on the same desire—to see that government met the needs of the "other half."

The regulation of child labor, for example, was one political issue in which Hull-House residents became involved because of their knowledge of the lives of the neighbors. The first juvenile court in Chicago was set up as a result of their efforts; it was a direct response to the anxious mothers who could not understand why Hull-House would not help get their boys out of jail. The first factory inspection law in Illinois was also credited to Hull-House, and Florence Kelley became the first inspector. Another Hull-House resident—Dr. Alice Hamilton—pioneered in the field of industrial medicine. Because of their intimate acquaintance with the human cost of industrialization, settlement workers became vigorous advocates of promoting social justice through law.

It was a long jump but not an illogical one from the campaign against Powers to the stage of the Chicago Coliseum in August, 1912, when Jane Addams arose to second the nomination of Teddy Roosevelt by the Progressive party on a platform of social welfare. More remarkable than the ovation—larger than that given to any other seconder—was the fact that the huge audience seemed to listen carefully to what she had to say.

Some newspapers grandly estimated her value to T.R. at a million votes. "Like the report of Mark Twain's death," she commented, "the report is greatly exaggerated." But she campaigned vigorously, in the face of criticism that this was not a proper role for a woman, and when the Bull Moose cause failed, she did not believe it had been a waste of time. It had brought about, she wrote Roosevelt, more discussion of social reform than she had dared to hope for in her lifetime. Alderman Powers was still in office—as were many like him—but the sources of his power were being attacked at the roots.

When the 1916 campaign came around, Democrats and Republicans alike made bids for Jane Addams' support. The outbreak of war in Europe had turned her attention, however, in a different direction. As early as 1907, in a book called *Newer Ideals of Peace,* she had begun to elaborate William James's notion of a "moral equivalent of war," and had suggested that the experience of polyglot immigrant populations in learning to live together might be laying the foundations for a true international order. Like her ideals of social justice, those that she conceived on international peace had their beginning in the nineteenth ward.

To her, as to so many idealistic progressives, world war came as a profound shock. Her response was a vigorous effort to bring together American women and women from all the European countries to urge upon their governments a negotiated peace. In Europe, where she went in 1915 for a meeting of the Women's International Peace Conference, she visited prime ministers; at the end of that year she planned to sail on Henry Ford's peace ship, but illness forced her to withdraw at the last moment. At home she appealed to President Wilson. Unshaken in her pacifism, she stood firmly against the war, even after the United States entered it.

Her popularity seemed to melt overnight. Many women's clubs and social workers, who owed so much to her vision, deserted her. An Illinois judge who thought it dangerous for her to speak in wartime was widely supported in the press. For most of 1917 and 1918 she was isolated as never before or again. But she did not waver.

When the war ended she began at once to work for means to

prevent another. Through the twenties she was constantly active in searching for ways in which women could cut across national lines in their work for peace. In 1931, in her seventy-first year, she received the Nobel Peace Prize—the second American to be so recognized. She died, full of honors, in 1935.

As for Johnny Powers, he had lived to a ripe old age and died in 1930, remaining alderman almost to the end, still fighting reform mayors, still protesting that he and Miss Addams were really friends, after all. From whichever department of the hereafter he ended up in, he must have looked down—or up—in amazement at the final achievements of his old enemy, who had been so little troubled by his insistence that there should be "no petticoats in politics."

The Fight for Women's Suffrage: An Interview with Alice Paul

ROBERT S. GALLAGHER

An increasingly popular technique being used by students of recent history, a kind of technological advance made possible by the tape recorder, is the personal interview. "Oral history," a term coined by Allan Nevins, who founded the great oral history archive at Columbia University, provides a method of preserving the recollections of participants in historical events. Superficially it resembles autobiography, an ancient literary form, but it has the great advantage of drawing out the speaker, prodding his or her memory, forcing him or her to confront contradictions and respond to criticism. The interviewer is able to direct the subject's thoughts toward the most significant and important aspects of the topic, matters which an autobiographer might ignore out of modesty or embarrassment. This type of research requires that the interviewer be thoroughly familiar with the interviewee's career and with the events surrounding it, and also that the interviewer be able to establish a rapport with the subject.

The following interview with Alice Paul, a leader in the early twentieth-century women's suffrage movement, is a fine example of the value of the interview technique. Ms. Paul is both frank and unprepossessing; she does not hesitate to speak her mind, yet she is perfectly capable of admitting sometimes that she no longer remembers all the details of her career. The interviewer, Robert S. Gallagher, formerly a contributing editor of American Heritage, *had done his "homework" well and, as the reader will quickly recognize, had gained Ms. Paul's confidence. Her responses tell us a great deal about the fight for women's suffrage and also about the mood and spirit of the suffragists.*
∎

American women won the right to vote in 1920 largely through the controversial efforts of a young Quaker named Alice Paul. She was born in Moorestown, New Jersey, on January 11, 1885, seven years after the woman-suffrage amendment was first introduced in Congress. Over the years the so-called Susan B. Anthony amendment had received sporadic attention from the national legislators, but from 1896 until Miss Paul's dramatic arrival in Washington in 1912 the amendment had never been reported out of committee and was considered moribund. As the Congressional Committee chairman of the National American Woman Suffrage Association, Miss Paul greeted incoming President Woodrow Wilson with a spectacular parade down Pennsylvania Avenue. Congress soon began debating the suffrage amendment again. For the next seven years—a tumultuous period of demonstrations, picketing, politicking, street violence, beatings, jailings, and hunger strikes—Miss Paul led a determined band of suffragists in the confrontation tactics she had learned from the militant British feminist Mrs. Emmeline Pankhurst. This unrelenting pressure on the Wilson administration finally paid off in 1918, when an embattled President Wilson reversed his position and declared that woman suffrage was an urgently needed "war measure."

The woman who, despite her modest disclaimers, is accorded major credit for adding the Nineteenth Amendment to the Constitution is a 1905 graduate of Swarthmore College. She received her master's degree (1907) and her Ph.D. (1912) from the University of Pennsylvania. Miss Paul combined her graduate studies in 1908 and 1909 at the London School of Economics with volunteer work for the British suffrage movement. Together with another American activist, Lucy Burns, she was jailed several times in England and Scotland and returned to this country in 1910 with a reputation as an energetic and resourceful worker for women's rights. She promptly enlisted in the American suffrage movement, and opponents and friends alike soon were—and still are—impressed by her unflinching fearlessness. "Alice Paul is tiny and her hair has turned gray," a sympathetic feminist writer recently observed, "but she is not a sweet little gray-haired lady."

Miss Paul's single-minded devotion to The Cause is, of course, legendary in the women's movement. . . .

How did you first become interested in woman suffrage?

It wasn't something I had to think about. When the Quakers were founded in England in the 1600's, one of their principles was and is equality of the sexes. So I never had any other idea. And long before my time the Yearly Meeting in Philadelphia, which I still belong to, formed a committee to work for votes for women. The principle was always there.

Then you had your family's encouragement in your work?

My father—he was president of the Burlington County [New Jersey] Trust Company—died when I was quite young, but he and Mother were both active in the Quaker movement. Mother was the clerk of the Friend's Meeting in our hometown. I would say that my parents supported all the ideals that I had.

In 1912 wasn't it a bit unusual for a woman to receive a Ph.D. degree?

Oh, no. There were no women admitted, of course, to the undergraduate school at the University of Pennsylvania, but there were a number of women graduate students.

When did you actually become involved in suffrage work?

Well, after I got my master's in 1907, my doctoral studies took me to the School of Economics in London. The English women were struggling hard to get the vote, and everyone was urged to come in and help. So I did. That's all there was to it. It was the same with Lucy Burns.

You met Miss Burns in London?

Yes, we met in a police station after we were both arrested. I had been asked to go on a little deputation that was being led by Mrs. [Emmeline] Pankhurst to interview the Prime Minister. I said I'd be delighted to go, but I had no idea that we'd be arrested. I don't know what the charge was. I suppose they hadn't made all the preparations for the interview with the Prime Minister or something. At any rate, I noticed that Miss Burns had a little American flag pin on her coat, so I went up to her, and we became great friends and allies and comrades. Well, we got out of that, and, of course, afterwards we were immediately asked to do something else. And that way you sort of get into the ranks.

What sort of things were you asked to do?

The next thing I was asked to do was to go up to Norwich and "rouse the town," as they say. Winston Churchill was in the British cabinet and was going to make a speech there. Well, the English suffragists knew that the government was completely opposed to suffrage, and they conceived this plan to publicly ask all the cabinet members what they were going to do about votes for women. For that moment at least, the whole audience would turn to the subject

This striking portrait of Alice Paul was taken at the same time as this interview. She was 87.

of suffrage. We considered it an inexpensive way of advertising our cause. I thought it was a very successful method.

What happened at Norwich?

I went to Norwich with one other young woman, who was as inexperienced as I was, and we had street meetings in the marketplace, where everyone assembled for several nights before Mr. Churchill's speech. I don't know whether we exactly "roused the town," but by the time he arrived, I think Norwich was pretty well aware of what we were trying to do. The night he spoke, we had another meeting outside the hall. We were immediately

arrested. You didn't have to be a good speaker, because the minute
you began, you were arrested.

Were you a good speaker?

Not particularly. Some people enjoyed getting up in public like
that, but I didn't. I did it, though. On the other hand, Lucy Burns
was a very good speaker—she had what you call that gift of the
Irish—and she was extremely courageous, a thousand times more
courageous than I was. I was the timid type, and she was just
naturally valiant. Lucy became one of the pillars of our movement.
We never, never, never could have had such a campaign in this
country without her.

*In her book about the suffrage movement Inez Haynes Irwin tells
about your hiding overnight on the roof of St. Andrew's Hall in
Glasgow, Scotland, in order to break up a political rally the next day.*

Did Mrs. Irwin say that? Oh, no. I never hid on any roof in my life.
In Glasgow I was arrested, but it was at a street meeting we
organized there. Maybe Mrs. Irwin was referring to the Lord
Mayor's banquet in London. I think it was in December of 1909,
and Miss Burns and I were asked to interrupt the Lord Mayor. I
went into the hall, not the night before but early in the morning
when the charwomen went to work, and I waited up in the gallery
all day. That night Lucy went in down below with the banquet
guests. I don't remember whether she got up and interrupted the
mayor. I only remember that I did.

What happened?

I was arrested, of course.

*Was this the time you were imprisoned for thirty days and forcibly fed
to break your hunger strike?*

I can't remember how long I was in jail that time. I was arrested a
number of times. As for forcible feeding, I'm certainly not going to
describe that.

The whole concept of forcible feeding sounds shocking.

Well, to me it was shocking that a government of men could look
with such extreme contempt on a movement that was asking
nothing except such a simple little thing as the right to vote. Seems
almost unthinkable now, doesn't it? With all these millions and
millions of women going out happily to work today, and nobody,
as far as I can see, thinking there's anything unusual about it. But,

of course, in some countries woman suffrage is still something that has to be won.

Do you credit Mrs. Pankhurst with having trained you in the militant tactics you subsequently introduced into the American campaign?

That wasn't the way the movement was, you know. Nobody was being trained. We were just going in and doing the simplest little things that we were asked to do. You see, the movement was very small in England, and small in this country, and small everywhere, I suppose. So I got to know Mrs. Pankhurst and her daughter, Christabel, quite well. I had, of course, a great veneration and admiration for Mrs. Pankhurst, but I wouldn't say that I was very much trained by her. What happened was that when Lucy Burns and I came back, having both been imprisoned in England, we were invited to take part in the campaign over here; otherwise nobody would have ever paid any attention to us.

That was in 1913?

I came back in 1910. It was in 1912 that I was appointed by the National American Woman Suffrage Association to the chairmanship of their Congressional Committee in Washington, which was to work for the passage of the amendment that Susan B. Anthony had helped draw up. And Lucy Burns was asked to go with me. Miss Jane Addams, who was on the national board, made the motion for our appointments. They didn't take the work at all seriously, or else they wouldn't have entrusted it to us, two young girls. They did make one condition, and that was that we should never send them any bills, for as much as one dollar. Everything we did, we must raise the money ourselves. My predecessor, Mrs. William Kent, the wife of the congressman from California, told me that she had been given ten dollars the previous year by the national association, and at the end of her term she gave back some change.

Weren't you discouraged by the national association's attitude?

Well, when we came along, we tried to do the work on a scale which we thought, in our great ignorance, might bring some success. I had an idea that it might be a one year's campaign. We would explain it to every congressman, and the amendment would go through. It was so clear. But it took us seven years. When you're young, when you've never done anything very much on your own, you imagine that it won't be so hard. We probably wouldn't have undertaken it if we had known the difficulties.

How did you begin?

I went down to Washington on the seventh of December, 1912. All
I had at the start was a list of people who had supported the
movement, but when I tried to see them, I found that almost all of
them had died or moved, and nobody knew much about them. So
we were left with a tiny handful of people.

*With all these obstacles how did you manage to organize the
tremendous parade that greeted President-elect Wilson three months
later?*

Well, it wasn't such a tremendous parade. We called it a
procession. I don't know whether there were five thousand or ten
thousand marchers, maybe, but it wasn't a very big one. The idea
for such a parade had been discussed at the 1912 suffrage
convention, although some of the delegates thought it was too big
an undertaking. It was unusual. There had never been a procession
of women for any cause under the sun, so people did want to go
and see it.

*The press estimated the crowd at a half million. Whose idea was it to
have the parade the day before Wilson's inaugural?*

That was the only day you could have it if you were trying to
impress the new President. The marchers came from all over the
country at their own expense. We just sent letters everywhere, to
every name we could find. And then we had a hospitality
committee headed by Mrs. Harvey Wiley, the wife of the man who
put through the first pure-food law in America. Mrs. Wiley
canvassed all her friends in Washington and came up with a
tremendous list of people who were willing to entertain the visiting
marchers for a day or two. I mention these names to show what a
wonderful group of people we had on our little committee. . . .

Didn't the parade start a riot?

The press reports said that the crowd was very hostile, but it
wasn't hostile at all. The spectators were practically all tourists who
had come for Wilson's inauguration. We knew there would be a
large turnout for our procession, because the company that put up
the grandstands was selling tickets and giving us a small
percentage. The money we got—it was a gift from heaven—helped
us pay for the procession. I suppose the police thought we were
only going to have a couple of hundred people, so they made no
preparations. We were worried about this, so another member of
our committee, Mrs. John Rogers, went the night before to see her

brother-in-law, Secretary of War [Henry L.] Stimson, and he promised to send over the cavalry from Fort Myer if there was any trouble.

Did you need his help?

Yes, but not because the crowd was hostile. There were just so many people that they poured into the street, and we were not able to walk very far. So we called Secretary Stimson, and he sent over the troops, and they cleared the way for us. I think it took us six hours to go from the Capitol to Constitution Hall. Of course, we did hear a lot of shouted insults, which we always expected. You know, the usual things about why aren't you home in the kitchen where you belong. But it wasn't anything violent. Later on, when we were actually picketing the White House, the people did become almost violent. They would tear our banners out of our hands and that sort of thing.

Were you in the front ranks of the 1913 parade?

No. The national board members were at the head of it. I walked in the college section. We all felt very proud of ourselves, walking along in our caps and gowns. One of the largest and loveliest sections was made up of uniformed nurses. It was very impressive. Then we had a foreign section, and a men's section, and a Negro women's section from the National Association of Colored Women, led by Mary Church Terrell. She was the first colored woman to graduate from Oberlin, and her husband was a judge in Washington. Well, Mrs. Terrell got together a wonderful group to march, and then, suddenly, our members from the South said they wouldn't march. Oh, the newspapers just thought this was a wonderful story and developed it to the utmost. I remember that that was when the men's section came to the rescue. The leader, a Quaker I knew, suggested that the men march between the southern delegations and the colored women's section, and that finally satisfied the southern women. That was the greatest hurdle we had.

If the parade didn't cause any real trouble, why was there a subsequent congressional investigation that resulted in the ouster of the district police chief?

The principal investigation was launched at the request of our women delegates from Washington, which was a suffrage state. These women were so indignant about the remarks from the crowd. And I remember that Congressman Kent was very aroused at the things that were shouted at his daughter, Elizabeth, who was riding on the California float, and he was among the first in Congress to demand an investigation into why the police hadn't been better prepared. As I said, the police just didn't take our little procession seriously. I don't think it was anything intentional. We didn't testify against the police, because we felt it was just a miscalculation on their part.

What was your next move after the parade?

A few weeks after Mr. Wilson became President, four of us went to see him. And the President, of course, was polite and as much of a gentleman as he always was. He told of his own support, when he had been governor of New Jersey, of a state referendum on suffrage, which had failed. He said that he thought this was the way suffrage should come, through state referendums, not through Congress. That's all we accomplished. We said we were going to try and get it through Congress, that we would like to have his help and needed his support very much. And then we sent him another delegation and another and another and another and another and another and another—every type of women's group we could get. We did this until 1917, when the war started and the President said he couldn't see any more delegations.

So you began picketing the White House?

We said we would have a perpetual delegation right in front of the White House, so he wouldn't forget. Then they called it picketing. We didn't know enough to know what picketing was, I guess.

How did you finance all this work?

Well, as I mentioned, we were instructed not to submit any bills to the National American. Anything we did, we had to raise the money for it ourselves. So to avoid any conflict with them we decided to form a group that would work exclusively on the Susan B. Anthony amendment. We called it the Congressional Union for Woman's Suffrage. You see, the Congressional Committee was a tiny group, so the Congressional Union was set up to help with the lobbying, to help with the speechmaking, and especially to help in raising money. The first year we raised $27,000. It just came from anybody who wanted to help. Mostly small contributions. John McLean, the owner of the Washington *Post,* I think, gave us a thousand dollars. That was the first big gift we ever got.

The records indicate that you raised more than $750,000 over the first eight years. Did your amazing fund-raising efforts cause you any difficulties with the National American?

I know that at the end of our first year, at the annual convention of the National American, the treasurer got up—and I suppose this would be the same with any society in the world—she got up and made a speech, saying, "Well, this group of women has raised a tremendous sum of money, and none of it has come to my treasury," and she was very displeased with this. Then I remember that Jane Addams stood up and reminded the convention that we had been instructed to pay our own debts, and so that was all there was to it. Incidentally, the Congressional Union paid *all* the bills of that national convention, which was held in Washington that year. I remember we paid a thousand dollars for the rent of the hall. If you spend a hard time raising the money, you remember about it.

Were you upset about not being reappointed chairman of the Congressional Committee?

No, because they asked me to continue. But they said if I were the committee chairman, I would have to drop the Congressional Union. I couldn't be chairman of both. Some of the members on the National American board felt that all the work being put into the federal amendment wasn't a good thing for the entire suffrage campaign. I told them I had formed this Congressional Union and that I wanted to keep on with it.

Was it true, as some historians of the movement maintain, that the National American's president, Dr. Anna Shaw, was "suspicious" of unusual activity in the ranks?

No, I don't think she was. She came down to Washington frequently and spoke at our meetings, and she walked at the head of our 1913 procession. But I think we did make the mistake perhaps of spending too much time and energy just on the campaign. We didn't take enough time, probably, to go and explain to all the leaders why we thought [the federal amendment] was something that could be accomplished. You see, the National American took the position—not Miss Anthony, but the later people—that suffrage was something that didn't exist anywhere in the world, and therefore we would have to go more slowly and have endless state referendums to indoctrinate the men of the country.

Obviously you didn't agree with this. Was this what caused the Congressional Union to break with the National American?

We didn't break with the National American. In a sense we were expelled. At the 1913 convention they made lots and lots of changes in the association's constitution. I don't recall what they were, and I didn't concern myself with the changes at the time. At any rate, the Congressional Union was affiliated with the National American under one classification, and they wrote to us and said if we would resign from that classification and apply for another classification, there would be a reduction in our dues. So we did what they told us, and then when we applied for the new classification, they refused to accept us, and we were out.

Why did the National American do this to your group?

The real division was over the Shafroth-Palmer amendment that the National American decided to substitute for the Anthony amendment in the spring of 1914. Under this proposal each state would hold a referendum on woman suffrage *if* more than 8 per cent of the legal voters in the last preceding election—males, of course—signed a petition for it. This tactic had been tried without much success before, and with all the time and money such campaigns involve, I don't think many women would have ever become voters. Our little group wanted to continue with the original amendment, which we called the Susan B. Anthony because the women of the country, if they knew anything about the movement, had heard the name Susan B. Anthony. Now the great part of the American women were very loyal to this amendment, and when the National American suddenly switched to Shafroth-Palmer, we thought that the whole movement was going off on a sidetrack. And that is the reason we later formed the National Woman's Party, because if we hadn't continued, there would have been nobody in Washington speaking up for the original amendment.

You didn't have much faith in state referendums?

The first thing I ever did—after I graduated from Swarthmore, I did some social work in New York City—one of the suffragists there asked me to go with her to get signatures for a suffrage referendum in New York State. So I went with her, and she was a great deal older and much more experienced than I was. I remember going into a little tenement room with her, and a man there spoke almost no English, but he could vote. Well, we went in and tried to talk to this man and ask him to vote for equality for women. And almost invariably these men said, "No, we don't think that it is the right thing. We don't do that in Italy, women don't vote in Italy." You can hardly go through one of those referendum campaigns and not think what a waste of the strength of women to try and convert a majority of men in the state. From that day on I was convinced that the way to do it was through Congress, where there was a smaller group of people to work with.

Then the National Woman's Party was formed to continue the work on the federal amendment?

We changed our name from the Congressional Union to the National Woman's Party in 1916, when we began to get so many new members and branches. Mainly people who disagreed with the National American's support of the Shafroth-Palmer. And the person who got us to change our name was Mrs. [Alva E.] Belmont.

Would you tell me about Mrs. Belmont?

She was, of course, a great supporter of the suffrage movement financially, and we didn't even know her the first year we were in Washington. People said to me that she was a wonderfully equipped person who was very fond of publicity, and they suggested that I invite her to come down and sit on one of the parade floats. Well, I didn't know who she was at all, but I wrote her an invitation, and I remember thinking what a queer person she must be to want to sit on a float. She turned out to be anything but the type she was described, and, of course, she didn't sit on any float. Anyway, a year later, after we had been expelled from the National American and couldn't have been more alone and more unpopular and more unimportant, one of our members, Crystal Eastman [Benedict], contacted Mrs. Belmont. And Mrs. Belmont invited me to come have dinner and spend the night at her home in New York City. Well, I like to go to bed early, but Mrs. Belmont was the type that liked to talk all night. So all night we talked about how we could probably get suffrage. A little later Mrs. Belmont withdrew entirely from the old National American and threw her whole strength into our movement. The first thing she did was give us five thousand dollars. We had never had such a gift before.

Why do you think Mrs. Belmont crossed over to your group?

She was entirely in favor of our approach to the problem. She wanted to be immediately put on our national board, so she could have some direction. And then, after suffrage was won, she became the president of the Woman's Party, and at that time she gave us most of the money to buy the house in Washington that is still the party's headquarters. Over the years Mrs. Belmont did an enormous amount for the cause of women's equality. She was just

one of those people who were born with the feeling of
independence for herself and for women.

*Did Mrs. Belmont have something to do with the decision to campaign
against the Democrats in the November, 1914, elections?*

Yes. You see, here we had an extremely powerful and wonderful
man—I thought Woodrow Wilson was a very wonderful man—the
leader of his party, in complete control of Congress. But when the
Democrats in Congress caucused, they voted against suffrage. You
just naturally felt that the Democratic Party was responsible. Of
course, in England they were up against the same thing. They
couldn't get this measure through Parliament without getting the
support of the party that was in complete control.

*Didn't this new policy of holding the party in power responsible
represent a drastic change in the strategy of the suffrage movement?*

Up to this point the suffrage movement in the United States had
regarded each congressman, each senator, as a friend or a foe. It
hadn't linked them together. And maybe these men were individual
friends or foes in the past. But we deliberately asked the
Democrats to bring it up in their caucus, and they did caucus
against us. So you couldn't regard them as your allies anymore. I
reported all this to the National American convention in 1913, and
I said that it seemed to us that we must begin to hold this party
responsible. And nobody objected to my report. But when we
began to put it into operation, there was tremendous opposition,
because people said that this or that man has been our great
friend, and here you are campaigning against him.

*Would you have taken the same position against the Republicans if
that party had been in power in 1914?*

Of course. You see, we tried very hard in 1916—wasn't it [Charles
Evans] Hughes running against Wilson that year?—to get the
Republicans to put federal suffrage in their platform, and we failed.
We also failed with the Democrats. Then we tried to get the
support of Mr. Hughes himself. Our New York State committee
worked very hard on Mr. Hughes, and they couldn't budge him. So
we went to see former President [Theodore] Roosevelt at his home
at Oyster Bay to see if *he* could influence Mr. Hughes. And I
remember so vividly what Mr. Roosevelt said. He said, "You know,
in political life you must always remember that you not only must
be on the right side of a measure, but you must be on the right
side at the right time." He told us that that was the great trouble

with Mr. Hughes, that Mr. Hughes is certainly for suffrage, but he can't seem to know that he must do it in time. So Mr. Hughes started on his campaign around the country, and when he came to Wyoming, where women were already voting, he couldn't say he was for the suffrage amendment. And he went on and on, all around the country. Finally, when he came to make his final speech of the campaign in New York, he had made up his mind, and he came out strongly for the federal suffrage amendment. So it was true what Mr. Roosevelt had said about him. . . .

In the 1914 elections women voted for forty-five members of Congress, and the Democrats won only nineteen of these races, often by drastically reduced pluralities. Weren't you at all concerned about defeating some of your strongest Democratic supporters in Congress?

Not really. Whoever was elected from a suffrage state was going to be prosuffrage in Congress anyway, whether he was Republican or Democrat. But how else were we going to demonstrate that women could be influential, independent voters? One of the men we campaigned against was Representative—later Senator—Carl Hayden of Arizona, and he finally became a very good friend of the movement, I thought. But it is true that most of them really did resent it very much. . . .

You were once quoted to the effect that in picking volunteers you preferred enthusiasm to experience.

Yes. Well, wouldn't you? I think everybody would. I think every reform movement needs people who are full of enthusiasm. It's the first thing you need. I was full of enthusiasm, and I didn't want any lukewarm person around. I still am, of course.

One of your most enthusiastic volunteers was Inez Milholland Boissevain, wasn't she?

Inez Milholland actually gave her life for the women's movement. I think Inez was our most beautiful member. We always had her on horseback at the head of our processions. You've probably read about this, but when Inez was a student at Vassar, she tried to get up a suffrage meeting, and the college president refused to let her hold the meeting. So she organized a little group, and they jumped over a wall at the edge of the college and held the first suffrage meeting at Vassar in a cemetery. Imagine such a thing happening at a women's college so short a time ago. You can hardly believe such things occurred. But they did.

How did Miss Milholland give her life for the movement?

After college Inez wanted to study law, but every prominant law school refused to admit a girl. She finally went to New York University, which wasn't considered much of a university then, and got her law degree. Then she threw her whole soul into the suffrage movement and really did nothing else but that. Well, in 1916, when we were trying to prevent the re-election of Woodrow Wilson, we sent speakers to all the suffrage states, asking people not to vote for Wilson, because he was opposing the suffrage which they already had. Inez and her sister, Vita, who was a beautiful singer, toured the suffrage states as a team. Vita would sing songs about the women's movement, and then Inez would speak. Their father, John Milholland, paid all the expenses for their tour, which began in Wyoming. Well, when they got to Los Angeles, Inez had just started to make her speech when she suddenly collapsed and fell to the floor, just from complete exhaustion. Her last words were "Mr. President, how long must women wait for liberty?" We used her words on picket banners outside the White House. I think she was about twenty-eight or twenty-nine. . . . She was brought back and buried near her family home in New York State. We decided to have a memorial service for her in Statuary Hall in the Capitol on Christmas Day. . . .

Did you invite President Wilson and his family?

Oh, no. We did send a delegation to him from the meeting, but he wouldn't receive them. Finally on January 9, 1917, he agreed to meet with women from all over the country who brought Milholland resolutions. The women asked him once more to lend the weight and influence of his great office to the federal amendment, but the President rejected the appeal and continued to insist that he was the follower, not the leader, of his party. The women were quite disappointed when they returned to Cameron House, where we had established our headquarters across Lafayette Square from the White House. That afternoon we made the decision to have a perpetual delegation, six days a week, from ten in the morning until half past five in the evening, around the White House. We began the next day.

And this perpetual delegation, or picketing, continued until the President changed his position?

Yes. Since the President had made it clear that he wouldn't see any more delegations in his office, we felt that pickets outside the White House would be the best way to remind him of our cause.

*Inez Milholland in a demonstration parade. She was
driving her own automobile, a most unusual thing for a
woman at that time.*

Every day when he went out for his daily ride, as he drove through
our picket line he always took off his hat and bowed to us. We
respected him very much. I always thought he was a great
President. Years later, when I was in Geneva [Switzerland] working
with the World Woman's Party, I was always so moved when I
would walk down to the League of Nations and see the little tribute
to Woodrow Wilson. . . .

*Do you want to talk about the violence that occurred on the White
House picket line?*

Not particularly. It is true that after the United States entered the war [April 6, 1917], there was some hostility, and some of the pickets were attacked and had their banners ripped out of their hands. The feeling was—and some of our own members shared this and left the movement—that the cause of suffrage should be abandoned during wartime, that we should work instead for peace. But this was the same argument used during the Civil War, after which they wrote the word "male" into the Constitution. Did you know that "male" appears three times in the Fourteenth Amendment? Well, it does. So we agreed that suffrage came *before* war. Indeed, if we had universal suffrage throughout the world, we might not even have wars. So we continued picketing the White House, even though we were called traitors and pro-German and all that. . . .

It is true, isn't it, that you were arrested outside the White House on October 20, 1917, and sentenced to seven months in the District of Columbia jail?

Yes.

And that when you were taken to the cell-block where the other suffragists were being held, you were so appalled by the stale air that you broke a window with a volume of Robert Browning's poetry you had brought along to read?

No. I think Florence Boeckel, our publicity girl, invented that business about the volume of Browning's poetry. What I actually broke the window with was a bowl I found in my cell.

Was this the reason you were transferred to solitary confinement in the jail's psychopathic ward?

I think the government's strategy was to discredit me. That the other leaders of the Woman's Party would say, well, we had better sort of disown this crazy person. But they didn't.

During the next three or four weeks you maintained your hunger strike. Was this the second or third time you underwent forcible feeding?

Probably, but I'm not sure how many times.

Is this done with liquids through a tube put down through your mouth?

I think it was done through the nose, if I remember right. And they didn't use the soft tubing that is available today.

While you were held in solitary confinement your own lawyer, Dudley Field Malone, could not get in to see you. And yet one day David Lawrence, the journalist, came in to interview you. How do you explain this?

I think he was a reporter at that time, but anyway he was a very great supporter of and, I guess, a personal friend of President Wilson's. I didn't know then what he was, except that he came in and said he had come to have an interview with me. Of course, a great many people thought that Lawrence, because of his close connection with the White House, had been encouraged to go look into what the women were doing and why they were making all this trouble and so on.

You and all the other suffragist prisoners were released on November 27 and 28, just a few days after Lawrence's visit. Could this action have been based on his report to the President?

I wouldn't know about that. Of course, the only way we could be released would be by act of the President.

And on January 9, 1918, President Wilson formally declared for federal suffrage. The next day the House passed the amendment 274-136, and the really critical phase of the legislative struggle began.

Yes. Well, when we began, Maud Younger, our congressional chairman, got up this card catalogue, which is now on loan to the Library of Congress. We had little leaflets printed, and each person who interviewed a congressman would write a little report on where this or that man stood. We knew we had the task of winning them over, man by man, and it was important to know what our actual strength was in Congress at all times. These records showed how, with each Congress, we were getting stronger and stronger, until we finally thought we were at the point of putting the Anthony amendment to a vote. And of course this information was very helpful to our supporters in Congress.

Yet when the Senate finally voted on October 1, 1918, the amendment failed by two votes of the necessary two thirds. What happened?

We realized that we were going to lose a few days before the vote. We sat there in the Senate gallery, and they talked on and on and on, and finally Maud Younger and I went down to see what was going on, why they wouldn't vote. People from all over the country had come. The galleries were filled with suffragists. We went to see

Senator Curtis, the Republican whip, and the Republican leader, Senator Gallinger. It was then a Republican Senate. And there they stood, each with a tally list in their hands. So we said, why don't you call the roll. And they said, well, Senator Borah has deserted us, he has decided to oppose the amendment, and there is no way on earth we can change his mind. . . .

Was it about this time that your members began burning the President's statements in public?

I'm not sure when it started. We had a sort of perpetual flame going in an urn outside our headquarters in Lafayette Square. I think we used rags soaked in kerosene. It was really very dramatic, because when President Wilson went to Paris for the peace conference, he was always issuing some wonderful, idealistic statement that was impossible to reconcile with what he was doing at home. And we had an enormous bell—I don't recall how we ever got such an enormous bell—and every time Wilson would make one of these speeches, we would toll this great bell, and then somebody would go outside with the President's speech and, with great dignity, burn it in our little caldron. I remember that Senator Medill McCormick lived just down the street from us, and we were constantly getting phone calls from him saying they couldn't sleep or conduct social affairs because our bell was always tolling away.

You had better results from the next Congress, the Sixty-sixth, didn't you?

Yes. President Wilson made a magnificent speech calling for the amendment as a war measure back in October, 1918, and on May 20, 1919, the House passed the amendment. Then on June 4 the Senate finally passed it.

Did you go to hear the President?

I don't believe we were there, because when the President spoke, everybody wanted tickets, and the Woman's Party has never asked for tickets, because we still don't want to be in any way under any obligation. I know we were in the gallery when the Senate actually voted, because nobody wanted tickets then. Our main concern was that the Senate might try to reinstate the seven-year clause that had been defeated in the House.

The seven-year clause?

This clause required the amendment to be ratified by the states within seven years or else the amendment would be defeated. We got the clause eliminated on the suffrage amendment, but we were unable to stop Congress from attaching it to the present equal rights amendment.

Were you relieved when the Anthony amendment finally passed?

Yes, for many reasons. But we still had to get it ratified. We went to work on that right away and worked continuously for the fourteen months it took. But that last state . . . we thought we never would get that last state. And, you know, President Wilson really got it for us. What happened was that Wilson went to the governor of Tennessee, who was a Democrat. The President asked him to call a special session of the state legislature so the amendment could be ratified in time for women to vote in the 1920 Presidential election.

That was on August 18, 1920, and there is a well-known photograph of you, on the balcony of your headquarters, unfurling the suffrage flag with thirty-six stars. What were your feelings that day?

You know, you are always so engrossed in the details that you probably don't have all the big and lofty thoughts you should be having. I think we had this anxiety about how we would pay all our bills at the end. So the first thing we did was to just do nothing. We closed our headquarters, stopped all our expenses, stopped publishing our weekly magazine, *The Suffragist,* stopped everything and started paying off the bills we had incurred. Maud Younger and I got the tiniest apartment we could get, and she took over the housekeeping, and we got a maid who came in, and we just devoted ourselves to raising this money. . . .

Then the following year, on February 15, 1921, we had our final convention to decide what to do. Whether to disband or whether to continue and take up the whole equality program— equality for women in all fields of life—that had been spelled out at the Seneca Falls convention in 1848. We decided to go on, and we elected a whole new national board, with Elsie Hill as our new chairman. We thought we ought to get another amendment to the Constitution, so we went to many lawyers—I remember we paid one lawyer quite a large sum, for us, at least—and asked them to draw up an amendment for equal rights. We had another meeting up in Seneca Falls on the seventy-fifth anniversary of the original meeting, and there we adopted the program we have followed ever since on the equal-rights amendment. That was 1923. So that is when we started.

Was that the year the first equal-rights amendment was introduced?

We hadn't been able to get any lawyer to draft an amendment that satisfied us, so I drafted one in simple ordinary English, not knowing anything about law, and we got it introduced in Congress. But at the first hearing our little group was the only one that supported it. All these other organizations of women that hadn't worked to get the vote, these professional groups and so on, opposed the amendment on the grounds that it would deprive them of alimony and force them to work in the mines, and they would lose these special labor laws that protect women. So it was obvious to us—and to the Congress—that we were going to have to change the thinking of American women first. So we began going to convention after convention of women, trying to get them to endorse E.R.A. It took many years. The American Association of University Women just endorsed it in 1972. Imagine, all the years and years and years that women have been going to universities. But the new generation of college women were so hopeless on this subject.

It was like forty years in the wilderness, wasn't it?

Yes, more or less. But during that time we opened—and by "we" I mean the whole women's movement—we opened a great many doors to women with the power of the vote, things like getting women into the diplomatic service. And don't forget we were successful in getting equality for women written into the charter of the United Nations in 1945.

Do you think the progress of the equal-rights amendment has been helped by the women's liberation movement?

I feel very strongly that if you are going to do anything, you have to take one thing and do it. You can't try lots and lots of reforms and get them all mixed up together. Now, I think the liberation movement has been a good thing, because it has aroused lots of women from their self-interest, and it has made everyone more aware of the inequalities that exist. But the ratification of the equal-rights amendment has been made a bit harder by these people who run around advocating, for instance, abortion. As far as I can see, E.R.A. has nothing whatsoever to do with abortion.

How did abortion become involved with equal rights?

At the 1968 Republican convention our representative went before the platform committee to present our request for a plank on equal rights, and as soon as she finished, up came one of the liberation ladies, a well-known feminist, who made a great speech on abortion. So then all the women on the platform committee said, well, we're not going to have the Republican Party campaigning for abortion. So they voted not to put *anything* in the party platform about women's rights. That was the first time since 1940 that we didn't get an equal-rights plank in the Republican platform. And then that feminist showed up at the Democratic convention, and the same thing happened with their platform. It was almost the same story at the 1972 conventions, but this time we managed to get equal rights back into the platforms.

It's really the principle of equal rights that you're concerned with, isn't it, not the specific applications?

I have never doubted that equal rights was the right direction. Most reforms, most problems are complicated. But to me there is nothing complicated about ordinary equality. Which is a nice thing about our campaign. It really is true, at least to my mind, that only good will come to everybody with equality. If we get to the point where everyone has equality of opportunity—and I don't expect to see it, we have such a long, long way ahead of us—then it seems to me it is not our problem how women use their equality or how men use their equality.

Miss Paul, how would you describe your contribution to the struggle for women's rights?

I always feel . . . the movement is a sort of mosaic. Each of us puts in one little stone, and then you get a great mosaic at the end.

Part Four

America in World Affairs

Battleships of the Great White Fleet en route to Japan lie at anchor in San Francisco harbor in this 1908 photograph.

The Needless War with Spain

WILLIAM E. LEUCHTENBURG

Seldom have events so pregnant with future significance occurred in an atmosphere so devoid of an understanding of their significance as in 1898 when the United States went to war with Spain. It is perhaps not quite accurate to say that the United States emerged from that war as a world power. In retrospect the nation was a world power well before the war began. But the war made Americans aware that the United States was a world power, and from that awareness flowed American imperialism, American participation in World War I, and much that followed.

As William E. Leuchtenburg explains in this essay, there was no shortage of "aggressive, expansionist, jingoistic" feeling in America during the early 1890s. But the conflict with Spain derived chiefly from the desire of Americans to help the beleaguered Cubans with their independence from Spain. Americans wanted the war (which could well have been avoided) but they had little understanding of what the results of that war would be.

Mr. Leuchtenburg, William Rand Kenan professor of history at the University of North Carolina, is the author of Franklin D. Roosevelt and the New Deal, 1932–1940, *which won a Francis Parkman Prize, awarded each year to the book in American history that best combines sound scholarship and literary distinction. This essay also combines these two qualities.* ∎

The United States in the 1890's became more aggressive, expansionistic, and jingoistic than it had been since the 1850's. In less than five years, we came to the brink of war with Italy, Chile, and Great Britain over three minor incidents in which no American national interest of major importance was involved. In each of these incidents, our secretary of state was highly aggressive, and the American people applauded. During these years, we completely overhauled our decrepit Navy, building fine new warships like the *Maine.* The martial virtues of Napoleon, the imperial doctrines of Rudyard Kipling, and the naval theories of Captain Alfred T. Mahan all enjoyed a considerable vogue.

There was an apparently insatiable hunger for foreign conquest. Senator Shelby M. Cullom declared in 1895: "It is time that some one woke up and realized the necessity of annexing some property. We want all this northern hemisphere, and when we begin to reach out to secure these advantages we will begin to have a nation and our lawmakers will rise above the grade of politicians and become true statesmen." When, in 1895, the United States almost became involved in a war with Great Britain over the Venezuelan boundary, Theodore Roosevelt noted: "The antics of the bankers, brokers and anglomaniacs generally are humiliating to a degree. . . . Personally I rather hope the fight will come soon. The clamor of the peace faction has convinced me that this country needs a war." The Washington *Post* concluded: "The taste of Empire is in the mouth of the people. . . ."

In the early nineteenth century, under the leadership of men like Simon Bolivar, Spain's colonies in the New World had launched a series of successful revolutions; of the great Spanish empire that Cortes and Pizarro had built, the island of Cuba, "the Ever Faithful Isle," was the only important Spanish possession to stay loyal to the Crown. Spain exploited the economy of the island mercilessly, forcing Cubans to buy Spanish goods at prices far above the world market, and Madrid sent to Cuba as colonial officials younger sons who had no interest in the island other than making a quick killing and returning to Spain. High taxes to support Spanish officialdom crippled the island; arbitrary arrests and arbitrary trials made a mockery of justice; and every attempt at public education was stifled.

The island of Cuba had been in a state of political turbulence for years when in 1894 the American Wilson-Gorman Tariff placed duties on Cuban sugar which, coupled with a world-wide depression, brought ruin to the economy of the island. The terrible hardship of the winter was the signal for revolution; on February 24, 1895, under the leadership of a junta in New York City headed by José Martí, rebels once more took the field against Spain. At first, the American people were too absorbed with the Venezuelan crisis to pay much attention to another revolt in Cuba. Then, in September, 1895, came the event which changed the course of the Cuban rebellion: William Randolph Hearst, a young man of 32 who had been operating the San Francisco *Examiner* in a sensational fashion, purchased the New York *Morning Journal,* and immediately locked horns with Joseph Pulitzer and the *World* in a circulation war that was to make newspaper history.

Hearst capitalized on the fact that the American people had only the most romantic notions of the nature of the Cuban conflict. The rebels under General Máximo Gómez, a tough Santo Domingan guerrilla fighter, embarked on a program of burning the cane fields in the hope not only of depriving the government of revenue but also of so disrupting the life of the island that the government would be forced to submit. Although there were some noble spirits in the group, much of the rebellion had an unsavory odor; one of the main financial supports for the uprising came from American property owners who feared that their sugar fields would be burned unless protection money was paid.

While Gómez was putting Cuba to the torch, American newsmen were filing reports describing the war in terms of nonexistent pitched battles between the liberty-loving Cubans and the cruel Spaniards. The war was presented, in short, as a Byronic conflict between the forces of freedom and the forces of tyranny, and the American people ate it up. When Hearst bought the *Journal* in late 1895, it had a circulation of 30,000; by 1897 it had bounded to over 400,000 daily, and during the Spanish-American War it was to go well over a million.

The sensational newspapers had influence, yet they represented no more than a minority of the press of the country; and in the South and the Middle West, where anti-Spanish feeling became most intense, the representative newspaper was much more conservative. Certainly the yellow press played a tremendous part in whipping up sentiment for intervention in Cuba, but these feelings could not be carried into action unless American political leaders of both parties were willing to assume the terrible responsibility of war.

By the beginning of 1896 the rebels had achieved such success in their guerrilla tactics that Madrid decided on firmer steps and sent General Don Valeriano Weyler y Nicolau to Cuba. When Weyler arrived in February, he found the sugar industry severely disrupted and the military at a loss to meet the rebel tactic of setting fire to the cane fields. Weyler declared martial law and announced that men guilty of incendiarism would be dealt with summarily; he was promptly dubbed "The Butcher" by American newspapermen.

By late 1896 Weyler still had not succeeded in crushing the insurrection, and his measures became more severe. On October 21 he issued his famous *reconcentrado* order, directing the "reconcentration"

This pro-McKinley cartoon, from Puck's *April 13, 1898, issue, applauded the President's efforts to restrain war hysteria; but two days earlier McKinley had reversed his pacifistic policy.*

of the people of Pinar del Río in the garrison towns, and forbidding the export of supplies from the towns to the countryside. Reasoning that he could never suppress the rebellion so long as the rebels could draw secret assistance from people in the fields, Weyler moved the people from the estates into the towns and stripped the countryside of supplies to starve out the rebellion. Since many of the people had already fled to the towns, the *reconcentrado* policy was not as drastic as it appeared; yet the suffering produced by the policy was undeniable. Lacking proper hygienic care, thousands of Cubans, especially women and children, died like flies.

When William McKinley entered the White House in 1897, he had no intention of joining the War Hawks. "If I can only go out of office . . . with the knowledge that I have done what lay in my power to avert this terrible calamity," McKinley told Grover Cleveland on the eve of his inauguration, "I shall be the happiest man in the world." McKinley came to power as the "advance agent of prosperity," and business interests were almost unanimous in opposing any agitation of the Cuban question that might lead to war. Contrary to the assumptions of Leninist historians, it was Wall Street which, first and last, resisted a war which was to bring America its overseas empire.

The country had been gripped since 1893 by the deepest industrial depression in its history, a depression that was to persist until the beginning of 1897. Each time it appeared recovery might be on its way, a national crisis had cut it off: first the Venezuelan boundary war scare of December, 1895, then the bitter free silver campaign of 1896. What business groups feared more than anything else was a new crisis. As Julius Pratt writes: "To this fair prospect of a great business revival the threat of war was like a specter at the feast."

McKinley was not a strong President, and he had no intention of being one. Of all the political figures of his day, he was the man most responsive to the popular will. It was his great virtue and, his critics declared, his great weakness. Uncle Joe Cannon once remarked: "McKinley keeps his ear to the ground so close that he gets it full of grasshoppers much of the time." If McKinley was not one of our greatest Presidents, he was certainly the most representative and the most responsive. Anyone who knew the man knew that, although he was strongly opposed to war, he would not hold out against war if the popular demand for war became unmistakable. "Let the voice of the people rule"—this was McKinley's credo, and he meant it.

The threat to peace came from a new quarter, from the South and West, the strongholds of Democracy and free silver. Many Bryanite leaders were convinced that a war would create such a strain on the currency system that the opposition to free silver would collapse. Moreover, with the opposition to war strongest in Wall Street, they found it easy to believe that Administration policy was the product of a conspiracy of bankers who would deny silver to the American people, who would deny liberty to the people of Cuba, who were concerned only with the morality of the countinghouse. Moreover, Bryan was the spokesman for rural Protestantism, which was already speaking in terms of a righteous war against Spain to free the Cubans from bondage. These were forces too powerful for McKinley to ignore. McKinley desired peace, but he was above all, a Republican partisan, and he had no intention of handing the Democrats in 1900 the campaign cry of Free Cuba and Free Silver.

While McKinley attempted to search out a policy that would preserve peace without bringing disaster to the Republican party, the yellow press made his job all the more difficult by whipping up popular anger against Spain. On February 12 the *Journal* published a dispatch from Richard Harding Davis, reporting that as the American steamship *Olivette* was about to leave Havana Harbor for the United States, it was boarded by Spanish police officers who searched three young Cuban women, one of whom was suspected of carrying messages from the rebels. The *Journal* ran the story under the headline, "Does Our Flag Protect Women?" with a vivid drawing by Frederic Remington across one half a page showing Spanish plainclothes men searching a wholly nude woman. War, declared the *Journal,* "is a dreadful thing, but there are things more dreadful than even war, and one of them is dishonor." It shocked the country, and Congressman Amos Cummings immediately resolved to launch a congressional inquiry into the *Olivette* out-

Frederic Remington's rendition of the Olivette
*incident was actually the work of Hearst, who had
Remington exaggerate the supposed impropriety.*

rage. Before any steps could be taken, the true story was revealed. The
World produced one of the young women who indignantly protested
the *Journal*'s version of the incident. Pressured by the *World,* the *Journal*
was forced to print a letter from Davis explaining that his article had
not said that male policemen had searched the women and that, in fact,
the search had been conducted quite properly by a police matron with
no men present.

The *Olivette* incident was manufactured by Hearst, but by the spring
of 1897 the American press had a new horror to report which was all
too true. Famine was stalking the island. Cuba had been in a serious
economic state when the rebellion broke out in 1895; two years of war
would, under any circumstances, have been disastrous, but the deliberate policies pursued both by the insurgents and by the government
forces made the situation desperate. It was a simple matter for Hearst
and Pulitzer reporters to pin the full responsibility on Weyler.

By the middle of July, McKinley had formulated a policy which he
set down in a letter of instructions to our new American minister to
Spain, General Stewart L. Woodford. The letter emphasized the need
of bringing the Cuban war to an end and said that this could be done
to the mutual advantage of both Spain and the Cubans by granting

some kind of autonomy to Cuba. If Spain did not make an offer to the rebels and if the "measures of unparalleled severity" were not ended, the United States threatened to intervene.

On August 8 an Italian anarchist assassinated the Spanish premier; and when Woodford reached Madrid in September, a new government was about to take over headed by Señor Sagasta and the Liberals, who had repeatedly denounced the "barbarity" of the previous government's policy in Cuba. Sagasta immediately removed General Weyler, and the prospects for an agreement between the United States and Spain took a decided turn for the better.

While Woodford was carrying on skillful diplomatic negotiations for peace in Madrid, the Hearst press was creating a new sensation in this country with the Cisneros affair. Evangelina Cisneros was a young Cuban woman who had been arrested and imprisoned in the Rocojidas in Havana, guilty, according to the American press, of no other crime than protecting her virtue from an unscrupulous Spanish colonel, an aide to Butcher Weyler. The Rocojidas, Hearst's reporter told American readers, was a cage where the innocent beauty was herded with women criminals of every type, subject to the taunts and vile invitations of men who gathered outside.

When it was reported that Señorita Cisneros, whose father was a rebel leader, was to be sent for a long term to a Spanish penal colony in Africa or in the Canaries, the *Journal* launched one of the most fabulous campaigns in newspaper history. "Enlist the women of America!" was the Hearst war cry, and the women of America proved willing recruits. Mrs. Julia Ward Howe signed an appeal to Pope Leo XIII, and Mrs. Jefferson Davis, the widow of the president of the Confederacy, appealed to the queen regent of Spain to "give Evangelina Cisneros to the women of America to save her from a fate worse than death." When the *Journal* prepared a petition on behalf of Señorita Cisneros, it obtained the names of Mrs. Nancy McKinley, the mother of the President, and Mrs. John Sherman, the wife of the secretary of state, as well as such other prominent ladies as Julia Dent Grant and Mrs. Mark Hanna.

It was a startling coup for Mr. Hearst, but he had not yet even begun to display his ingenuity. On October 10, 1897, the *Journal* erupted across its front page with the banner headline: "An American Newspaper Accomplishes at a Single Stroke What the Best Efforts of Diplomacy Failed Utterly to Bring About in Many Months." Hearst had sent Karl Decker, one of his most reliable correspondents, to Havana in late August with orders to rescue the Cuban Girl Martyr "at any hazard"; and Decker had climbed to the roof of a house near the prison, broken the bar of a window of the jail, lifted Evangelina out, and, after hiding her for a few days in Havana, smuggled her onto an American steamer. Decker, signing his dispatch to the *Journal* "Charles Duval," wrote: "I have broken the bars of Rocojidas and have set free the beautiful captive of monster Weyler. Weyler could blind the Queen to the real character of Evangelina, but he could not build a jail that would hold against *Journal* enterprise when properly set to work." The Cuban Girl Martyr was met at the pier by a great throng, led up Broadway in a triumphal procession, taken to a reception at Delmonico's where 120,000 people milled about the streets surrounding the restaurant, and hailed at a monster reception in Madison Square Garden. The Bishop of London cabled his congratulations to the *Journal*, while Governor Stephens of Missouri proposed that the *Journal* send down 500 of its reporters to free the entire island.

On October 23 Sagasta announced a "total change of immense scope" in Spanish policy in Cuba. He promised to grant local autonomy to the Cubans immediately, reserving justice, the armed forces, and foreign relations to Spain. On November 13 Weyler's successor, Captain-General Blanco, issued a decree modifying considerably the *reconcentrado* policy, and on November 25 the queen regent signed the edicts creating an autonomous government for the island. In essence, Madrid had acceded to the American demands.

While Woodford was conducting negotiations with a conciliatory Liberal government in Madrid and while there was still hope for peace, the fatal incident occurred which made war virtually inevitable. On January 12, 1898, a riot broke out in Havana, and Spanish officers attacked newspaper offices. The nature of the riot is still not clear; it was over in an hour, and it had no anti-American aspects. If the United States now sent a naval vessel to Havana, it might be buying trouble with Spain. Yet if a riot did break out and Americans were killed, the Administration would be stoned for not having a ship there to protect them. For several days McKinley wavered; then he ordered the *Maine* to Havana, but with the explanation that this was a courtesy visit demonstrating that so nonsensical were the rumors of danger to American citizens that our ships could again resume their visits to the island.

As the *Maine* lay at anchor in Havana Harbor, the rebels, with a perfect sense of timing, released a new propaganda bombshell. In December, 1897, in a private letter, Señor Enrique Dupuy de Lôme, the Spanish minister at Washington, had set down his opinions of President McKinley's annual message to Congress: "Besides the ingrained and inevitable bluntness (*grosería*) with which it repeated all that the press and public opinion in Spain have said about Weyler," De Lôme wrote, "it once more shows what McKinley is, weak and a bidder for the admiration of the crowd, besides being a would-be politician (*politicastro*) who tries to leave a door open behind himself while keeping on good terms with the jingoes of his party." De Lôme added: "It would be very advantageous to take up, even if only for effect, the question of commercial relations, and to have a man of some prominence sent here in order that I may make use of him to carry on a propaganda among the Senators and others in opposition to the junta."

De Lôme had, to be sure, written all this in a private letter (which was stolen by an insurgent spy in the Havana post office), not in his official capacity, and his characterization of McKinley was not wholly without merit, but it was a blunder of the highest magnitude. Not only had De Lôme attacked the President, but he had gone on to suggest that the negotiations then going on over a commercial treaty were not being conducted in good faith. Throughout the letter ran precisely the tone which Hearst had been arguing expressed the Spanish temper— a cold, arrogant contempt for democratic institutions. The State Department immediately cabled Woodford to demand the recall of the Spanish minister, but Madrid had the good fortune of being able to tell Woodford that De Lôme, informed of the disaster the night before, had already resigned.

A week after the publication of the De Lôme indiscretion, at 9:40 on the night of February 15, 1898, came the terrible blow which ended all real hope for peace. In the harbor of Havana, the *Maine* was blown up by an explosion of unknown origin. In an instant, the ship was filled with the sounds of shrieking men and rushing water. The blast occurred in the forward part of the ship where, a half hour before, most of the men had turned in for the night; they were killed in their hammocks. Of the 350 officers and men on board, 260 were killed. By morning the proud *Maine* had sunk into the mud of Havana Harbor.

"Public opinion should be suspended until further report," Captain Sigsbee cabled to Washington, but even Sigsbee could not down his suspicions. The *Maine* had gone to a Spanish possession on a courtesy call, and the *Maine* now lay at the bottom of Havana Harbor. What could it mean but war? "I would give anything if President McKinley would order the fleet to Havana tomorrow," wrote Theodore Roosevelt. "The *Maine* was sunk by an act of dirty treachery on the part of the Spaniards." Volunteers lined up for war service, even though there was no one to enlist them; in New York 500 sharpshooting Westchester businessmen volunteered as a unit for the colors. The *Journal* reported: "The Whole Country Thrills With War Fever."

The cause of the explosion of the *Maine* has never been finally established. That Spain deliberately decided to blow up the *Maine* is

On February 15, 1898, the battleship **Maine** *exploded;
with it went any chance for peace.*

inconceivable, although it is possible that it might have been the work
of unauthorized Spanish extremists. The one group which had everything to gain from such an episode was the rebels; yet it seems unlikely
that either they or Spanish hotheads could have carried out such an act
and remained undetected. The most likely explanation is that it was
caused by an explosion of internal origin; yet the evidence for this is
not conclusive. In any event, this was the explanation that the Navy in
1898 was least willing to consider since it would reflect seriously on
the care with which the Navy was operating the *Maine.*

The move toward war seemed relentless. On March 9 Congress
unanimously voted $50,000,000 for war preparations. Yet the days
went by and there was no war, in part because important sectors of
American opinion viewed Hearst's stories of the atrocious conditions
on the island with profound skepticism. Senator Redfield Proctor of
Vermont decided to launch his own investigation into conditions on
the island. On March 17, after a tour of Cuba, Proctor made one of the
most influential speeches in the history of the United States Senate.

Proctor, who Roosevelt reported was "very ardent for the war," had not generally been regarded as a jingo, and no man in the Senate commanded greater respect for personal integrity. Proctor declared that he had gone to Cuba skeptical of reports of suffering there, and he had come back convinced. "Torn from their homes, with foul earth, foul air, foul water, and foul food or none, what wonder that one-half have died and that one-quarter of the living are so diseased that they can not be saved?" Proctor asked. "Little children are still walking about with arms and chest terribly emaciated, eyes swollen, and abdomen bloated to three times the natural size. . . . I was told by one of our consuls that they have been found dead about the markets in the morning, where they had crawled, hoping to get some stray bits of food from the early hucksters."

The question of peace or war now lay with McKinley. The Spaniards, Woodford had conceded, had gone about as far as they could go; but with the *Maine* in the mud of Havana Harbor, with the country, following Proctor's speech, crying for war, how much longer could McKinley hold out? The jingoes were treating his attempt to preserve peace with outright contempt; McKinley, Roosevelt told his friends, "has no more backbone than a chocolate éclair."

"We will have this war for the freedom of Cuba," Roosevelt shouted at a Gridiron Dinner on March 26, shaking his fist at Senator Hanna, "in spite of the timidity of the commercial interests." Nor was McKinley permitted to forget the political consequences. The Chicago *Times-Herald* warned: "Intervention in Cuba, peacefully if we can, forcibly if we must, is immediately inevitable. Our own internal political conditions will not permit its postponement. . . . Let President McKinley hesitate to rise to the just expectations of the American people, and who can doubt that 'war for Cuban liberty' will be the crown of thorns the free silver Democrats and Populists will adopt at the elections this fall?"

On March 28 the President released the report of the naval court of inquiry on the *Maine* disaster. "In the opinion of the court the *Maine* was destroyed by the explosion of a submarine mine, which caused the partial explosion of two or more of the forward magazines," the report concluded. Although no one was singled out for blame, the conclusion was inescapable that if Spain had not willfully done it, Spain had failed to provide proper protection to a friendly vessel on a courtesy visit in its waters. Overnight a slogan with the ring of a child's street chant caught the fancy of the country:

Remember the Maine!
To hell with Spain!

"I have no more doubt than that I am now standing in the Senate of the United States," declared Henry Cabot Lodge, "that that ship was blown up by a government mine, fired by, or with the connivance of, Spanish officials."

Desiring peace yet afraid of its consequences, McKinley embarked on a policy of attempting to gain the fruits of war without fighting. On March 29 Woodford demanded that Spain agree to an immediate armistice, revoke the reconcentration order, and co-operate with the United States to provide relief; Spain was given 48 hours to reply. On March 31 Spain replied that it had finally revoked the reconcentration orders in the western provinces; that it had made available a credit of three million pesetas to resettle the natives; that it was willing to submit the *Maine* controversy to arbitration; and that it would grant a truce if the insurgents would ask for it. In short, Spain would yield everything we demanded, except that it would not concede defeat; the appeal for a truce would have to come from the rebels. Since the rebels would not make such an appeal, since they were confident of ultimate American intervention, the situation was hopeless; yet Spain had come a long way. Woodford cabled to Washington: "The ministry have gone as far as they dare go to-day. . . . No Spanish ministry would have dared to do one month ago what this ministry has proposed to-day."

For a week the Spaniards attempted to cling to their last shreds of dignity. On Saturday, April 9, Madrid surrendered. Driven to the wall by the American demands, the Spanish foreign minister informed Woodford that the government had decided to grant an armistice in Cuba immediately. Gratified at achieving the final concession, Woodford cabled McKinley: "I hope that nothing will now be done to humiliate Spain, as I am satisfied that the present Government is going, and is loyally ready to go, as fast and as far as it can."

It was too late. McKinley had decided on war. Spain had conceded everything, but Spain had waited too long. Up until the very last moment, Spanish officials had feared that if they yielded to American demands in Cuba, it might mean the overturn of the dynasty, and they preferred even a disastrous war to that. Proud but helpless in the face of American might, many Spanish officials appeared to prefer the dignity of being driven from the island in a heroic defensive war to meek surrender to an American ultimatum. In the end they surrendered and promised reforms. But they had promised reforms before— after the Ten Years' War which ended in 1878—and they had not kept these promises. Throughout the nineteenth century, constitutions had been made and remade, but nothing had changed. Even in the last hours of negotiations with the American minister, they had told Woodford that the President had asked the Pope to intervene, when the President had done nothing of the sort. Even if their intentions were of the best, could they carry them out? Spain had had three full years to end the war in Cuba and, with vastly superior numbers of troops,

had not been able to do it. And the insurgents would accept nothing
from Madrid, not even peace.

On Monday, April 11, McKinley sent his message to Congress,
declaring that "the forcible intervention of the United States as a
neutral to stop the war, according to the large dictates of humanity and
following many historical precedents" was "justifiable on rational
grounds." The fact that Spain had met everything we had asked was
buried in two paragraphs of a long plea for war. It took Congress a full
week to act. On Monday night, April 18, while the resolution shuttled
back and forth between the two chambers and the conference room,
congressmen sang "The Battle Hymn of the Republic" and "Dixie"
and shook the chamber with the refrain of "Hang General Weyler to
a Sour Apple Tree." At three o'clock the next morning the two houses
reached an agreement—the United States recognized the independence of Cuba, asserted that we would not acquire Cuba for ourselves,
and issued an ultimatum to Spain to withdraw within three days. On
April 20 President McKinley signed the resolution. War had come at
last. But not quite. Although hostilities had begun, not until four days
later did Congress declare war. When it did declare war, it dated it
from McKinley's action in establishing a blockade four days before. To
the very end, we protested our peaceful intentions as we stumbled
headlong into war.

We entered a war in which no vital American interest was involved,
and without any concept of its consequences. Although McKinley declared that to enter such a war for high purposes, and then annex
territory, would be "criminal aggression," we acquired as a result of
the war the Philippines and other parts of an overseas empire we had
not intended to get and had no idea how to defend. Although we
roundly attacked Spain for not recognizing the rebel government, we,
in our turn, refused to recognize the rebels. Although we were shocked
by Weyler's policies in Cuba, we were soon in the unhappy position
of using savage methods to put down a rebel uprising in the Philippines, employing violence in a measure that easily matched what Weyler had done.

It would be easy to condemn McKinley for not holding out against
war, but McKinley showed considerable courage in bucking the tide.
McKinley's personal sympathy for the Cubans was sincere; only after
his death was it revealed that he had contributed $5,000 anonymously
for Cuban relief. It would be even easier to blame it all on Hearst; yet
no newspaper can arouse a people that is not willing to be aroused.
At root lay the American gullibility about foreign affairs, with the
penchant for viewing politics in terms of a simple morality play; equally
important were the contempt of the American people for Spain as a

cruel but weak Latin nation and the desire for war and expansion which permeated the decade. The American people were not led into war; they got the war they wanted. "I think," observed Senator J. C. Spooner, "possibly the President could have worked out the business without war, but the current was too strong, the demagogues too numerous, the fall elections too near."

The Enemies of Empire

HAROLD A. LARRABEE

When the war with Spain ended, the United States found itself in control of Spain's Pacific and Caribbean colonies; what to do with them was the first problem the new proprietor had to confront. The controversy that developed over this issue in America was relatively brief—by 1900 it appeared to have been settled in favor of those who wanted to create an American empire. However, the basic issues raised in this debate have never been settled; the history of American foreign policy in the twentieth century is full of the repercussions and elaborations of the arguments of 1898–1900. To what extent, if any, should questions of national interest and honor take precedence over those of morality and the national interests of other peoples? What is "national honor"? Is colonialism always evil, no matter how administered or for what end?

Professor Harold A. Larrabee of Union College and author of Decision at the Chesapeake *describes the argument as it first developed between imperialists and anti-imperialists after the Spanish-American War. He takes a strong anti-imperialist position, and few today would disagree. That he is probably too favorable in his estimate of the anti-imperialists of that day—many of them, for example, opposed annexing colonies because they disliked bringing nonwhites under the American flag—detracts little from the value of his essay as a graphic re-creation of the mood of the times. Larrabee provides fascinating glimpses into the minds of the anti-imperialists, the defenders of expansionism, and those many sincere but somewhat befuddled citizens who, like President McKinley, had great trouble deciding between these two positions.* ∎

We know, to the hour and minute, when this country reached the point of no return on its way to becoming a world power. It was at exactly 5:39 A.M., Manila time, on Sunday, May 1, 1898, when Commodore George Dewey, U.S.N., commanding the Asiatic Squadron of four small cruisers and two gunboats, coolly turned from his position on the bridge of his flagship *Olympia*, and said to its captain in words that were to echo across distant America: "You may fire when you are ready, Gridley." The command loosed salvos of shells that swiftly crushed the decrepit fleet of the Spanish Admiral Montojo (two cruisers and seven small gunboats of an antiquated type), which had been huddling under the defenses of Manila. The battle was, in the words of the English historian Herbert W. Wilson, "a military execution rather than a real contest."

Its effects on American foreign policy, however, were incalculable, and the end is not yet. Hawaii was swiftly annexed as a territory on July 7, 1898; and by the ratification of the Treaty of Paris ending the war on February 6, 1899, we found ourselves the sovereign rulers of all the Spanish colonial possessions in the Philippines, there to remain for the next forty-seven years. The Pacific Ocean was thenceforth to be regarded as "an American lake." What we now often forget, however, is how many Americans were in those early days opposed to the idea of an American Empire. Sixty years ago imperialism, then defined as the raising of the flag by force over noncontiguous territory, and called by its friends "expansionism," was the burning issue of the day. It was bitterly contested, largely on abstract moral grounds as a gross betrayal of American principles, by a small but tenacious band of New England reformers.

The hard core of the anti-imperialist movement, both at the start and at the finish, was composed of conservative Boston lawyers and bankers, many of them lineal descendants of the Pilgrims. They soon gathered about them a remarkable nationwide galaxy of literary lights, college presidents, leaders of industry and labor, editors, and politicians, constituting what has been called "the first great national propaganda organization of the twentieth century." Their achievements were greater in the vigorous expression of their views than in practical politics. Yet they lost one of their major battles in the Senate by only one vote; for a time they threatened to endanger McKinley's re-election in 1900; and there can be no doubt that their tireless needling of the American conscience about colonialism, which continued until 1920, hastened the eventual independence of the Philippines.

Crusades being somewhat out of fashion nowadays, it may be difficult to recover the fervor of these heirs of Wendell Phillips and Charles Sumner as they denounced the extension of American rule by force in the Philippines, not because of what it might do to the Filipinos, but

In Rufus Zogbaum's canvas, Commodore George Dewey directs the American victory at the Battle of Manila Bay from the bridge of the Olympia.

because of what they were convinced it was bound to do to American democratic ideals. They saw in the American seizure and retention of the Islands "the infamy of the doctrine that a people may be governed without their consent." At least some of the Filipinos, under Emilio Aguinaldo, were not "consenting" to their "pacification" by our troops. A spineless administration in Washington, too much influenced by a group of jingoes in high places and by the yellow press, had liberated the Islanders from Spain only to try to enslave them again. This was rank apostasy from our professed principles in the Declaration of Independence and the Gettysburg Address. Could it be that Aguinaldo was fighting for *our* principles, while we had succumbed to the evil colonial policy of defeated Spain?

The expansionists' reply to this plea for democracy was the twin slogan: duty and destiny. It was, they said, the moral and religious duty of a civilized nation to accept the white man's burden, imposed upon us, in this instance, by our own idealistic crusade to free the Spanish possessions from centuries of misrule. As a moral aristocrat among nations, blessed with so many special advantages, America must, as a matter of *noblesse oblige,* undertake a self-sacrificing mission of political education in a world of backward peoples. In the words of the archexpansionist Theodore Roosevelt: "Peace cannot be had until the civi-

lized nations have expanded in some shape over the barbarous nations." And besides, such expansion was inevitable. What John Hay
called "cosmic tendency" and others invoked as Manifest Destiny (now
enlarged to a global scale) was irresistibly impelling the onward march
of the white men who spoke what Sir Cecil Spring-Rice called "God's
language." Richard Croker, the boss of Tammany, remarked that "My
idea of anti-imperialism is opposition to the fashion of shooting everybody who doesn't speak English."

What intensified and prolonged the conflict was the fact that both
sides professed to want liberty for the Filipinos: the anti-imperialists
believed that for us, as democrats, to deny them *immediate* liberty was
to stultify our own ideals; while the expansionists maintained that the
hopelessly backward Islanders were to be granted *eventual* liberty after
a sufficient but indefinite period of Yankee tutelage. On both sides,
then, there was an appeal to conscience by sincere but profoundly
ignorant American patriots who found themselves enmeshed in the
toils and tangles of historical circumstances, including domestic party
politics. Since a moral issue was involved, the other side was not only
wrong, but wicked, and words like "blood lust" and "murderer" were
hurled at the imperialists, while the antis were denounced as "cowards" and "traitors." Nothing stirs the American people so deeply as
a controversy in which both parties claim to be morally right: witness
the battles over slavery, woman suffrage, and prohibition. In our day,
"imperialism" has become a term battered almost beyond recognition
in the cold war. But the central issue of 1898–1902—what constitutes
the consent of the governed, and who is qualified to give it—has never
been more alive than today, as one former colonial possession after
another struggles toward a precariously independent nationhood.

"You have a wolf by the ears in the Philippines. You cannot let go
of him with either dignity or safety, and he will not be easy to tame,"
said an anonymous American diplomat to one of our peace commissioners who was leaving for Paris in the fall of 1898. Even some of the
expansionists themselves deplored our grip on the wolf in the first
place, but were nevertheless extremely reluctant to let go. This was at
once the strength and the weakness of the anti-imperialists' case. The
imperialists had to admit, in the words of one of their leaders, Ambassador Whitelaw Reid, that "it was perfectly true that the American
people did not wish for more territory, and never dreamed of distant
colonies." Yet the grip on the wolf was an accomplished fact, and the
practical difficulty of letting go with dignity and safety was the fatal flaw
in the position into which the anti-imperialists found themselves ma-
neuvered.

The clinching argument of the imperialists was "where once the
flag goes up, it must never come down." The crucial decisions that sent

Dewey to Manila in the first place, and ordered troops to his support as early as May 4, even before the news of his victory had reached Washington, were the work of a small elite group in the Republican administration who had managed to convert a pliable President. In 1897, McKinley had told Carl Schurz, "Ah, you may be sure there will be no jingo nonsense under my administration." But there was some truth in the popular conundrum: "Why is McKinley's mind like an unmade bed? Answer: Because it has to be made up for him every time he wants to use it." Theodore Roosevelt's friend Henry Adams spoke of his "alarm and horror of seeing poor weak McKinley, in gaiety . . . plunge into an inevitable war to conquer the Philippines contrary to every profession or so-called principle of our lives and history."

The ringleaders in the open conspiracy to move into the Orient via Hawaii and an isthmian canal, without ever consulting the American people, were two ardent disciples of Captain Alfred Thayer Mahan, U.S.N., the author of *The Influence of Sea Power Upon History, 1660–1783,* namely—Senator Henry Cabot Lodge of Massachusetts and the young and aggressive Assistant Secretary of the Navy, Theodore Roosevelt. It is one of the ironies of history that Captain Mahan himself was an anti-imperialist until the year 1885, and for precisely the reason most often advanced against his later followers: empire "would destroy free government." By 1890, however, a study of British sea power had converted him to the belief that the United States could take "a larger part in external affairs without risk to their institutions and with benefit to the world at large." Theodore Roosevelt, then a civil service commissioner, devoured Mahan's book, and reviewed it with enthusiasm in the *Atlantic Monthly,* later proclaiming Mahan "the only great naval expert who also possessed in international matters the mind of a statesman of the first rank."

Mahan's advice to Roosevelt in May, 1897, was: "Do nothing unrighteous; but take the [Hawaiian] islands first, and solve afterwards." The Roosevelt of 1898, described by William James as "still mentally in the *Sturm und Drang* period of early adolescence," needed little urging. He had been frustrated by President Cleveland's blocking of the annexation of Hawaii, but with the advent of a Republican administration his hopes were high. He was, however, soon indignant over the hesitancy of President McKinley, who, he said, "has no more backbone than a chocolate éclair." Behind McKinley stirred the powerful boss Mark Hanna, senator from Ohio, who flatly opposed the coming Spanish war at a Gridiron dinner on March 26, 1898, less than three weeks before it was declared. Introduced by the toastmaster at the same dinner as "At least one man connected with this administration who is not afraid to fight," Theodore Roosevelt, by that time in the Navy

Department, declared: "We will have this war for the freedom of Cuba, Senator Hanna, in spite of the timidity of commercial interests." As William James put it, "Roosevelt gushes over war as the ideal condition of human society, for the manly strenuousness which it involves, and treats peace as a condition of blubberlike and swollen ignobility, fit only for huckstering weaklings, dwelling in gray twilight and heedless of the higher life. . . . One foe is as good as another, for aught he tells us."

Roosevelt's superior, Secretary John D. Long, seems to have had few inklings of what was to come, and "every time his back was turned," says David S. Barry, "Roosevelt would issue some kind of order in the line of military preparedness. . . ." On February 25, 1898, Long went home early, and as Acting Secretary of the Navy for a few hours, Roosevelt proceeded to sent his momentous cable to Dewey in Hong Kong specifying "offensive operations in the Philipine [*sic*] islands." Next morning Long found that "in his precipitate way," his assistant had "come very near causing more of an explosion than happened to the *Maine* . . . He has gone at things like a bull in a china shop." Roosevelt was never again left in charge of the Navy Department for even part of a day, but his order to Dewey was not rescinded. Long seems to have thought he was dealing merely with a young subordinate who was unduly impetuous, rather than with the representative of a coterie with an elaborate imperialist philosophy and the determination to do something about it. Roosevelt was showing what a man of daring with a plan, influential associates, amenable superiors, and a little brief authority could do in the making of American foreign policy.

That the American people were unprepared for the new possessions supposedly "flung into their arms by Dewey's guns" is a gross understatement of the facts. McKinley freely confessed that, before consulting a globe, he could not have told "within two thousand miles" where the Philippines were. Incredible as it may seem to us, Dewey's staff did not include a public relations officer, and the presence of two newspapermen on board the revenue cutter *McCulloch* was a pure accident.

The public's state of bewilderment, after the first delirious celebrations of Dewey's bloodless victory had subsided, was best expressed by Finley Peter Dunne, editor of the Chicago *Journal,* whose Mr. Dooley conversed with his friend Mr. Hennessy "On the Philippines."

"I know what I'd do if I was Mack," said Mr. Hennessy, "I'd hist a flag over th' Ph'lipeens, an' I'd take in th' whole lot iv thim."

"An' yet," said Mr. Dooley, " 'tis not more thin two months since ye larned whether they were islands or canned goods . . . If yer son Packy was to ask ye where th' Ph'lipeens is, cud ye give him anny good idea whether they was in Rooshia or jus' west iv th' thracks?"

"Mebbe I cudden't," said Mr. Hennessy, haughtily, "but I'm f'r taking thim in, annyhow."

Not everyone in the country, however, went along with the bulk of the press and the expansionist-led administration. One month and one day after Dewey's triumph, the first recorded protest was made against "the insane and wicked ambition which is driving this country to ruin . . . and a slavery worse for Massachusetts, at least, than that of the Negro." It came in the form, classically correct for a proper Bostonian, of a letter to the editor of the *Evening Transcript* of June 2, 1898, entitled "A Cry for Help." It was written by Gamaliel Bradford, father of the well-known biographer. He was a seventh-generation descendant of Governor William Bradford of Plymouth, a retired banker, a Republican mugwump (he had deserted Blaine for Cleveland in 1884), and the author of several thousand letters to the newspapers in behalf of various reforms. His offer to join with any others who would help him in securing Boston's traditional Cradle of Liberty, Faneuil Hall, resulted in the first public meeting "to protest against the adoption of a so-called imperial policy by the United States."

Bradford was soon joined by another Pilgrim descendant, Erving Winslow, who was to prove the most undiscourageable of all the anti-imperialists, and by the able Boston lawyer Moorfield Storey, who was to become the acknowledged long-time champion of the movement. Presiding at the June 15 meeting that he had convened, Bradford took good care to say that its purpose was not to oppose "the vigorous prosecution of the war," but rather to check "the rush of reckless and unbridled ambition for dominion" evident in "a certain faction in Congress," which might turn "a war of liberation into a war of conquest." Storey laid down what was to be the most enduring plank in the anti-imperialist platform when he declared: "When Rome began her career of conquest, the Roman Republic began to decline . . . Let us once govern any considerable body of men without their consent, and it is a question of time how soon this republic shares the fate of Rome." The *Evening Transcript* spoke of the meeting as "a solemn warning against surrendering to the madness of the hour"; but Lodge depicted it to Roosevelt (en route to Cuba with his Rough Riders) as "a very comic incident."

The strange mixture of popular war hysteria, whipped up for their own purposes by Joseph Pulitzer of the *World* and William Randolph Hearst of the *Journal,* and the as-yet-unshaken confidence of many intellectuals in the pacific intentions of McKinley was vividly portrayed and analyzed by the philosopher William James in a letter written to his French friend François Pillon, just before James left his house in Cambridge to attend the Faneuil Hall meeting:

> A curious episode of history, showing how a nation's ideals can be changed in the twinkling of an eye, by a succession of outward events partly accidental. It is quite possible that, without the explosion of the *Maine,* we should still be at peace . . . The actual declaration of war by Congress, however, was a case of *psychologie des foules,* a genuine hysteric stampede at the last moment . . . Our Executive has behaved very well. The European nations of the Continent cannot believe that our pretense of humanity, and our disclaiming of all ideas of conquest, is sincere. It has been *absolutely* sincere! The self-conscious feeling of our people has been entirely based in a sense of philanthropic duty . . . But here comes in the psychologic factor: once the excitement of action gets loose, the taxes levied, the victories achieved, etc., the old human instincts will get into play with all their old strength, and the ambition and sense of mastery which our nation has will set up new demands. We shall never take Cuba . . . But Porto Rico, and even the Philippines, are not so sure. We had supposed ourselves (with all our crudity and barbarity in certain ways) a better nation morally than the rest, safe at home, and without the old savage ambition, destined to exert great international influence by throwing in our "moral weight," etc. Dreams! Human Nature is everywhere the same, and at the least temptation all the old military passions rise, and sweep everything before them . . . It all shows by what short steps progress is made . . .

It soon became evident that William James had not overestimated the immense task facing the small band of anti-imperialists: no less than the complete reversal of public opinion in the face of easy victories, promised spoils, and a flag-waving press. For one thing, during the summer of 1898, history was being made at a furious pace. Whether one accepts the John Hay version, "a splendid little war," or "a jolly war," or the London *Saturday Review*'s estimate, "never a more shabby war," it was decidedly a short one. In less than four months it was all over but the disposition of "the waifs of the world deposited on our doorsteps." At a foreign policy conference at Saratoga Springs, New York, on August 18, 1898, just five days after the armistice, Carl Schurz, who had embarked upon a one-man crusade to impress McKinley, delivered a vigorous anti-imperialist address in which, ironically, he used against Senator Lodge and his fellow expansionists "the very principles which Lodge was to exalt so extravagantly twenty years later in the fight against the Covenant of the League of Nations." A delegation from the Sarotoga conference, with Samuel Gompers as one of its members, waited upon McKinley but was received only with suave hospitality.

To the public in the fall of 1898 the President offered the image of a sorely tried pacifist in doubt about the propriety of retaining the

In this cartoon from Frank Leslie's Official History of the Spanish-American War, *captioned "Better rags with honor than patches with dishonor," Uncle Sam peers angrily over his shoulder at patches showing the* Maine *exploding and Spanish soldiers blowing off the heads of members of the* Virginius' *crew.*

Philippines, even speculating that "if old Dewey had just sailed away after he had smashed the Spanish fleet, what a lot of trouble he would have saved us." But his every action was in line with what Lodge called "our large policy" of complete possession. McKinley packed the peace commission virtually four-to-one in favor of expansionism (three of them senators who would later have to vote on their own work), and gave them ever more sweeping instructions about what was to be demanded of the Spaniards, even though his Cabinet was divided on the issue. How he arrived at his final decision to tell the peace commission to demand "the whole archipelago or none" was told by the President himself on November 21, 1899, to a committee representing the General Missionary Committee of the Methodist Episcopal Church, then in session in Washington. Surely it is one of the most amazing descriptions of the workings of a Chief Executive's conscience in the field of foreign policy that has ever been recorded.

The delegation was about to leave the White House, when McKinley turned to them, and said earnestly:

Hold a moment longer! Not quite yet, gentlemen! Before you go I would like to say just a word about the Philippine business. I have been criticized a good deal about the Philippines, but don't deserve it. The truth is I didn't want the Philippines, and when they came to us, as a gift from the gods, I did not know what to do with them. . . . I sought counsel from all sides—Democrats as well as Republicans—but got little help. I thought first we would take only Manila; then Luzon; then other islands, perhaps, also. I walked the floor of the White House night after night until midnight; and I am not ashamed to tell you, gentlemen, that I went down on my knees and prayed Almighty God for light and guidance more than one night. And one night late it came to me this way—I don't know how it was, but it came: (1) That we could not give them back to Spain—that would be cowardly and dishonorable; (2) that we could not turn them over to France or Germany—our commercial rivals in the Orient—that would be bad business and discreditable; (3) that we could not leave them to themselves—they were unfit for self-government—and they would soon have anarchy and misrule over there worse than Spain's was; and (4) that there was nothing left for us to do but take them all, and to educate the Filipinos, and uplift and civilize and Christianize them, and by God's grace do the very best we could by them, as our fellow men for whom Christ also died. And then I went to bed, and went to sleep, and slept soundly, and the next morning I sent for the chief engineer of the War Department (our map-maker), and I told him to put the Philippines on the map of the United States [pointing to a large map on the wall of his office], and there they are, and there they will stay while I am President!

The anti-imperialists' first battle, for the mind of the President as the chief architect of the nation's foreign policy, was thus lost to higher authority before it had hardly begun. But the country might still be persuaded to reject McKinley's Philippine policy. On November 19, 1898, in the Boston office of Edward Atkinson, retired textile manufacturer—later to become notorious because of the Postmaster General's closing of the mails to his publications—the Anti-Imperialist League was organized. Its object was: "to oppose, by every legitimate means, the acquisition of the Philippine Islands, or of any colonies away from our shores, by the United States."

The only thing more remarkable than the high quality of the League's adherents was their extreme diversity. As its perpetual secretary, Erving Winslow, remarked: "We must in our organization stand shoulder to shoulder: Republican, Democrat, Socialist, Populist, Gold-Man, Silver-Man, and Mugwump, for the one momentous, vital, paramount issue, Anti-Imperialism and the preservation of the Republic." Such advice, however, was not always easy to follow, since the anti-imperialist leader in the Senate, George F. Hoar, regular Republican, had once called the Mugwumps "the vilest set of political assassins that ever disgraced this or any other country."

Besides every shade in the country's political spectrum, the League's ever-lengthening list of vice presidents, many of whom lent only their names to the movement, included every variety of American reformer: municipal, civil service, social welfare, single-taxer, free-trader, pacifist, and prohibitionist. Education furnished a long list of college presidents: Eliot, Jordan, Rogers, Alderman, Stanley Hall, Schurman, King, and Faunce, with such distinguished teachers as Charles Eliot Norton, George Herbert Palmer, William Graham Sumner, Felix Adler, William James, John Dewey, and Franklin H. Giddings. From industry and finance came the extremely active donor Andrew Carnegie, and Richard T. Crane and George Foster Peabody. The contribution of "interest" groups (beet sugar and tobacco), which wanted no Philippine competition, was remarkably small.

At the peak of the League's activities in 1899, it claimed thirty thousand members and "half a million contributors" in branches located in a dozen large cities from Boston to Portland, Oregon. One of its conferences, in Chicago on October 17–18, 1899, attracted ten thousand delegates; and by 1900 the League claimed to have distributed four hundred thousand pieces of literature. This spreading of its work enhanced its prestige, no doubt, but it proved to be a handicap in exerting political influence. For what leader could be found who could win and keep the confidence of quite so many kinds of followers?

The first political battle fought by the anti-imperialists was the one in which they came the closest to victory: the heated conflict over the ratification of the treaty of peace with Spain in January and February, 1899. The only controversial section in the document was the article providing for the cession of the whole Philippine archipelago to the United States. As Peace Commissioner Whitelaw Reid put it: he and his associates were accused of "overdoing the business, looking after the interests of the country too thoroughly . . ." Since a two-thirds vote was required for ratification in a Senate composed of forty-six Republicans, thirty-four Democrats, and ten members of minor parties, it was evident that a substantial number of Democratic senators would have to be won over.

Fresh from his discharge from the Army, William Jennings Bryan announced in an interview at Savannah, Georgia, on December 13, 1898, that although he was firmly anti-imperialist, he believed that the treaty should be ratified and the issue of imperialism settled by resolution at a later date. The less politically minded anti-imperialists (Carnegie, Schurz, and Storey) regarded this as a sacrifice of principle in order to secure a campaign issue to go along with free silver (which they detested) in the election of 1900. Ten Democratic senators helped to ratify the treaty by only one vote more than the necessary two thirds, and although two or three of them may have been swayed by the outbreak of fighting, two days earlier, between Filipino and American soldiers, Bryan has generally been credited with influencing the key votes. Many senators were undoubtedly influenced by Lodge's argument that failure to ratify would be a repudiation of McKinley and a continuation of the war. If there could have been a clear-cut decision regarding the retention of the Philippines, "the imperialists," says the diplomatic historian Thomas A. Bailey, "would almost certainly have failed to obtain a two-thirds majority." A few days later the Bacon amendment, pledging ultimate independence to the Filipinos, resulted in a tie vote, decided in the negative by the vote of Vice President Garret A. Hobart.

Despite this setback, the movement grew, rather than declined, as the 1900 election approached, although Bryan had created an amount of distrust in the minds of the "true" anti-imperialists, which led to talk of a third-party ticket designed to split the McKinley vote. Bryan agreed to make anti-imperialism "the paramount issue" of his campaign, and was finally endorsed by the League's Liberty Congress in Indianapolis in August, 1900. But many of the anti-imperialists refused to stomach Bryan's continued insistence upon free silver, and either voted for McKinley or held aloof from both candidates. Bryan secured fewer votes in 1900 than in 1896, and his defeat "marked the end of anti-imperialism as an important factor in American politics."

Political failure did not prevent literary success for the cause, although most of the blows struck by the pen came too late to turn the tide of public opinion. The one man whose emotional response to imperialism became enduring literature was the poet William Vaughn Moody. He risked his position as teacher of English at the University of Chicago by publishing several anti-imperialist poems in the *Atlantic Monthly*. In contrast to its noble sacrifices in the Civil War, Moody saw his country engaged in "ignoble battle," but protested:

> *We have not sold our loftiest heritage*
> *The proud republic hath not stooped to cheat and scramble in the market*
>   *place of war . . .*
> *That so our hand with better ease*
> *May wield the driver's whip and grasp the jailer's keys.*

Warning the country's leaders to "tempt not our weakness, our cupidity," the poet declares that "save we let the island men go free," our soldiers will have died in vain. In a shorter poem entitled "On a Soldier Fallen in the Philippines," (*Atlantic Monthly*, February, 1901), Moody makes use of the poignant contradiction between the honor due to the fallen and the dishonor of his cause:

Toll! Let him never guess
What work we set him to . . .
Let him never dream that his bullet's scream went wide of its island
*   mark,*
Home to the heart of his darling land where she stumbled and sinned in
*   the dark.*

Moody's language was mild and temperate compared with that of his fellow Chicagoan, the novelist Henry Blake Fuller, who became convinced that McKinley's policies were not only ignorant and stupid but actually vicious. Fuller addressed the President:

Thou sweating chattel slave to swine!
Who dost befoul the holy shrine
Of liberty with murder! . . .

A much saner poetic approach was that of Ernest Crosby, president of the New York branch of the movement, whose Whitmanesque lines ran:

There is only one possession worth the capturing, and that is the hearts of
*   men;*
And these hearts can never be won by a nation of slaves.
Be free, and all mankind will flock to your standard.

Mark Twain was one literary figure who was won over from the opposition, in part by the urging of his friend William Dean Howells. "I left these shores at Vancouver [on his way to Vienna]," he wrote, "a red-hot imperialist. I wanted the American eagle to go screaming into the Pacific. It seemed tiresome and tame for it to content itself with the Rockies. Why not spread its wings over the Philippines, I asked myself? And I thought it would be a real good thing to do." But gradually Twain began to see the Philippines in a different light, for early in 1900 he wrote to Joseph Twichell: "Apparently we are not proposing to set the Filipinos free and give their islands to them . . . If these things are so, the war out there has no interest for me." From the day of Twain's triumphant return to this country in October, 1900, he joined forces with Howells in a steady barrage of articles, interviews, petitions, and pamphlets in behalf of anti-imperialism. The League made extensive use on cards of his "salutation-speech from the Nineteenth Century to the Twentieth," in which he said:

I bring you the stately matron named Christendom, returning bedraggled, besmirched, and dishonored from pirate-raids in Kiao-Chou, Manchuria, South Africa, & the Philippines, with her soul full of meanness, her pocket full of boodle and her mouth full of pious hypocrisies. Give her soap and a towel, but hide the looking glass.

In this 1899 cartoon from
Puck, *E. L. Godkin, William
Jennings Bryan, and other
anti-imperialists are pictured
defiling the favorable image
that imperial adventures had
won for the United States.*

At a welcoming dinner for the young English war correspondent Winston Spencer Churchill in the Waldorf-Astoria Hotel on December 13, 1900, Mark Twain introduced the half-English, half-American speaker with these words: "I think that England sinned when she got herself into a war in South Africa which she could have avoided, just as we have sinned in getting into a similar war in the Philippines . . . yes, we are kin. And now that we are also kin in sin, there is nothing more to be desired. The harmony is complete, the blend is perfect—like Mr. Churchill himself, whom I now have the honor to present to you."

One of the most effective presentations of the case for anti-imperialism was made by the peppery Yale sociologist William Graham Sumner under the striking title, "The Conquest of the United States by Spain," but it was buried in the *Yale Law Journal* for January, 1899. Logic in terms of political theory, however, proved a poor match for the logic of events. Professor Richard Hofstadter has acutely observed that the Spanish-American War was fought because the American people wanted "not so much the freedom of Cuba as a *war* for the freedom of Cuba." Once war was under way, in the opinion of the late Vice

President Charles G. Dawes, who was a close McKinley associate, "the
retention of the Philippines was inevitable. . . . No man, or no party,
could have prevented it." Yet in the sober judgment of Samuel Flagg
Bemis, "looking back on those years of adolescent irresponsibility, we
can now see the acquisition of the Philippines, the climax of American
expansion, as a great national aberration."

But it was in vain that the anti-imperialists of that era cited the
words of Abraham Lincoln: "No man is good enough to govern another without that other's consent." The missing premise in the arguments of both sides was the lack of adequate knowledge of the Filipinos
and their capacity for solving their immediate political problems. The
anti-imperialists saw them as ready and able to govern themselves
democratically; the imperialists were just as convinced that they were
mostly untutored barbarians. Neither side had enough facts, and as a
result both substituted passion for logic.

The anti-imperialists saw the whole problem as a simple matter of
political morality, which could never be settled until settled "right."
By their indefatigable agitating they administered such a shock to
sensitive American consciences that the burden of guilt could not be
lifted. In time it came to be assumed that the pledge of Philippine
independence defeated by a single vote in 1899 had, morally speaking,
been given.

What the imperialists, notably Theodore Roosevelt, could never
grasp was the Filipinos' yearning for *self*-government. Both sides en-
tertained illusions: the imperialists saw a mirage of untold wealth in
trade with the Orient, which did not materialize; the anti-imperialists
foresaw "tyranny at home" as the sure result of "tyranny abroad." The
latter were also incorrect in their belief that their opponents would
never "let go" of the archipelago, although it was not until 1935 that
the Commonwealth was established, with complete independence promised in 1946. The promise was kept, and the Philippines became "the
first colony ever to be surrendered voluntarily."

The annual reports of the Anti-Imperialist League, which continued until its nineteenth and last meeting in 1917, make melancholy
reading as the necrology lengthened and the budgets shrank. Treasurer Greene declared doggedly: "Anti-Imperialists are not quitters";
but when Erving Winslow died in 1923, Moorfield Storey wrote: "Almost everybody who belonged to the League is dead, and the young
men do not take up the work. I am still its representative, but I have
no followers."

One of the striking characteristics of the League in its heyday was
the lack of contact between its zealous leaders in America and the
Filipinos in whose behalf they were enduring a steady rain of epithets:

little Americans, seditionists, cowards, and traitors. But the Filipinos had subtle ways of showing their appreciation. Long before they were allowed the privilege of self-government, they named the square directly in front of the Malacañang Palace in Manila, the official residence of the American Governor General, *La Liga Anti-Imperialistica.*

Woodrow Wilson and the League of Nations

THOMAS A. BAILEY

Woodrow Wilson was surely one of the most paradoxical figures in American history. He was both a great idealist and a shrewd practical politician; a man capable of enormous achievements yet physically delicate; one who concealed hot emotional fires beneath an icy exterior; a brilliant public orator but a man who could seldom persuade or inspire other individuals in private confrontations.

In this essay Thomas A. Bailey, professor emeritus of history at Stanford University, analyzes the role played by Wilson's complex personality in the great tragedy that closed his brilliant career—the defeat of his plan to enroll the United States in the League of Nations. That Wilson's personal qualities had a great deal to do with the Senate's rejection of the League goes without saying. However, as Bailey makes clear, forces far larger than those exerted by any man were also involved. Thus his discussion serves as a case study of the interaction of great men with their times. It is one of Bailey's strengths as a historian that he is able to describe the difficult and tangled events of 1918–1920 briefly and simply without doing violence to truth and to carry the narrative of events along swiftly and smoothly at the same time that he is focusing the attention of the reader on the personal qualities of Wilson and the other principal actors in the drama.

Among Professor Bailey's many books are Woodrow Wilson and the Lost Peace, Woodrow Wilson and the Great Betrayal, Presidential Greatness, *and two popular textbooks,* A Diplomatic History of the American People, *and* The American Pageant. ∎

The story of America's rejection of the League of Nations revolves largely around the personality and character of Thomas Woodrow Wilson, the twenty-eighth President of the United States. Born in Virginia and reared in Yankee-gutted Georgia and the Carolinas, Wilson early developed a burning hatred of war and a passionate attachment to the Confederate-embraced principle of self-determination for minority peoples. From the writings of Thomas Jefferson he derived much of his democratic idealism and his invincible faith in the judgment of the masses, if properly informed. From his stiff-backed Scotch-Presbyterian forebears, he inherited a high degree of inflexibility; from his father, a dedicated Presbyterian minister, he learned a stern moral code that would tolerate no compromise with wrong, as defined by Woodrow Wilson.

As a leading academician who had first failed at law, he betrayed a contempt for "money-grubbing" lawyers, many of whom sat in the Senate, and an arrogance toward lesser intellects, including those of the "pygmy-minded" senators. As a devout Christian keenly aware of the wickedness of this world, he emerged as a fighting reformer, whether as president of Princeton, governor of New Jersey, or President of the United States.

As a war leader, Wilson was superb. Holding aloft the torch of idealism in one hand and the flaming sword of righteousness in the other, he aroused the masses to a holy crusade. We would fight a war to end wars; we would make the world safe for democracy. The phrase was not a mockery then. The American people, with an amazing display of self-sacrifice, supported the war effort unswervingly.

The noblest expression of Wilson's idealism was his Fourteen Points address to Congress in January, 1918. It compressed his war aims into punchy, placard-like paragraphs, expressly designed for propaganda purposes. It appealed tremendously to oppressed peoples everywhere by promising such goals as the end of secret treaties, freedom of the seas, the removal of economic barriers, a reduction of arms burdens, a fair adjustment of colonial claims, and self-determination for oppressed minorities. In Poland university men would meet on the streets of Warsaw, clasp hands, and soulfully utter one word, "Wilson." In remote regions of Italy peasants burned candles before poster portraits of the mighty new prophet arisen in the West.

The fourteenth and capstone point was a league of nations, designed to avert future wars. The basic idea was not original with Wilson; numerous thinkers, including Frenchmen and Britons, had been working on the concept long before he embraced it. Even Henry Cabot Lodge, the Republican senator from Massachusetts, had already spoken publicly in favor of *a* league of nations. But the more he heard about the Wilsonian League of Nations, the more critical of it he became.

A knowledge of the Wilson-Lodge feud is basic to an understanding of the tragedy that unfolded. Tall, slender, aristocratically bewhiskered, Dr. Henry Cabot Lodge (Ph.D., Harvard), had published a number of books and had been known as the scholar in politics before the appearance of Dr. Woodrow Wilson (Ph.D., Johns Hopkins). The Presbyterian professor had gone further in both scholarship and politics than the Boston Brahmin, whose mind was once described as resembling the soil of his native New England: "naturally barren but highly cultivated." Wilson and Lodge, two icy men, developed a mutual antipathy, which soon turned into freezing hatred.

The German armies, reeling under the blows of the Allies, were ready to give in by November, 1918. The formal armistice terms stipulated that Germany was to be guaranteed a peace based on the Fourteen Points, with two reservations concerning freedom of the seas and reparations.

Meanwhile the American people had keyed themselves up to the long-awaited march on Berlin; eager voices clamored to hang the Kaiser. Thus the sudden end of the shooting left inflamed patriots with a sense of frustration and letdown that boded ill for Wilson's policies. The red-faced Theodore Roosevelt, Lodge's intimate of long standing, cried that peace should be dictated by the chatter of machine guns and not the clicking of typewriters.

Wilson now towered at the dizzy pinnacle of his popularity and power. He had emerged as the moral arbiter of the world and the hope of all peoples for a better tomorrow. But regrettably his wartime sureness of touch began to desert him, and he made a series of costly fumbles. He was so preoccupied with reordering the world, someone has said, that he reminded one of the baseball player who knocks the ball into the bleachers and then forgets to touch home plate.

First came his brutally direct appeal for a Democratic Congress in October, 1918. The voters trooped to the polls the next month and, by a narrow margin, returned a Republican Congress. Wilson had not only goaded his partisan foes to fresh outbursts of fury, but he had unnecessarily staked his prestige on the outcome—and lost. When the Allied leaders met at the Paris peace table, he was the only one not entitled to be there, at least on the European basis of a parliamentary majority.

Wilson next announced that he was sailing for France, presumably to use his still enormous prestige to fashion an enduring peace. At this time no President had ever gone abroad, and Republicans condemned the decision as evidence of a dangerous Messiah complex—of a desire, as former President Taft put it, "to hog the whole show."

Woodrow Wilson acknowledging a cheering crowd at the Waldorf-Astoria in New York.

The naming of the remaining five men to the peace delegation caused partisans further anguish. Only one, Henry White, was a Republican, and he was a minor figure at that. The Republicans, now the majority party, complained that they had been good enough to die on the battlefield; they ought to have at least an equal voice at the peace table. Nor were any United States senators included, even though they would have a final whack at the treaty. Wilson did not have much respect for the "bungalow-minded" senators, and if he took one, the logical choice would be Henry Cabot Lodge. There were already enough feuds brewing at Paris without taking one along.

Doubtless some of the Big Business Republicans were out to "get" the President who had been responsible for the hated reformist legislation of 1913–14. If he managed to put over the League of Nations, his prestige would soar to new heights. He might even arrange—unspeakable thought!—to be elected again and again and again. Much of the partisan smog that finally suffocated the League would have been cleared away if Wilson had publicly declared, as he was urged to do, that in no circumstances would he run again. But he spurned such counsel, partly because he was actually receptive to the idea of a third term.

The American President, hysterically hailed by European crowds as "Voovro Veelson," came to the Paris peace table in January, 1919, to meet with Lloyd George of Britain, Clemenceau of France, and Orlando of Italy. To his dismay, he soon discovered that they were far more interested in imperialism than in idealism. When they sought to carve up the territorial booty without regard for the colonials, contrary to the Fourteen Points, the stern-jawed Presbyterian moralist interposed a ringing veto. The end result was the mandate system—a compromise between idealism and imperialism that turned out to be more imperialistic than idealistic.

Wilson's overriding concern was the League of Nations. He feared that if he did not get it completed and embedded in the treaty, the imperialistic powers might sidetrack it. Working at an incredible pace after hours, Wilson headed the commission that drafted the League Covenant in ten meetings and some thirty hours. He then persuaded the conference not only to approve the hastily constructed Covenant but to incorporate it bodily in the peace treaty. In support of his adopted brain child he spoke so movingly on one occasion that even the hard-boiled reporters forgot to take notes.

Wilson now had to return hurriedly to the United States to sign bills and take care of other pressing business. Shortly after his arrival the mounting Republican opposition in the Senate flared up angrily. On March 4, 1919, 39 senators or senators-elect—more than enough to defeat the treaty—published a round robin to the effect that they would not approve the League in its existing form. This meant that Wilson had to return to Paris, hat in hand, and there weaken his position by having to seek modifications.

Stung to the quick, he struck back at his senatorial foes in an indiscreet speech in New York just before his departure. He boasted that when he brought the treaty back from Paris, the League Covenant would not only be tied in but so thoroughly tied in that it could not be cut out without killing the entire pact. The Senate, he assumed, would not dare to kill the treaty of peace outright.

At Paris the battle was now joined in deadly earnest. Clemenceau, the French realist, had little use for Wilson, the American idealist. "God gave us the ten commandments and we broke them," he reportedly sneered. "Wilson gave us the Fourteen Points—we shall see." Clemenceau's most disruptive demand was for the German Rhineland; but Wilson, the champion of self-determination, would never consent to handing several million Germans over to the tender mercies of the French. After a furious struggle, during which Wilson was stricken with influenza, Clemenceau was finally persuaded to yield the Rhineland and other demands in return for a security treaty. Under it, Britain and America agreed to come to the aid of France in the event of another unprovoked aggression. The United States Senate shortsightedly pigeonholed the pact, and France was left with neither the Rhineland nor security.

Two other deadlocks almost broke up the conference. Italy claimed the Adriatic port of Fiume, an area inhabited chiefly by Yugoslavs. In his battle for self-determination, Wilson dramatically appealed over the head of the Italian delegation to the Italian people, whereupon the delegates went home in a huff to receive popular endorsement. The final adjustment was a hollow victory for self-determination.

The politely bowing Japanese now stepped forward to press their economic claims to China's Shantung, which they had captured from the Germans early in the war. But to submit 30,000,000 Chinese to the influence of the Japanese would be another glaring violation of self-determination. The Japanese threatened to bolt the conference, as the Italians had already done, with consequent jeopardy to the League. In the end, Wilson reluctantly consented to a compromise that left the Japanese temporarily in possession of Shantung.

The Treaty of Versailles, as finally signed in June, 1919, included only about four of the original Fourteen Points. The Germans, with considerable justification, gave vent to loud cries of betrayal. But the iron hand of circumstance had forced Wilson to compromise away many of his points in order to salvage his fourteenth point, the League of Nations, which he hoped would iron out the injustices that had crept into the treaty. He was like the mother who throws her younger children to the pursuing wolves in order to save her sturdy first-born son.

Bitter opposition to the completed treaty had already begun to form in America. Tens of thousands of homesick and disillusioned soldiers were pouring home, determined to let Europe "stew in its own juice." The wartime idealism, inevitably doomed to slump, was now plunging to alarming depths. The beloved Allies had apparently turned out to be greedy imperialists. The war to make the world safe for democracy had obviously fallen dismally short of the goal. And at the end of the war to end wars there were about twenty conflicts of varying intensity being waged all over the globe.

The critics increased their clamor. Various foreign groups, including the Irish-Americans and the Italian-Americans, were complaining that the interests of the old country had been neglected. Professional liberals, for example the editors of the *New Republic,* were denouncing the treaty as too harsh. The illiberals, far more numerous, were denouncing it as not harsh enough. The Britain-haters, like the buzz-saw Senator James Reed of Missouri and the acid-penned William R. Hearst, were proclaiming that England had emerged with undue influence. Such ultra-nationalists as the isolationist Senator William E. Borah of Idaho were insisting that the flag of no superstate should be hoisted above the glorious Stars and Stripes.

When the treaty came back from Paris, with the League firmly riveted in, Senator Lodge despaired of stopping it.

Henry Cabot Lodge in 1909.

"What are you going to do? It's hopeless," he complained to Borah. "All the newspapers in my state are for it." The best that he could hope for was to add a few reservations. The Republicans had been given little opportunity to help write the treaty in Paris; they now felt that they were entitled to do a little rewriting in Washington.

Lodge deliberately adopted the technique of delay. As chairman of the powerful Senate Committee on Foreign Relations, he consumed two weeks by reading aloud the entire pact of 264 pages, even though it had already been printed. He then held time-consuming public hearings, during which persons with unpronounceable foreign names aired their grievances against the pact.

Lodge finally adopted the strategy of tacking reservations onto the treaty, and he was able to achieve his goal because of the peculiar composition of the Senate. There were 49 Republicans and 47 Democrats. The Republicans consisted of about twenty "strong reservationists" like Lodge, about twelve "mild reservationists" like future Secretary of State Kellogg, and about a dozen "irreconcilables." This last group was headed by Senator Borah and the no less isolationist Senator Hiram Johnson of California, a fiery spellbinder.

The Lodge reservations finally broke the back of the treaty. They were all added by a simple majority vote, even though the entire pact would have to be approved by a two-thirds vote. The dozen or so Republican mild reservationists were not happy over the strong Lodge reservations, and if Wilson had deferred sufficiently to these men, he might have persuaded them to vote with the Democrats. Had they done so, the Lodge reservations could have all been voted down, and a milder version, perhaps acceptable to Wilson, could have been substituted.

As the hot summer of 1919 wore on, Wilson became increasingly impatient with the deadlock in the Senate. Finally he decided to take his case to the country, as he had so often done in response to his ingrained "appeal habit." He had never been robust, and his friends urged him not to risk breaking himself down in a strenuous barnstorming campaign. But Wilson, having made up his mind, was unyielding. He had sent American boys into battle in a war to end wars; why should he not risk his life in a battle for a League to end wars?

Wilson's spectacular tour met with limited enthusiasm in the Middle West, the home of several million German-Americans. After him, like baying bloodhounds, trailed Senators Borah and Johnson, sometimes speaking in the same halls a day or so later, to the accompaniment of cries of "Impeach him, impeach him!" But on the Pacific Coast and in the Rocky Mountain area the enthusiasm for Wilson and the League was overwhelming. The high point—and the breaking point— of the trip came at Pueblo, Colorado, where Wilson, with tears streaming down his cheeks, pleaded for his beloved League of Nations.

That night Wilson's weary body rebelled. He was whisked back to Washington, where he suffered a stroke that paralyzed the left side of his body. For weeks he lay in bed, a desperately sick man. The Democrats, who had no first-rate leader in the Senate, were left rudderless. With the wisdom of hindsight, we may say that Wilson might better have stayed in Washington, providing the necessary leadership and compromising with the opposition, insofar as compromise was possible. A good deal of compromise had already gone into the treaty, and a little more might have saved it.

Senator Lodge, cold and decisive, was now in the driver's seat. His Fourteen Reservations, a sardonic parallel to Wilson's Fourteen Points, had been whipped into shape. Most of them now seem either irrelevant, inconsequential, or unnecessary; some of them merely reaffirmed principles and policies, including the Monroe Doctrine, already guaranteed by the treaty or by the Constitution.

But Wilson, who hated the sound of Lodge's name, would have no part of the Lodge reservations. They would, he insisted, emasculate the entire treaty. Yet the curious fact is that he had privately worked out his own set of reservations with the Democratic leader in the Senate, Gilbert M. Hitchcock, and these differed only in slight degree from those of Senator Lodge.

As the hour approached for the crucial vote in the Senate, it ap-

A cartoon by Bronstrup in the San Francisco Chronicle *captioned, "They Won't Dovetail" summed up the attitude of many opponents of the League.*

peared that public opinion had veered a little. Although confused by the angry debate, it still favored the treaty—but with some safeguarding reservations. A stubborn Wilson was unwilling to accept this disheartening fact, or perhaps he was not made aware of it. Mrs. Wilson, backed by the President's personal physician, Dr. Cary Grayson, kept vigil at his bedside to warn the few visitors that disagreeable news might shock the invalid into a relapse.

In this highly unfavorable atmosphere, Senator Hitchcock had two conferences with Wilson on the eve of the Senate voting. He suggested compromise on a certain point, but Wilson shot back, "Let Lodge compromise!" Hitchcock conceded that the Senator would have to give ground but suggested that the White House might also hold out the olive branch. "Let Lodge hold out the olive branch," came the stern reply. On this inflexible note, and with Mrs. Wilson's anxiety mounting, the interview ended.

The Senate was ready for final action on November 19, 1919. At the critical moment Wilson sent a fateful letter to the Democratic minority in the Senate, urging them to vote down the treaty with the hated Lodge reservations so that a true ratification could be achieved. The Democrats, with more than the necessary one-third veto, heeded the voice of their crippled leader and rejected the treaty with reservations. The Republicans, with more than the necessary one-third veto, rejected the treaty without reservations.

The country was shocked by this exhibition of legislative paralysis. About four fifths of the senators professed to favor the treaty in some form, yet they were unable to agree on anything. An aroused public opinion forced the Senate to reconsider, and Lodge secretly entered into negotiations with the Democrats in an effort to work out acceptable reservations. He was making promising progress when Senator Borah got wind of his maneuvers through an anonymous telephone call. The leading irreconcilables hastily summoned a council of war, hauled Lodge before them, and bluntly accused him of treachery. Deeply disturbed, the Massachusetts Senator said: "Well, I suppose I'll have to resign as majority leader."

"No, by God!" burst out Borah. "You won't have a chance to resign! On Monday, I'll move for the election of a new majority leader and give the reasons for my action." Faced with an upheaval within his party such as had insured Wilson's election in 1912, Lodge agreed to drop his backstage negotiations.

The second-chance vote in the Senate came on March 19, 1920. Wilson again directed his loyal Democratic following to reject the treaty, disfigured as it was by the hateful Lodge reservations. But by this time there was no other form in which the pact could possibly be ratified. Twenty-one realistic Democrats turned their backs on Wilson and voted Yea; 23 loyal Democrats, mostly from the rock-ribbed South, joined with the irreconcilables to do the bidding of the White House. The treaty, though commanding a simple majority this time of 49 Yeas to 35 Nays, failed of the necessary two-thirds vote.

Wilson, struggling desperately against the Lodge reservation trap, had already summoned the nation in "solemn referendum" to give him a vote in favor of the League in the forthcoming presidential election of 1920. His hope was that he could then get the treaty approved without reservations. But this course was plainly futile. Even if all the anti-League senators up for re-election in 1920 had been replaced by the pro-League senators, Wilson would still have lacked the necessary two-thirds majority for an unreserved treaty.

The American people were never given a chance to express their views directly on the League of Nations. All they could do was vote either for the weak Democratic candidate, Cox, who stood for the League, and the stuffed-shirt Republican candidate, Harding, who wobbled all over the map of the League arguments. If the electorate had been given an opportunity to express itself, a powerful majority probably would have favored the world organization, with at least some reservations. But wearied of Wilsonism, idealism, and self-denial, and confused by the wordy fight over the treaty, the voters rose

*By 1919, when this
Bronstrup cartoon appeared,
Wilson was sinking rapidly in
a whirlpool of adverse public
opinion.*

up and swept Harding into the White House. The winner had been more anti-League than pro-League, and his prodigious plurality of 7,000,000 votes condemned the League to death in America.

What caused this costly failure of American statesmanship?

Wilson's physical collapse intensified his native stubbornness. A judicious compromise here and there no doubt would have secured Senate approval of the treaty, though of course with modifications. Wilson believed that in any event the Allies would reject the Lodge reservations. The probabilities are that the Allies would have worked out some kind of acceptance, so dire was their need of America's economic support, but Wilson never gave them a chance to act.

Senator Lodge was also inflexible, but prior to the second rejection he was evidently trying to get the treaty through—on his own terms. As majority leader of the Republicans, his primary task was to avoid another fatal split in his party. Wilson's primary task was to get the pact approved. From a purely political point of view, the Republicans had little to gain by engineering ratification of a Democratic treaty.

The two-thirds rule in the Senate, often singled out as the culprit, is of little relevance. Wilson almost certainly would have pigeonholed the treaty if it had passed with the Lodge reservations appended.

Wilson's insistence that the League be wedded to the treaty actually contributed to the final defeat of both. Either would have had a better chance if it had not been burdened by the enemies of the other. The United Nations, one should note, was set up in 1945 independently of any peace treaty.

Finally, American public opinion in 1919–20 was not yet ready for the onerous new world responsibilities that had suddenly been forced upon it. The isolationist tradition was still potent, and it was fortified by postwar disillusionment. If the sovereign voters had spoken out for the League with one voice, they almost certainly would have had their way. A treaty without reservations, or with a few reservations acceptable to Wilson, doubtless would have slipped through the Senate. But the American people were one war short of accepting leadership in a world organization for peace.

Pearl Harbor: Who Blundered?

COLONEL T. N. DUPUY

The Japanese attack on Pearl Harbor, aptly characterized in this essay by the military historian Colonel Trevor N. Dupuy as "the worst disaster in the military annals of the United States," was an event so implausible, so shocking, and so enormous in its results that it has been studied exhaustively—by politicians, by military men, by plain citizens, and, of course, by historians. "What happened" was never difficult to determine; why it happened—who was responsible for the unpreparedness of the American forces in Hawaii—is a question that has excited the bitterest of controversies.

Colonel Dupuy's effort to untangle the events of late November and early December, 1941, takes an unusual but interesting and effective form. Superficially his essay appears almost a chronicle. He describes day by day from November 25 to December 7 what was going on in Washington, in Hawaii, and in the western Pacific, where the Japanese attack force was steaming toward its destination. The dramatic force of this approach is considerable, but alone it would not produce a sound history of the affair. To it Dupuy adds both a prologue, setting the stage and introducing the main characters in the tragedy, and a conclusion, in which he weighs and balances the evidence and offers his own explanation of what went wrong. ∎

Precisely at 7:55 A.M. on Sunday, December 7, 1941, a most devastating Japanese aerial attack struck the island of Oahu, Territory of Hawaii. When it was all over, the battleships of our Pacific Fleet, moored by pairs in their Pearl Harbor base, had received a mortal blow. Our army air strength in Hawaii—the Japanese found its planes ranged neatly wing to wing on airfield ramps— was a tangled mass of smoking wreckage.

The worst disaster in the military annals of the United States had ushered us into World War II. As in most wars, the political and diplomatic background was so complex and confused as to defy definitive analysis—though this has not prevented historians and others from making the attempt. But as to the disaster itself, the military record is clear.

A well-planned and brilliantly executed surprise attack by Japanese carrier-based aircraft was launched against the major American bastion in the Pacific. The United States government, its senior military leaders, and its commanders in Hawaii had had sufficient information to be adequately warned that an attack was possible, and had had time to be prepared to thwart or to blunt the blow. The information was largely ignored; the preparations were utterly inadequate.

Someone had blundered. Who? And how?

At the moment of the attack four professional military men filled posts of vital importance. In Washington, General George C. Marshall, Chief of Staff, was responsible for the entire United States Army and all of its installations. In a nearby office sat his Navy counterpart, Admiral Harold R. Stark, Chief of Naval Operations. On the Hawaiian island of Oahu, Lieutenant General Walter C. Short commanded the Hawaiian Department, the Army's most vital overseas outpost. Commanding the United States Pacific Fleet was Rear Admiral Husband E. Kimmel; his headquarters was also on Oahu, overlooking the great Navy base at Pearl Harbor.

Marshall, product of the Virginia Military Institute, had a well-deserved reputation for brilliant staff work under Pershing in France in World War I. Later he had taken a prominent part in developing the Army's Infantry School at Fort Benning, Georgia. Short, a graduate of the University of Illinois, had entered the Army from civilian life in 1901. Early in 1941 he had been chosen by Marshall to command the Hawaiian Department.

Both Stark and Kimmel had graduated from the United States Naval Academy at Annapolis—Stark in 1903, Kimmel a year later. Both had risen to their high positions in the Navy following exemplary command and staff service at sea and on shore. Close personal friends, both were highly respected by their naval colleagues.

The thinking and attitudes of these four men were shaped by two

247

decades of unanimous opinion among American soldiers and sailors that someday Japan would clash with the United States in a struggle for predominance in the vast Pacific Ocean. All accepted without question the basic elements of U.S. doctrine for the defense of the Pacific in such a war.

The doctrine was that the United States Navy—and in particular its Pacific Fleet—was the essential element to American success in a Pacific war. Immobilization or destruction of that fleet would be the greatest damage Japan could inflict on the United States. Upon the Army lay the responsibility for furthering the offensive powers of the fleet by protecting its great Pearl Harbor base; by safeguarding the Panama Canal, the Navy's life line from the Atlantic to the Pacific; and by defending the advanced Philippine delaying position, which in military opinion was likely to be Japan's initial target.

Since 1939 the top military authorities of the nation, including President Franklin D. Roosevelt, had understood the almost inexorable logic of events that pointed to our eventual involvement either in the conflict which Hitler had begun in Europe or that in Asia between Japan and China—or both. And under Roosevelt's skillful guidance the nation, albeit grudgingly, was very slowly building up its military strength.

As 1941 rolled along, it became apparent, even to the man in the street, that the most pressing danger lay in the Far East. Our diplomatic relations with Japan were worsening; by November they appeared to be almost at the breaking point. The long-continued diplomatic bickering between the two nations on a variety of subjects had resulted in the arrival in Washington of a special envoy, Saburo Kurusu, who—with Ambassador Kichisaburo Nomura—had on November 20 presented the State Department with a document that was practically an ultimatum.

Japan would acquiesce to our government's demands that she withdraw from Indochina only upon "establishment of an equitable peace in the Pacific area" and, further, upon "supply to Japan [by the U.S. of] a required quantity of oil."

In 1940, our cipher experts had cracked the Japanese secret codes—a cryptoanalytical procedure known in the War Department as "Magic." Hence our government knew that the envoys had received instructions to press for American acceptance of this "final proposal" by November 25. The ambassadors had been warned that for reasons "beyond your ability to guess" this was essential, but that if the "signing can be completed by the 29th" the Imperial Japanese government would wait. "After that things are automatically going to happen."

It was also known through Magic radio intercepts that a large proportion of Japanese military strength—land, sea, and air—was con-

*Saburo Kurusu (right) and Kichisaburo Nomura (left) with
Secretary of State Cordell Hull arriving at the White House
on November 17 for a conference with President Roosevelt.*

centrating in the Indochina and South China Sea areas. No evidence
of aircraft carriers had been found, however, either in those areas or
in the Japanese mandated islands. Intelligence agencies, monitoring
Japanese radio traffic, considered it probable that the carriers were still
in their home waters, but they were not certain.

On this basis Marshall, Stark, and their respective staffs concluded
that the Japanese were preparing to strike in Southeast Asia; this

threat, of course, included the Philippine Commonwealth. Accordingly our Army and Navy commanders in the Philippines and at Guam had been specifically warned. The commanders in Hawaii, Panama, Alaska, and on the West Coast were kept informed of important developments.

This was the situation as Marshall and Stark saw it early on November 25. From that time on events succeeded one another with increasing rapidity, both in Washington and in Hawaii. This is how they unfolded:

Washington, Tuesday, November 25

Marshall and Stark attended a "War Council" meeting with the President, Secretary of State Cordell Hull, Secretary of War Henry L. Stimson, and Secretary of the Navy Frank Knox. Were the Japanese bluffing? Hull thought not; rejection of their terms would mean war. "These fellows mean to fight," he told the group. "You [Marshall and Stark] will have to be prepared."

Adequate preparation could not be guaranteed by either service chief. The great draft army was still only a partly disciplined mass. The Navy, better prepared for an immediate fight, was still far from ready for an extended period of combat. Marshall urged diplomatic delay. If the State Department could hold war off for even three months, the time gained would be precious, especially in the Philippines, where Douglas MacArthur's newly raised Commonwealth Army was only partly organized and equipped.

Perhaps the State Department's formula—*modus vivendi* they called it—which had been sent by cable to our British, Chinese, Australian, and Dutch allies for comment—would gain the needed time. This was a proposal for a three-month truce in Sino-Japanese hostilities, during which the United States, in return for Japan's withdrawal from southern Indochina, would make limited economic concessions to her.

It was evident to all concerned that otherwise hostilities were almost certain to break out within a few days. The President, noting Japan's proclivity for attacking without a declaration of war, impressed on all concerned that if war came, it must result from an initial blow by Japan. How, then, asked Roosevelt, could the United States permit this without too much danger to itself?*

*The claim has been advanced—notably by Rear Admiral Robert A. Theobald in *The Final Secret of Pearl Harbor* (Devin-Adair, 1954)—that President Roosevelt abetted the Japanese surprise "by causing the Hawaiian Commanders to be denied invaluable information from decoded Japanese dispatches concerning the rapid approach of the war and the strong probability that the attack would be directed at Pearl Harbor." He did so, according to now-retired Admiral Kimmel in a recent interview with United Press International, to "induce the Japanese to attack Pearl Harbor and thus permit him to honor

That evening Stark wrote a lengthy warning to Kimmel in Hawaii, informing him that neither the President nor the Secretary of State "would be surprised over a Japanese surprise attack," adding that while "an attack upon the Philippines would be the most embarrassing thing that could happen to us . . . I still rather look for an advance into Thailand, Indochina, Burma Road areas as the most likely." Marshall reviewed the incoming and outgoing messages to overseas commanders, and busied himself with the almost numberless duties of his most important task: preparing our Army for combat.

Honolulu, Tuesday, November 25

Kimmel and Short had more than a passing interest in the status of our negotiations with Japan. Admiral Kimmel had been kept informed of the increasingly strained relations by frequent frank and newsy letters from Admiral Stark. One of these, dated November 7, had said in part: "Things seem to be moving steadily towards a crisis in the Pacific. . . . A month may see, literally, most anything . . . It doesn't look good."

Admiral Kimmel undoubtedly was thinking of that letter when he reread the official radio message which he had received the day before, November 24:

> Chances of favorable outcomes of negotiations with Japan very doubtful . . . A surprise aggressive movement in any direction including attack on Philippines or Guam is a possibility. Chief of Staff has seen this dispatch, concurs and requests action addressees to inform senior Army officers their areas. Utmost secrecy necessary in order not to complicate an already tense situation or precipitate Japanese action.

Admiral Kimmel promptly sent a copy of the message to General Short. He had standing instructions to show such messages to the Army commander: the most critical messages from Washington were usually sent over Navy channels because the Army code was consid-

---

his secret commitments to Great Britain and the Netherlands with the full support of the American people."

The report of the Army Pearl Harbor Board, submitted to the Secretary of War on October 20, 1944, apportioned a share of the blame for the surprise to the War and Navy Departments and their top military officers in Washington. Even so, the service inquiries concluded that General Short and Admiral Kimmel had sufficient information to realize that war was imminent and had no excuse for inadequate security measures. They were not court-martialed, despite their requests, largely for political reasons. In this they were grievously wronged, for they had a right to be heard in their own defense. On the other hand, although I am not an apologist for the late President Roosevelt, it is simply ridiculous to suggest that he, who loved the Navy perhaps more than did any of our Presidents, would deliberately offer the Pacific Fleet as a sacrifice to entice Japan into war, and that this scheme was abetted by other responsible military men and statesmen. So many people would have known of such a nefarious plot that it would in fact have been impossible to muffle it.—T.N.D.

ered to be less secure. The Admiral saw no need for further action. After receiving a warning message on October 16 he had taken some measures for a partial alert and reported those promptly to Stark, who replied: "OK on the disposition which you made."

Admiral Kimmel and General Short had a cordial personal relationship, despite subsequent widespread but unfounded allegations to the contrary. They had frequently discussed, officially and personally, the possibility of a surprise Japanese attack and the measures to be taken to prepare for it and to thwart it if it should come. These plans had been approved in Washington. The Navy was responsible for long-range reconnaissance up to 700 miles, while the Army, with its land-based aircraft, was responsible for inshore reconnaissance for a distance up to twenty miles from shore. The Army's new radar would provide additional reconnaissance and air-warning service for a distance of up to 130 miles from Oahu. Periodically the commanders held joint maneuvers to test the plans and the readiness of their forces to carry them out.

They commanded large forces which might soon be called upon to fight, and it was essential that they maintain an intensive training schedule to assure the highest possible standard of combat efficiency. This was a formidable task, since many of their officers and men were inexperienced and untrained, having only recently been brought into our rapidly expanding armed forces. At the same time, as outpost commanders, both Short and Kimmel were well aware of their responsibilities for assuring the security of the fleet and of the island of Oahu.

Moreover, each commander assumed the other knew his business; each assumed the other's command was running on a full-time status. Each felt—as shown by later testimony—that to probe into the other's shop would be an unpardonable and resented intrusion. As a result, the liaison essential to any sort of joint or concerted operation—the daily constant and intimate exchange of details of command operations between Army and Navy staffs—was almost nonexistent. Each commander, then, was working in a partial vacuum.

On the single island of Oahu were concentrated most of the 42,857 troops that comprised the units of General Short's department. Carrying out the intensive training schedule was the bulk of two infantry divisions, less one regiment scattered in detachments on the other islands of the group. Also on Oahu were most of the antiaircraft and coast defense units of the Coast Artillery Command, and more than 250 aircraft of the Army's Hawaiian air force. Some of these aircraft, aloft on routine training exercises, were being tracked by the inexperienced crews of six Army mobile radar units newly installed at different points on the island.

There was comparable activity at the great Pearl Harbor Navy Yard, on the southern coast of the island, close by the bustling metropolis of Honolulu. Quite a few vessels of the U.S. Pacific Fleet were in port. Here Kimmel, the fleet's commander in chief, had his headquarters, from which he and his staff closely supervised the intense training programs of their ships in Hawaiian waters. The fleet comprised eight battleships, two aircraft carriers (with a total of 180 planes), sixteen cruisers, forty-five destroyers, twelve submarines, and slightly more than 300 land-based aircraft. In addition another battleship, an aircraft carrier, four cruisers, and various smaller vessels were temporarily absent, many being in mainland yards for repairs.

The Navy Yard itself was the principal installation of the Fourteenth Naval District; both base and the district were commanded by Rear Admiral Claude C. Bloch, who was a direct subordinate of Kimmel both as base commander and as a Pacific Fleet staff officer—a setup which bred no little confusion and which was not helped by the fact that Bloch was Kimmel's senior in the service, though not in command. Kimmel properly held Bloch responsible for the functioning and local security of all the land-based installations of the fleet in Hawaii, while he himself devoted his principal attention to the readiness of the fleet to function offensively at sea. He considered Bloch to be Short's naval counterpart, so far as local protection of the fleet in Hawaii was concerned. Formal co-ordination of Army and Navy activities in Hawaii and nearby Pacific areas, however, was done at conferences—fairly frequent—between Kimmel and Short.

[*On November 25 (Washington date line), Vice Admiral Chuichi Nagumo's First Air Fleet—six aircraft carriers and 414 combat planes, escorted by two battleships, two heavy cruisers and one light, and nine destroyers—put to sea from Tankan Bay in the southern Kurile Islands. Eight tank ships trailed it. Screening the advance were twenty-eight submarines which had left Kure a few days earlier.*

This powerful naval striking force had long been preparing for a surprise attack on the United States Pacific Fleet at Pearl Harbor. It did not, however, have a final directive to carry it out. The First Air Fleet was to leave the Kurile Islands and steam slowly east into the North Pacific to await orders either to attack or, if negotiations with the United States reached a conclusion satisfactory to Japan, to return home.]

Washington, Wednesday, November 26

Before attending a meeting of the Army-Navy Joint Board, both General Marshall and Admiral Stark had learned that Secretary of State Hull, with the full approval of the President, had made a momentous decision.

During the evening of the twenty-fifth and the early hours of the twenty-sixth, the State Department received the comments of our allies on the *modus vivendi* reply to the Japanese ultimatum. The British, Australians, and Dutch gave lukewarm approval to the proposal for a three-month truce, though in a personal message to the President, Prime Minister Winston Churchill remarked pointedly, "What about Chiang Kai-shek? Is he not having a very thin diet?"

Chiang, in fact, had protested violently against the truce proposal, which, with its relaxation of economic pressure on Japan, could only work to the psychological and military disadvantage of China. The protest, as well as information gleaned from more intercepted messages indicating that the Japanese would accept nothing less than complete agreement to their demands of November 20, caused Secretary Hull to doubt the wisdom of the *modus vivendi*. Obviously, these concessions were inadequate to satisfy Japanese demands, yet, because they would seem like American appeasement they would strike a major blow to Chinese morale.

Hull therefore recommended a different reply, which the President approved. After a calm but firm restatement of the principles which had guided the American negotiations, the new note proposed, in essence: withdrawal of Japanese military forces from China and Indochina, recognition of the territorial integrity of those countries, unqualified acceptance of the National Government of China, and, finally, negotiation of a liberal U.S.-Japanese trade treaty once the other conditions had been met.

At 5 P.M. on November 26 Secretary Hull met with the two Japanese ambassadors and presented this reply to them. Special envoy Kurusu read the note, then commented that his government would "throw up its hands" and that the American position practically "put an end to the negotiations."

By frequent phone calls, Secretary Hull had kept both Stimson and Knox informed of these rapid developments, and the two service secretaries had passed on the information to their senior military subordinates. So it was that when they met at a Joint Board conference that same day, Marshall and Stark were well aware of the course of the events still in progress at the State Department. Agreeing that war was now almost certain, they both felt that it was incumbent upon them to remind the President once more of the dangerous weakness of the Army and the Navy and particularly the grave danger of disaster in the Philippines if war were to break out before further reinforcements of men and matériel could reach General MacArthur. They directed their subordinates to have ready for their signatures the next day a joint memorandum to the President which would urge avoidance of hostilities for as long as possible consistent with national policy and national honor.

Late in the afternoon General Marshall held a conference with Major General Leonard T. Gerow, Chief of the War Plans Division, to discuss what should be done the next day, November 27. Marshall had planned to be in North Carolina that day to observe the final phases of the largest maneuvers in the Army's peacetime history; he felt he should carry out that intention, despite his concern about a report that a large Japanese troop convoy had moved into the South China Sea. The two officers discussed the grave implications of the growing Japanese concentrations in the Southeast Asia region. Even though he intended to be back at his desk on the twenty-eighth, General Marshall authorized Gerow to send overseas commanders a warning in his name if further information next day—the twenty-seventh—should point to the possibility of a surprise Japanese attack.

Honolulu, Wednesday, November 26

Admiral Kimmel received a report from the radio intelligence unit in Hawaii of a strong concentration of Japanese submarines and carrier aircraft in the Marshall Islands. This implied, but did not definitely prove, that some Japanese carriers were there as well. This information was perhaps inconsistent with a somewhat more definite report from the Philippines saying that radio traffic indicated all known Japanese carriers to be in home waters. Neither Admiral Kimmel nor members of his staff saw any need to inform General Short of these reports.

Short, meanwhile, had received an official message directing him to send two long-range B-24 bombers—due from the mainland—to photograph and observe the Japanese bases of Truk in the Caroline Islands and Jaluit in the Marshalls, reporting the number and locations of all Japanese naval vessels. He was to make sure both planes were "fully equipped with gun ammunition." But neither mission was ever flown: only one B-24 reached Short, and it was not properly equipped.

[*On the high seas, their bleak rendezvous at Tankan far astern, Nagumo's task force was steaming eastward. Radio silence was absolute. High-grade fuel kept smoke to a minimum. No waste was thrown overboard to leave telltale tracks; blackout on board was complete. Only the Admiral and a handful of his staff knew their orders; the rest of the command buzzed with speculation like so many hornets.*]

Washington, Thursday, November 27

General Gerow, summoned to Mr. Stimson's office, found Secretary Knox and Admiral Stark already there. The Secretary of War felt the time had come to alert General MacArthur in the Philippines. He told his listeners that Secretary Hull had warned him no peaceful solution was apparent. "I have washed my hands of it," Hull had said, "and it is now in the hands of you and Knox, the Army and the Navy."

Stimson added word of a telephone discussion with the President, who, agreeing that an alert order be sent out, desired all commanders to be cautioned that Japan must commit the first overt act of war. All four in Stimson's office then prepared drafts of alert messages to be sent to General MacArthur and Admiral Hart in the Philippines and to Army and Navy commanders in Hawaii, Panama, and on the West Coast.

Early in the afternoon Gerow sent out the warning:

> Negotiations with Japan appear to be terminated to all practicable purposes with only the barest possibilities that the Japanese Government might . . . offer to continue.

The message then reiterated Mr. Roosevelt's desire that Japan commit the first overt act. But this, it was pointed out,

> should not repeat not be construed as restricting you to a course . . . that might jeopardize your defense. *Prior to hostile Japanese action you are directed to undertake such reconnaissance and other measures as you deem necessary* [italics supplied], but these measures should be carried out so as not repeat not to alarm civil population or disclose intent. Report measures taken . . .

The message further directed that, should hostilities occur, commanders would undertake offensive tasks in accordance with existing war plans. It concluded with the caution that dissemination of "this highly secret information" should be limited to the essential minimum.

Stark's message to Navy commanders (as well as to our special naval observer in London, who was to advise the British) was sent at the same time; it opened bluntly: "This dispatch is to be considered a war warning." It related the end of negotiations and the expectation that "an aggressive move" might come within the next few days. Then, in contrast to the more general Army warning, it added the information that known military activities of the Japanese indicated they probably intended to launch "an amphibious expedition against either the Philippines, Thai or Kra peninsula or possibly Borneo." Like the Army warning, it directed execution of existing war plans in the event of hostilities. Naval commanders in the continental United States, Guam, and Samoa were cautioned to take antisabotage measures.

If read together, these two messages definitely pointed a finger at Southeast Asia as the expected enemy target. This, of course, in no way excuses any of the subsequent actions of our commanders in Hawaii, whose paramount responsibility was the security of their post. But it must have influenced their thinking.

Honolulu, Thursday, November 27

The official warnings from Washington confirmed to Short and Kimmel the seriousness of the international situation. Short, who noted that he was expected to report the measures he was taking, sent the following reply: "Report Department alerted to prevent sabotage. Liaison with the Navy."

The Hawaiian Department plans provided for three kinds of alert. Number 1, which was what Short had ordered, was to guard against sabotage and uprisings—long a preoccupation of all Hawaiian commanders because of the high proportion of Japanese in the Islands. Number 2 included security against possible isolated, external air or naval attacks. Number 3 was a full-scale deployment for maximum defense of the Islands, and particularly of Oahu—heart of the military organization. Only in the two higher stages of alert was ammunition to be distributed to the antiaircraft batteries; in Alert No. 1 all ammunition was to be kept stored in the dumps. Under Alert No. 1, planes would be parked closely for easy guarding; under the others they would be dispersed.

General Short felt he was confirmed in his concern over sabotage when his intelligence officer—or G-2—presented a message from the War Department G-2, warning that "subversive activities may be expected."

In obedience to the instruction to make such reconnaissance as he might "deem necessary," Short did, however, order his newly installed radar stations to operate daily from 4 A.M. to 7 A.M.; these were the dawn hours when surprise attack was most likely. Further reconnaissance, he felt, was the Navy's responsibility. He didn't know that Kimmel was having troubles of his own in attempting any sustained offshore reconnaissance. Nor was Kimmel aware that Short's radar was operating only on a curtailed basis.

Kimmel pondered over what steps he should take. Though he was already alerted to some extent, he knew that for the moment he could do little in the way of "defensive deployment" in his war plan tasks—most specifically, raids into the Japanese mandated islands. Should he then prepare for an attack against Oahu? The Washington message implied that this was not a probability. Even so, he didn't have sufficient planes for a 360 degree, distant reconnaissance from Oahu.

In compliance with instructions from Washington, Kimmel was sending some Marine planes to Wake and Midway islands. He decided that the two carrier task forces he was ordering to carry out this instruction could, en route, conduct long-range searches to the west, over the direct route from Japan to Oahu.

Task Force 8, under Vice Admiral William F. Halsey, including the

carrier *Enterprise* and three cruisers, was leaving that day. In conference
with Halsey before departure, Kimmel showed him the "war warning"
message. Halsey asked how far he should go if he met any Japanese
ships while searching. "Use your common sense," was Kimmel's reply.
Halsey, it is understood, commented that these were the best orders
he could receive, adding that if he found as much as one Japanese
sampan, he would sink it. Kimmel, by making no further comment,
apparently acquiesced.

Pending the arrival of Halsey at Wake, Kimmel sent orders to a
patrol plane squadron based on Midway to proceed to Wake and
return, searching ocean areas and covering a 525-mile area around
Wake itself.

Kimmel felt that he had done all he could in that line without
completely halting fleet training and exhausting the pilots of his relatively weak air command. But he did order immediate attack on any
and all unidentified submarines discovered in the vicinity of Oahu and
other fleet operating zones. Neither then nor later, apparently, did he
check on the local security measures undertaken by Admiral Bloch's
command, nor did he suggest any co-ordination between Bloch and
Short.

[*Nagumo's force was steady on a course laid between the Aleutians and Midway
Island, the carriers in two parallel rows of three each. Battleships and cruisers
guarded the flanks, destroyers screened wide, and submarines were scouting far
ahead.*]

Washington, Friday, November 28

General Marshall, back from his North Carolina inspection, was
briefed by Gerow on the previous day's happenings. He read and
approved the joint memorandum, already signed by Admiral Stark,
which urged on the President the need for gaining time, particularly
until troops—some already at sea and nearing Guam, others about to
embark on the West Coast—could reach the Philippines. He also approved the warning message Gerow had sent to the overseas commanders.

At noon he attended the President's "War Council" meeting at the
White House. The implications of a large Japanese amphibious force,
known to be sailing southward through the South China Sea, were
discussed. British Malaya, the Netherlands East Indies, and the Philippines were potential targets, the invasion of which would immediately
involve us in war. But unless Congress should previously declare war,
the United States could not attack this force. It was agreed that the

President should send a message to Emperor Hirohito urging him to preserve peace, and that Mr. Roosevelt should also address Congress, explaining the dangers being created by this Japanese aggressive action. The President then left for a short vacation at Warm Springs, Georgia, directing his advisers to have the two documents prepared in his absence.

Marshall, back at his desk, thumbed through a sheaf of radio replies to the "war warning" message. Lieutenant General John L. DeWitt, commanding on the Pacific Coast, reported instituting a harbor alert at San Francisco and similar precautions in Alaska in liaison with naval authorities. He requested permission to direct air as well as ground deployment of his far-flung command. It was a long message, contrasting sharply with Short's succinct report of sabotage defense measures in Hawaii. But the Chief of Staff didn't pay much attention; it would be Gerow's job to handle any necessary responses. So Marshall initialed most of the messages and then forgot about them.

Short's message, however, was not initialed by Marshall. He would later testify he had no recollection of ever having seen it, although it bore the routine rubber stamp, "Noted by Chief of Staff."

As for Admiral Stark, he was pushing off a long message to Navy commanders on the West Coast, and to Admiral Kimmel, quoting the Army alert message of the twenty-seventh, including its admonition that Japan must commit the first "overt act."

Honolulu, Friday, November 28

Kimmel read Stark's long quote of the Army's alert message. He was particularly interested in its stress that "if hostilities cannot . . . be avoided the United States desires that Japan commit the first overt act." This appeared to confirm his decision of the previous day: limiting defensive deployment to one patrol squadron cruising from Wake to Midway and sending carrier task forces for local defense of those outposts.

Admiral Kimmel received several other interesting reports. The U.S.S. *Helena* reported contact with an unidentified submarine. An intelligence estimate based on radio intercepts indicated Japanese carriers were still in their own home waters. Another report on intercepted Japanese messages established a "winds code," by means of which Japan would notify its diplomatic and consular representatives abroad of a decision to go to war: "east wind rain" meant war with the United States; "north wind cloudy," war with Russia; "west wind clear," war with England and invasion of Thailand, Malaya, and the Dutch East Indies.

It was all very interesting. However, the Admiral never thought of mentioning any of these reports during his conference with General Short that day. They discussed mutual responsibility for security of Wake and Midway—in light of the mixed Army-Navy garrisons at both places. But neither thought of asking the other what action he had taken on the November 27 warnings, nor did either volunteer any information on matters he considered to be of interest to his own individual service only.

[*Admiral Nagumo's fleet spent the day in attempts to refuel in a plunging sea—an operation which, as it turned out, would continue for several days under almost heartbreaking conditions of bad weather.*]

Washington, Saturday, November 29

Both General Marshall and Admiral Stark received Magic copies of more intercepted Japanese messages. One of these from Premier Tojo in Tokyo to the ambassadors in Washington was quite ominous:

> The United States' . . . humiliating proposal . . . was quite unexpected and extremely regrettable. The Imperial Government can by no means use it as a basis for negotiations. Therefore . . . in two or three days the negotiations will be de facto ruptured. . . . However, I did not wish you to give the impression that the negotiations are broken off. Merely say to them that you are awaiting instructions. . . . From now on, do the best you can.

To Marshall and Stark this was clear evidence indeed that the Japanese were stalling for time only long enough to get their forces ready to attack in the Indonesia-Southeast Asia area. It seemed now only a question of time, as more reports streamed in about Japanese convoys moving into the South China Sea.

For a good part of the morning Stark and Marshall were working closely with Secretaries Knox and Stimson in preparing and revising drafts of the presidential messages to Congress and to Emperor Hirohito, in accordance with the agreement at the previous day's meeting of the War Council. Finally, about noon, the two secretaries were satisfied, and their proposed drafts were sent to Secretary Hull.

Late in the afternoon both read with considerable interest reports of a warlike speech which Premier Tojo had delivered that day (November 30, Tokyo time). The twenty-ninth had been the deadline established in the messages from Tokyo to the ambassadors. The speech, while warlike, failed to give any indication of Japanese intentions.

Honolulu, Saturday, November 29

Things were generally quiet on Oahu and in the outlying waters, as the Army and Navy both began a weekend of relaxation after five days of strenuous training. There was considerable bustle, however, at the Army's headquarters at Fort Shafter, as well as at Navy headquarters at nearby Pearl Harbor. General Short approved a message in reply to the latest sabotage warning from Washington, outlining in detail the security measures which had been taken. Admiral Kimmel received another message from Washington reminding him once more that he was to be prepared to carry out existing war plans in the event of hostilities with Japan. Thus, once again, the two commanders were reminded of the alert messages they had received on the twenty-seventh, and once again they found themselves satisfied with the actions they had then taken.

[*In the North Pacific Admiral Nagumo's fleet continued refueling.*]

Washington, Sunday, November 30

General Marshall, returning from his usual Sunday morning horseback ride at Fort Myer, found another intercepted Japanese message awaiting him; the Foreign Ministry was cautioning its envoys in Washington to keep talking and "be careful that this does not lead to anything like a breaking-off of negotiations." He agreed with G-2's conclusion that the Japanese were stalling until their South China Sea assault was ready.

Stark, at his desk, was called that morning by Secretary of State Hull, gravely concerned about Premier Tojo's warlike speech. The Secretary told him he was going to urge the President's return from Warm Springs. A later call from Hull informed Stark that President Roosevelt would be back Monday morning; Stark must see the President and report on the naval developments in the Far East.

Honolulu, Sunday, November 30

General Short, in light of his instructions "not to alarm the civil population," must have been annoyed to read the Honolulu *Advertiser* headlines that morning: "Hawaii Troops Alerted." There wasn't anything he could do about it, however; even the limited nature of his Alert No. 1 would draw newspaper attention in a critical time such as this. He also read that "Leaders Call Troops Back in Singapore—Hope Wanes as Nations Fail at Parleys" and "Kurusu Bluntly Warned Nation Ready for Battle."

General George Catlett Marshall, Chief of Staff of the United States Army, December 1941.

Kimmel ordered a squadron of patrol planes to Midway, to replace temporarily the squadron which he had ordered to reconnoiter about Wake. He was also interested in an information copy of a Navy Department message to Admiral Hart, commanding our Asiatic Fleet at Manila, directing him to scout for information as to an intended Japanese attack on the Kra Isthmus of Thailand, just north of Malaya.

Kimmel didn't think that war could be delayed much longer. He wrote on the top of a piece of paper the words—"Steps to be taken in case of American-Japanese war within the next twenty-four hours," an *aide-mémoire* of the orders he must issue to his fleet.

[*The Japanese First Air Fleet was still engaged in the arduous refueling job, while continuing its eastward course at slow speed.*]

Washington, Monday, December 1

A busy day. Stark learned from his intelligence staff that the Japanese Navy had changed service radio frequencies and call letters for all units afloat—a normal prewar step. He went to the White House with Secretary Hull and briefed the President.

In the afternoon both Stark and Marshall digested an unusual number of important Magic intercepts of Japanese messages. Japan's Foreign Minister was urging his ambassadors to prevent the United States "from becoming unduly suspicious," emphasizing that it was important to give the impression to the Americans that "negotiations are continuing." Tokyo also had ordered its diplomatic offices in London, Hong Kong, Singapore, and Manila "to abandon the use of code machines and to dispose of them." Japan's ambassador at Bangkok reported his intrigues to maneuver Thailand into a declaration of war on Great Britain.

But most significant was an exchange between Japan's ambassador to Berlin and his foreign office. The ambassador reported that Foreign Minister von Ribbentrop had given him Hitler's unequivocal assurance that "should Japan become engaged in a war against the United States, Germany, of course, would join the war immediately." Tojo promptly told the ambassador to inform the German government that "war may suddenly break out between the Anglo-Saxon nations and Japan through some clash of arms. . . . This war may come quicker than anyone dreams."

And how quickly would that be? This was the question which sprang immediately to the minds of Admiral Stark and General Marshall, the men responsible for readying the armed forces of the United States for the coming clash of arms. They had no way of knowing that the answer lay in a brief uncoded message picked up by several American radio intelligence intercept stations just a few hours earlier. "Climb Mount Niitaka," was the message. No significance could be attached to it, so it never came to the attention of Marshall or Stark. Nor would it have meant anything to either of them.

Honolulu, Monday, December 1

Kimmel and Short held another routine conference. Presumably they discussed at some length the grave international situation. Supplementing the cryptic but alarming official intelligence reports and warnings were the headlines blazoning the Honolulu newspapers.

But neither Kimmel nor Short in their conversation discussed local security precautions or a possible threat to Oahu. Politely but inconclusively they continued discussion of the divided responsibility at Wake and Midway. Kimmel never thought to mention to Short that he had received another Washington warning about the "winds code" and that he had also been informed of the change in Japanese military frequencies and call letters. It never occurred to Kimmel that Short might not have been told about either matter.

Routine training continued in Army posts. General Short was quite pleased that his limited alert—which the War Department had apparently approved—had not interfered noticeably with training programs.

[*"Climb Mount Niitaka!"*

Admiral Nagumo sucked in his breath as the message was laid before him this day. This was it; the prearranged code which meant "Proceed with attack."

Obedient to the signal flags broken out aboard the flagship, the gray ships came foaming about to a southeasterly course, vibrating to the thrust of increased propeller speed. Inside the steel hulls the mustered crews, learning the news, cheered, quaffed sake, and burned incense to the spirits of their ancestors.]

Washington, Tuesday, December 2

Additional Magic intercepts indicated further Japanese preparations for war, with the enemy's known offensive weight still massing in Southeast Asia.

Honolulu, Tuesday, December 2

Kimmel, discussing intelligence reports with his staff, noted the change in Japanese radio frequencies as related in the Navy Department's fortnightly intelligence summary, received late the previous day. The gist of it was that Tokyo was preparing for "operations on a large scale."

Then Kimmel called for intelligence estimates on the location of

Japanese aircraft carriers. Captain Edwin T. Layton, his intelligence officer, gave estimated locations for all except Divisions 1 and 2—four carriers.

"What!" exclaimed Kimmel, "you don't know where [they] are?"

"No, sir, I do not. I think they are in home waters, but—"

Sternly, but with a suspicion of a twinkle in his eyes, Kimmel delivered himself of a masterpiece of unconscious irony.

"Do you mean to say they could be rounding Diamond Head and you wouldn't know it?"

The conference ended after a discussion on the difficulty of locating a force operating under sealed orders while preserving radio silence.

Short met Kimmel that day again. They continued debate over jurisdiction at Wake and Midway.

[*Nagumo's fleet was steadily driving south toward Oahu. In prearranged code— unintelligible to American Magic interceptors—Tokyo had confirmed the target date: "X-Day will be 8 December"—December 7, Honolulu time.*]

Washington, Wednesday, December 3

Along with the other recipients of Magic information, General Marshall and Admiral Stark noted but attached no particular significance to a pair of intercepted messages made available to them that day.

One, dated November 15, was already old; its translation had been deferred for several days in order to take care of messages considered more urgent. It referred to an earlier message directing the Japanese consulate at Honolulu to make periodic reports on the location of American warships in Pearl Harbor, and requested the Honolulu consulate to step up these reports to twice a week.

No particular importance was attributed to this by Admiral Stark or his senior naval intelligence officers, since the Japanese had long been making efforts to obtain information about the activities and number of ships in harbor at other naval bases on the West Coast and at Panama. The fact that the Japanese wanted more complete data, including exact locations of specific vessels in Pearl Harbor, was assumed to be merely an indication of their thoroughness in evaluating intelligence on America's main Pacific combat force.

The other message was a reply by Prime Minister Tojo to the suggestion of his ambassadors at Washington that peace could perhaps be preserved through a high-level conference—they had proposed former Premier Prince Konoye as the Japanese envoy and Vice President Henry Wallace or Presidential Assistant Harry Hopkins for the United States—at "some midway point, such as Honolulu." Tojo's response, that "it would be inappropriate for us to propose such a meeting," seemed a less significant indication of Japan's immediate intentions than the continuing reports of her movements in and near Indochina.

Honolulu, Wednesday, December 3

Admiral Kimmel noted the continuing and surprising lack of information on Japanese carriers contained in the latest daily radio intelligence summary, which stated that "carrier traffic is at a low ebb."

That day, too, he received Admiral Stark's letter of November 25. He agreed with Stark's view that "an attack on the Philippines" might be embarrassing, but that "an advance into Thailand, Indochina, Burma Road area [was] most likely."

In the afternoon Short and Kimmel conferred. They soon got into a grim discussion of what they could do to carry out assigned war plans when and if war broke out. Both were thinking, of course, of planned naval and air raids into the Marshall Islands and of security measures for Wake and Midway. There was no mention of like measures for Oahu. Nor did Admiral Kimmel think to mention to General Short his latest intelligence reports about the burning of Japanese codes or the missing aircraft carriers.

[*Nagumo's planners on the high seas were busy marking on their charts of Pearl Harbor the exact locations of six of the U.S. battle fleet—the* Pennsylvania, Arizona, California, Tennessee, Maryland, *and* West Virginia. *The data came from Honolulu, relayed by radio through Imperial Navy Headquarters in Tokyo.*]

Washington, Thursday, December 4

A mixed bag of Magic intercepts available to both Stark and Marshall gave clear indication of Japanese intentions to go to war. Instructions came to Ambassador Nomura to completely destroy one of the two special machines for secret coding, but to hold the other and its cipher key—which should be in his personal possession—"until the last minute." One intercepted message, considered to be relatively insignificant, was to the Japanese consul at Honolulu; he was to "investigate completely the fleet-bases in the neighborhood of the Hawaiian military reservation."

Stark and Marshall concerned themselves with routine activities.

Honolulu, Thursday, December 4

Admiral Kimmel conferred with two of his senior task-force commanders, scheduled to sail the next day on combined training-alert missions. One, under Vice Admiral Wilson Brown, was to proceed to Johnson Island, 700 miles southwest of Oahu, on a joint Navy-Marine bombardment and landing exercise. The other, under Rear Admiral T. H. Newton, included the carrier *Lexington*. This force was to go to Midway Island, fly off a squadron of Marine planes to reinforce the local garrison, and then rendezvous with Brown at Johnson Island. En route the *Lexington*'s planes would conduct routine scouting flights.

Kimmel's intention was that, should war break out, these forces would be available for raids into the Marshall Island group in accordance with existing war plans. Both task-force commanders understood their war-plan missions; both were aware in general of the tense international situation. Kimmel, therefore, felt he was under no obligation to inform either of Washington's November 27 "war warning" message.

The net naval situation on Oahu now was that the entire carrier force of the Pacific Fleet was either at sea or about to steam and that the approaches to the island from the west would be scouted for several days to come.

Kimmel felt that these steps would ensure a reconnaissance search of a large portion of the central Pacific Ocean, as extensive as his limited aircraft strength would permit. But, from the Hawaiian Islands north to the Aleutians, both sea and air were still bare of American reconnaissance.

Kimmel and Short did not meet that day.

[Admiral Nagumo, watching the intermittent refueling being carried on during the day, was intrigued to learn from Honolulu, via Tokyo, that watchful Japanese eyes were "unable to ascertain whether air alert had been issued. There are no indications of sea alert. . . ."]

Washington, Friday, December 5

Both War and Navy departments were busy compiling data for President Roosevelt on Japanese sea, land, and air strength concentrating in French Indochina and adjacent areas. In an intercepted Japanese message from Washington, Ambassador Nomura told Tokyo that in case of Japanese invasion of Thailand, joint military action by Great Britain and the United States "is a definite certainty, with or without a declaration of war." Another, from Tokyo, reiterated the previous instructions about destruction of codes and coding machines.

Admiral Stark, conferring with staff officers, decided no further warning orders need be sent to overseas naval commanders; the message of November 27 was adequate. All concurred.

Honolulu, Friday, December 5

General Short read with interest a cryptic message from G-2 in Washington to his intelligence officer, directing him to get in touch with the Navy immediately "regarding broadcasts from Tokyo reference weather." So Lieutenant Colonel George W. Bicknell, assistant G-2, gave the General all facts obtainable from his own office and from Kimmel's headquarters. Short was informed by Kimmel of the departure of the two naval task forces of Admirals Brown and Newton.

[*While pilots and squadron leaders on board Nagumo's fleet studied and restudied their coming roles, the ships—900 miles north of Midway and 1,300 miles northwest of Oahu—slid slowly down the North Pacific rollers, still far beyond the range of any American search plane.*]

Washington, Saturday, December 6

Reports of increasing Japanese concentration and movements in Indochina, South China, and the South China Sea absorbed Stark and Marshall, as well as all the other members of the War Cabinet from the President down. Mr. Roosevelt, the service chiefs were glad to learn, had decided that he would personally warn Emperor Hirohito that further aggressions might lead to war and urge the Japanese ruler that withdrawal of his forces from Indochina "would result in the assurance of peace throughout the whole of the South Pacific area."

Late in the afternoon Magic plucked out of the air thirteen parts of a fourteen-part memorandum from Tokyo to the Japanese envoys. This much of the message summarized negotiations from the Japanese viewpoint, concluding that the American note of November 26 was not "a basis of negotiations." The envoys were instructed to handle it carefully, since "the situation is extremely delicate."

Distribution of this intercept was curious. Decoding was completed after office hours. General Sherman A. Miles, Army G-2, saw no need to disturb either the Secretary of War, General Marshall, or General Gerow at their homes. (In passing it might be mentioned that one didn't disturb General Marshall at home without extremely good reason.) Some Navy people saw the message. Stark, who was at the theater, learned of it when he returned home and found that he was expected to call the White House. The President had received the intercept, as had the State Department. The details of the conversation are not known, but presumably the President told Stark, as he had earlier said to Harry Hopkins: "This means war!"

Honolulu, Saturday, December 6

In the daily radio intelligence summary received that morning from Washington, Admiral Kimmel was again struck by lack of information on the location of Japanese carriers. In other dispatches, however, there was considerable information about different kinds of Japanese activity. He received a copy of Admiral Hart's message reporting on the movement of the two convoys south of Indochina. And he received a message from Washington authorizing him, "in view of the international situation and the exposed position of our outlying Pacific Islands," to order the destruction of classified documents at these islands, "now or under later conditions of greater emergency." Neither the Admiral nor any member of his staff saw any need to pass on any information to the Army. Presumably General Short was getting it all through Army channels.

Carefully checking the reported locations of all fleet units and projecting their planned routes for the next twenty-four hours, Admiral Kimmel again made his daily revision of his personal check-list memorandum: "Steps to be taken in case of American-Japanese war within the next twenty-four hours."

Over at Fort Shafter, Army headquarters, the daily staff conference was as usual presided over by Colonel Walter C. Phillips, chief of staff. General Short did not normally attend these meetings. Bicknell, assistant G-2, who seems to have been on his toes those days, reported the Japanese consulate in Honolulu was busily burning and destroying secret papers, significant in light of similar reports throughout the world already noted in the intercepts. The chief of staff and G-2 reported this information later to General Short.

And so Oahu drifted into another weekend: a time of relaxation for both Army and Navy. Short, however, was interrupted by Bicknell early that evening at his quarters while he and his G-2—Colonel Kendall Fielder—and their wives were about to drive to a dinner dance.

Bicknell, with some sense of urgency, reported that the local FBI agent had passed to him and to Navy intelligence a transcript of a suspicious long-distance telephone message. A Japanese named Mori, talking to someone in Tokyo, mentioned flights of airplanes, searchlights, and the number of ships in Pearl Harbor, along with cryptic reference to various flowers—apparently part of some sort of code.

*An unusual photo of the crew of a Japanese aircraft carrier
cheering as the planes take off to attack Pearl Harbor.*

Both the FBI man and Bicknell were alarmed at the implications
of this flower code. Neither Short nor Fielder, however, was disturbed. Short, before they hurried to the car where their wives
awaited them impatiently, told Bicknell he was, perhaps, "too intelli-
gence-conscious." In any event they could talk about it again in the
morning.

The district intelligence officer of the Navy decided that the transcript should be studied further by a Japanese linguist and so put the
FBI report away until Monday morning. Admiral Kimmel was not
informed.

[*Nagumo's fleet, the wallowing tankers now left behind, was churning southward
at twenty-four-knot speed. By 6 A.M. next day it would be 230 miles north of
Oahu with its planes thrusting skyward. And at dawn, five midget two-man
submarines—disgorged from five large Japanese submarines gathered offshore that
night—poked their way around Diamond Head, Pearl Harbor-bound.*]

Washington, Sunday, December 7

By 8 A.M. the last part of the Japanese memorandum—Part Four-teen—had been intercepted, transcribed, and was ready for distribu-tion. Both Army and Navy intelligence officers were slightly surprised at its mild tone: "The Japanese Government regrets . . . that it is impossible to reach an agreement through further negotiations."

Stark got it in his office. Marshall was taking his Sunday morning recreational ride at Fort Myer: the message would await his arrival—usually at about 11 A.M. All others concerned got it. Meanwhile two other messages had been intercepted by Magic, and Colonel Rufus Bratton, executive officer in G-2, was so upset by them he tried vainly to get them to the Chief of Staff.

One of the messages ordered the embassy to destroy immediately its one remaining cipher machine plus all codes and secret documents. The other read:

"Will the Ambassador please submit to the United States Govern-ment (if possible to the Secretary of State) our reply to the United States at 1 P.M. on the 7th, your time."

It will be remembered that General Marshall did not take kindly to interruptions in his off-duty hours. So, despite the limited area of his ride—an automobile or motorcycle from Fort Myers headquarters could have intercepted him in fifteen minutes at most—not until his return to his quarters at ten-thirty did Marshall learn that an important message was awaiting him. He reached his office in the Munitions Building at about 11:15, to find General Gerow, General Miles, and Colonel Bratton there. Bratton handed him the three intercepted mes-sages—the memorandum, the instructions to destroy codes and pa-pers, and the instruction to deliver the Japanese answer at 1 P.M. precisely. Marshall read quickly but carefully, as was usual with him. Then—

"Something is going to happen at one o'clock," he told the officers. "When they specified a day, that of course had significance, but not comparable to an hour."

He immediately called Stark, who had read all three messages. A warning should be sent at once to all Pacific commanders, Marshall felt. Stark hesitated; he felt all had already been alerted. Marshall stated that in view of the "one o'clock" item he would apprise Army commanders anyway.

Hanging up, he reached for a pencil and drafted his instruction to DeWitt, Western Defense Command; Andrews, Panama Command; Short, Hawaiian Command; and MacArthur, Philippine Command. It took him about three minutes. He read it to the group:

"The Japanese are presenting at 1 P.M. E.S.T. today, what amounts to an ultimatum. Also they are under orders to destroy their code machine immediately. Just what significance the hour set may have, we do not know, but be on alert accordingly."

As he was ordering Bratton to send it out at once, Stark telephoned back. Would Marshall please include in his dispatch the "usual expression to inform the naval officer?" Marshall quickly added the words "Inform naval authorities of this communication." He sent Bratton on his way, instructing him to return as soon as the message had been delivered to the message center.

Bratton was back in five minutes; he had delivered the message personally to the officer in charge of the message center, Colonel French.

Marshall, obviously more perturbed than any of those present had ever before seen him, asked Bratton how much time would be consumed in enciphering and dispatching the message. Bratton didn't know. So back he was rushed to find out.

Marshall, it developed, was pondering whether or not he should telephone a warning—especially to MacArthur. Time was running out; not much more than one hour remained. Marshall had a "scrambler" phone on his desk, which permitted secure long-distance conversations with similar phones in the headquarters of overseas commanders; eavesdroppers would hear only unintelligible gibberish. Marshall, however, must have had some private reservations as to the efficacy of the scrambler mechanism, and apparently feared that the Japanese might have some way of deciphering the conversation. A telephone call which could not be kept secret might precipitate Japanese action; it would almost certainly indicate we had broken their secret code. Would it be worth it?

Bratton reported back that the process would take about thirty minutes.

"Thirty minutes until it is dispatched, or thirty minutes until it is received and decoded at the other end?"

Business of rushing back to the message center again, while the big office clock ticked away. Bratton, charging back, announced that the message, decoded, would be in the hands of the addressees in thirty minutes. It was now precisely noon. In Hawaii it was only 6:30 A.M. Marshall, satisfied, made no further follow-up.

Had he done so he would have found out that Colonel French at the message center was having some troubles. To San Francisco, Panama, and Manila the warning sped without delay. But the War Department radio, so Colonel French was informed, had been out of contact with Hawaii since 10:20 that morning. French decided to use commercial facilities: Western Union to San Francisco, thence commercial radio to Honolulu. This was a normal procedure; usually it would mean but little further delay. French never dreamed of disturbing the Chief of Staff by reporting such trivia. So Marshall's warning was filed at the Army Signal Center at 12:01 P.M. (6:31 A.M. in Hawaii); teletype transmission to San Francisco was completed by 12:17 P.M. (6:47 A.M. in Hawaii), and was in the Honolulu office of RCA at 1:03 P.M. Washington time (7:33 A.M. in Hawaii). Since that was too early for teletype traffic to Fort Shafter, RCA sent it by motorcycle messenger. He would, as it turned out, be delayed through extraordinary circumstances.

Honolulu, Sunday, December 7

Extraordinary circumstances had become almost commonplace on and near Oahu as early as 3:42 A.M. At that hour the mine sweeper *Condor,* conducting a routine sweep of the harbor entrance, sighted a submarine periscope. This was a defensive area where American submarines were prohibited from operating submerged. The *Condor* flashed a report of the sighting to the destroyer *Ward,* of the inshore patrol. For two hours the *Ward* searched the harbor entrance in vain; meanwhile the *Condor* and another mine sweeper had entered the harbor at about 5 A.M.; for some reason the antisubmarine net, opened to permit the entrance of the mine sweepers, was not closed.

At 6:30 the U.S.S. *Antares*—a repair ship towing a steel barge—was approaching the harbor entrance when she sighted a suspicious object, which looked like a midget submarine. The *Antares* immediately notified the *Ward.* At 6:55 a Navy patrol plane sighted the same object and dropped two smoke pots on the spot. The *Ward* hastened to the scene, spotting the sub—her superstructure just above the surface— at 6:40, and promptly opened fire. At the same time the patrol plane dropped bombs or depth charges. The submarine keeled over and began to sink, as the *Ward* dropped more depth charges. Shortly after 6:50 the destroyer sent a coded message that it had attacked a submarine in the defensive sea area.

At about 7:40 Admiral Kimmel received a telephone call from the staff duty officer, reporting the *Ward*-submarine incident. Kimmel replied, "I will be right down." Quickly he completed dressing and left for his headquarters.

Meanwhile, the Army's six mobile radar stations on Oahu had been on the alert since 4 A.M. in compliance with General Short's Alert No. 1 instructions. At 7 A.M. five of these stations ceased operations, in accordance with these same instructions. At the remote Opana station at the northern tip of the island, Privates Joseph Lockard and George Elliott kept their set on while waiting for the truck which was to pick them up to take them to breakfast. Lockard, an experienced radar operator, planned to use this time to give Elliott a bit more instruction. At this moment an unusual formation appeared at the edge of the screen; Lockard checked the machine, found it operating properly, and at 7:02 A.M. concluded that a large number of aircraft, approximately 130 miles distant, was approaching Oahu from the north. For fifteen minutes Lockard and Elliott observed the approach of the formation, debating whether they should report it. Finally, at 7:20, Lockard called the radar information center. The switchboard operator informed him that the center had closed down twenty minutes before, that everyone had left except one Air Corps officer, First Lieutenant Kermet Tyler. Lockard reported the approaching flight to Tyler, who thought for a moment; the flight was undoubtedly either a naval patrol, a formation of Hickam Field bombers, or—most likely—a number of B-17's due from the mainland. "Forget it," he told Lockard.

Twenty minutes later—about 7:50—there was a bustle of activity on the decks of the ninety-four vessels of the Pacific Fleet in Pearl Harbor. It was almost time for morning colors on each vessel, and white-garbed sailors were briskly preparing for the daily flag-raising ceremony. Except for one destroyer, moving slowly toward the entrance, each ship was motionless at its moorings.

At 7:55 boatswains' whistles piped, and the preparatory signal for the colors ceremony was hoisted on each ship. At the same moment a low-flying plane, approaching over the hills to the northeast, swooped low over Ford Island, in the middle of the harbor. A bomb dropped on the seaplane ramp, close by the eight battleships moored next to the island. As the plane zoomed upward, displaying the red sun emblem of Japan, it was followed closely by others. By 9:45 some 260 Japanese planes had flashed that emblem over Oahu, and when the dreadful 110 minutes were over, 2,403 Americans—mostly sailors on the battleships—were dead or dying; 1,178 more had been wounded; the battle force of the Pacific Fleet had been destroyed, with four battleships sunk or capsized and the remaining four damaged, while several smaller vessels were sunk or damaged severely. The Japanese lost twenty-nine planes, five midget submarines, and less than a hundred men.

One small further incident is pertinent to our assessment of United States leadership in high places just before Pearl Harbor.

The Nisei RCA messenger boy carrying General Marshall's message speedily found himself involved in trouble. Not until 11:45 could he thread his way through traffic jams, road blocks, and general confusion to reach the Fort Shafter signal office, which was itself swamped in traffic by this time.

Not until 2:58 P.M. Hawaiian time—9:58 that evening in bewildered Washington—was the message decoded and placed on Short's desk. He rushed a copy to Admiral Kimmel, who read it, remarked—perhaps unnecessarily—that it was not of the slightest interest any more, and dropped it into the wastebasket.

It had been a pretty long thirty minutes.

Who was responsible?

No disaster of the magnitude of Pearl Harbor could have occurred without the failure—somewhere and somehow—of leadership. A total of eight separate official investigations searched for scapegoats, and found them. The disaster remained a political football long after the last three of these investigations. And much confusion and argument still exist.

Yet through this welter of discord, some facts and conclusions stand out. Today, nearly thirty years later, in another time of crisis, they hold important lessons.

It makes no difference, in assessing responsibility, that exceptional Japanese military skill, shrouded by deceit and assisted by almost incredible luck, accomplished its mission. Nor, indeed, does it matter that—as adjudicated in the always brilliant light of afterthought—Japan might well have inflicted defeat upon our Pacific Fleet and our Army forces in Hawaii regardless of how well alerted they may have been on December 7, 1941.

It makes no difference, so far as responsibility for the disaster itself was concerned, whether the war could have been prevented by wiser statesmanship or more astute diplomacy—though this would have required a wholehearted and unified national determination which did not exist in America in 1941 and the years before. It makes no difference that on December 7 the President and the Secretary of State—like the civilian Secretaries of War and Navy—had their eyes fixed on the Japanese threat in Southeast Asia. They had repeatedly warned the military men that war had probably become unavoidable.

What *does* matter is that the civilian statesmen—however deft or clumsy, shrewd or shortsighted—performed their difficult tasks of diplomacy and of administration confident that the military men would carry out their professional responsibilities by doing everything humanly possible to prepare for a war so clearly impending. They had every right to expect that—within the limits of scanty means available—the Armed Forces would be ready for any contingency.

The confidence and expectations of civilian leadership and of the nation were tragically dashed that Sunday almost thirty years ago.

Military failures were responsible for Pearl Harbor.

In Washington the most important of these were the following:
1. The War Department staff, over which General Marshall presided, was at the time a complicated but "one-man" shop, where delegation of responsibility was the exception rather than the rule. When Marshall

Scene at Pearl Harbor during December 7, 1941 attack.

was absent, the operational wheels tended to freeze. This situation was
to some extent due to cumbersome organization, to some extent due
to the personality of the Chief of Staff.

2. General Marshall, in a letter to General Short on February 7, 1941,
stressed that "the risk of sabotage and the *risk involved in a surprise raid
by air and submarine* [italics supplied] constitute the real perils of the
[Hawaiian] situation." Yet, although definitely warning General Short
on November 27 of the threat of war, and ordering him to report the
measures he would take in response, Marshall did not check up on
those measures; moreover, he was unaware that Short had done no
more than to take routine precautions against sabotage. And General
Gerow, heading the War Plans Division of General Marshall's General
Staff—as he testified later in taking full responsibility for this slip—had
not made any provision for following up operational orders. The net

result was that both Marshall and Short remained the whole time in blissful ignorance of a vital misinterpretation of orders.

3. Marshall and Admiral Stark—and indeed all members of their staffs who knew the situation—permitted themselves to be hypnotized by the concrete evidence of the aggressive Japanese build-up in Southeast Asia which threatened our Philippines outpost. This theme, it will be remembered, ran as background to nearly all the warnings sent Hawaii. Thus succumbing to the illusory diagnosis of "enemy probable intentions," both top commanders ignored the danger implicit in our inability to locate at least four Japanese carriers.

4. Finally, on December 7, having indicated his full realization of the significance of the "one o'clock" intercept—that less than two hours now separated peace and war—and having decided not to use his "scrambler" telephone, Marshall failed to require surveillance and positive report on the delivery of his final warning.

These certainly were grave lapses in leadership. Yet in fairness, it should be noted that the consequences might not have been disastrous if all subordinate commanders had taken adequate security measures on the basis of the instructions, information, and warnings which they had received. To General Marshall's credit one must also chalk up his ability to profit by his mistakes. In less than three months after Pearl Harbor, he completely reorganized the War Department, decentralizing the mass of relatively minor administrative and executive matters that choked major strategical and tactical decisions. His newly created Operations Division of the General Staff— which he aptly termed his "command post"—ensured co-ordinated action and direction of Army activities in theaters of war all around the globe. On Oahu the situation was less ambiguous: military leadership at the top failed utterly.

Almost three decades later, with war clouds still lowering over most of the world, the story of the Pearl Harbor disaster has more significance than mere passing memorials to the brave men who lost their lives that day. If the lessons are heeded, our surviving descendants may never again have to commemorate another "day of infamy."

The Cold War

CHARLES L. MEE, JR.

During the latter stages of World War II, the American people were subjected to a barrage of propaganda designed to convince them that the Soviet Union was fighting democracy's battle against fascist tyranny (as indeed it was) and that the Russian dictator Joseph Stalin was somehow a benevolent grandfather who puffed amiably at an old pipe while dispensing shrewd bits of folk wisdom to millions of loyal and admiring followers (which was utterly preposterous). Then, almost before the echoes of the last shots of the war had faded, the United States and the Soviet Union were engaged in the first of that long series of crises and confrontations that are known as the Cold War. American historians have written about this conflict at great length, and in recent years many of them have argued that the Cold War was largely the responsibility of the United States. Apparently aggressive Soviet actions, these historians insist, were in reality Russian attempts at self-protection. Stalin, if not the kindly character depicted in the early 1940s, was not an aggressor; he was primarily interested in protecting his nation from a possible invasion from the West.

What distinguishes the work of Charles L. Mee, Jr., from that of most other historians who are critical of American Cold War policy is that his interpretation is so nicely balanced. He understands the problems American leaders faced and has no illusions about the character of Soviet leadership. No one will be able to write the definitive history of the Cold War until the Russian archives are opened, but Mee's account is as definitive as possible at this time. Mee is a former editor of Horizon *and the author of* Meeting at Potsdam. ■

On April 12, 1945, Franklin Roosevelt died, and soon afterward Vyascheslav M. Molotov, the Russian foreign minister, stopped by in Washington to pay his respects to Harry Truman, the new President. Truman received Molotov in the Oval Office and, as Truman recalled it, chewed him out "bluntly" for the way the Russians were behaving in Poland. Molotov was stunned. He had never, he told Truman, "been talked to like that in my life."

"Carry out your agreements," Truman responded, "and you won't get talked to like that."

That's a good way to talk, if you want to start an argument . . .

In Europe, Germany surrendered to the Allies on May 8. On May 12, Prime Minister Winston Churchill sent Truman an ominous cable about the Russians: "An iron curtain is drawn down upon their front," Churchill said, and, moreover, "it would be open to the Russians in a very short time to advance if they chose to the waters of the North Sea and the Atlantic." On May 17, Churchill ordered his officers not to destroy any German planes. In fact, Churchill kept 700,000 captured German troops in military readiness, prepared to be turned against the Russians.

That, too, is a good way to behave, if you are looking for trouble . . .

Joseph Stalin said little: he did not advance his troops to the Atlantic, but he planted them firmly throughout eastern Europe and, in violation of previous agreements with the British and Americans, systematically crushed all vestiges of democratic government in Poland, Hungary, Czechoslovakia, Bulgaria, Rumania, Yugoslavia, and Finland. In truth, not quite: the Finns had managed to salvage a few bits and scraps of democratic usage for themselves. At dinner one night in the Kremlin, Andrei Zhdanov, one of Stalin's propagandists, complained that the Russians should have occupied Finland. "Akh, Finland," said Molotov, "that is a peanut."

And that, too, is a nice way to behave, if you are trying to stir up a fight . . .

Most people, most of the time, want peace in the world, and they imagine that most politicians, being human, share the same wishes. At the end of a war, presumably, the desire for peace is most intense and most widely shared. Lamentably, that is not always the case. At the end of World War II the Russians, as Churchill remarked, feared "our friendship more than our enmity."

The Russians had both immediate cause and long-standing historical reasons for anxiety.

"From the beginning of the ninth century," as Louis Halle, a former State Department historian, has written, "and even today, the prime driving force in Russia has been fear. . . . The Russians as we know them today have experienced ten centuries of constant, mortal fear. This has not been a disarming experience. It has not been an experience calculated to produce a simple, open, innocent, and guileless society." Scattered over a vast land with no natural frontiers for protection, as Halle remarks, the Russians have been overrun "generation after generation, by fresh waves of invaders. . . . Lying defenseless on the plain, they were slaughtered and subjugated and humiliated by the invaders time and again."

Thus the Russians sought to secure their borders along eastern Europe. The czars attempted this, time and again: to secure a buffer zone, on their European frontier, a zone that would run down along a line that would later be called the Iron Curtain.

Yet, at the end of World War II, Stalin's fears were not just fears of outsiders. World War II had shown that his dictatorship was not only brutal but also brutally inept; he was neither a great military leader nor a good administrator; and the Russian soldiers returning from the Western Front had seen much evidence of Western prosperity. Stalin needed the Cold War, not to venture out into the world again after an exhausting war, but to discipline his restless people at home. He had need of that ancient stratagem of monarchs—the threat of an implacable external enemy to be used to unite his own people in Russia.

Churchill, on the other hand, emerged from World War II with a ruined empire irretrievably in debt, an empire losing its colonies and headed inevitably toward bankruptcy. Churchill's scheme for saving Great Britain was suitably inspired and grand: he would, in effect, reinvent the British Empire; he would establish an economic union of Europe (much like what the Common Market actually became); this union would certainly not be led by vanquished Germany or Italy, not by so small a power as the Netherlands, not by devastated France, but by Great Britain. To accomplish this aim, unfortunately, Churchill had almost nothing in the way of genuine economic or military power left; he had only his own force of persuasion and rhetoric. He would try to parlay those gifts into American backing for England's move into Europe. The way to bring about American backing was for Churchill to arrange to have America and Russia quarrel; while America and Russia quarreled, England would—as American diplomats delicately put it—"lead" Europe.

Truman, for his part, led a nation that was strong and getting stronger. Henry Luce, the publisher of the influential *Time* and *Life* magazines, declared that this was to be the beginning of "the American Century"—and such a moment is rarely one in which a national leader wants to maintain a status quo. The United States was securing the Western Hemisphere, moving forcefully into England's collapsing "sterling bloc," acquiring military and economic positions over an area of the planet so extensive that the sun could never set on it.

The promise was extraordinary, the threat equally so. The United States did not practice Keynesian economics during the 1930's. It was not Roosevelt's New Deal that ran up the enormous federal deficit or built the huge, wheezing federal bureaucracy of today. War ran up the deficit; war licked the depression; war made the big federal government. In 1939, after a decade of depression, after the Civilian Conservation Corps, the Public Works Administration, the Civil Works Administration, the Agricultural Adjustment Act, the Social Security Act, and all the rest of the New Deal efforts on behalf of social justice, the federal budget was $9 billion. In 1945 it was $100 billion.

American prosperity was built upon deficit spending for war. President Truman knew it, and maintained deficit spending with the Cold War. Eventually, with the Truman Doctrine and the Marshall Plan, the encouragement of American multinational companies, and a set of defense treaties that came finally to encompass the world, he institutionalized it. The American people might find this easier to damn if they had not enjoyed the uncommon prosperity it brought them.

In October, 1944, Churchill visited Stalin in Moscow. The need then, clearly, was for cooperation among the Allies in order to win the war—and it appeared at the time that the cooperativeness nurtured during the war could be continued afterward. Each had only to recognize the other's vital interests. Churchill commenced to outline those interests to be recognized for the sake of the postwar cooperation.

"I said," Churchill recalled, " 'Let us settle about our affairs in the Balkans. Your armies are in Rumania and Bulgaria. We have interests, missions, and agents there. Don't let us get at cross-purposes in small ways. So far as Britain and Russia are concerned, how would it do for you to have ninety percent predominance in Rumania, for us to have ninety per cent of the say in Greece, and go fifty-fifty about Yugoslavia?' "

Churchill wrote this out on a piece of paper, noting, too, a split of Bulgaria that gave Russia 75 per cent interest, and a fifty-fifty split of Hungary. He pushed the piece of paper across the table to Stalin, who placed a check mark on it and handed it back. There was a silence. "At length I said, 'Might it not be thought rather cynical if it seemed we had disposed of these issues, so fateful to millions of people, in such an offhand manner? Let us burn the paper.' 'No, you keep it,' said Stalin."

Such casual and roughshod "agreements" could hardly be the last word on the matter; yet, they signified a mutual recognition of one another's essential interests and a willingness to accommodate one another's needs—while, to be sure, the smaller powers were sold out by all sides. At this same time, in October, 1944, and later on in January, 1945, Roosevelt entered into armistice agreements with Britain and Russia that gave Stalin almost complete control of the internal affairs of the ex-Nazi satellites in eastern Europe. As a briefing paper that the State Department prepared in the spring of 1945 for President Truman said, "spheres of influence do in fact exist," and "eastern Europe is, in fact, a Soviet sphere of influence."

In short, the stage was set for postwar peace: spheres of influence had been recognized; a tradition of negotiation had been established. Yet, the European phase of World War II was no sooner ended than symptoms of the Cold War began to appear. The Big Three no longer needed one another to help in the fight against Hitler, and the atomic bomb would soon settle the war against Japan.

Toward the end of May, 1945, Harry Hopkins arrived in Moscow to talk with Stalin, to feel out the Russians now that the war in Europe had ended, and to prepare the agenda for discussion at the Potsdam Conference that would be held in Germany in mid-July. The United States had a problem, Hopkins informed Stalin, a problem so serious that it threatened "to affect adversely the relations between our two countries." The problem was, Hopkins said, Poland: "our inability to carry into effect the Yalta Agreement on Poland."

But, what was the problem? Stalin wanted to know. A government had been established there, under the auspices of the occupying Red Army, a government that was, naturally, "friendly" to the Soviet Union. There could be no problem—unless others did not wish to allow the Soviet Union to ensure a friendly government in Poland.

"Mr. Hopkins stated," according to the notes taken by his interpreter, Charles Bohlen, "that the United States would desire a Poland friendly to the Soviet Union and in fact desired to see friendly countries all along the Soviet borders.

"Marshal Stalin replied if that be so we can easily come to terms in regard to Poland."

But, said Hopkins, Stalin must remember the Declaration on Liberated Europe (signed at the Yalta Conference in February, 1945) and its guarantees for democratic governments; there was a serious difference between them; Poland had become the issue over which cooperation between Russia and America would flourish or fail.

Evidently Stalin could not understand this demand; apparently he could not believe that Americans were sincerely so idealistic. Did not America, after all, support a manifestly undemocratic dictatorship in Franco's Spain? "I am afraid," Averell Harriman, the U.S. ambassador to the Soviet Union, cabled home to Truman, "Stalin does not and never will fully understand our interest in a free Poland as a matter of principle. He is a realist in all of his actions, and it is hard for him to appreciate our faith in abstract principles. It is difficult for him to understand why we should want to interfere with Soviet policy in a country like Poland, which he considers so important to Russia's security, unless we have some ulterior motive."

And indeed, Russia's sphere of influence was recognized, it seemed, only so that it might serve as a bone of contention. Poland, Czechoslovakia, Bulgaria, Rumania, Hungary, all became bones of contention. It is not clear that any one of the Big Three deeply cared what happened to these eastern European countries so long as the countries served as useful pawns. Hopkins insisted that Stalin must recognize freedom of speech, assembly, movement, and religious worship in Poland and that all political parties (except fascists) must be "permitted the free use, without distinction, of the press, radio, meetings and other facilities of political expression." Furthermore, all citizens must have "the right of public trial, defense by counsel of their own choosing, and the right of habeas corpus."

Of course, Stalin said, of course, "these principles of democracy are well known and would find no objection on the part of the Soviet Government." To be sure, he said, "in regard to the *specific* [italics added] freedoms mentioned by Mr. Hopkins, they could only be applied in full in peace time, and even then with certain limitations."

In the latter two weeks of July, 1945, the Big Three gathered at Potsdam, just outside of Berlin, for the last of the wartime conferences. They discussed the issues with which the war in Europe had left them, and with which the war in the Far East would leave them when it came to an end. They discussed spheres of influence, the disposition of Germany, the spoils of war, reparations, and, of course, eastern Europe.

At one of the plenary sessions of the Potsdam Conference, they outlined the spheres of influence precisely, clearly, and in detail during a discussion of the issue of "German shares, gold, and assets abroad." To whom did these items belong? What, for instance, did Stalin mean when he said "abroad"?

STALIN: ". . . the Soviet delegation . . . will regard the whole of Western Germany as falling within your sphere, and Eastern Germany, within ours."

Truman asked whether Stalin meant to establish "a line running from the Baltic to the Adriatic." Stalin replied that he did.

STALIN: "As to the German investments, I should put the question this way: as to the German investments in Eastern Europe, they remain with us, and the rest, with you. . . ."
TRUMAN: "Does this apply only to German investments in Europe or in other countries as well?"

The Big Three at Potsdam: Joseph Stalin, Harry Truman, and Winston Churchill.

STALIN: "Let me put it more specifically: the German investments in Ru-
mania, Bulgaria, Hungary, and Finland go to us, and all the rest to you."
FOREIGN MINISTER ERNEST BEVIN: "The German investments in other coun-
tries go to us?"
STALIN: "In all other countries, in South America, in Canada, etc., all this
is yours. . . ."
SECRETARY OF STATE JAMES BYRNES: "If an enterprise is not in Eastern
Europe but in Western Europe or in other parts of the world, that
enterprise remains ours?"
STALIN: "In the United States, in Norway, in Switzerland, in Sweden, in
Argentina [general laughter], etc.—all that is yours."

A delegation of Poles arrived at Potsdam to argue their own case
before the Big Three. The Poles, struggling desperately and vainly for

their land, their borders, their freedoms, did not seem to understand that their fate was being settled for reasons that had nothing to do with them. They wandered about Potsdam, trying to impress their wishes on the Big Three. "I'm sick of the bloody Poles," Churchill said when they came to call on him. "I don't want to see them. Why can't Anthony [Eden] talk to them?" Alexander Cadogan, Permanent Undersecretary for Foreign Affairs, found the Poles at Eden's house late one night and "had to entertain them as best I could, and went on entertaining them—no signs of A. He didn't turn up till 11:30. . . . So then we got down to it, and talked shop till 1:30. Then filled the Poles (and ourselves) with sandwiches and whiskies and sodas and I went to bed at 2 A.M." Altogether, it had been an agreeable enough evening, although in general, Cadogan confided to his diary, he found the Poles to be "dreadful people. . . ."

Germany, too, provided a rich field for contention. The answer to the German question became a simple but ticklish matter of keeping Germany sufficiently weak so that it could not start another war and yet, at the same time, sufficiently strong to serve as a buffer against Russia, or, from Russia's point of view, against the Western powers. To achieve this delicate balance, the Big Three haggled at Potsdam over a complex set of agreements about zones of authority, permissible levels of postwar industry, allocation of resources of coal and foodstuffs, spoils of war reparations, and other matters. The country as a whole was divided into administrative zones in which Allied commanders had absolute veto powers over some matters, and, in other respects, had to defer to a central governmental council for measures to be applied uniformly to Germany.

Out of all these careful negotiations came the astonishing fact that Germany was established as the very center and source of much of the anxiety and conflict of the Cold War. How this could have happened is one of the wonders of the history of diplomacy. The discussions and bargaining at Potsdam among Churchill, Truman, and Stalin, and among the foreign ministers, and on lower levels, among economic committees and subcommittees, is maddeningly tangled; but, once all of the nettlesome complexities are cleared away, the postwar arrangement for Germany can be seen with sudden and arresting clarity. The Big Three agreed to have a Germany that would be politically united—but, at the very same time, economically divided. They agreed, then, to create a country that could never be either wholly united nor entirely divided, neither one Germany nor two Germanies, but rather a country that would be perpetually at war with itself, and, since its two halves would have two patrons, would keep its two patrons in continuous conflict. Whether this postwar arrangement for Germany was intentional or inadvertent, it was certainly a diplomatic tour de force. In

1949, with the formation of the West German and East German governments, the contradictions of the Potsdam policy became overt.

Eastern Europe, Germany, and the atomic bomb were the three most striking elements of the early Cold War. It was while he was at the Potsdam Conference that President Truman received news that the test of the bomb at Alamogordo had been successful. By that time the bomb was no longer militarily necessary to end the war against Japan; the Japanese were near the end and were attempting to negotiate peace by way of their ambassador to Moscow. After the bomb was dropped, Truman would maintain that it had avoided the invasion of the Japanese mainland and so saved a million American lives. But was that true?

General Henry (Hap) Arnold, chief of the Army Air Forces, said, before the atomic device was dropped on Japan, that conventional bombing would end the war without an invasion. Admiral Ernest J. King, chief of U.S. naval operations, advised that a naval blockade alone would end the war. General Eisenhower said it was "completely unnecessary" to drop the bomb, and that the weapon was "no longer mandatory as a measure to save American lives." Even General George Marshall, U.S. chief of staff and the strongest advocate at that late hour for the bomb's use, advised that the Japanese at least be forewarned to give them a chance to surrender. Diplomats advised Truman that he need only have Russia sign his proclamation calling for Japanese surrender; the Russians had not yet declared war against Japan, and so the Japanese still had hopes that the Russians would help them negotiate peace; if Russia signed the proclamation, the Japanese would see that their last chance was gone and would surrender. None of this advice was followed.

After the war, the United States Strategic Bombing Command issued a study confirming the advice Truman had been getting before he gave the order to drop the atomic bomb: "Japan would have surrendered even if the atomic bombs had not been dropped, even if Russia had not entered the war, and even if no invasion had been planned or contemplated." Then why was it dropped? Admiral William Leahy, Truman's top aide, was unable to offer the puzzled British chiefs of staff a better explanation than that it was "because of the vast sums that had been spent on the project," although he commented that in using the bomb, the Americans "had adopted an ethical standard common to the barbarians of the Dark Ages."

However that may be, its use must have been chilling to Stalin; doubly chilling if Stalin realized that the United States had used the bomb even when it was not militarily necessary. Indeed, according to Secretary of State James Byrnes, that was the real reason why the bomb was used after all—"to make Russia," as he said, "more manageable

The August 6, 1945 bombing of Hiroshima—the first of two atomic bombings of Japan.

in Europe." Perhaps it is because that constituted a war crime—to kill people when it is not militarily necessary is a war crime according to international accord—that Truman insisted to his death, and in obstinate defiance of all other opinion, that it was militarily necessary.

The bomb may have been dropped, too, in order to end the war against Japan without Russian help. The Russians had promised to enter the war in the Far East exactly three months after the war in Europe ended—which it did on May 8. Truman's aim was not merely to end the war against Japan, but to end it before August 8.

When word reached Potsdam that the atomic bomb had been successfully tested, Truman was enormously pleased. When the news was passed along to Churchill, the prime minister was overcome with delight at the "vision—fair and bright indeed it seemed—of the end of the whole war in one or two violent shocks." Churchill understood at once that "we should not need the Russians," and he concluded that "we seemed suddenly to have become possessed of a merciful abridgment of the slaughter in the East and of a far happier prospect in Europe. I have no doubt that these thoughts were present in the minds of my American friends."

The problem was what to tell the Russians. Presumably, as allies of the Americans and British, they needed to be told of this new weapon in which Truman and Churchill placed such tremendous hopes. Yet, if the Russians were told, they might rush to enter the war against Japan and so share in the victory. "The President and I no longer felt that we needed [Stalin's] aid to conquer Japan," Churchill wrote. And so Stalin must be told about the existence of the bomb—and at the same time he must not be told. In short, Truman and Churchill decided, Stalin must be informed so casually as not to understand that he was being informed of much of anything.

On July 24, after one of the sessions of the Potsdam Conference, Truman got up from the baize-covered table and sauntered around to Stalin. The President had left his interpreter, Charles Bohlen, behind and relied on Stalin's personal translator—signifying that he had nothing important to say, just idle, end-of-the-day chit-chat.

"I was perhaps five yards away," Churchill recalled, "and I watched with the closest attention the momentous talk. I knew what the President was going to do. What was vital to measure was its effect on Stalin. I can see it all as if it were yesterday."

"I casually mentioned to Stalin," Truman wrote in his memoirs, "that we had a new weapon of unusual destructive force. The Russian Premier showed no special interest. All he said was that he was glad to hear it and hoped we would make 'good use of it against the Japanese.'"

"I was sure," Churchill said, "that [Stalin] had no idea of the significance of what he was being told . . . his face remained gay and genial and the talk between these two potentates soon came to an end. As we were waiting for our cars I found myself near Truman. 'How did it go?' I asked. 'He never asked a question,' he replied."

According to the Russian General Shtemenko, the ploy worked: the Russian Army staff "received no special instructions" after this meeting. According to Marshal Georgi K. Zhukov, commander of the Russian zone of occupation in Germany, Stalin returned from the meeting and told Molotov about Truman's remarks. Molotov "reacted immediately: 'Let them. We'll have to talk it over with Kurchatov and get him to speed things up.' I realized they were talking about research on the atomic bomb."

Whatever the case, whether Stalin realized what he had been told at the time, or only in retrospect, the nuclear arms race began, in effect, at Potsdam, on July 24, 1945, at 7:30 P.M.

Distrust, suspicion, anxiety, fear—all were intensified at Potsdam, and to them were added harshness and provocation, from all sides. During the next few months the agreements that had been reached were violated, or used as the bases for accusations of duplicity and bad faith. Many of the questions raised at Potsdam had been postponed and delegated to a Council of Foreign Ministers that was established to deal with these questions, and new ones, as they arose. The first meeting of the council was set for September, 1945. James Byrnes, before he left Washington to attend the meeting, had chatted with Secretary of War Henry Stimson. "I found that Byrnes was very much against any attempt to cooperate with Russia," Stimson noted in his diary. "His mind is full of his problems with the coming meeting of foreign ministers and he looks to have the presence of the bomb in his pocket, so to speak, as a great weapon to get through the thing. . . ." The British Chancellor of the Exchequer, Rt. Hon. Hugh Dalton, asked Foreign Minister Ernest Bevin how things were going, once the meeting started. "Like the strike leader said," Bevin replied, "thank God there is no danger of a settlement."

Not everyone was so quick or so eager to encourage the start of the Cold War. Henry Stimson was very much the elder statesman in 1945; he had spent more than fifty years in assorted government positions, and he foresaw dread consequences in Truman's developing policies toward Russia. Stimson had long thought that America should be tough with the Soviet Union, but he now believed that toughness was turning into harshness and harshness into provocativeness. In a memo that he wrote Truman in the autumn of 1945, he focused his thoughts around one of the most vexing problems of the postwar world:

". . . I consider the problem of our satisfactory relations with Russia as not merely connected with but as virtually dominated by the prob-

Secretary of War Henry Stimson with Chief of Staff George
C. Marshall in early 1945. Marshall later became
Secretary of State and developer of the Marshall Plan—a
key feature of the Cold War.

lem of the atomic bomb. Except for the problem of the control of that
bomb, those relations, while vitally important, might not be immediately pressing. . . . But with the discovery of the bomb, they became
immediately emergent. These relations may be perhaps irretrievably
embittered by the way in which we approach the solution of the bomb
with Russia. For if we fail to approach them now and merely continue
to negotiate with them having this weapon rather ostentatiously on our
hip, their suspicions and their distrust of our purposes and motives will
increase. . . .

"The chief lesson I have learned in a long life is that the only way
you can make a man trustworthy is to trust him; and the surest way to
make him untrustworthy is to distrust him and show your distrust."

Men like Stimson—and Henry Wallace, then Secretary of Commerce—were allowed, or forced, to resign. Others, those who tended
to believe in an aggressive attitude toward Russia, were spotted, and
promoted—young men such as John Foster Dulles and Dean Rusk.
George Kennan, then in the American embassy in Moscow, was discovered after he sent a perfervid 8,000-word cable back to Washington:

"We have here a political force committed fanatically to the belief that with U.S. there can be no permanent modus vivendi, that it is desirable and necessary that the internal harmony of our society be disrupted, our traditional way of life be destroyed, the international authority of our state be broken. . . ." In his memoirs, Kennan says that he now looks back on his cable "with horrified amusement." At the time, however, he was ideal for Truman's use, and he was recalled from Moscow and made chairman of the State Department's Policy Planning Committee, or as the *New York Times* called him, "America's global planner."

At Potsdam, the Big Three had all agreed to remove their troops from Iran. They set a deadline of March 2, 1946, and, as the deadline approached, the British announced that they would be leaving. The Russians, however, let it be known that they were somewhat reluctant to leave until they had made an agreement with the Iranians for an oil concession, and, regardless even of that agreement, Stalin rather thought he would like to withdraw only from central Iran and keep some troops in northern Iran. Not all these matters were immediately clarified and so, on March 1, 1946, Stalin announced that Russian soldiers would remain in Iran "pending clarification of the situation."

President Truman, meanwhile, invited Winston Churchill to deliver an address in March, 1946, at Fulton, Missouri: "A shadow has fallen upon the scenes so lately lighted by the Allied victory," said the former prime minister. "Nobody knows what Soviet Russia and its Communist international organization intends to do in the immediate future, or what are the limits, if any, to their expansive and proselytising tendencies. . . . From Stettin in the Baltic to Trieste in the Adriatic [the line, as Churchill neglected to mention, to which he and Truman had agreed at Potsdam], an iron curtain had descended across the Continent. Behind that line lie all the capitals of the ancient states of Central and Eastern Europe . . . in what I must call the Soviet sphere. . . . this is certainly not the Liberated Europe we fought to build up. Nor is it one which contains the essentials of permanent peace."

In Moscow, a well-rehearsed Russian reporter quizzed Stalin.

QUESTION: "How do you appraise Mr. Churchill's latest speech in the United States?"

STALIN: "I appraise it as a dangerous act, calculated to sow the seeds of dissension among the Allied states and impede their collaboration."

QUESTION: "Can it be considered that Mr. Churchill's speech is prejudicial to the cause of peace and security?"

STALIN: "Yes, unquestionably. As a matter of fact, Mr. Churchill now takes the stand of the warmongers, and in this Mr. Churchill is not alone. He has friends not only in Britain but in the United States of America as well."

During the winter of 1946–47, a succession of snowstorms hit Britain. Coal was already in short supply; factories had already closed for lack of fuel that winter. With the blizzards came rationing, first of electricity and then of food; finally heat was cut off. Britain, as Louis Halle wrote, "was like a soldier wounded in war who, now that fighting was over, was bleeding to death." The empire was at last dying.

In Washington, on February 21, 1947, a Friday afternoon, First Secretary H. M. Sichel of the British embassy delivered two notes to Loy Henderson at the State Department. Until that moment, Britain had been the principal support for the economy of Greece and the provider for the Turkish Army. The first of Sichel's notes said that Britain could no longer support Greece; the second said Britain could no longer underwrite the Turkish Army. "What the two notes reported," Halle observed, "was the final end of the *Pax Britannica.*"

The following week, on February 27, Truman met with congressional leaders in the White House. Undersecretary of State Dean Acheson was present at the meeting, and Truman had him tell the congressmen what was at stake. Acheson spoke for ten minutes, informing the legislators that nothing less than the survival of the whole of Western civilization was in the balance at that moment; he worked in references to ancient Athens, Rome, and the course of Western civilization and freedoms since those times. The congressmen were silent for a few moments, and then, at last, Senator Arthur Vandenberg of Michigan, a prominent Republican who had come to support an active foreign policy, spoke up. All this might be true, Vandenberg said; but, if the President wished to sell his program to the American people, he would have to "scare hell out of the country." It was at that moment that the Cold War began in earnest for the United States.

It would be nice to be able to say that one nation held back from the nattering and abusiveness, that one seemed reluctant to start a conflict with its former allies, that one tried to compose the differences that had predictably arisen at the end of the war, that this one was the first to make a provocative move or charge and that one was last—but in truth all three leaped into the fray with such haste and determination that the origins of the Cold War are lost in a blur of all three sides hastening to be first in battle.

It is difficult to know the effects the Cold War had upon the Russian people in these years. But America paid heavy costs. When a nation has an actively internationalist, interventionist foreign policy, political power in that country tends to flow to the central government, and, within the central government, to the executive branch. That there was, in recent times, the creation of an "imperial presidency" in the U.S. was no quirk or happenstance; it was the natural outgrowth of the

Cold War. From the imperial presidency, from the disorientation of the constitutional system of checks and balances, Watergate, proteiform and proliferating spy organizations, the impotence and decadence of Congress—all these were almost inevitable. That is why George Washington, a profoundly sophisticated man, advised Americans to avoid foreign entanglements; and that is why Americans who prize their freedom have always been a peace-loving people.

Part Five

Great Depression and the New Deal

In 1932 thousands of World War I veterans marched on Washington to demand payment of a cash bonus. This California group camped on the Capitol grounds.

The Causes of the Great Crash

JOHN KENNETH GALBRAITH

The following essay is an example of analytical history at its best. Without relying on narrative techniques, the Harvard economist John Kenneth Galbraith takes apart the economy of the 1920s and shows us how its weaknesses led to the Great Depression of the 1930s. In the course of doing so, he also "takes apart," in the colloquial sense of that expression, the presidents of the 1920s and a number of their leading advisers.

The effectiveness and power of the essay depend upon a number of factors. One is Galbraith's mastery both of the facts he deals with and of the economic mechanisms of the society; he discusses few events that are not thoroughly familiar to students of the subject, but he has an unfailing eye for what is significant. Another is his gift for anecdote and the pithy phrase. As he says, the epigram that Elbert H. Gary of U.S. Steel "never saw a blast furnace until his death" is well known; but not everyone who writes about Gary knows enough to use it. Still a third is Galbraith's ability to state his own opinions without qualification and at the same time without passion, to make the kind of calm, reasoned judgments that are characteristic of a convinced but unprejudiced and intelligent mind. All these qualities explain why his books, such as American Capitalism, The Affluent Society, *and* The Great Crash, 1929 *(a fuller treatment of the subject of this essay), have been both popular and critical successes.* ∎

The decade of the twenties, or more exactly the eight years between the postwar depression of 1920–21 and the sudden collapse of the stock market in October, 1929, were prosperous ones in the United States. The total output of the economy increased by more than 50 per cent. The preceding decades had brought the automobile; now came many more and also roads on which they could be driven with reasonable reliability and comfort. There was much building. The downtown section of the mid-continent city—Des Moines, Omaha, Minneapolis—dates from these years. It was then, more likely than not, that what is still the leading hotel, the tallest office building, and the biggest department store went up. Radio arrived, as of course did gin and jazz.

These years were also remarkable in another respect, for as time passed it became increasingly evident that the prosperity could not last. Contained within it were the seeds of its own destruction. The country was heading into the gravest kind of trouble. Herein lies the peculiar fascination of the period for a study in the problem of leadership. For almost no steps were taken during these years to arrest the tendencies which were obviously leading, and did lead, to disaster.

At least four things were seriously wrong, and they worsened as the decade passed. And knowledge of them does not depend on the always brilliant assistance of hindsight. At least three of these flaws were highly visible and widely discussed. In ascending order, not of importance but of visibility, they were as follows:

First, income in these prosperous years was being distributed with marked inequality. Although output per worker rose steadily during the period, wages were fairly stable, as also were prices. As a result, business profits increased rapidly and so did incomes of the wealthy and the well-to-do. This tendency was nurtured by assiduous and successful efforts of Secretary of the Treasury Andrew W. Mellon to reduce income taxes with special attention to the higher brackets. In 1929 the 5 per cent of the people with the highest incomes received perhaps a quarter of all personal income. Between 1919 and 1929 the share of the one per cent who received the highest incomes increased by approximately one seventh. This meant that the economy was heavily and increasingly dependent on the luxury consumption of the well-to-do and their willingness to reinvest what they did not or could not spend on themselves. Anything that shocked the confidence of the rich either in their personal or in their business future would have a bad effect on total spending and hence on the behavior of the economy.

This was the least visible flaw. To be sure, farmers, who were not participating in the general advance, were making themselves heard; and twice during the period the Congress passed far-reaching relief legislation which was vetoed by Coolidge. But other groups were much less vocal. Income distribution in the United States had long been unequal. The inequality of these years did not seem exceptional. The trade-union movement was also far from strong. In the early twenties the steel industry was still working a twelve-hour day and, in some jobs, a seven-day week. (Every two weeks when the shift changed a man worked twice around the clock.) Workers lacked the organization or the power to deal with conditions like this; the twelve-hour day was, in fact, ended as the result of personal pressure by President Harding on the steel companies, particularly on Judge Elbert H. Gary, head of the United States Steel Corporation. Judge Gary's personal acquaintance with these working conditions was thought to be slight, and this gave rise to Benjamin Stolberg's now classic observation that the Judge "never saw a blast furnace until his death." In all these circumstances the increasingly lopsided income distribution did not excite much comment or alarm. Perhaps it would have been surprising if it had.

But the other three flaws in the economy were far less subtle. During World War I the United States ceased to be the world's greatest debtor country and became its greatest creditor. The consequences of this change have so often been described that they have the standing of a cliché. A debtor country could export a greater value of goods than it imported and use the difference for interest and debt repayment. This was what we did before the war. But a creditor must import a greater value than it exports if those who owe it money are to have the wherewithal to pay interest and principal. Otherwise the creditor must either forgive the debts or make new loans to pay off the old.

During the twenties the balance was maintained by making new foreign loans. Their promotion was profitable to domestic investment houses. And when the supply of honest and competent foreign borrowers ran out, dishonest, incompetent, or fanciful borrowers were invited to borrow and, on occasion, bribed to do so. In 1927 Juan Leguia, the son of the then dictator of Peru, was paid $450,000 by the National City Company and J. & W. Seligman for his services in promoting a $50,000,000 loan to Peru which these houses marketed. Americans lost and the Peruvians didn't gain appreciably. Other Latin American republics got equally dubious loans by equally dubious devices. And, for reasons that now tax the imagination, so did a large number of German cities and municipalities. Obviously, once investors awoke to the character of these loans or there was any other shock to confidence, they would no longer be made. There would be nothing with which to pay the old loans. Given this arithmetic, there would be either a sharp reduction in exports or a wholesale default on the outstanding loans, or more likely both. Wheat and cotton farmers and others who depended on exports would suffer. So would those who owned the bonds. The buying power of both would be reduced. These consequences were freely predicted at the time.

The second weakness of the economy was the large-scale corporate thimblerigging that was going on. This took a variety of forms, of which by far the most common was the organization of corporations to hold stock in yet other corporations, which in tui n held stock in yet other corporations. In the case of the railroads and the utilities, the purpose of this pyramid of holding companies was to obtain control of a very large number of operating companies with a very small investment in the ultimate holding company. A $100,000,000 electric utility, of which the capitalization was represented half by bonds and half by common stock, could be controlled with an investment of a little over $25,000,000—the value of just over half the common stock. Were a company then formed with the same capital structure to hold *this* $25,000,000 worth of common stock, it could be controlled with an investment of $6,250,000. On the next round the amount required would be less than $2,000,000. That $2,000,000 would still control the entire $100,000,000 edifice. By the end of the twenties, holding-company structures six or eight tiers high were a commonplace. Some of them—the utility pyramids of Insull and Associated Gas & Electric, and the railroad pyramid of the Van Sweringens—were marvelously complex. It is unlikely that anyone fully understood them or could.

In other cases companies were organized to hold securities in other companies in order to manufacture more securities to sell to the public. This was true of the great investment trusts. During 1929 one investment house, Goldman, Sachs & Company, organized and sold nearly a billion dollars' worth of securities in three interconnected investment trusts—Goldman Sachs Trading Corporation; Shenandoah Corporation; and Blue Ridge Corporation. All eventually depreciated virtually to nothing.

This corporate insanity was also highly visible. So was the damage. The pyramids would last only so long as earnings of the company at the bottom were secure. If anything happened to the dividends of the underlying company, there would be trouble, for upstream companies had issued bonds (or in practice sometimes preferred stock) against the dividends on the stock of the downstream companies. Once the earnings stopped, the bonds would go into default or the preferred stock would take over and the pyramid would collapse. Such a collapse would have a bad effect not only on the orderly prosecution of business and investment by the operating companies but also on confidence, investment, and spending by the community at large. The likelihood was increased because in any number of cities—Cleveland, Detroit, and Chicago were notable examples—the banks were deeply committed to these pyramids or had fallen under the control of the pyramiders.

Finally, and most evident of all, there was the stock market boom. Month after month and year after year the great bull market of the twenties roared on. Sometimes there were setbacks, but more often there were fantastic forward surges. In May of 1924 the New York *Times* industrials stood at 106; by the end of the year they were 134; by the end of 1925 they were up to 181. In 1927 the advance began in earnest—to 245 by the end of that year and on to 331 by the end of 1928. There were some setbacks in early 1929, but then came the fantastic summer explosion when in a matter of three months the averages went up another 110 points. This was the most frantic summer in our financial history. By its end, stock prices had nearly quadrupled as compared with four years earlier. Transactions on the New York Stock Exchange regularly ran to 5,000,000 or more shares a day. Radio Corporation of America went to 573¾ (adjusted) without ever having paid a dividend. Only the hopelessly eccentric, so it seemed, held securities for their income. What counted was the increase in capital values.

And since capital gains were what counted, one could vastly increase his opportunities by extending his holdings with borrowed funds—by buying on margin. Margin accounts expanded enormously, and from all over the country—indeed from all over the world—money poured into New York to finance these transactions. During the summer, brokers' loans increased at the rate of $400,000,000 a month. By September they totaled more than $7,000,000,000. The rate of interest on these loans varied from 7 to 12 per cent and went as high as 15.

This boom was also inherently self-liquidating. It could last only so long as new people, or at least new money, were swarming into the market in pursuit of the capital gains. This new demand bid up the stocks and made the capital gains. Once the supply of new customers began to falter, the market would cease to rise. Once the market stopped rising, some, and perhaps a good many, would start to cash in. If you are concerned with capital gains, you must get them while the getting is good. But the getting may start the market down, and this will one day be the signal for much more selling—both by those who are trying to get out and those who are being forced to sell securities that are no longer safely margined. Thus it was certain that the market would one day go down, and far more rapidly than it went up. Down it went with a thunderous crash in October of 1929. In a series of terrible days, of which Thursday, October 24, and Tuesday, October 29, were the most terrifying, billions in values were lost, and thousands of speculators—they had been called investors—were utterly and totally ruined.

This too had far-reaching effects. Economists have always deprecated the tendency to attribute too much to the great stock market

collapse of 1929: this was the drama; the causes of the subsequent
depression really lay deeper. In fact, the stock market crash was very
important. It exposed the other weakness of the economy. The overseas loans on which the payments balance depended came to an end.
The jerry-built holding-company structures came tumbling down. The
investment-trust stocks collapsed. The crash put a marked crimp on
borrowing for investment and therewith on business spending. It also
removed from the economy some billions of consumer spending that
was either based on, sanctioned by, or encouraged by the fact that the
spenders had stock market gains. The crash was an intensely damaging
thing.

And this damage, too, was not only foreseeable but foreseen. For
months the speculative frenzy had all but dominated American life.
Many times before in history—the South Sea Bubble, John Law's
speculations, the recurrent real-estate booms of the last century, the
great Florida land boom earlier in the same decade—there had been
similar frenzy. And the end had always come, not with a whimper but
a bang. Many men, including in 1929 the President of the United
States, knew it would again be so.

The increasingly perilous trade balance, the corporate buccaneer-
ing, and the Wall Street boom—along with the less visible tendencies
in income distribution—were all allowed to proceed to the ultimate
disaster without effective hindrance. How much blame attaches to the
men who occupied the presidency?

Warren G. Harding died on August 2, 1923. This, as only death can
do, exonerates him. The disorders that led eventually to such trouble
had only started when the fatal blood clot destroyed this now sad and
deeply disillusioned man. Some would argue that his legacy was bad.
Harding had but a vague perception of the economic processes over
which he presided. He died owing his broker $180,000 in a blind
account—he had been speculating disastrously while he was President,
and no one so inclined would have been a good bet to curb the coming
boom. Two of Harding's Cabinet officers, his secretary of the interior
and his attorney general, were to plead the Fifth Amendment when
faced with questions concerning their official acts, and the first of these
went to jail. Harding brought his fellow townsman Daniel R. Crissinger
to be his comptroller of the currency, although he was qualified for this
task, as Samuel Hopkins Adams has suggested, only by the fact that he
and the young Harding had stolen watermelons together. When Crissinger had had an ample opportunity to demonstrate his incompetence
in his first post, he was made head of the Federal Reserve System. Here
he had the central responsibility for action on the ensuing boom. Jack
Dempsey, Paul Whiteman, or F. Scott Fitzgerald would have been at
least equally qualified.

Cartoonist Forbell titled this 1929 drawing "Club Life in America—The Stock Brokers."

Yet it remains that Harding was dead before the real trouble started. And while he left in office some very poor men, he also left some very competent ones. Charles Evans Hughes, his secretary of state; Herbert Hoover, his secretary of commerce; and Henry C. Wallace, his secretary of agriculture, were public servants of vigor and judgment.

The problem of Herbert Hoover's responsibility is more complicated. He became President on March 4, 1929. At first glance this seems far too late for effective action. By then the damage had been done, and while the crash might come a little sooner or a little later, it was now inevitable. Yet Hoover's involvement was deeper than this—and certainly much deeper than Harding's. This he tacitly concedes in his memoirs, for he is at great pains to explain and, in some degree, to excuse himself.

For one thing, Hoover was no newcomer to Washington. He had been secretary of commerce under Harding and Coolidge. He had also been the strongest figure (not entirely excluding the President) in both Administration and party for almost eight years. He had a clear view of what was going on. As early as 1922, in a letter to Hughes, he expressed grave concern over the quality of the foreign loans that were being floated in New York. He returned several times to the subject. He knew about the corporate excesses. In the latter twenties he wrote to his colleagues and fellow officials (including Crissinger) expressing his grave concern over the Wall Street orgy. Yet he was content to express himself—to write letters and memoranda, or at most, as in the case of the foreign loans, to make an occasional speech. He could with propriety have presented his views of the stock market more strongly to the Congress and the public. He could also have maintained a more vigorous and persistent agitation within the Administration. He did neither. His views of the market were so little known that it celebrated his election and inauguration with a great upsurge. Hoover was in the boat and, as he himself tells, he knew where it was headed. But, having warned the man at the tiller, he rode along into the reef.

And even though trouble was inevitable, by March, 1929, a truly committed leader would still have wanted to do something. Nothing else was so important. The resources of the Executive, one might expect, would have been mobilized in a search for some formula to mitigate the current frenzy and to temper the coming crash. The assistance of the bankers, congressional leaders, and the Exchange authorities would have been sought. Nothing of the sort was done. As secretary of commerce, as he subsequently explained, he had thought himself frustrated by Mellon. But he continued Mellon in office. Henry M. Robinson, a sympathetic Los Angeles banker, was commissioned to go to New York to see his colleagues there and report. He returned to say that the New York bankers regarded things as sound. Richard Whitney, the vice-president of the Stock Exchange, was summoned to the White House for a conference on how to curb speculation. Nothing came of this either. Whitney also thought things were sound.

Both Mr. Hoover and his official biographers carefully explained that the primary responsibility for the goings on in New York City rested not with Washington but with the governor of New York State. That was Franklin D. Roosevelt. It was he who failed to rise to his responsibilities. The explanation is far too formal. The future of the whole country was involved. Mr. Hoover was the President of the whole country. If he lacked authority commensurate with this responsibility, he could have requested it. This, at a later date, President Roosevelt did not hesitate to do.

Finally, while by March of 1929 the stock market collapse was inevitable, something could still be done about the other accumulating disorders. The balance of payments is an obvious case. In 1931 Mr. Hoover did request a one-year moratorium on the inter-Allied (war) debts. This was a courageous and constructive step which came directly to grips with the problem. But the year before, Mr. Hoover, though not without reluctance, had signed the Hawley-Smoot tariff. "I shall approve the Tariff Bill. . . . It was undertaken as the result of pledges given by the Republican Party at Kansas City. . . . Platform promises must not be empty gestures." Hundreds of people—from Albert H. Wiggin, the head of the Chase National Bank, to Oswald Garrison Villard, the editor of the *Nation*—felt that no step could have been more directly designed to make things worse. Countries would have even more trouble earning the dollars of which they were so desperately short. But Mr. Hoover signed the bill.

Anyone familiar with this particular race of men knows that a dour, flinty, inscrutable visage such as that of Calvin Coolidge can be the mask for a calm and acutely perceptive intellect. And he knows equally that it can conceal a mind of singular aridity. The difficulty, given the inscrutability, is in knowing which. However, in the case of Coolidge the evidence is in favor of the second. In some sense, he certainly knew what was going on. He would not have been unaware of what was called the Coolidge market. But he connected developments neither with the well-being of the country nor with his own responsibilities. In his memoirs Hoover goes to great lengths to show how closely he was in touch with events and how clearly he foresaw their consequences. In his *Autobiography*, a notably barren document, Coolidge did not refer to the accumulating troubles. He confines himself to such unequivocal truths as "Every day of Presidential life is crowded with activities" (which in his case, indeed, was not true); and "The Congress makes the laws, but it is the President who causes them to be executed."

At various times during his years in office, men called on Coolidge to warn him of the impending trouble. And in 1927, at the instigation of a former White House aide, he sent for William Z. Ripley of Harvard, the most articulate critic of the corporate machinations of the period. The President became so interested that he invited him to stay

March 4, 1929: President Coolidge (left) and President-Elect Hoover drive from the White House to Hoover's inauguration at the Capitol.

for lunch, and listened carefully while his guest outlined (as Ripley later related) the "prestidigitation, double-shuffling, honey-fugling, hornswoggling, and skulduggery" that characterized the current Wall Street scene. But Ripley made the mistake of telling Coolidge that regulation was the responsibility of the states (as was then the case). At this intelligence Coolidge's face lit up and he dismissed the entire matter from his mind. Others who warned of the impending disaster got even less far.

And on some occasions Coolidge added fuel to the fire. If the market seemed to be faltering, a timely statement from the White House—or possibly from Secretary Mellon—would often brace it up. William Allen White, by no means an unfriendly observer, noted that after one such comment the market staged a 26-point rise. He went on to say that a careful search "during these halcyon years . . . discloses this fact: Whenever the stock market showed signs of weakness, the President or the Secretary of the Treasury or some important dignitary of the administration . . . issued a statement. The statement invariably declared that business was 'fundamentally sound,' that continued prosperity had arrived, and that the slump of the moment was 'seasonal.' "

Such was the Coolidge role. Coolidge was fond of observing that "if you see ten troubles coming down the road, you can be sure that nine will run into the ditch before they reach you and you have to battle

Andrew Mellon, Secretary of the Treasury under Harding,
Coolidge, and Hoover, in a 1927 photo.

with only one of them." A critic noted that "the trouble with this
philosophy was that when the tenth trouble reached him he was wholly
unprepared. . . . The outstanding instance was the rising boom and
orgy of mad speculation which began in 1927." The critic was Herbert
Hoover.

Plainly; in these years, leadership failed. Events whose tragic culmi-
nation could be foreseen—and was foreseen—were allowed to work
themselves out to the final disaster. The country and the world paid.
For a time, indeed, the very reputation of capitalism itself was in the
balance. It survived in the years following perhaps less because of its
own power or the esteem in which it was held, then because of the
absence of an organized and plausible alternative. Yet one important
question remains. Would it have been possible even for a strong Presi-

dent to arrest the plunge? Were not the opposing forces too strong? Isn't one asking the impossible?

No one can say for sure. But the answer depends at least partly on the political context in which the Presidency was cast. That of Coolidge and Hoover may well have made decisive leadership impossible. These were conservative Administrations in which, in addition, the influence of the businessman was strong. At the core of the business faith was an intuitive belief in *laissez faire*—the benign tendency of things that are left alone. The man who wanted to intervene was a meddler. Perhaps, indeed, he was a planner. In any case, he was to be regarded with mistrust. And, on the businessman's side, it must be borne in mind that high government office often nurtures a spurious sense of urgency. There is no more important public function than the suppression of proposals for unneeded action. But these should have been distinguished from action necessary to economic survival.

A bitterly criticized figure of the Harding-Coolidge-Hoover era was Secretary of the Treasury Andrew W. Mellon. He opposed all action to curb the boom, although once in 1929 he was persuaded to say that bonds (as distinct from stocks) were a good buy. And when the depression came, he was against doing anything about that. Even Mr. Hoover was shocked by his insistence that the only remedy was (as Mr. Hoover characterized it) to "liquidate labor, liquidate stocks, liquidate the farmers, liquidate real estate." Yet Mellon reflected only in extreme form the conviction that things would work out, that the real enemies were those who interfered.

Outside of Washington in the twenties, the business and banking community, or at least the articulate part of it, was overwhelmingly opposed to any public intervention. The tentative and ineffective steps which the Federal Reserve did take were strongly criticized. In the spring of 1929 when the Reserve system seemed to be on the verge of taking more decisive action, there was an anticipatory tightening of money rates and a sharp drop in the market. On his own initiative Charles E. Mitchell, the head of the National City Bank, poured in new funds. He had an obligation, he said, that was "paramount to any Federal Reserve warning, or anything else" to avert a crisis in the money market. In brief, he was determined, whatever the government thought, to keep the boom going. In that same spring Paul M. Warburg, a distinguished and respected Wall Street leader, warned of the dangers of the boom and called for action to restrain it. He was deluged with criticism and even abuse and later said that the subsequent days were the most difficult of his life. There were some businessmen and bankers—like Mitchell and Albert Wiggin of the Chase National Bank—who may have vaguely sensed that the end of the boom would mean their own business demise. Many more had per-

*Poverty makes strange bedfellows: In Everett Shinn's
depression drawing of a breadline, former businessmen and
bums queue up.*

suaded themselves that the dream would last. But we should not com-
plicate things. Many others were making money and took a short-run
view—or no view—either of their own survival or of the system of
which they were a part. They merely wanted to be left alone to get a
few more dollars.

And the opposition to government intervention would have been
nonpartisan. In 1929 one of the very largest of the Wall Street operators was John J. Raskob. Raskob was also chairman of the Democratic
National Committee. So far from calling for preventive measures, Raskob in 1929 was explaining how, through stock market speculation,
literally anyone could be a millionaire. Nor would the press have been
enthusiastic about, say, legislation to control holding companies and
investment trusts or to give authority to regulate margin trading. The
financial pages of many of the papers were riding the boom. And from
the speculating public, which was dreaming dreams of riches and had
yet to learn that it had been fleeced, there would have been no thanks.
Perhaps a President of phenomenal power and determination might
have overcome the Coolidge-Hoover environment. But it is easier to
argue that this context made inaction inevitable for almost any President. There were too many people who, given a choice between disaster and the measures that would have prevented it, opted for disaster
without either a second or even a first thought.

On the other hand, in a different context a strong President might
have taken effective preventive action. Congress in these years was
becoming increasingly critical of the Wall Street speculation and cor-

porate piggery-pokery. The liberal Republicans—the men whom Senator George H. Moses called the Sons of the Wild Jackass—were especially vehement. But conservatives like Carter Glass were also critical. These men correctly sensed that things were going wrong. A President such as Wilson or either of the Roosevelts (the case of Theodore is perhaps less certain than that of Franklin) who was surrounded in his Cabinet by such men would have been sensitive to this criticism. As a leader he could both have reinforced and drawn strength from the contemporary criticism. Thus he might have been able to arrest the destructive madness as it became recognizable. The American government works far better—perhaps it only works—when the Executive, the business power, and the press are in some degree at odds. Only then can we be sure that abuse or neglect, either private or public, will be given the notoriety that is needed.

Perhaps it is too much to hope that by effective and timely criticism and action the Great Depression might have been avoided. A lot was required in those days to make the United States in any degree depression-proof. But perhaps by preventive action the ensuing depression might have been made less severe. And certainly in the ensuing years the travail of bankers and businessmen before congressional committees, in the courts, and before the bar of public opinion would have been less severe. Here is the paradox. In the full perspective of history, American businessmen never had enemies as damaging as the men who grouped themselves around Calvin Coolidge and supported and applauded him in what William Allen White called "that masterly inactivity for which he was so splendidly equipped."

The Poor in the Great Depression

DAVID J. ROTHMAN

In this essay, David J. Rothman of Columbia University carries the story of how Americans have dealt with the problem of poverty in the twentieth century down to the 1930s. The tale, inspiring in the sense that it reveals how American reformers have struggled to help the poor, is also discouraging in that despite all efforts the problem of poverty was not eliminated. Even more disturbing is the fact that with all our fantastic expansion and new technology, poverty continues to exist among us today. ∎

The years of the progressive era marked a major shift in public attitudes and policies toward the poor. Beginning in the 1890's and culminating in the administrations of Theodore Roosevelt and Woodrow Wilson, a new and more complex understanding of the origins of dependency spread through the nation, together with a host of fresh alternatives to institutionalization. The innovations were the work of clergymen like Washington Gladden and Walter Rauschenbusch, who preached a new social gospel; of social workers like Robert Hunter, Jane Addams, and Robert Woods, who practiced community work in their settlement houses; of sociologists like Margaret Byington and Crystal Eastman, who provided the first sophisticated and detailed studies of the causes and conditions of poverty; and of popularizers like Jacob Riis, who wrote newspaper articles and books to arouse the American conscience. Taken together, these groups influenced the thinking and responses of ordinary citizens and political leaders.

The new view toward poverty rested first on an understanding of the shortcomings of the economy—the periodic unemployment that forced many laborers below the subsistence line, the prevalent low wages that did not allow even the thrifty among them to accumulate savings. ("Many, many thousand families," wrote Robert Hunter in *Poverty* [1904], "receive wages so inadequate that no care in spending, however wise it may be, will make them suffice for the family needs.") It also was sensitive to the debilitating effects of slums, the crowded and unsanitary tenements through which disease rapidly spread, particularly tuberculosis, robbing households of their main providers. ("Penury and poverty," declared Jacob Riis in *How the Other Half Lives* [1890], "are wedded everywhere to dirt and disease.") It emphasized the dangers inherent in work itself—the inevitable accidents that occurred when managers neglected to install safety devices; when employees were crowded into sweatshops that were firetraps; when laborers, after ten or twelve hours on the job, grew fatigued and careless. (We must do something, pleaded Crystal Eastman in *Work Accidents and the Law* [1910], to insure that modern industry is conducted "without the present wholesale destruction of the workers.") Critics recognized, too, the general misery of life for those at the bottom of society, a misery that drove them to the tavern to gain a temporary respite from their troubles. And they understood how generation after generation would remain trapped in poverty: families, hard pressed to make ends meet, would put young children out to work, depriving them of the education necessary to take skilled jobs. In brief, these reformers taught Americans to think of the needy as the laboring poor who, as Robert Hunter put it, "live miserably . . . [and] know not why. They work sore, and yet gain nothing."

To some degree these conclusions almost forced themselves upon social observers. Forays into the urban slums, whether to bring the gospel to the unchurched or to ameliorate their need, taught ministers and charity workers that the poor were victims not of immorality but of forces beyond their control. The deeper sociologists probed, the more apparent it became that the moralism traditionally characterizing American attitudes toward poverty explained only a fraction of the problem. Ten million Americans, it was reliably estimated in 1904— an eighth of the population—earned less than subsistence incomes, and clearly the great majority of them were feeling the effects of social and economic dislocations. When newly graduated college students went into the ghettos to learn about the poor and to offer their help, whether at Chicago's Hull House or New York's Henry Street Settlement, they too immediately recognized the many disadvantages that the poor could not escape. To all these commentators it was obvious that America had become, once and for all, an urban and industrial nation, with a frontier that was now practically settled and, given successive waves of immigrants, a surplus of labor. The emphasis of earlier reformers on personal reformation and rehabilitation now seemed largely irrelevant, and the isolation of the poor in an almshouse an inadequate response.

The new outlook on poverty also reflected special fears and hopes for American society. The majority of the urban poor (and it was the city's needs that monopolized attention) were also immigrants. To reformers, the newcomers represented both a major threat to the national well-being and an unusual opportunity to do good. Two intimately related problems demanded resolution: the immigrant had to be assimilated into American life, and his standard of living had to be improved. The prospect of failure was haunting, for progressives were deeply suspicious of the aliens, disturbed by many of their idiosyncratic customs (from their strange modes of dress to worshipping in Roman Catholic churches), and frightened that they might act on foreign principles (be it a slavish obedience to Rome or a dedicated allegiance to European socialism). And yet, these critics were also confident that American society had the resources to counter these threats. They pinned their hopes on the opportunities for all men to climb the ladder of success and for all families to enjoy an unprecedented material well-being. Once the several barriers that penned the immigrant into his ghetto poverty were removed, once ambitious and energetic foreigners enjoyed the full chance to succeed, then the nation's stability and security would be assured.

Still, the reformers themselves, and many more of their countrymen, could not completely escape a moralistic view of poverty. The equation of the immigrant with the poor kept alive the conviction that vice helped generate dependency. After all, one had only to walk through an ethnic ghetto to discover the omnipresence of taverns, beer halls, dance halls, and houses of prostitution. Even Robert Hunter, as sympathetic an observer as one can find in this period, maintained the older distinction between the worthy and the unworthy poor. "There is unquestionably," he conceded, "a poverty which men deserve, and by such poverty men are perhaps taught needful lessons. It would be unwise to legislate out of existence . . . that poverty which penalizes the voluntarily idle and vicious." And progressives, like others before and after them, could not altogether reconcile the presence of poverty with their deep sense of the munificence of American life. A tone of condescension entered their rhetoric, reflecting a certain disdain not only for the "wretched refuse" of European shores but also for those who had not been clever or ambitious enough to profit in the land of opportunity.

Despite such doubts, reformers did put an end to the almshouse monopoly, establishing new procedures that kept at least some of the poor within the community. The persons who benefited immediately were widows with small children—the group least suspect among the needy. In 1909 President Roosevelt convened the White House Conference on the Care of Dependent Children and happily publicized its major findings. "Poverty alone should not disrupt the home," he announced. "Parents of good character, suffering from temporary misfortune, and above all deserving mothers . . . deprived of the support of the normal breadwinner, should be given such aid as may be necessary to enable them to maintain suitable homes for the rearing of their children." To this end, Illinois in 1911 passed a widow's pension bill, and by the close of World War I nearly every industrial state had followed its example. The worthy widow and her children would no longer suffer separation and incarceration in almshouses and orphan asylums.

Reformers also moved to protect the lower classes both on the job and in their communities, to enable them to enjoy more of the advantages of industrialism. They enacted accident insurance to compensate injured laborers and regulated the number of hours women and children could work. They passed stringent building and fire codes to offset the most glaring dangers of slum living. They also tried to rescue the children of the poor from their parents' fate, enacting compulsory school laws and establishing a minimum age (ranging from twelve to sixteen) for factory work.

There was an enormous amount progressives did not do. They paid little attention to the plight of the black, his economic or social disabilities, and they almost completely ignored the rural poverty of tenant farmers, sharecroppers, and migrant laborers. They neither enacted health-care programs nor extended government pension provisions to the general work force. Although proposals for unemployment compensation and retirement benefits were heard between 1890 and 1914 (and indeed, several European countries were already administering them), no such advances were made here. Even the innovations that did occur were carefully circumscribed. Widow's pensions were limited to only the most deserving, so that mothers whose husbands had deserted them were not eligible, nor those with illegitimate children. As a result the majority of the poor still had to rely upon the limited funds of private charities, or turn to public relief for some coal or wood, or suffer a stint in the almshouse. Nevertheless, the progressives did signal a new departure. In attitude and practice, it was they who first broke with tradition.

Few advances in policy or thought occurred during the 1920's. In fact, given the severe tensions that pervaded the nation, it is noteworthy that the moderate advances of the progressives were not eradicated. This was the decade when the K.K.K. and the temperance movement and immigration restriction reached the zenith of their power and appeal, and antialien, antiurban sentiments also led to a resurgence of harsh and critical judgments on the poor, especially those who were first- or second-generation immigrants. If only they would stop drinking, gambling, and paying obeisance to Rome, the argument went, if only they would become full-fledged Americans, then poverty would disappear. To be sure, a few social critics who did not embrace these prejudices continued to circulate among themselves analytic studies of the poor in the best reformist tradition. Some explored the most efficient methods for organizing a national old-age assistance and pension program; others undertook the first investigations of conditions in black ghettos and among tenant farmers. And an occasional state legislature did manage to widen the eligibility requirements for widows' pensions. But in all, the 1920's was not an auspicious time to innovate, and the public achievement against poverty was not impressive.

The one significant change in this period affecting the poor was the organization and professionalization of social work. The good-hearted but casual home visitor to the needy, who dispensed a little cash and a lot of homilies, gave way to the college- and university-trained full-time social worker. The founding ideology of the discipline looked both to helping the poor adjust to society and to encouraging society to offer more help. But not surprisingly, in the 1920's it was the poor who had to do all the accommodating. Casework lost sight of social reform, focusing instead on teaching the lower classes to cope with their situation, to budget more carefully, to be more industrious, to emulate those above them. Part of the severity of this vision reflected

Among the earliest "social workers," as we would use the term, was the visiting nurse. This nurse is talking with a tenement family of the 1890s.

the inhospitable climate of public opinion. But it also reflected the impact of Freudian theory and the eagerness of social workers to become professionals. Using psychological therapy as a way to establish and exert their expertise, social workers insisted that many of the difficulties confronting the poor resulted from their emotional problems. The needy were not the victims of vice but of maladjustment, and careful and sympathetic counselling would teach them to achieve. But the net result of this new doctrine was to couch in modern terminology some very traditional ideas. The poor remained essentially responsible for their difficulties. Reformation and rehabilitation returned to the center of the stage, now rationalized in updated language. The "unworthy" poor had become the "emotionally deprived" poor. Hence,

by the close of this decade, public programs and attitudes had rigi-
dified. The nation was not well equipped to confront the phenomenon
of the Great Depression.

Suddenly, the poor had more than enough company. The crash of
1929 sparked the most massive economic dislocation in our history, at
its peak leaving 25 per cent of the work force unemployed. Poverty was
no longer the exclusive fate of the ghetto immigrant or the migrant
farmer but of blue-collar workers laid off the assembly line and white-
collar workers dismissed from brokerage houses. The problem had
unexpectedly become national.

At first, both powerful and ordinary Americans denied the magnitude of the crisis, insisting that recovery was imminent. Herbert
Hoover, wedded to an older American credo and fearful of undermining the country's moral fiber, refused to involve the federal government in relief. "I am opposed," he declared in 1931, "to any direct or
indirect government dole. . . . Our people are providing against distress from unemployment in true American fashion." But true American fashion meant that local governments and private charities had to
carry all of the burden, and by 1932 they were without the resources.
Cities lacked funds and the taxing power to raise them. The Red Cross
distributed bags of flour and the community chest armfuls of coal.
Distress was everywhere apparent: migrants pitched camps at one
water spot and then another, their life's possessions piled on the back
of a broken-down truck. The urban poor pasted together shacks in
shantytowns in the parks and along the river banks. Those with some
savings cut corners, awaiting a bank's foreclosure or a landlord's evic-
tion. Often unable to clothe their families decently, they kept their
children out of school and shunned their neighbors.

New Deal legislation alleviated some of this misery. Less bound by
tradition, Franklin D. Roosevelt plunged the national government into
the business of relief. By 1936, with the passage of the Social Security
Act and the establishment of the Works Progress Administration,
Washington was providing the states with relief funds and the unemployed with jobs. New Deal legislation did alter permanently the character of public programs. To meet immediate problems, the unem-
ployable (the aged, blind, and very young) received, after passing a
means test, direct relief at home; at the same time, federally sponsored
projects made jobs available for destitute but able-bodied workers.
Unemployment compensation, funded by a tax on employers, provided incomes for the temporarily unemployed; and retirement pensions, paid for by employee contributions, gave the aged a new measure of security. The almshouse became a thing of the past, abolished
through the effects of these innovations.

Still, the New Deal investment in relief fell considerably short of the nation's need. Afraid to violate the sanctity of the balanced budget or the prerogatives of the states, and committed first and foremost to work relief, President Roosevelt insisted on funding relief through the states but would not set national standards. (Thus, the poor in Mississippi received about one third the support of those in Massachusetts.) The sums allotted to the aged were far below subsistence—nineteen dollars a month when forty dollars would barely do. WPA regulations required men to leave the rolls after eighteen months, no matter how grim their economic condition. Social security was not to take effect until 1942—and even then the pension sums were too small to support recipients. The states were no more generous. California, for example, packed migrant workers and the young unmarried unemployed off to work camps that bordered on penal colonies. The states also tried to seal their borders by reviving stringent residence laws.

Despite the magnitude of the problem and the unprecedented government response, a very traditional attitude toward poverty persisted through the Depression. The new leadership continued to preach many ancient axioms, and the average citizen retained older beliefs. F.D.R. himself denigrated direct relief, keeping alive the term "dole." To some degree this was a conscious strategy to swell public support for the millions expended on W.P.A. But it also reflected his inner conviction that relief corrupted and weakened the recipient. Those on relief, or who tottered on the brink, felt an acute sense of dread and guilt, a painful reluctance to take what they still defined as charity. Hence, just when one might have anticipated a public furor over real suffering, when widespread turmoil and vicious riots might have broken out, the nation remained remarkably quiescent. Most Americans remained silent, suffering alone.

In essence, poverty demoralized rather than activated the country. The unemployed insisted on blaming themselves for their misery, defining their problems as internal, not external. If only they looked harder or put up a better front, they would find a job. Instead of joining with others in faulting the system, they became immobilized and isolated. One after another they passionately and honestly told the interviewers that before taking relief they would "rather be dead and buried." Years later, when good times returned, they still vividly recalled these feelings. "I didn't want to go on relief," one small businessman remembered. "Believe me, when I was forced to go to the office of relief, the tears were running out of my eyes. I couldn't bear myself to take money from anybody for nothing." Their actions did not belie their words. Of nearly one thousand unemployed in New Haven, Connecticut, less than one quarter had asked for relief after being without a job for over a year.

Desperation also took more comic or pathetic turns in the Depres-

A group of unemployed men camped in a shantytown along the Hudson River in New York City in 1932. On the table is one of the few remaining comforts of home: a hand-cranked gramophone.

sion. The board game called Monopoly swept the country. If one could not eke out a living in the real world, one could accumulate a paper fortune in a fantasy one. Dale Carnegie's *How to Win Friends and Influence People* became a best seller with an overt message of doubtful relevance: confidence, grace, personal style, and sensitive shrewdness would bring success. Its latent message was also obvious: failures had only their own personalities to blame. Soap operas, which fastened themselves on the radio public in the 1930's, provided a catalogue of troubles for the listener to compare with his own. But the serials usually blamed failure on personal and emotional inadequacy, rarely on external and social events.

Public-opinion polls during the Depression accurately gauged the degree of persistence and change in American attitudes toward poverty and the poor. There can be no doubt of the popularity of the federal involvement in relief among all the sectors of society. In March, 1939, a Roper poll indicated that three-quarters of the American public affirmed the government's obligation to relieve all persons who had no other means of subsistence. Yet, at the same time, a majority of the public continued to think of the poor in hostile and pejorative terms. Reliefers could get jobs, they believed, if only they tried. The New Deal did institute new and important and widely supported relief programs, but the welfare recipient remained a target of suspicion, disparaged by himself and others. Even the Great Depression could not wipe away the stigma of poverty. . . .

The Revolt of the Old Folks

DAVID H. BENNETT

One of the most important achievements of the New Deal was the social security system. It is easy to forget that until the passage of the Social Security Act of 1935 there was no national system of old age pensions, and that only a small fraction of the working population was covered by any kind of pension plan at all. How frightening it must have been to have approached retirement age during the Depression under these circumstances!

In this article Professor David H. Bennett of Syracuse University describes the rise and fall of Dr. Francis E. Townsend's Old Age Revolving Pension Plan. The passion with which so many elderly people embraced this impractical scheme is a measure of the desperation felt by millions of old people living on the edge of poverty. Movements like Dr. Townsend's served a useful purpose in pushing the Roosevelt administration in the direction of reform. Professor Bennett's story also illustrates the fine line that sometimes separates genuine social reform movements from the crackpot schemes of fanatics, well meaning and otherwise. Bennett is the author of Demagogues in the Depression: American Radicals and the Union Party. ∎

For Cleveland, Ohio, the summer of 1936 was a time to remember. In the steaming month of July, during which a twelve-day heat wave in the Midwest and East cost 3,000 lives, there came to the great lake-front city a procession of people—gray, simple, sixty-ish, and poor—from all across the nation. They came in buses and railroad coaches and broken-down Fords. Carrying their battered suitcases, they found dollar-a-night lodgings on the city's outskirts and travelled to the downtown convention hall in trolleys, eating bananas and oranges out of bags to save lunch money. They had calloused hands and wore clean but threadbare Sears, Roebuck clothing. They were the delegates to the second annual convention of Old Age Revolving Pensions, Ltd.—disciples of Dr. Francis E. Townsend, whom they fervently believed had been sent by God to save the old people of America in their time of deepest need.

The year before, at Chicago, the first national meeting of the organization had attracted 7,000 delegates. The Cleveland convention drew 11,000. Banners proclaimed "The Three Emancipators: Washington, Lincoln, Townsend." One speaker suggested that "God almighty placed this great idea in the mind of one of His servants." Another announced that "the Doctor is the leader of a greater army than any known to history." Yet another wondered why no star had hung over Dr. Townsend's birthplace to "guide Wise Men of that generation to his side."

If the Townsend Plan was an idea so explosive as to merit this kind of response, then in the presidential election year of 1936 it could prove to be political dynamite. Of this the organizers of the meeting were very much aware. Indeed, the Townsendites were assembling in the very hall where, only a month earlier, the Republican party had met to nominate Alfred M. Landon. As one journalist pointed out, Townsend's convention had at least two advantages over Landon's: it was bigger and it was livelier.

The Cleveland gathering of Townsendites marked the high point of one of the most curious and potentially formidable mass movements in modern American history. The road which led to Cleveland began some three years before in Long Beach, California, where Francis Everett Townsend had his great vision. In 1933 Townsend was almost sixty-seven—a country-bred physician who had come to the retirement community of Long Beach in 1919 to recover his health and seek a livelihood. Educated in rural Illinois schools, he was successively a ranch hand and farm laborer in the West; a mucker in Colorado mines; a homesteader, teacher, and salesman in Kansas. Finally, at the age of thirty-one, he entered medical school in Omaha and after graduation practiced medicine in South Dakota, where he was driven out of Belle Fourche for fighting local political corruption. In 1927–28 he was a real-estate promoter in Long Beach. When the Depression struck, most of his savings were wiped out, and he had to accept an appointment as assistant director of the City Health Office. There he could see just how cruelly the economic crisis was ravaging the old people of America. Years later he recalled that "I stepped into such distress, pain and horror as to shake me even today with its memory. . . . They were good men and women, they had done all they could, had played the game as they had been taught to play it, and suddenly, when there was no chance to start over again, they were let down."

In 1933 the Doctor lost his job when the City Health Office ran out of funds: his own crisis seemed only to intensify a growing feeling that something had to be done to help the old people of America.

For most men the years after age sixty-five are the twilight of their careers, but for Dr. Townsend, all the years that went before seemed to serve only as a prelude for the great work he was now to undertake.

For Townsend had a vision of America's elderly people permanently freed from economic privation by means of a substantial pension, disbursed monthly by the federal government to every citizen aged sixty and over. The government was to raise this money through a small "transaction tax," a multiple sales tax, levied not just at the point of ultimate sale but at each point that a commodity changed hands along the way from raw material to finished product.

The Doctor had read somewhere that in 1929 the gross business done in the United States amounted to $935 billion. He deduced that it could be possible, by tapping this enormous business transaction with a sales tax, to produce twenty to twenty-four billion dollars per year, enough to give $150 a month—later he raised it to $200—to everyone over sixty.

As the months rolled by, Townsend began to advertise his program as a solution to the economic woes of not only the aged but the rest of the population as well. He decided that spending the $200 within thirty days should be made mandatory, and thus began to stress the revolving aspect of his proposal—that twenty to twenty-four billion dollars paid to the elderly every year would tend to stimulate the entire economy as the old people spent their pensions on all manner of consumer goods. He now spoke in terms of the "velocity of money," pointing out, for example, that the dollar spent by an old man for food would be used by his grocer to pay the wholesaler, and so on down the line. In this way, the pension money would "revolve" and would multiply; the pension checks coursing through the economy would stimulate every aspect of American enterprise and finally would end the Depression.

Townsend began to make even more sweeping claims for his plan. Millions of new jobs, he promised, would be made available to younger men by withdrawing the aged from the employment rolls. State and local governments would save the billions of dollars consumed yearly by crime and crime prevention as his plan eliminated poverty and privation: even more billions would be saved which were now spent on charity.

When Townsend described his dream to the aged, it did not seem too far-fetched. To them, the economy of abundance of the 1920's had come to be the normal thing; the Depression, a grotesquely atypical phenomenon. When Townsend drew upon these memories of prosperity and added to them his own thesis, few old people challenged his arguments.

Indeed, there were few who would have wanted to doubt the plan's validity, so bleak were the prospects for the elderly during the Depression. In 1934, only twenty-eight of the forty-eight states had any pension plan at all; three of those were bankrupt and the others were woefully inadequate. Almost three-quarters of a million Americans aged sixty-five and over were on some form of federal relief, and the situation appeared to be getting worse. For, while the elderly were relentlessly being displaced in the job market, they were steadily increasing both in absolute numbers and in percentage of the total population. In 1930 the aged comprised 6.6 million, or 5.4 per cent of all the people in the United States; by 1935 these figures had grown to 7.5 million and 6 per cent.

Thus it was not surprising that when Dr. Townsend first proposed his plan in late 1933, almost immediately support for it sprang up across America.

The plan grew out of a letter Townsend wrote to the "People's Forum" column of a Long Beach newspaper in late September. At the time, he planned no program of action. But within days of the letter's appearance, replies flooded the paper, which soon devoted a daily page to discussion of Townsend's ideas. At the same time he was approached directly by people who wanted concrete proposals for putting his ideas into action. By November, Townsend had decided to devote his life to realizing his plan. When the Doctor advertised for canvassers to obtain signatures on petitions for congressional action, he was overwhelmed by replies. Within a matter of days he had received completed petitions containing the names of 2,000 supporters.

The Doctor now searched about for a promoter, a person to help him set up the organization that would push the Townsend Plan into law. He turned to Robert Earl Clements, a young, driving real-estate broker.

The two men began collecting names and sending out Old Age Revolving Pensions literature. After five weeks, they were getting an average of one hundred replies a day. Physicians and ministers in the

Long Beach area became spokesmen for the plan, and a newspaper, *The Townsend Weekly,* was started. As the movement continued to grow, local Townsend clubs began to spring up, and by January, 1935, five months after the first of these had been founded, the leaders proudly announced that more than 3,000, with a total membership approaching one-half million, were operating—actually there were only 1,200 clubs, but even that figure was impressive. Organizers were soon at work across the nation setting up more clubs, and the Doctor had to hire a staff of ninety-five to handle his mounting flow of mail. Almost overnight, the Townsend movement had become a force to be reckoned with.

The fanaticism with which Townsend's growing thousands of followers promoted his plan astounded and finally frightened journalists and politicians throughout the nation. There were ugly rumors that newly organized Townsend clubs in the Pacific Northwest were threatening merchants and newspaper publishers with economic boycotts if they refused to support the plan. "This thing's become a religion," one alarmed editor said. "It holds the whole town in its grasp."

Clearly, Dr. Townsend had struck into a subsoil of fear and discontent which went far deeper than the immediate material privations of the Depression. Most Townsendites had grown to adulthood believing that they were heirs to a tradition of self-reliance and rugged individualism. The America of their youth was a land in which opportunity abounded, in which a man's failure was seen generally as the result of his own inadequacy, in which the thrifty could count on security in their old age. It was also a land of close family ties, where age was respected.

But in the 1930's, these ideas were becoming only memories. Industrialization and urbanization were destroying the nation's traditional rural and small-town way of life. A man was less independent and less secure in the new America: the factory assembly line robbed him of his individualism and the economics of industrial capitalism subjected him to the vagaries of the business cycle. Family ties were all too often broken as children moved far from their parental homes. Even old age seemed to lose its dignity: the highest premium in the land now seemed to be on youth.

Dr. Townsend appeared on the scene to soothe and comfort the aged. By arguing that a comfortable pension was fully deserved after a lifetime of sacrifice and devotion, he appealed to their hurt pride. He appealed also to their self-esteem, asserting that "people over sixty were selected to be the circulators of large sums of money because they have more buying experience than those of fewer years." He called old people "Civil Veterans of the Republic" and told them that they could

Dr. Townsend reaches out to greet his devoted followers at
a rally in Indianapolis, one of many held during the great
days of the movement.

become a "research, educational, and corrective force in both a material and spiritual way in the United States."

Thus were the aged offered the best of all possible worlds. They
might live in comfort, but they need not feel idle or useless, for as
"circulators of money" or, as Townsend preferred to call them, "dis-
tributor custodians," they would be serving a vital function.

Furthermore, Townsend did not force his followers to choose between his plan and basic American values. One could be a Townsend-
ite without the risk of being called a foreigner, a "red," or an atheist.
The leaders proclaimed their faith in the political and economic system
of the nation, and although their solution was clearly a radical one, it
was presented in conservative terms. It offered to preserve the "American way of life." It became for its followers, in the words of a contemporary observer, "simply the means of redeeming the promises of the
little red school house."

Along with this wholesomely patriotic tone, the movement had a
definite religious content. The aura of the evangelist's camp meeting
surrounded Townsendism. The leadership included many clergymen;
the spokesmen described their cause as being "God-given" and "or-

dained by the Lord"; well-known religious songs became anthems of the movement; and Bible reading was a part of most of its gatherings.

Aided by this combination of religiosity and patriotism, the Townsend organization, by the start of the election year of 1936, claimed a membership of some 2.2 million in 7,000 local clubs operating across the nation. Dr. Townsend liked to tell his followers that "the movement is all yours, my friends; it belongs to you." In reality, it was very much the property of Francis E. Townsend and the few leaders who surrounded him. Moreover, the old physician began to be affected by his meteoric rise to fame. The speechmaking, the plane trips, the cheering throngs, made him feel, as he confessed to one interviewer, that he "had been chosen by God to accomplish this mission." The movement's newspaper began to compare him to the great men of the past—to Washington and Lincoln, to Columbus and Copernicus, to Franklin and Luther, and even to Christ.

Townsend revelled in the praise, but he did not change his speaking style. His soft, warm voice was not fitted for oratory, and even after delivering dozens of addresses, the old man still seemed ill at ease on the speaker's platform. This very ineptitude proved to be an asset, for the old folks in the Townsend crusade did not want their leader to be too articulate and dynamic; they wanted him to be like themselves. And this the Doctor knew. His conversation was punctuated with homely phrases such as "dang" and "by gum." His publicists pictured him as the folksy older American who had triumphed over adversity and who was now helping all America overcome its troubles.

But Dr. Townsend was not an organizer. He needed a covey of sleek and efficient proselyters, men who were accustomed to talking for their living, men who were willing to serve as the salesmen of Utopia—men, in short, like Robert E. Clements.

Clements, who insisted on calling himself the "cofounder" of the movement, was its manager and fund-raiser. It was he who devised its authoritarian system of centralized control, which Townsend eventually employed to dispose of those dissidents who rebelled against official policy. Clements made the promotion of the Townsend Plan a big business. He marketed Townsend emblems and stickers for automobiles, pictures, pamphlets, songs, buttons, badges, and banners, all sold at a handsome profit. But of all his lucrative schemes, none was so profitable as the *Townsend Weekly*. Its circulation rose steadily to over 300,000; this and other publications of their Prosperity Publishing Company were soon grossing Townsend and Clements $200,000 a year. The bulk of the income from the *Weekly* came from advertisements, many of which preyed on the fears and anxieties of old people, filling the newspaper with testimonials to the magical qualities of bladder tablets, gland stimulants, and kidney pills.

The intensive campaign to build the organization was paying rich dividends by late 1935. Townsend headquarters announced that in the first fifteen months of its existence, total receipts approached three-quarters of a million dollars. In order to justify this growth the Townsend leaders had to exert political pressure for legislative adoption of the plan. . . .

Early in December, the Townsend Plan high command wrote to all 531 congressmen, asking whether they would vote for a Townsend bill in the next session. Only sixty answered, and only thirty-nine said yes. The old doctor was angry. He could not understand the rebuff when all across the country there was new evidence of the movement's strength.

Townsend decided that there must be a congressional "conspiracy" against his plan, and that the New Deal was behind it. Although President Roosevelt himself had carefully avoided making a public statement on the pension proposal, his lieutenants—Labor Secretary Frances Perkins, Harry Hopkins, and Senate Majority Leader Joseph Robinson among them—had clearly indicated the administration's opposition.

A major cause of Townsend's irritation with the New Deal was that F. D. R. had once refused to see him. Another and more important reason was the Social Security bill. The Doctor considered its provision of $30 a month for people age seventy and over to be "a miserable dole," an "insult to elderly Americans," and "a mere bid for political support." There may have been some grain of truth in Townsend's charge that Social Security was an attempt to take the spotlight off his plan. The Social Security bill would probably have become law even if Townsend had never come on the scene, but there is little doubt that the existence of the O.A.R.P. organization did speed its adoption. As F. D. R. said to Secretary Perkins: "We have to have it. . . . The Congress can't stand the pressure . . . unless we have a real old-age insurance system. . . ."

The Roosevelt administration never seriously considered adopting even a modified version of the Townsend Plan The President had been advised by professional economists that if put into practice, it would not only be unworkable but might well destroy the nation.

Merely reviewing the price of implementing the plan stunned economists; they estimated that its yearly cost would be one and one-half times the amount spent by all government—federal, state, and local—in 1932, and almost one-half the total national income for 1934.

The transaction tax, they decided, would almost certainly fail to produce the requisite income, for while the Townsendites based their estimates of income on the gross national product of the last of the pre-Depression years, 1929, their taxing program would operate in a far less prosperous America. Moreover, the argument concerning the velocity of money, the economists said, was mythical—a dollar would not "turn over" ten times within a month, for even in the boom years of the 1920's the average turnover amounted to less than three times monthly. And although Townsend looked for economic wonders through money distribution, the promised goods and services simply could not be produced because of the limitations of existing plant capacity. But the transaction tax had still another defect. It was essentially a sales tax, and as such, it was ungraduated. The burden would have fallen on those least able to afford it. Paul Douglas, professor of economics at the University of Chicago (now U.S. Senator from Illinois), estimated that if this tax had become law, the real income of most workers would have been reduced by about one-half.

Economists of the day asked another question: How would the government make sure the elderly spent their monthly payments promptly? Frugal oldsters, unaccustomed to such a sizable income, might well have attempted to save part of their monthly checks in case the golden faucet should ever be turned off.

When all of its deficiencies had been uncovered, the plan became the butt of economists' jokes. Dr. Louis Haney of New York University wryly suggested that Townsend had not gone far enough, that $200 should be given to everyone every week. If the government can afford $24 billion, Haney said, it can afford $2,400 billion. In Battle Creek, Michigan, a "rival" to the O.A.R.P. was announced. The "Retire at Birth Plan" proposed that every newborn child receive $20,000, payable with interest at age twenty.

Townsend's supporters tried to counterattack. "The politicians should stop listening to these academics," one urged, "for they are but husk-dry pedants, who rely upon books, formal rules, and abstract theories." And a leading publicist for the plan even asserted that "the physician, understanding physiology, may be especially qualified to feel, by the process of intuitive analogy, the most fundamental economic principles."

Convinced of the absurdity of the Townsend Plan, F. D. R. moved to meet the political threat it represented by encouraging, in early 1936, a new series of attacks on it by Democratic congressmen.

Senator Kenneth McKellar of Tennessee opened the assault by stating that the plan was nothing more than a "fantastic . . . devastating . . . wild-eyed scheme for looting the treasury of the United States." Representative Phillip Ferguson of Oklahoma termed it "a racket," and Representative Maury Maverick of Texas argued that it was "a way of avoiding discussion of the real issues."

Dr. Townsend, now certain that "the politicians" were his enemies, was ready to fight back. He accused the New Deal of being "a misdeal . . . where political appointees experiment in human misery." He termed certain actions of the administration "nothing more than Mussolini Fascism." And he even hinted at the formation of a new political party.

Townsend had declared war on Congress and on the White House; retaliation was inevitable. The weapon was a new congressional subcommittee, headed by Missouri Democrat C. Jasper Bell.

The Bell committee's formally stated purpose was to investigate old-age pension plans in order to propose legislation to prevent frauds, but its unstated purpose was to undermine the Townsend organization's effectiveness as a political force in the 1936 elections. . . .

Midway in its weeks of hearings, the committee called Townsend himself to the witness stand. The Doctor, sensitive to the harsh questions, began to crack under the pressure. His economic naïveté was revealed time and time again. As E. B. White put it, "When forced to deal with the fundamental problems, he quietly came apart, like an inexpensive toy."

For Townsend, the Bell committee hearings represented a disaster. . . . Clements resigned from the movement the day after he was called to appear at the Bell hearings. And once he faced the congressional investigators, he proved willing to give damaging anti-Townsend testimony.

Dr. Townsend was now in trouble. But his followers rallied to their leader. Angry letters poured into the White House, and many Townsendites travelled to Washington to provide moral support for the Doctor, some bearing petitions with hundreds of thousands of signatures attesting that members had "donated the money to be used as the leader saw fit."

Heartened by the evidence of widespread support, Dr. Townsend decided to defy the committee and the New Deal. He lashed out at the hearing, calling it an "inquisition," and he shrewdly played the part of the innocent victim of slander, while his newspaper headlined MOSES BEFORE PHARAOH. Then, after several days of particularly gruelling questioning, Townsend finally had had enough. Suddenly saying, "Good day, gentlemen," the Doctor stood up and walked toward the exit. The congressmen were flabbergasted. The frail old physician had trouble pushing through the crowd, but a large, powerful man leaped to his feet, seized Townsend's arm, and helped him through the throng to the corridor and safety.

The Doctor's savior was the Reverend Gerald L. K. Smith, an experienced and ambitious leader of mass movements, who had his eye on the O.A.R.P. After several years as a successful minister in Indiana and Louisiana, Smith had joined forces with Senator Huey

Long and had become the organizer of the national Share-Our-Wealth movement, the vehicle which Long hoped to ride to the Presidency. Spreading rapidly across the South, the Share-Our-Wealth clubs appealed to poor white farmers and small-town merchants, men who wanted to believe that money and power could be wrenched from the leaders of southern society and the captains of eastern industry and be redistributed. Like Long, Smith was a master of the art of crossroads oratory upon which demagogues in the South had for generations built a following among the poverty-stricken "redneck" farmers. Shrewdly exploiting the wealth-sharing theme in the depths of the Depression, the minister was making political headway when, in 1935, the assassination of the "Kingfish" robbed him of his chance for glory. The heirs to Long's Louisiana machine quickly thrust Smith out of his seat of influence, leaving him desperately hungry for power.

Smith's career to that date had been short but spectacular. The roster of organizations he had flirted with included William Dudley Pelley's fascistic Silver Shirt Legion of America and Georgia Governor Eugene Talmadge's violently anti-New Deal Grass Roots Convention. But in the spring of 1936 Smith was without an organization, and he saw Dr. Townsend as the answer to his prayer.

After his rescue in the hearing room, the Doctor took Smith to the Baltimore office of the O.A.R.P., spoke briefly to reporters, and then saw his impromptu press conference taken over by Smith. The following day Smith grandly told newsmen that "we here and now join hands in what shall result in a nation-wide protest against this Communistic dictatorship in Washington."

Townsend seemed dazzled by the powerful personality of his new ally, and Smith persuaded the Doctor to join him on a speechmaking tour of eastern Pennsylvania. In a dramatic climax to that trip, he took the old man to Valley Forge, where, as he told the press, "the Doctor and I stood under the historic arch and vowed to take over the government." By this time Townsend was parroting his younger companion: "We are presenting a common front against the dictatorship in Washington."

Townsend's other subordinates were greatly disturbed: they felt that the Doctor might soon find himself playing Trilby to Gerald Smith's Svengali. But even before meeting Smith, Townsend had become convinced that radical action was necessary if his pension scheme was to become a reality. He had told his followers:

> The only way for us to lick the stuffing out of the old parties is to become militant and go after them hammer and tongs for being totally incompetent . . . We should begin to talk about the Townsend Party and not wait

in the foolish hope that one of the old groups will adopt us. If they do, they will treat us like poor adopted trash. To hell with them.

Aware of newspaper reports which indicated that Townsendites were in practical control of at least eight and probably ten states, he began to boast that "we have strength enough to elect a candidate. We have at least thirty million votes."

Now Smith heightened the old man's anger and channeled his thinking along more radical lines. And Smith was anxious to play a role in the formation of the new third party. He told an interviewer at this time, "You know what my ambition is? I think chaos is inevitable. I want to get as many people as I can now, so that when chaos comes, I'll be a leader."

Townsend had been rather hazy about the political nature of the new Townsend party of which he had talked, and he acquiesced when Smith proclaimed himself "director in charge of political policy." The Doctor was naïve enough to believe in Smith's simple but startling arithmetic: six million Townsend Planners plus four million Share-Our-Wealth members equals ten million votes "to start with." Smith could thus convince the unsophisticated old pension promoter that the Share-Our-Wealth movement was a formidable political force, but he himself knew that this was only a dream. In fact, Gerald L. K. Smith had lost control of the Share-Our-Wealth mailing lists after Long's assassination and his organization was now defunct. He knew that he and Dr. Townsend would need allies if they were to achieve a political revolution.

Such allies were readily available. The Reverend Charles E. Coughlin, a Catholic priest with a parish in a Detroit suburb, had experienced a meteoric rise to fame and power during the Depression years by effectively utilizing that new tool of mass communication, the radio. The "radio priest" advocated a strong central bank and the distribution of large amounts of unbacked currency as a means of bringing the United States out of the Depression. He accused international bankers and the Roosevelt brain trusters alike of being part of a conspiracy to undermine America's position at home and abroad.

His audience was composed mainly of lower and lower-middle class Irish and German Catholics living in large cities. For these people Coughlin offered both an explanation of their Depression-born woes and an emotional outlet for their frustration. By identifying their oppressors as rich eastern bankers, white Anglo-Saxon Protestant aristocrats, and Ivy League intellectuals, he appealed both to a hidden ethnic and religious bias and to the insecurity of his listeners as relative newcomers still not fully assimilated into the American melting pot. In accusing these "oppressors" of being somehow un-American—that is, both communistic and capitalistic in an evil "international" sense—he gave his followers at once more security in their own Americanization and a scapegoat for their anger.

The priest had organized his followers into a huge, active movement, the National Union for Social Justice, and by the spring of the presidential election year, he, like Townsend, was talking in terms of a new political party. His candidate was to be William Lemke, a Republican congressman from North Dakota, a veteran of third-party organizing efforts in his home state, and a man who commanded a wide following among the dissatisfied farmers of the northern Plains.

The Coughlin and Lemke forces soon became the prime object of Gerald Smith's plans. At first Townsend balked. He had, in the past, made derogatory statements about both the Congressman and the priest. But Smith slowly built a bridge between Father Coughlin and the Doctor. Coughlin's strong support for Townsend after the Bell committee hearings softened the pension leader's attitude, and Lemke's defense of the plan made him more palatable to Townsend.

In May, Smith told the press that he, Coughlin, and Townsend were about to "congeal under a leadership with guts." By June 16 he was asserting that "more than twenty million votes" could be controlled by. a "Smith-Townsend-Coughlin-Lemke Axis." A working agreement was developing among the four. On June 19, Lemke announced the formation of the new Union party, with himself as the presidential candidate. . . .

The new third party, then, came into the world as the product of a curious coalition, bound together by somewhat similar inflationist programs and a unifying hatred of Franklin D. Roosevelt. But there were significant divisive factors: the rival personal ambitions of the leaders and the strikingly different groups of supporters to which each appealed. If the Union party was to be successful, its disparate elements would have to work together.

One of these elements was already facing an internal test. In July, the Townsend National Recovery Plan, as it was now called, prepared to hold its second annual convention in Cleveland. As thousands of aged Americans trekked to the Lake Erie city for the event, the road that had begun in Long Beach, California, two years earlier reached its most important turning point.

On the first day of the convention, good fellowship overflowed. A man on the rostrum instructed each member of the audience to shake hands with the neighbor sitting at each side. Another told everybody to shout, "God bless you." But the warm glow experienced that first day was cooled by the proceedings of the next, when Representative Gomer Smith—a Democrat from Oklahoma, a famous lawyer of Indian blood, and a stirring orator—stood up to speak. Gomer Smith was a

*Gerald L. K. Smith in a moment of triumph embraces Dr.
Townsend (left) and Father Coughlin (right) after speaking
at the convention of Townsend followers in Cleveland,
Ohio, in the summer of 1936.*

power in the movement, and he was angry at recent developments.
Now he blasted Father Coughlin and Gerald L. K. Smith, accusing
them of trying to use Townsend for their own purposes. He praised
F.D.R. and spoke against endorsement of the Union Party.

The crowd gave Gomer Smith a rousing ovation. An angry Dr.
Townsend hurried to the microphone to say that "poor Gomer" was
a "troublemaker" and should not be applauded. The permanent chairman of the convention then stated that "there will be no more free
speech at these meetings." But the trouble was not over. The whole
question of the Townsend movement's role in the coming campaign
had been opened, and by the end of the day some fifteen state delegations had caucused and voted against backing Lemke.

Townsend and Gerald L. K. Smith were prepared for this revolt.
They had already decided that they would follow the course which the
dissenters were now demanding: no "official" endorsement of the new
party by the organization. Townsend now pushed on with the remain-
der of the convention program: speeches by the four key men of the
Union party.

Gerald L. K. Smith was first. He had been having a fine time at the convention. He roamed the floor of the auditorium, shaking hands with the delegates and looking the part, as one newsman put it, of "the irrepressible young man smashing his way into the leadership of the movement."

Smith's speech was perhaps the best of his career. An astounded H. L. Mencken wrote:

> His speech was a magnificent amalgam of each and every American species of rabble-rousing, with embellishments borrowed from the Algonquin Indians and the Cossacks of the Don. It ran the keyboard from the softest sobs and gurgles to the most ear-splitting whoops and howls, and when it was over the thousands of delegates simply lay back in their pews and yelled. Never in my life, in truth, have I heard a more effective speech.

Smith spoke clutching a Bible. Coatless, sweat plastering his shirt to his broad shoulders and barrel chest, he roared hatred of Wall Street bankers, millionaire steel magnates, Chicago wheat speculators, and New Deal social engineers who "sneezed at the Doctor's great vision." He issued his call to arms and bellowed:

> We must make our choice in the presence of atheistic Communistic influences! It is Tammany or Independence Hall! It is the Russian primer or the Holy Bible! It is the Red Flag or the Stars and Stripes! It is Lenin or Lincoln! Stalin or Jefferson! James A. Farley or Francis E. Townsend!

As the crowd gave Smith a standing, screaming ovation, the next speaker fidgeted nervously. Jealous of his new ally's platform delivery, Father Coughlin had sulked at the back of the auditorium through most of Smith's address. And as Smith concluded, the priest decided to make a dramatic gesture.

Midway through his address, Coughlin halted for an electric pause. He stepped back from the microphone and, peeling off his black coat and his Roman collar, literally unfrocked himself before the audience of 10,000 people. Striding back to the rostrum, he roared: "As far as the National Union is concerned, no candidate who is endorsed for Congress can campaign, go electioneering for, or support the great betrayer and liar, Franklin D. Roosevelt." And then he concluded: "I ask you to purge the man who claims to be a Democrat from the Democratic Party—I mean Franklin Double-Crossing Roosevelt."

After a moment of stunned silence, the delegates stamped and shouted their approval of this vicious assault upon the nation's President. And they kept on shouting as Coughlin proclaimed Townsend, Smith, and himself as the "trinity of hope" against the "unholy trinity of Roosevelt, Landon, and Browder."

Now, Charles E. Coughlin made his bid:

> . . . there is Dr. Townsend and there is the Reverend Gerald L. K. Smith. By those two leaders I stand foursquare. Ladies and gentlemen, you haven't come here to endorse any political party. [Their principles] have been incorporated in the new Union party. You are not asked to endorse it. Your beloved leader endorses them and how many of you will follow Dr. Townsend?

The Townsendites, almost to a man, rose in response to Coughlin's question.

After such oratorical pyrotechnics, Dr. Townsend's speech seemed tepid stuff. But his adoring followers did not care. Making his position in the coming election clear, he affirmed that he "could not do otherwise" than to support William Lemke for President. . . .

Throughout July and August, Townsend relentlessly toured the nation for the Union ticket, and when Coughlin's National Union for Social Justice held its own convention in mid-August, the old doctor was on hand to make a speech along with Lemke, Smith, and the radio priest. It seemed as if the strange coalition of radical leaders was indeed going to hold together.

This proved to be an illusion. Except for the curious hold that Gerald Smith had over Townsend, relations among the four key men of the Union party were never cordial. Each was primarily concerned with promoting his own program and/or personality. . . .

By late August, pressures began building up within the Townsend movement which were to cause the Doctor to lose heart for the Union crusade. Several of his important subordinates had been complaining about the influence of Gerald L. K. Smith and had been opposing the founder's endorsement of Lemke. When Townsend fired these men, they brought suit against the Townsend National Recovery Plan, Ltd., asking that Townsend be ousted as president. The Doctor survived this attack only after lengthy court action.

Townsend's troubles were compounded by the poor showing of candidates endorsed by his movement in various primary elections held in the late summer. And in September and October, the pension promoter began to receive disturbing reports about the reaction of his large California following to the Lemke candidacy. A presidential preference poll of 50,000 California Townsendites showed 28 per cent for Roosevelt, 52 for Landon, 4 neutral and only 6 per cent for Lemke. . . .

In the weeks before the election Townsend began moving toward Landon, telling the press, "I shall cast my vote for an untried man in hope that he may prove of greater value to the nation than the incumbent. . . . I do this because I will not be permitted to vote for Mr. Lemke, my choice for the office." He referred to the fact that in his own state of California—and in thirteen others as well—Lemke's name would not be on the ballot. In these areas, as the days passed, Townsend widened his appeal for Landon support. "Lemke has my endorsement," he proclaimed, "but remember, Roosevelt is our sworn enemy. . . . He must be beaten!" This last-minute switch confused his supporters and seriously weakened the Union party.

When the returns came in on November 3, the dream of power that the radical leaders had shared when they had made their summer alliance was blasted. William Lemke received less than 900,000 votes as Franklin D. Roosevelt, the hated foe, rolled up the most one-sided Electoral College victory in American history; he received more than 27 million popular votes, to Alfred Landon's 16 million.

All of the leaders of the new political organization were to pay a severe price for the horrendous defeat. And after the election their careers curved downhill. . . .

Townsend returned to diligent work for the group whose support had brought him into the limelight, . . . but his organization was faltering. Membership fell off, and from the decay of the plan sprang other panaceas, such as the "Thirty Dollars Every Thursday" clubs in California. Although Dr. Townsend pushed on, continuing to lead his dwindling band of followers, publishing his newspaper, and maintaining a national headquarters throughout the war and postwar years, nothing could reverse the growing tide of unconcern among the elderly toward the movement and its founder. The end of the depression and the prosperity of the 1940's and 1950's eliminated the fear and privation upon which the plan had fed. Yet Francis E. Townsend carried on until 1960, when, still speaking hopefully of the future, the man who had found a career when most men think of retirement died in Los Angeles at ninety-three.

Dr. Townsend did not achieve his long-sought goal. But in the Depression decade this dedicated, sincere man, despite his ignorance of economics and naïveté about politics, carved out an important place for himself in American life. "It is dissatisfaction with the attainable," Raymond Gram Swing has written, "which leads to fanaticism and at last to social fury. . . . When great masses are ready to believe the impossible, that is an ominous political fact." In the 1930's, when the great Depression created a crisis in which messianic leaders could flourish, millions of pathetically eager, infinitely hopeful, and dangerously credulous people trooped blindly after Dr. Francis E. Townsend. The old Doctor pushed his followers too far and too fast in the election campaign of 1936, but for many hectic months his movement was a

A cartoon by Brown that appeared in the New York Herald Tribune *in the mid-1930s.*

force to be reckoned with in the United States. Winston Churchill, then sixty-two years old, came to this country during those months and dismissed the Townsend Plan as "an attempt to mint the moonlight into silver and coin the sunshine into gold." Perhaps it was. But for a time millions of Americans fervently believed in it. The year was 1936—the year of the old folks' revolt.

The Place of Franklin D. Roosevelt in History

ALLAN NEVINS

This essay brings together a great historian and a great subject. Allan Nevins's estimation of Franklin D. Roosevelt is complicated. He says as much about Roosevelt's weaknesses as about his strengths. He looks at Roosevelt through the eyes of the president's friends and his enemies; he refers to his personal observations of the man and also makes the broadest of generalizations, based on his amazing understanding not only of the whole course of American history but of much of the history of the western world. He tells us funny stories that reveal Roosevelt in moments of relaxation and quotes from formal state papers which show him center stage at crucial points in his career. Above all, like a great conductor interpreting a symphony, he is at every stage absolute master of his subject and his materials, devoting exquisite care to every detail yet never forgetting that each separate passage contributes vitally to the total effect.

That effect is, in a word, sunny. Nevins, despite his awareness of Roosevelt's limits and defects, admired the man because of what he calls his "effective greatness," which he believed was produced by qualities of spirit rather than of intellect or even of moral fiber. ∎

Seldom has an eminent man been more conscious of his special place in history than was Franklin D. Roosevelt. He thought of history as an imposing drama and himself as a conspicuous actor. Again and again he carefully staged a historic scene: as when, going before Congress on December 8, 1941, to call for a recognition of war with Japan, he took pains to see that Mrs. Woodrow Wilson accompanied Mrs. Roosevelt to the Capitol, thus linking the First and Second World Wars. As governor and as President, he adopted for the benefit of future historians the rule that every letter addressed to him, however insignificant, and copies of every document issued from his office, should be preserved. This mass of papers, mounting into the millions, soon became almost overwhelming. It might have been added, with some difficulty, to the many other official collections in the Library of Congress. But, with a strong sense of his special place in history, Roosevelt wanted a memorial all his own, a place of resort for scholars, connected uniquely with his name and his administrations. He announced the gift of his papers to the nation; his mother gave sixteen acres of land for a building at Hyde Park; some 28,000 donors subscribed $400,000 for an edifice; and Congress made the Roosevelt Library a federal institution.

In this Library at Hyde Park, as a token of his place in history, he took an almost naïve pride. I well recall the dinner he gave early in 1939 to the trustees and a select number of historians to discuss plans for its management. It took place at the Mayflower Hotel in Washington; he was wheeled up an inclined ramp to his place at a central table; he waved joyously to everyone; he enjoyed his stewed mulligatawny turtle—a favorite dish—his companions, his sense of launching another original enterprise. In a long informal speech he talked of certain predecessors: of Lincoln, of Grover Cleveland, whom he had known, and of his cousin Theodore Roosevelt; he dwelt on Woodrow Wilson's sense of history—Wilson in 1917 had forbidden young Roosevelt, then Assistant Secretary of the Navy, to bring warships up from Cuban waters to the United States lest future historians should accuse him of making a provocative gesture on the eve of our first war with Germany. I well recall, too, the still more interesting occasion when he laid the cornerstone of the Hyde Park Library on November 19, 1939. Trustees, historians, and editors lunched with him; he gaily drove his own specially equipped car to the site; he chatted blithely with everyone; and he watched the cornerstone slip into place with a gratified smile.

Today his grave lies close by that Library, and by the family home that has become a national shrine, visited by hundreds of thousands every year. To the collections there shelved, multitudes of scholars annually repair, for they are open to all. Roosevelt's own deposits, including letters, documents, books, pamphlets, films, photographs,

As this 1938 cartoon from the Columbus Dispatch *suggests, Roosevelt was exceedingly interested in assuring himself a place among the outstanding presidents of American history.*

speeches, and museum pieces, have exceeded a total of fifty million items; and to them are being added the papers of Cabinet officers and other official associates. The career of no other American President has so vast a documentation for history.

Is it too soon to estimate the place of Franklin D. Roosevelt in the stream of American and world events? It is never too soon for such a task. History is not a remote Olympian bar of judgment, but a controversial arena in which each generation must make its own estimate of the past. We have every right to fix the historical position of Roosevelt as we see it today, knowing that it will be reassessed from the vantage point of a longer perspective and fuller knowledge in 1975, and re-estimated again in 2065. That it will be a great place we may already be certain. A statue to Roosevelt has been reared in Oslo. When a statue was proposed in London, five-shilling subscriptions were opened one morning; they were closed that night with the sum over-subscribed; had they been kept open a few days money would have poured in for five statues. Streets have been named for him around the world. Fifty American historians, interrogated by Arthur M. Schlesinger, Sr., of Harvard, have all but unanimously agreed that in the roster of Presidents Lincoln stands first, Washington second, and Franklin D. Roosevelt third. Hearing of that verdict, Winston Churchill declared that in impact upon world history Roosevelt unquestionably stood first.

We have this advantage in attempting the task, that a great part of the necessary evidence is already at hand. Never before in human annals has so huge a volume of reminiscences, autobiographies, impressions, letters, official documents, and other data bearing on one man been issued within twenty years of his death. The thirteen volumes of Roosevelt's official papers edited by Judge Samuel I. Rosenman and the four volumes of personal letters edited by Elliot Roosevelt; the memoirs of Cordell Hull, Harry Hopkins, Henry Morgenthau, Harold Ickes, Henry L. Stimson, James Farley, Edward J. Flynn, Mrs. Franklin D. Roosevelt, Frances Perkins, Grace Tully, Hugh Johnson, Dwight Eisenhower, Omar Bradley, and a hundred others; the mass of comment by Washington reporters and war correspondents who watched history being made; the procession of European histories and memoirs so impressively headed by Winston Churchill's volumes—this already forms a corpus too great for one student to explore fully in a lifetime. But while we shall have immense fresh accretions of detail, it is unlikely that we shall receive any startling new "revelations," any facts that will offer a basis for sweeping revisions of judgment.

In dealing with every commanding figure of history, a fundamental question presents itself: To what extent did greatness inhere in the man, and to what degree was it a product of the situation? If great men have their stars, as Napoleon said he did, it is often because a national or world crisis favors greatness. The reason why fifty American historians did not wholly agree with Winston Churchill upon Roosevelt's rank among the nation's Presidents is, I think, simple. Washington had indisputable greatness in himself. "The first, the last, the best, the Cincinnatus of the West," as Lord Byron called him, he was great in character, great in traits of leadership, great in insight and wisdom. Lincoln had an even more manifest and appealing personal greatness. His public utterances, from the House Divided address to the Gettysburg Address, his state papers, from the First Inaugural to the final pronouncements on Reconstruction, attest a rare intellectual power. The wisdom of his principal public acts, his magnanimity toward all foes public and private, his firmness under adversity, his elevation of spirit, his power of strengthening the best purposes and suppressing the worst instincts of a broad, motley democracy, place him in the front rank of modern statesmen.

But with Franklin D. Roosevelt we feel no such assurance of transcendent personal eminence. We feel that he lacked the steadfast elevation of character exhibited by George Washington. We find in him distinctly less intellectual power than in Jefferson, Lincoln, or perhaps Woodrow Wilson. We conclude, in short, that his tremendous place in history was in lesser degree the product of his special personal endowments, and in larger degree the handiwork of his stormy times, than that occupied by George Washington or Abraham Lincoln.

That Roosevelt had remarkable intellectual gifts is plain; but these gifts fell short of the highest distinction. He possessed a quick, re-sourceful, and flexible mind. This fact is illustrated on an elevated level by his ability to deal with fifty important issues in a day, making shrewd decisions on each; by his power in wartime of efficiently coordinating departments, industries, and armies, of gaining the teamwork of generals, admirals, and business leaders, as no other President has ever done. He organized the national energies with unique success. His intellectual proficiency is illustrated on a lower plane by almost any of the press conferences recorded in Judge Rosenman's volumes; by his deft tact in handling two-score quick-witted newspapermen, evading some questions, dissecting the fatuity of others, using a few to touch a needed chord of public opinion, and responding to many with concise, expert answers. Like his cousin Theodore Roosevelt, he had an insatiable curiosity about books, about men, about events. It was linked with an unquenchable zest for experience; the zest expressed in his famous wartime message to Churchill, "It is fun to be in the same century with you."

He had a talent for quick parliamentary hits. He could make his enemies ridiculous by a few pungent words, as in the happy rhythmical phrase about "Martin, Barton, and Fish" that, recited over the radio, exposed these three reactionary congressmen to a continental gale of laughter in 1940; or by a lambent flare of humor, as in his speech of 1944 picturing the Scottish unhappiness of his dog Fala over an accusation of extravagance. He had flashes of daring imagination. He had a remarkable gift of rapid improvisation, as he showed in all the recurrent crises of his twelve crowded years in office. In part this consisted of his ability to use other men's thought; "he is the best picker of brains who ever lived," his intimates used to say. His power of application was remarkable even among our overworked Presidents. He had an average working day of fourteen hours (Truman later boasted of sixteen), and he told Governor James M. Cox: "I never get tired."

But of pre-eminent intellectual talent he had little. I recall Walter Lippmann saying in the second administration: "He has never written a real state paper." In a sense that is true. No paper signed by him equals Washington's Farewell Address, Lincoln's great papers, Theodore Roosevelt's first annual message, or Woodrow Wilson's nobler productions. Nearly all his speeches were in fact largely written for him by others. Robert Sherwood describes a typical scene: Judge Rosenman, Harry Hopkins, and Sherwood gathered about a table discussing the material for an imminent presidential address, and threshing it over and over until Judge Rosenman impatiently flung down a pencil with the words, "There comes a time in the life of every speech when it's got to be *written!*" Roosevelt wrote no books; he was probably incapable of matching such a work as Theodore Roosevelt's *The Win-*

ning of the West. He threw out no such immortal epigrams as Churchill's sentence challenging Britons to face a future of "blood, sweat, and tears." His best phrases, like "the forgotten man" and "the new deal," were borrowed from other men.

A capacity for abstract thought was largely omitted from his equipment. The idea once current that he had a special intimacy with Maynard Keynes was obviously erroneous, for he was simply incapable of following a mind so analytical, an intellect so subtle, as that of Lord Keynes. When John Gunther asked one of Roosevelt's friends, "Just how does the President think?" he met the reply: "The President never *thinks.*" Like Theodore Roosevelt, he was primarily a man of action. His mental processes, as many friends have said, were intuitive rather than logical. He reacted rather than reflected. A President is not necessarily too busy to do abstract thinking. Newton D. Baker, who held a minor post in Grover Cleveland's administration and a major office under Woodrow Wilson, once observed to me that while Cleveland shouldered his way through difficulties like a buffalo charging a thicket, Wilson "dissolved his problems by an acid process of thought." This acid process was beyond Roosevelt. All that is told us of his reading suggests that it was rather adolescent: either escapist, like the detective stories carried on every long trip; or attached to a hobby, like naval history; or journalistic. His humor lacked the philosophic overtones of Lincoln's or even the saltiness of Harry Truman's; it too was somewhat adolescent. It was usually the humor of the quip, as when he said to his secretary, Grace Tully, over-addicted to punctuation, "Grace, how often do I have to tell you not to waste the taxpayer's commas?" Or it was the humor of the wisecrack, as when he remarked to the six New England governors who startled him in 1933 by suddenly appearing at the White House in a body: "What, all six of you? You're not going to secede from the Union, are you?"

We all know what Lord Bacon said makes a ready man; and intellectually, the talkative Roosevelt was a ready leader—perhaps the readiest of all the world's leaders in his exigent time. This power to act quickly, shrewdly, and earnestly was a gift that served the nation and the free world with unforgettable dexterity and force. Honoring this princely capacity, we can afford to give minor weight to the fact that his mind, compared with that of Woodrow Wilson, sometimes appears superficial, and that he possessed no such intellectual versatility as Thomas Jefferson—to say nothing of Winston Churchill.

In respect to character, similarly, he had traits of an admirable kind; but we must add that even in combination, they fell short of a truly Roman weight of virtue. He held sincere religious convictions, and it was no mere gesture that led him to take his Cabinet, on the morn of his first inauguration, to divine service at St. John's. "I think," writes

Mrs. Roosevelt in *This I Remember,* "he actually felt he could ask God for guidance and receive it. That was why he loved the Twenty-third Psalm, the Beatitudes, and the thirteenth chapter of First Corinthians." He was one of the unflinching optimists of his time. Having conquered a prostrating illness and horrible physical handicap, he felt an inner faith in man's power to conquer anything. When his aides made estimates of American industrial capacity, he raised them; when the Combined Chiefs of Staff set down dates for the various goals in the invasion of Europe, he revised them forward. Because of his religious faith and his ingrained optimism, he possessed an unfailing serenity. In the stormiest of hours his nerve was never shaken.

On his first day in the Presidency in 1933, with the banks of the nation closed down and the country almost prostrate with anxiety, he found his desk at six o'clock in the afternoon quite clear. He pressed a button. Four secretaries appeared at four doors to the room. "Is there anything more, boys?" he inquired. "No, Mr. President," they chorused. And Roosevelt remarked with his happy smile: "This job is a cinch!"

Equally admirable were his idealism, his consciousness of high objectives, and his frequent nobility of spirit. He was willing to sacrifice himself for the public weal. When in 1928 Alfred E. Smith, the Democratic presidential candidate, asked him to run for governor of New York, he was told by physicians that if he kept out of public life another year or two, he could regain the use of his left leg, while if he did not he would be incurably lame; but he answered the call of duty. His concern for the poor, the friendless, the unfortunate, was more keenly humane than that of any leader since Lincoln. "I see one-third of a nation," he said in his Second Inaugural, "ill-housed, ill-clad, ill-nourished"—and meant to do something about it. Moderately rich himself, he disliked those who were too rich. The steel magnate Eugene Grace, who took a bonus of a million dollars a year without the knowledge of his stockholders, aroused his bitter scorn. "Tell Gene he'll never make a million a year again!" was the angry message he sent the man. Frances Perkins, who had known him as a rather arrogant, snobbish young man before his seizure by infantile paralysis, and who knew him as a battler for social justice afterward, believed that this physical ordeal taught him sympathy for the afflicted and underprivileged.

Yet, we must add, these impressive virtues were flawed by certain grievous defects. He had flashes of insincerity which sometimes impaired the confidence even of close friends. Henry L. Stimson mentions in his memoirs the fact that, having found out Roosevelt in a quite needless bit of duplicity, for several years he avoided all contact with him. Henry A. Wallace committed to paper an account of Roosevelt's double-dealing (as Wallace saw it) in handling the Vice Presidential nomination in 1944. Other men have penned different stories. Even the President's defenders could not deny that his treatment of that critical problem showed a certain irresponsibility, to be excused perhaps by the fact that he was already more ill than he realized. Because of this instability, Roosevelt was ready at times to abandon principle for expediency. Cordell Hull has described how unfortunate were the results of such an abandonment in the Neutrality Acts. And Mrs. Roosevelt writes: "While I often felt strongly on various subjects, Franklin frequently refrained from supporting causes in which he believed, because of political realities. There were times when this annoyed me very much. In the case of the Spanish Civil War, for instance, we had to remain neutral, though Franklin knew quite well he wanted the democratic government to be successful. But he also knew he could not get Congress to go along with him. To justify his action, or lack of action, he explained to me, when I complained, that the League of Nations had asked us to remain neutral. . . . He was simply trying to salve his own conscience. It was one of the many times I felt akin to a hair shirt."

Edward J. Flynn writes flatly: "The President did not keep his word on many appointments." There exists no question that he promised to make Louis Johnson Secretary of War, and broke the promise. All statesmen have to adjust principle to events and to public sentiment, and are sometimes compelled to revoke promises. But Roosevelt was at times indefensibly evasive even with intimates like Flynn and Louis Johnson, and lacked straightforwardness. It can be said, too, that he often followed a Machiavellian technique in administration. He liked, for example, to put two or three men in positions of conflicting authority, so that they worked at loggerheads, with himself as ultimate arbiter. It was in part his fault that Sumner Welles and Cordell Hull made the State Department for several years a maelstrom of rival policies and ambitions—although this is a complex story; it was in part his fault that Jesse Jones and Henry Wallace engaged at one time in a feud which sadly injured both the administration and the country.

Other unhappy traits might be copiously illustrated. Roosevelt could seem dismayingly casual about everything from a political speech to some of the issues at Yalta. He could be reprehensibly secretive; he kept the minutes of the Teheran Conference from Secretary of State Hull, and withheld from the American people the concession he made at Yalta to Russia on votes in the United Nations Assembly. He was pettily vindictive toward some opponents, as Raymond B. Moley and James Farley testify in detail, and his attempted purge of certain southern leaders in 1938 is far from the happiest chapter in his career. All in all, we must repeat our conclusion that his character lacked the symmetry, harmony, and weight found in that of Washington and of Lincoln.

Yet without the highest inner greatness Roosevelt had an effective greatness of action, in relation to his time, which will cause him to be remembered as happily as any American leader. It is significant that Churchill, intellectually so much superior, always treated him with manifest deference, as a lesser man bowing to a greater. Was this simply because Roosevelt headed the more powerful state? I think not. We must here face what seems to me a salient fact of history. A leader who puts second-rate qualities of intellect and character into first-rate application to the needs of his time may be a greater man than the leader who puts first-rate qualities into a second-rate application. Roosevelt signally illustrates this aphorism. He had, to begin with, the gift of address: a gift for doing the right thing at just the right time. He had, in the second place, the greater gift of being able to put his personal forces into harmony with the best forces of his era.

Roosevelt's effective greatness included an unrivalled power of matching the urgent crisis with the adequate act; a power of timing an impressive measure to meet a desperate need. Take the first days of 1933, after his election. Never in a period of peace—never since the days of British invasion in 1814, or Confederate victory in 1863—had the nation been in such straits. Between twelve and fifteen million men were out of work. Five million families, one seventh of the population, were supported by public relief or private charity. Since the beginning of the depression, 4,600 banks had failed. Travellers through the broad industrial belt from Chicago to New York seemed to pass nothing but closed factory gates. Half the automobile plants of Michigan had shut down. Along the Great Lakes, path of the largest marine commerce of the world, ships had almost ceased to move. In the iron beds of the Mesabi and Vermilion ranges scarcely a shovel dipped into the riches ores of the globe; in the copper mountain at Butte scarcely a drill was at work. The looms of southern textile factories were cob-webbed. On railway sidings locomotives gathered rust in long rows; behind them huddled passenger and freight cars in idle hundreds, their paint fading. Middle-western farmers gazed bitterly at crops whose market value was less than the cost of harvesting; on the high plains, ranchers turned cattle loose to graze at will because it did not pay to send them to the stockyards. In Pennsylvania and New England desperate men and women offered to work for anything, and some did work for a dollar a week.

Worst of all was the fear which gripped the nerves of the nation. To observers who travelled across the country in trains almost empty, through factory districts with hardly a wisp of smoke, the helpless populations sent up an almost audible cry of anger, bewilderment, and

An ebullient F.D.R. holding an outdoor press conference at Warm Springs, Georgia, in 1939.

panic. The day before Roosevelt took office the crisis gathered to a climax. By midnight of March 3 the closing of all remaining banks had been or was being ordered in every state. Never before had a change of Presidents taken place against a background so dramatic. The people, awakening on March 4 to read that their financial system was prostrate, gathered at noon by millions about their radios to listen in anguish, in anxiety, but in hope, to the voice of their new national leader.

There ensued four of the most brilliantly successful months in the history of American government. Roosevelt's first words promised energy: "I assume unhesitatingly the leadership of this great army of our people, dedicated to a disciplined attack upon our common problems." He improvised a series of policies, and mobilized an administrative machine, with a vigor that would have done credit to any wartime executive. Within thirty-six hours he had taken absolute control of the currency and banking system, and called Congress in extraordinary session. He forthwith launched an aggressive attack along half a dozen fronts; upon banking problems, industrial prostration, farm distress, unemployment, public works, the burden of public and private debt. One reporter wrote that the change in Washington was like that from oxcart to airplane. Congress labored for ninety-nine days under the President's all-but-complete sway. Almost his every wish was obeyed by immediate votes. One staggered member said of the program: "It reads like the first chapter of Genesis."

And as Roosevelt took these steps his courage, his resourcefulness, his blithe optimism, infected the spirit of the people; he gave Americans new confidence and the *élan* of a new national unity. When he gaily signed his last bills and departed for a brief sail up the Atlantic coast as skipper of a 45-foot sailing boat, the nation realized that it had turned from stagnation to a bright adventure. As the President put it, we were "on our way."

Nor was this an isolated spasm of leadership; for each recurrent crisis found the same resourcefulness called into effective play. When France fell, when the British Commonwealth stood alone against the deadliest foe that modern civilization had known, Americans gazed at the European scene in fear, in gloom, in perplexity. With a sense of dumb helplessness, tens of millions put their intensest feeling into the hope for Britain's survival. Those tens of millions never forgot the morning of September 3, 1940, when they read the headlines announcing that Roosevelt had told a startled Congress of the transfer of fifty destroyers to embattled Britain; a defiance of Hitler, a defiance of home isolationists, a first long stride toward ranging America against the Fascist despots. Nor could lovers of world freedom ever forget the dramatic steps that followed hard upon British victory over Hitler's air force and upon Roosevelt's re-election: the Four Freedoms speech of January 6, 1941; the introduction of the Lend-Lease Bill four days later, a measure which completely transformed American foreign policy; the establishment of naval and military posts in Greenland and Iceland; the proclamation of an unlimited national emergency; the seizure of all Axis ships and Axis credits; the Atlantic Charter meeting with Churchill off Newfoundland; the establishment of convoys for American ships carrying aid to Britain; and, in the background, the stimulation of American production to an unprecedented flow of guns, tanks, shells, and airplanes, with factories roaring day and night for the defense of democracy.

These years 1940–41 were, as we see now, among the greatest crises in modern history. They were met with an imagination, boldness, and ingenuity that can hardly be overpraised. Parochialism, timidity, or fumbling might have been fatal; even a pause for too much reflection might have been fatal. We knew then that Roosevelt was determined to face the exigency with an intrepidity worthy of the republic. But his intention was even more courageous than we supposed. For we know now that Harry Hopkins told Churchill in London early in 1941: "The President is determined that we shall win the war together. Make no mistake about it. He sent me here to tell you that at all costs and by all means he will carry you through."

Roosevelt's second quality of effective greatness was his ability to vindicate the American method of pragmatic experiment, of practical *ad hoc* action, step by step. He was essentially a Jeffersonian. He belonged to the school which, following the historic Anglo-American bent of mind, is attached to facts rather than ideas, to the enlargement of precedents rather than the formulation of dazzling visions. Like all Anglo-American statesmen, he disliked sweeping generalizations of an intolerant, exclusive nature. He loved experimental advance, and was wont to say that if he were right sixty per cent of the time, he would be satisfied. Like Jefferson, he was willing to scrap a theory the moment a brute fact collided with it; he trusted experience, and distrusted flights into the empyrean. His so-called revolution, though unprecedentedly broad and swift, was like Jefferson's "revolution"; it was simply a combination of numerous practical changes, the main test of which was whether or not they worked.

The Rooseveltian changes did work. They did transform American life and the American outlook in two distinct ways. They converted a nation of aggressive individualists into a social-minded nation accepting the principles of the welfare state. They changed an isolationist or largely isolationist nation into one committed to world partnership and world leadership. The New Deal in home affairs was empirical, not ideological. The emergency program I have sketched was a stop-gap affair put together to tide over a crisis, and as Mrs. Roosevelt once put it, "give us time to think." It succeeded. Taken as a whole, the New Deal passed through two phases. In the first, 1933–35, the government tried scarcity economics, reducing factory production, farm output, and hours of work, and doing what it could to cut off the American economy from the outside world. In the second and better phase, 1935–50, it tried full employment, full production, enlarged distribution of goods, and freer international trade. This led directly toward the acceptance of Cordell Hull's ideal of co-operative internationalism. American participation in world affairs after 1938 similarly passed through two phases. In the first, all the nation's energies were devoted to the defeat of the Axis. In the second, Roosevelt, Hull, Welles, and Stettinius moved step by step to construct a new world order, an enduring fabric of the United Nations. In home and foreign affairs alike action was always direct, experimental, and pragmatic.

It gave America a new social order at home, and a new orientation in global affairs. It worked; it is still working. But because it never approached a sweeping ideological revolution of the Marxist or totalitarian type, it was the despair of certain impractical theorists *pur sang.*

For example, readers of that brilliant but extraordinarily half-informed and error-streaked book, Harold Laski's *The American Democracy,* will find an almost incredible analysis of what the author regards as Mr. Roosevelt's fundamental failure. This was his failure to smash the old America completely, and build a quite new America on the theories that pleased Mr. Laski. The author draws an illuminating comparison between Lenin and Roosevelt. Lenin, it appears, made a marvelously precise and correct analysis of the maladies of modern society and economics; and he applied it with revolutionary courage. Roosevelt, on the other hand, was never converted—he never learned that "the foundations of the Americanism he inherited were really inadequate to the demands made upon its institutional expression." In particular, writes Laski, he failed to see that he should destroy "private ownership of the means of production"; that is, that the state should take over all mines, factories, transport, workshops, and farms. Roosevelt, as a result of his faulty analysis, unhappily failed to carry through a real revolution. What was the upshot? In Russia, admits Laski, life became nearly intolerable. The price of revolution proved "almost overwhelming"—starvation of millions, wholesale executions, vast concentration camps, the extinction of freedom. In America, Laski admits, life was immensely improved. Industrial production became enormous; farm output grew tremendous; the standard of living steadily rose. But theory (says Mr. Laski) is everything. Lenin with his ideology was right; Roosevelt with his practical experimentalism was a failure!

This view of the matter would be emphatically rejected by all but a handful of Americans, including those who do not admire Roosevelt. Like Jefferson, like Lincoln, like Wilson, he was innovator and conservator at once; he made daring new additions to the American fabric, but he kept the best of the old structure. While he converted Americans to the new ideal of social security, he strengthened their old faith in individual opportunity. He proved again that America needs no ideological revolution. He vindicated our traditional method of solving problems one at a time by pragmatic trial and error. As one journalist wrote: "One remembers him as a kind of smiling bus driver, with that cigarette holder pointed upward, listening to the uproar from behind as he took the sharp turns. They used to tell him that he had not loaded his vehicle right for all eternity. But he knew that he had stacked it well enough to round the next corner, and he knew when the yells were false, and when they were real, and he loved the passengers."

Roosevelt's third and most important quality of effective greatness lay in his ability to imbue Americans, and to some extent even citizens of other lands, with a new spiritual strength. Well into the twentieth century, most men in the New World had shared a dream of ever-widening adventure, a sense of elated achievement. They had dared much in coming to the new continent, and still more in mastering it. They were optimistic, self-confident, exuberant. The heavy costs of the First World War, the disillusionments of its aftermath, the pressure of complex new social problems, and above all the staggering blows of the Great Depression darkened our horizons. We had entered the Shadow Belt which Bryce predicted in his book on *The American Commonwealth*. From that zone of gloom, that numbed consciousness of frustration and failure, Roosevelt lifted Americans on the wings of his great new adventures—the alphabetical adventures of the AAA, the NRA, the TVA; above all, on the wings of the greatest adventure in our history, the effort to rescue democracy from totalitarianism, and to organize the world to safeguard freedom.

For a few years Americans had felt lost, bewildered, paralyzed. Roosevelt carried them to a Moabite peak whence once more they saw promised lands. They threw off their frustrations; he gave them a feeling that they were participating in a life far wider than their every-day parochial concerns. His self-confidence, his enthusiasm, his happy faculty of obliterating old failures by bold new plans, taught them that they were not imprisoned in a dead past but were helping build a living future. In the three centuries 1607–1907 Americans had triumphantly mastered their physical environment. Just so, in the next century to come, they would master their social and economic environment at home, and join other nations in a mastery of the world environment. As the storm thickened after 1940, Roosevelt's rich voice grew more urgent—"bidding the eagles of the West fly on." Here at last, he seemed to say, is a task worthy of you; tyranny like Hell is not easily conquered. Lincoln had once used a phrase which haunts his country-men. "Thanks to all," he exclaimed after Gettysburg and Vicksburg, "thanks to all: for the great republic—for the principle it lives by and keeps alive—for man's vast future—thanks to all." A sense of man's vast future, a hope of shaping it for the better, never left Roosevelt's cheerful heart.

It is not often realized to what a degree the spirit of adventure kindled at home under the New Deal was carried over into world affairs when the United States faced the Axis menace. The defeatism of Hoover's day was gone. A hundred and sixty million citizens had been morally prepared to undertake unprecedented tasks. They grumbled; they cursed the hard luck of their grim era; they shuddered over the mounting costs—the colossal debt, the wasted resources; but they never doubted their ability to put the job through. That change in temper was primarily Roosevelt's accomplishment. It threw open, tem-porarily, the portals of a wider world. The change from oxcart was a spiritual, not a material, change. Never in our history have the emotion and resolution of the American people been so completely fused as when, as the first waves of American and British troops stormed across the Normandy beaches, Roosevelt sat at the radio leading the nation in prayer.

Effective greatness—that is Roosevelt's title to a high place in the world's history. Intellect and character are not enough; to them must be added personality, energy, and an accurate sense for the proper timing of action. Roosevelt was not an intellectual giant; but what of the personality that made the Arkansas sharecropper and the Harlem Negro feel they shared all the destinies of the republic? His character did not awe men by its massive strength; but what of the gifts that made him so efficient in harmonizing labor, capital, and agriculture at home, and getting discordant nations to pool their wartime efforts? He lacked the iron traits of Cromwell—but how incomparably more successful he was! He did not have the powerful grasp of Bismarck, but how much more beneficent was his career! In time his specific achievements may be blurred, but the qualities of his spirit will be remembered. For centuries Americans will think of him as one of those spirits who ride in front; we shall see his jaunty figure, his gaily poised head, still in advance of us. We shall hear his blithe voice in his words just before his death at Warm Springs on April 12, 1945:

"The only limit to our realization of tomorrow will be our doubts of today. Let us move forward with strong and active faith."

The Rise of the Supermarket

J. TEVERE MacFAYDEN

As J. Tevere MacFayden remarks in this essay, many important changes in the way people live and even in the way they view the world occur without attracting much public notice. Such changes more or less insinuate themselves into our lives. Before we know it, so to speak, things that yesterday were unknown become routine aspects of every-day existence. The supermarkets that are the centerpieces of so many suburban shopping centers and that extend their facades along so many city streets (and whose advertisements fill page after page in our daily newspapers) are a prime example of this phenomenon. MacFay-den points out that although it is not possible to say with absolute assurance who "invented" the supermarket, his own candidate is Mike Cullen, founder of the King Kullen chain. But whether invented by a single person or simply a "product of the times," the supermarket was created in America, and from America, has spread throughout the world. MacFayden is the author of Gaining Ground: The Renewal of America's Small Farms. ∎

Late last year, on its obituary page, *The New York Times* acknowledged the passing of a multimillionaire Oklahoma businessman named Sylvan Goldman. SYLVAN N. GOLDMAN, 86, DIES; the headline read. INVENTOR OF THE SHOPPING CART.

Born before the turn of the century in what was still officially designated the Indian Territory, Sylvan Goldman fought in the Argonne during World War I and returned to join his brother and uncle in establishing a wholesale grocery venture.

By 1936, the Goldmans had absorbed their principal competitor, Humpty Dumpty, and were expanding their Oklahoma City-based chain of Standard Food Stores. Everything seemed to be going well, but early that year Sylvan perceived a distressing phenomenon. He was watching women walk through the aisles of one of his stores, putting their prospective purchases into the wicker baskets supplied for the purpose, and as Goldman remembered it, "They had a tendency to stop shopping when the baskets became too heavy or too full." Not long afterward, Goldman's attention fell upon a pair of plain folding chairs. Inspiration struck. What if the chairs were fitted with wheels and baskets were attached to their seats? Wouldn't that make shopping easier and shoppers thus inclined to purchase more? Goldman sought out a company carpenter and began a series of experiments. Initial prototypes proved unsatisfactory. They folded up on themselves at the slightest provocation and capsized entirely too easily. It took a year to perfect what he dubbed his "folding basket carrier," a wheeled cart with two wire baskets mounted on it, one offset above the other. In June 1937 the contraption made its debut in Standard stores. The reception, Goldman recalled in a 1977 interview with Charles Kuralt of CBS News, was less than encouraging.

"I went to our biggest store—there wasn't a soul using a basket carrier." This despite the fact that an "attractive girl" was posted at the entrance offering shoppers the new cart. "The housewives, most of 'em decided, 'No more carts for me. I have been pushing enough baby carriages. I don't want to push anymore.'"

Goldman's only takers seemed to be pensioners, and it occurred to the inventor that the public might benefit from some subliminal indoctrination. At each store where the carts were available, Goldman installed a covey of young and middle-aged men and women. He instructed them to wander about incognito, filling their folding carriers. "I told this young lady that was offering carts to the customers to say, 'Look, everybody's using them—why not you?'" She did, and they did.

On the short list of those things that Americans take most for granted, the shopping cart must rank fairly high. I am in my thirties. I proudly tell ten-year-old acquaintances that I somehow survived a life without pocket calculators, home computers, or video games. My par-

355

ents used to say as much to me, only substituting different examples: television, jet travel, the Pill, or the Bomb. We divide our personal histories into eras, and our markers are for the most part tangible and technological. When less concrete events serve to separate these chunks of time, they tend to be grand in scale: wars, coronations, assassinations, and the like. This seems curious in light of the fact that the institutional transformations that have often had the most profound influence over the way we actually live are far less celebrated. Take supermarkets, for example.

Between 1916, when a maverick entrepreneur in Tennessee opened what is generally thought to have been the first self-service grocery in the United States, and roughly 1960, by which time supermarkets were selling 70 percent of the nation's groceries, the evolution of the American supermarket irrevocably altered not only the way Americans bought food but, indeed, the very way they lived. . . . Supermarkets have been so tightly woven into the fabric of our daily lives that it has become practically impossible to imagine the condition of being without them. And because supermarkets seem so basic, so intrinsically unremarkable, it's difficult for most of us to comprehend the true impact of their invention. Supermarkets are not like telephones, for instance. Telephones are historically tidy. We can intellectually accommodate the notion of a time before and a time after telephones. Supermarkets, by contrast, seem timeless. They have permeated our entire existence. Even if we accept the proposition that once upon a time there were none, we're tempted to regard their evolution, in retrospect, as almost imperceptibly gradual. It wasn't.

Attempts to fix with any degree of certainty the precise time and location of the modern supermarket's conception are clouded by a welter of competing claims, but the story has to begin somewhere, and Memphis, Tennessee, is as good a place as any, at Clarence Saunders's self-service grocery on Jefferson Street in 1916.

U.S. Patent No. 1,242,872 was issued on October 9, 1917, to Saunders for "certain new and useful improvements in Self-Serving Stores." The legitimacy of his claims would subsequently be challenged in the courts and partially voided, but industry historians still count him as the progenitor of self-service food shopping. Saunders, who had entered the business as a fourteen-year-old clerk in a rural Virginia general store, called his new shop Piggly Wiggly—a name inspired by a plump shoat he chanced to see escaping through a fence— and it was an emporium like no other of that time. It had turnstiles at the entrance and a check-out counter at the exit. In between wound a single serpentine aisle lined with easy-to-reach goods. Customers took what they wanted and paid cash.

Simple as it sounds now, Saunders's idea constituted a radical revision of retailing orthodoxy. Previously, groceries and dry goods had been sold on a credit-and-delivery basis. Customers presented their orders to clerks, and the clerks filled them. Accounts were periodically tallied, and bills prepared. After considerable scrutiny Saunders determined these practices to be massively wrongheaded and created his alternative. (In the interests of historical balance, it should be acknowledged that several merchants in the West, principally in Texas and Southern California, seem to have come to similar conclusions at approximately the same time. But Saunders got the patent.) Having eliminated much of his standing overhead, he slashed prices, and on a masterfully hyped mixture of novelty and economy he proceeded to build an empire.

Clarence Saunders stuck with his formula, and Piggly Wigglys proliferated. At the apex of the company's growth there were nearly three thousand of them throughout the United States, and they all went by the book. Saunders's instruction manuals were lengthy and complete, spelling out every aspect of the operation in exhaustive detail. His formula worked, and his corporate worth soared, eventually leading to his undoing. Armed with a satchelful of cash and determined to protect the value of his stock, Saunders stormed Wall Street in 1923. He began placing orders and driving the share price up until, on paper anyway, he held virtually all of the company's outstanding common stock. At that point the New York Stock Exchange declared a corner, demanded that he pay for stock that he was buying on margin, and the whole precarious construction came tumbling down.

In the decades that followed, Saunders grew crankier and more iconoclastic. He'd built a fabulous pink palace in Memphis, but he never got the chance to live in it. His patent protection diluted, he turned to a new idea and set up a string of Clarence Saunders Sole-Owner-of-My-Name stores. When these foundered, he poured his energies into a futuristic merchandising format that he christened Keydoozle—key does all—a kind of grocery and dry goods automat where shoppers would use special "electric keys" to select items from closed display cases. The goods would then be ferried by conveyor to a check-out counter, there to be picked up and paid for. "Then she gives her tape to the cashier," Saunders explained to a *Forbes* magazine reporter in 1941. "It is fed into automatic machinery that uses the punched holes to activate a sorting apparatus backstage. And as if by magic a moving belt produces her beans, butter, bread, cauliflower, Tabasco sauce and scallions. She pays her bill and walks out popeyed." But popeyed was apparently not enough, for Keydoozle never got off the ground. After losing Piggly Wiggly, Saunders never flew quite so high again. Nevertheless, fully fourteen years before the first

*Clarence Saunders, after the initial success of his Piggly
Wiggly stores, tried to promote other new shopping concepts.
One was a type of store, called a Keydoozle, in which
packaged food was automatically dispensed. He poses here
with a prototype.*

real supermarket is judged to have been born, Clarence Saunders had
anticipated many of its essential elements.

During the early decades of this century a few major grocery
chains—the Krogers and Safeways, the Grand Unions, and most of all
the Hartford brothers' Great Atlantic & Pacific Tea Company—came
to dominate the nation's retail food trade. The first A&P opened in
1859. By 1930 there were almost 16,000 of them. Between 1914 and

1930 the number of corporate chains more than tripled, while their cumulative retail outlets increased from 24,000 to some 200,000. The keystone of chain store development was an equation that linked efficiency and expansion. Independent stores were owner operated. Owners purchased their stock from wholesale distributors and sold it to consumers, earning a profit on the markup. Chain stores were operated by salaried clerks and supplied by the parent company, which bought goods directly from the manufacturers. The more outlets that were added to a chain, the greater was the portion of a producer's output controlled by buyers for that chain, and thus they exerted an inescapable influence over price. As the chains' range and power grew, they commanded ever more potent economies of scale and tightened the screws on independents.

Not surprisingly, the independents fought back, enlisting their customers and communities in what they cast as a struggle for the preservation of local ownership and accountability and a decentralized economic structure—to say nothing of their own livelihoods. A raft of anti-chain store legislation was spawned, mostly at the municipal level, culminating in 1936 with the passage of the Robinson-Patman Act, which mandated federal regulation of wholesale pricing and distribution. The independents also formed so-called voluntary chains, seeking to match the corporate chains' economies. The best known of these cooperatives is probably the Independent Grocers Alliance of America, or IGA, whose signs still decorate corner groceries everywhere.

Prior to 1912 all grocery stores, chain and independent alike, were fully clerked, credit-and-delivery affairs. In that year A&P began tentatively to introduce what it described as "economy stores" into its system. The clerks remained, but credit and free delivery disappeared. Operating costs were also trimmed by standardization and restriction of store fixtures and stock. A small portion of savings was passed along to the consumer in the form of lower prices. Customers responded, albeit a bit reluctantly at first, by switching their allegiances from more expensive, locally owned establishments to the new economy stores. The independents and conventional chains initially saw little cause for concern. The attrition among their clientele did not yet seem significant, and besides, they retained the lure of liberal credit. In what was still a predominantly agrarian society, cash flow was a sometime and seasonal thing. Credit—be it at the grocer's or the feed and grain dealer's, the hardware store or the milliner's—was not a luxury but a necessity. The independents confidently predicted that the cash-and-carry chains would never gain more than a toehold.

But the nation was already transforming itself around them. The population was becoming measurably more urban, and it was also becoming wealthier, especially in the midst of the euphoric recovery that followed World War I, when the manufacturing and service sectors of the economy waxed in importance, and agriculture waned. An extraordinary transition was taking place. What had formerly been an overwhelmingly self-reliant, even a subsistence economy, was giving way to what was primarily a cash economy. That shift paved the way for the supermarket movement to come.

Society was changing in other ways as well. What would be called the mass media surfaced in the form of national weeklies and monthlies and in the burgeoning public appetite for radio entertainment; the automobile rolled into the mainstream; mobility increased, and distances shrank. Suburbs and planned communities sprang up, residential hermaphrodites that claimed to blend the best aspects of country living with the most desirable qualities of a life in town.

With the nation rearranging itself at such a rate, new retail forms tailored to changing needs prospered. As of 1918, every A&P store in the United States had converted to cash-and-carry. All the ingredients necessary for the creation of the modern supermarket were now in place. It remained only for someone to see them successfully combined.

To that role I nominate Michael Cullen, grocer *extraordinaire* and leading contender for the title of father of the American supermarket. . . . The term *supermarket* itself seems to have been formally adopted for the first time by William H. Albers, a former Kroger's president, who in 1933 founded his own company and called it Albers Super Markets. But it seems to have fallen to Michael Cullen finally to marry the individual elements that, united, form our understanding of what a supermarket is.

In his 1955 manifesto *The Super Market: A Revolution in Distribution,* M. M. ("Zim") Zimmerman, a trade editor and publicity man who became one of the supermarket's earliest champions and, over the course of his long career, indisputably its preeminent proselytizer, defines the creature as follows: "A Super Market is a highly departmentalized retail establishment, dealing in foods or other merchandise, either wholly owned, or concession operated, with adequate parking space, doing a minimum of $250,000 annually. The grocery department, however, must be on a self-service basis." Updated somewhat, that definition still holds, though it was drawn from the first number of the first volume—dated 1936—of Zimmerman's defunct trade publication *Super Market Merchandising.* The business has grown some. The Food Marketing Institute reports that 1983 average sales per store, industry-wide, hovered near the eight-million-dollar mark. Concession operations, whereby independently owned departments— a butcher, for instance, or a baker or a greengrocer—did business under the supermarket's aegis, have long since been abandoned. Several other defining characteristics also apply. Supermarkets are super. When the first of them burst upon the scene more than fifty years ago, they were often eight or ten times the size of standard groceries. Supermarkets, now as then, deal in low margins and high volumes. They are amply stocked, usually offering a wide variety of national and private-label brands. They often feature loss leaders, goods sold at or below cost for the sole purpose of attracting customers. They tend to be located away from crowded downtown centers, within driving distance of large populations. They emphasize convenience and price, and they are, like Ernest Hemingway's famous café, reliably clean and well-lighted places.

Michael Cullen's was a life in the grocery trade. He joined A&P as a clerk at eighteen and stayed for seventeen years before moving on. In 1929, when he was forty-five years old and employed as the manager of a Kroger's branch store in Herrin, Illinois, he addressed a long letter to the company president, William Albers. In it he presented the essence of a career's worth of experience and observation. He knew how the grocery business operated, he said, and he believed he could do better. Cullen sought Albers's and Kroger's backing for a string of five prototype supermarkets, "monstrous in size," to be opened in low-rent facilities several blocks off any main drag. The key to his plans lay in the conviction that by moving a great quantity of merchandise rapidly through his stores, he would be able to show a profit with much lower markups than had hitherto been thought possible. "This is the kind of cut-rate Chain of Wholesale selling direct to the public that I want to operate," he explained in his splendid harangue.

"I want to sell 300 items at cost.

"I want to sell 200 items at 5% above cost.

"I want to sell 300 items at 15% above cost.

"I want to sell 300 items at 20% above cost.

"I want to gross 9% and do a grocery, fruit and vegetable business of $10,000.00 per week, and make a net profit of 2½% on the grocery department, and 3% on the meat department. . . .

"Can you imagine how the public would respond to a store of this kind? To think of it—a man selling 300 items at cost and another 200 items at 5% above cost—nobody in the world ever did this before. Nobody ever flew the Atlantic either, until Lindbergh did it.

"When I come out with a two page ad and advertise 300 items at cost and 200 items at practically cost, which would probably be all the advertising that I would ever have to do, the public, regardless of their present feeling towards Chain Stores, because in reality I would not be a Chain Store, would break my front doors down to get in. It would be a riot. I would have to call out the police and let the public in so many at a time. I would lead the public out of the high priced

houses of bondage into the low prices of the house of the promised
land.

"I would convince the public that I would be able to save them from
one to three dollars on their food bills. I would be the 'miracle man'
of the grocery business. The public would not, and could not believe
their eyes. Week days would be Saturdays—rainy days would be sunny
days, and then when the great crowd of American people came to buy
all those low priced and 5% items, I would have them surrounded with
15%, 20%, and in some cases, 25% items. In other words, I could
afford to sell a can of Milk at cost if I could sell a can of Peas and make
2¢, and so on all through the grocery line.

"The fruit and vegetable department of a store of this kind would
be a gold mine. This department alone may make a net profit of 7%
due to the tremendous turnover we would have after selling out daily
and not throwing half the profit away, which is done at present time
in 25% of the Chain Stores throughout the land.

"Then the big meat department. This would be a bee-hive. We
would have the confidence of the public. They knew that every other
grocery item they picked up they saved money on same, and our meat
department would show us a very handsome profit. . . .

"I was never so confident in my life as I am at the present time; and
in order to prove to you my sincerity and my good faith, I am willing
to invest $15,000.00 of my own money to prove that this will be the
biggest money maker you have ever invested yourself in. . . .

"Again you may object to my locating two or three blocks from the
business center of a big city. One great asset in being away from the
business section is parking space. Another is, you can get generally the
kind of store you want, and on your own terms. The public will walk
an extra block or two if they can save money, and one of our talking
points would be, the reason we sell at wholesale prices are that we are
out of the high rent district. . . .

"Before you throw this letter in the wastebasket, read it again and
then wire me to come to Cincinnati, so I can tell you more about this
plan, and what it will do for you and your company.

"The one thought always uppermost in mind—How can I undersell
the other fellow? How can I beat the other fellow? How can I make my
company more money? The answer is very simple:—by keeping my
overhead down, and only by keeping this overhead down can I beat the
other fellow.

"What is your verdict?"

The verdict, despite Cullen's impassioned prospectus, was negative. . . . Mike Cullen resigned and moved East. In New York City he
found a willing partner in Harry Socoloff, a wholesale grocer, and
shortly thereafter took out a lease on a vacant garage at 171-06 Jamaica

*Mike Cullen opened his first King Kullen supermarket in
1930 in Jamaica in the New York City borough of Queens.*

Avenue, in the borough of Queens. There, in August of 1930, the first
King Kullen Grocery Company store—the first true supermarket—
opened its doors.

"Mike Cullen came out with his first newspaper advertising," Zim
Zimmerman writes in *The Super Market.* "It was fantastic, unorthodox,
contrary to what any experienced advertising man would have considered good copy, but it caught the attention of the people around Long
Island." As well it might have. Mike Cullen's advertisements ran across
whole pages and two-page spreads. Columns of brand names and
prices were capped with screaming boldface banner headlines. KING
KULLEN, WORLD'S GREATEST PRICE WRECKER, the tag lines declared, and
then was posed the rhetorical question, HOW DOES HE DO IT? Here and
there were inserted blocks of pithy, combative text. "Chain Stores read
these prices and weep. You Wall Street Chain Stores have been making
millions from the public for years with your outrageous prices. Chain
Stores, drop your prices, give the poor buying public a chance." When
the local papers resisted running his incendiary notices, he had them
printed as broadsides and delivered door to door.

The buying public, as prophesied, came in droves. A second store
soon followed, and then a third. Cullen's plan proved popular even
beyond his superheated expectations. He threw himself into spreading
the gospel so vigorously that when he died suddenly in April 1936 of
complications following an appendicitis operation, his friends and
family believed he'd worked himself to death. His wife, Nan, took over
the reins; the chain her late husband had founded only six years earlier
had grown to include fifteen stores, and King Kullen's competitors,
having begun to despair of ever beating him, were moving to join him.

Before long there were dozens of entrepreneurs "wrecking prices" nationwide. . . . Zim Zimmerman's 1934 survey counted ninety-four supermarkets. By 1936 his census had jumped to some twelve hundred stores in eighty-five different cities. The major chains balked briefly, then plunged. A&P opened its initial supermarket in Ypsilanti, Michigan, in 1936. The company opened approximately three hundred more in the ensuing twelve months. In the Middle West, Kroger weighed in with its Pay 'N Takit Supers, and Safeway was hastily converting its units on the West Coast. The chains underwent a sharp contraction, closing smaller neighborhood stores and consolidating their operations into fewer, larger outlets. Assertions that supermarkets were merely a Depression-fueled passing fad proved no more prescient than had the independents' earlier assessments of the long-term prognosis for chains.

A symbiosis quickly evolved between the nascent supermarketing and mass-merchandising movement and American business and popular culture. The rise of the supermarket was changing the way we live even as advancing technologies and changing social norms were making that rise possible.

Consider, for example, the business of food processing, packaging, and distribution. Without dramatic changes in each of these areas the supermarket as we know it today could not exist. Because supermarkets depend for their profits on high sales volumes, it follows that consumers must buy in large quantities. But in the absence of hygienic processing and packaging and of any sort of efficient means of home refrigeration, buying perishable foods in bulk was simply inconceivable. New packaging and processing methods and the advent of the domestic refrigerator changed that forever.

Similarly, supermarkets, to maintain their low overheads, were obliged to seek alternatives to hiring an army of clerks to cut and package meats, produce, and even some groceries. Thus demand grew for precut and prepackaged products. Clarence Birdseye had perfected his process for flash-freezing foods in 1927 and sold it to the General Foods Corporation, but before frozen food could gain any broad popularity, better commercial freezer cases had to make their way into supermarkets. To facilitate self-service shopping, packaging took on a markedly increased importance. Where previously many items had been distributed to stores in bulk containers and broken down, or packaged individually for each patron, most groceries now had to arrive at the store already wrapped and boxed in what producers judged to be convenient sizes. Finally, as more women joined the work force during the Second World War, the time set aside for cooking the family meals dwindled. Processed and precooked foods came along to fill the gap.

It is probably fair to suggest that the advent of mass marketing made mass media advertising inevitable. It seems equally valid, though, to surmise that without advertising mass marketing could not have endured. Again a mutually dependent relationship evolved. In the supermarket, advertising and packaging merged. The product's package acquired an added responsibility, having not only to supply protection in transit to the store but also to project a unique and identifiable image on the shelf. Much of what we have come to regard as typical about consumer advertising developed in conjunction with the supermarket. . . .

From the first, supermarkets sought to make shopping an entertainment rather than a chore. In the main they succeeded. Piped-in music, bright lights, and colorful displays, in some cases even in-house child care, coffee shops, and lounges—all contribute to the sense of a visit to the supermarket as a pleasure trip. Indeed, shopping has become a social phenomenon. In Washington, D.C., where there is a preponderance of young, single people, the Georgetown Safeway is highly regarded as a place to go looking for potential dates. And the suburban shopping mall—the supermarket's direct descendant—is typically filled with browsers who go there primarily to pass the time.

Supermarkets cannot be called the cause of highway shopping malls and strip development, nor are they to blame for the decline of the nation's downtowns. That unhappy honor belongs to the automobile. But the supermarket undeniably blazed trail by demonstrating conclusively that consumers would go out of their way to shop. The same reasoning that led Mike Cullen to an empty garage in Queens prodded other sorts of merchants to follow, taking up residence on the city's edge. Large spaces, low rents, easy access by car, and ample parking are as important to supermarkets today as they were to Cullen in the thirties.

The markets themselves have changed, of course. The first King Kullen unit occupied six thousand square feet and stocked about a thousand items. By the 1950s, when three new supermarkets were opening daily, stores averaged twenty thousand square feet and carried six thousand items. Nowadays an up-to-date standard supermarket might sprawl over more than thirty thousand square feet of floor space and sell as many as eighteen thousand different items. . . .

I drove out to Queens not long ago, on a sort of pilgrimage, to seek out the site of the first supermarket. The day was cold and gray under a slanting winter rain. The decades have not been kind to Jamaica Avenue, as the neighborhoods it crosses have slipped inexorably from suburb to slum. At the corner of 171st Street I found Quasar Liquors, whose owner conducts business from behind a bulletproof Plexiglas shield. Most of the rest of the stores on that side of the street were long gone.

Across the avenue, where I figure King Kullen's must have stood, the World's Greatest Price Wrecker was nowhere in evidence. There was a discount auto parts supplier, a machine shop, and a nameless corner bar whose curled and faded window placard promised "Topless Go-Go Dancers 7 Nites." The sidewalk was deserted.

This is America, land of the possible, where we keep our eyes fixed on the future and our backs turned toward the past, and nobody, I suppose, understood that better than Mike Cullen. The chain he established is still thriving, an institution on Long Island. Still, it seems a shame to me that this spot goes unmarked. If every inn where George Washington ever slept can count itself a shrine, then surely King Kullen deserves at least a small sign, one of those dignified little bronze tablets you find posted alongside secondary routes, framed in black and gilt. HERE STOOD THE FIRST SUPERMARKET IN AMERICA, it might say, and then, if Mike Cullen could have anything to do with it, SALE IN PROGRESS.

Part Six

Modern America

The Vietnam Memorial wall, carrying the names of those killed in action, was controversial when first installed, but soon became one of the most visited monuments in the nation's capitol.

Desegregating the Schools

LIVA BAKER

Any list of major events in American history and any account of the shifting course of race relations in the United States is bound to include the Supreme Court case known officially as Brown v. the Board of Education of the City of Topeka. The importance of key Supreme Court decisions has already been pointed out in my article on the case of Marbury v. Madison and in Alan F. Westin's essay "Ride-In." In 1896, in the case known as Plessy v. Ferguson, the Court had decided that blacks could be segregated from whites in railroad cars (and by implication in schools) provided that the facilities provided them were equal in quality to those provided whites. Over the years this "separate but equal" rule determined how the Court dealt with racial questions. Segregation was broken down to some extent, but only after it had been conclusively demonstrated that the facilities provided for blacks were inferior to those available to whites.

Liva Baker's account of how the Court reached the contrary conclusion in Brown v. Board of Education begins with an earlier case involving voting (Smith v. Allwright, 1944). She goes on to show how the members of the Court came finally to conclude that separate was inherently unequal, and therefore unconstitutional. Beyond this, she explains how the justices dealt with the socially explosive question, "how and when was desegregation to be achieved?" Baker is the author of Felix Frankfurter, *a biography of a key actor in the drama she describes here.* ■

On May 17, 1954, the Supreme Court of the United States destroyed the legal basis for racial segregation in public schools. As it almost had to be in a case that stirred elemental passions, the decision was unanimous. It was also, as Chief Justice Earl Warren had told the other justices ten days earlier it must be, "short, readable by the lay public, non-rhetorical, unemotional, and, above all, non-accusatory."

As the Chief Justice read the historic and potentially divisive opinion the nine justices—Justice Robert H. Jackson had left his hospital bed to be present—sat expressionless and calm, the rare picture of august solidarity belying three years of judicial soul-searching that had led to this moment.

. . . The 1954 desegregation decision, which still is attended by controversy, not only altered the nation's educational patterns but also eroded a way of life and touched people's most sensitive nerves.

Like most cases that come to the Supreme Court, *Brown v. Board of Education* was begun in a small way by quite ordinary people. Linda Brown, of Topeka, Kansas, in 1951 a fourth-grade student at a public elementary school for Negroes a long walk and a bus trip from her home, wanted to attend a nearby public elementary school for white children. She was turned away. Her father, the Reverend Oliver Brown, and twelve other parents sued the Topeka Board of Education in the local federal court. A special three-judge panel heard the case and decided that since Negro and white schools in Topeka were substantially equal, the Negroes were not discriminated against and they could not attend white schools. The Browns and the other parents appealed to the Supreme Court.

Since the Constitutional Convention of 1789 the issue of race had either been compromised or evaded, except during Reconstruction. No branch of government had been willing to confront it squarely, and as Justice Jackson commented during the oral argument of *Brown*, "I suppose that realistically the reason this case is here is that action couldn't be obtained from Congress." Beginning in the late 1930's, the Supreme Court had begun gradually but steadily desegregating American life; restrictive covenants that insured residential segregation, the white primary, segregated education in graduate schools, Jim Crow laws—these and others had collapsed before the Supreme Court. Now the court was forced to face the most explosive issue of all: segregation in public elementary schools.

The justices were not unworldly men, however avidly they sometimes seemed to cultivate an aura of monasticism. Before appointment to the Supreme Court each of them had held some public office. During their deliberations they were grimly aware that their decisions—whether they would hear the case or not hear it; whether, if they did hear it, they declared racial segregation in public schools constitutional or unconstitutional—presaged resentment at best, and probably resistance, from a large segment of the population.

They spent an extraordinary amount of time discussing the problem, examining it from historical, legal, political, and social perspectives. When the Brown case first reached the Supreme Court late in 1951, the justices spent seven months discussing whether they would even hear it. Finally, on June 7, 1952, they agreed that the court could note *probable* jurisdiction. . . .

Once that jurisdictional obstacle was hurdled, however, the court added other school segregation cases and combined them for argument until they had a total of five cases: one from the border state of Kansas, one each from rural Virginia and South Carolina, one from North-oriented Delaware, and one from federally administered District of Columbia. Together these cases gave the Supreme Court a detailed picture of racial segregation by law in American public schools. (At the time, state constitutional provisions and laws or local ordinances required the schools of seventeen southern and border states and the District of Columbia to be segregated; in four other states—Arizona, Kansas, New Mexico, and Wyoming—segregated schools were legally permitted on an optional basis.)

The court that was to hear these five segregation cases argued in December, 1952, was judicially unpredictable. At one end were two liberal activists: justices Hugo L. Black, former United States senator from Alabama, and William O. Douglas, former Yale law professor and chairman of the Securities and Exchange Commission. Appointed to the Supreme Court by President Franklin D. Roosevelt, both were quick to use the power of the court in the name of "social justice."

The rest of the court was enigmatic on the issue of racial segregation in public schools. Indianian Sherman Minton had been an administrative aide to President Franklin D. Roosevelt and a close friend of Harry S. Truman, with whom he entered the Senate in 1935. He was appointed to the Supreme Court by President Truman in 1949. Nothing in his writings indicated his position in these segregation cases.

The *New York Times* described Justice Harold H. Burton, on his appointment to the Supreme Court in 1945, as a "liberal of marked independence." As a justice, however, he seemed to lean toward a conservative stance; on civil rights he had voted both ways.

Justice Jackson, Solicitor General and Attorney General under Roosevelt, vigorous prosecutor of war criminals at Nuremberg, assumed the mantle of judicial restraint when he was appointed to the Supreme Court in 1941; he was hesitant to overrule state and federal enactments, believing, like his frequent judicial ally Justice Frankfurter, that undesirability could not be equated with unconstitutionality.

Linda Brown of Topeka, Kansas, posed for the camera in 1953. She was turned away from her neighborhood white elementary school, and that action set in motion the events that led to the momentous Brown v. Board of Education *decision.*

At the Senate hearings on his appointment to the Supreme Court in 1949, Justice Tom C. Clark, a Texas protégé of Senator Tom Connally and Representative Sam Rayburn, had been denounced by Negro groups for failing to protect Negro civil rights when he was Attorney General. Yet it was under Clark's stewardship that the Justice Department began to file amicus curiae (friend of the court) briefs defining the administration's legal positions; these consistently argued against racial discrimination and became a significant part of later civil-rights litigation. Clark had also, as president of the Federal Bar Association, demanded admission of Negro lawyers, and in 1950 had written a concurring opinion when the Supreme Court quashed a criminal indictment of a Negro on the grounds that Negroes had been discriminated against in the selection of grand jury panels. Clark's record looked "liberal" in 1952; however, he had not yet had to face the question whether racial segregation in public schools denied "equal protection of the laws."

Justice Stanley F. Reed came from the border state of Kentucky and had been Solicitor General under Roosevelt, arguing for the validity of NRA, TVA, the Wagner Act, and other of the President's measures. Appointed to the Supreme Court in 1938, he had become somewhat conservative but had also written a vigorous defense of Negro voting rights in 1944. How Reed came to write that 1944 opinion reveals not a little of the political consideration that goes into a major decision of the Supreme Court.

At conference on January 15, 1944, the Supreme Court decided to declare the Texas exclusion of Negroes from primary elections unconstitutional. Felix Frankfurter was assigned to write the opinion. The case was called *Smith v. Allwright.*

". . . That afternoon," a Frankfurter memorandum reads, "Bob Jackson came to see me. . . . He thought it was a very great mistake to have me write the *Allwright* opinion. For a good part of the country the subject—Negro disenfranchisement—was in the domain of the irrational and we have to take account of such facts. At best it will be very unpalatable to the South and should not be exacerbated by having the opinion written by a member of the Court who has, from the point of view of Southern prejudice, three disqualifications: 'You are a New Englander, you are a Jew and you are not a Democrat—at least not recognized as such.' " Frankfurter replied that he saw Jackson's point; Jackson was free, Frankfurter said, to suggest to the Chief Justice— Harlan Fiske Stone at that time—that the opinion be reassigned. When Stone later asked Frankfurter to suggest a name, Frankfurter declared that "the job required, of course, delicacy of treatment and absence of a raucous voice and that I thought of the Southerners Reed was the better of the two for the job. He agreed to that. . . ."

Thus, on April 3, 1944, in the case of *Smith v. Allwright,* the Texas white primary was invalidated. Justice Reed—Southerner, Protestant, and Democrat—spoke for the majority: "The United States is a constitutional democracy. Its organic law grants to all citizens a right to participate in the choice of elected officials without restriction by any State because of race."

In 1952, in addition to these seven justices, there were two crucial men on the court that was to hear the school segregation cases: Chief Justice Fred M. Vinson and Felix Frankfurter. But Vinson died before the school segregation cases were decided, and so what he would have done can only be a matter of speculation.

He was succeeded by Earl Warren, three-term governor of California and Republican candidate for Vice President in 1948. A hearty, amiable man on the surface, he was expected to be, as one of his biographers put it, "the colorless manager of a team of all-stars." No one, including President Dwight D. Eisenhower, who appointed him, expected a courageous, reforming chief justice. Justice Frankfurter wrote his impressions of Warren to a young English friend at the time of the appointment:

> . . . He has not had an eminent legal career, but he might well have had had he not been deflected from the practice of law into public life. He brings to his work that largeness of experience and breadth of outlook which may well make him a very good Chief Justice provided he has some other qualities which, from what I have seen, I believe he has. First and foremost, complete absorption in the work of the Court is demanded. That is not as easy to attain as you might think, because this is a very foolish and distracting town. Secondly, he must have great industry because . . . for about nine months of the year it is a steady grind. Further, he must have the capacity to learn, he must be alert to the range and complexities of the problems that come before this Court. . . . One more requisite. . . . Intent, open-minded, patient listening is a surprisingly rare faculty even of judges. The new Chief Justice has it, I believe, to a rare degree.

Warren seemed, like most of the court, judicially unpredictable. He had never been able to live down his major role as California attorney general in sending Japanese and Japanese-Americans in the state to detention camps at the outbreak of World War II. But beyond this questionable moment in his career, there was a bold record as crusading district attorney in Alameda County and a progressive governorship during which Warren battled annually against a hostile legislature for social legislation and reforms.

The other crucial man on the Supreme Court in 1952 was Felix Frankfurter. Appointed to the Supreme Court in 1939 by Roosevelt, Justice Frankfurter had eagerly joined in the decisions invalidating legal segregation prior to the Brown case. He had, however, consistently laid a light restraining hand on his brethren.

He was a sworn enemy of racial discrimination; he had served on the legal committee of the NAACP from 1929 until he was appointed to the Supreme Court (when he scrupulously severed connections with all organizations). He was, however, aware of the potential for divisiveness in racial discrimination cases before the court. He wrote in a note to Justice Wiley B. Rutledge regarding a 1948 case of racial discrimination on an excursion boat: ". . . Considerable practical experience with problems of race relations led me to the conclusion that the ugly practices of racial discrimination should be dealt with by eloquence of action but with austerity of speech. . . ." Likewise, when Chief Justice Vinson's draft opinion in a 1950 case involving segregation in graduate schools was circulated among the justices for suggestions—as is customary on the court—Frankfurter urged restraint in the rhetoric. The opinion, he said, ought to accomplish "the desired result without needlessly stirring the kind of feelings that are felt even by truly liberal and high-minded southerners. . . . One does not have to say everything that is so. . . . The shorter the opinion, the more there is an appearance of unexcitement and inevitability about it, the better. . . ."

The school desegregation decisions of 1952–1955 were broken into two parts. The first was *whether* racial segregation in public schools was constitutional or unconstitutional; inherent in this question was whether it was the business of the court or the business of Congress to deal with the problem. The court struggled nearly a year before making up its mind on that question.

The second part of the decisions was the question of remedy: *How* and *when* was desegregation to be achieved? This question was not answered for a full year after the court declared racial segregation in public schools unconstitutional, in May of 1954. The delay—which gave the South a breathing spell—was used to forge a compromise between immediate wholesale desegregation and gradual adjustment to the court's decision; between Negro rights and southern hostility. That year was full of judicial pondering and introspection that scotch any notion that the court arbitrarily exerted its power.

The segregation cases had been argued the first time in December, 1952. Lawyers—mostly from the NAACP—argued for the Negro plaintiffs that state school segregation laws denied to Negroes the equal protection guaranteed under the Fourteenth Amendment of the Constitution. Attorneys for the southern school districts countered that school segregation involved no constitutional rights; it was, they said, strictly a state legislative matter. The court listened, waited six months, and then in June, 1953, scheduled the cases for reargument the following term, with counsel for both sides instructed this time to address themselves to five specific questions.

The first three questions concerned the original intent of the framers of the Fourteenth Amendment regarding racial segregation in public schools.

That amendment, passed by a Republican Congress in 1866 in the heat of post-Civil War passion, says nothing about racial segregation in public schools; but neither does it say anything about housing or transportation or juries, areas in which the Supreme Court had, by 1953, already used it to invalidate discriminatory practices. Like the rest of the Constitution, the Fourteenth Amendment is a vessel into which judges had, over the years, poured many meanings. Its crucial first section merely said: "No State shall . . . deny to any person within its jurisdiction the equal protection of the laws." Section 5 gives Congress the power to enforce the amendment's provisions "by appropriate legislation."

Now in 1953 the Supreme Court wanted to know: Did the authors of the Fourteenth Amendment in fact intend desegregation of public schools either at the time of their writing or in the future? Exhaustive research by the court and the contending parties never revealed a clear answer to that.

Questions four and five asked how desegregation might be achieved, prompting observers to speculate that the court—still headed by Chief Justice Vinson—had already decided to declare racial segregation in public schools unconstitutional.

For the scheduled rehearing the court extended an invitation to the Attorney General of the United States to participate in oral arguments. A Frankfurter memorandum of June 8, 1953, explained that the new administration under Eisenhower "may have the responsibility of carrying out a decision full of perplexities; it should therefore be asked to face that responsibility as part of our process of adjudication. . . ." When the rearguments were heard in December, 1953, their significant portions turned out to be those dealing with the question of a remedy for segregation if deemed warranted.

NAACP lawyers, led by Thurgood Marshall, later to be appointed to the Supreme Court himself, urged immediate admission of Negro children to the schools of their choice, but reluctantly acknowledged that the Supreme Court had the power to effect instead a gradual adjustment. The southern states, whose chief attorney was John W. Davis, 1924 Democratic Presidential candidate, argued that the Supreme Court had the power to order a gradual process, but no effective way of mandating the details. "Your Honors do not sit, and cannot sit, as a glorified Board of Education for the State of South Carolina or any other State," John Davis declared.

Thurgood Marshall (center), then special counsel of the NAACP, with the two other attorneys who successfully argued the landmark case. Marshall was later appointed to the Supreme Court in 1967.

At this stage of the proceedings the government's position was anomalous. The brief filed by the Eisenhower administration did not urge the court to hold public school segregation unconstitutional, although its overall tenor supported such a holding. Some of the lawyers who worked on it have said that an original version did include a direct call for the court to declare public school segregation unconstitutional but that it was diluted by either Attorney General Herbert Brownell or President Eisenhower. Brownell has denied this, saying that the brief never contained such a call. But he agreed—and advised Eisenhower—that if J. Lee Rankin, the Assistant Attorney General who was to argue for the government in court, was asked during oral argument for the administration's position, he would answer that the court should hold public school segregation unconstitutional—which was what Rankin actually did.

On the question of how desegregation could be accomplished, the government suggested remanding the cases to the lower courts, where, in the light of local conditions, decrees would be formulated and a gradual adjustment be made.

Shortly after this December reargument and four months before the Supreme Court would officially declare public school segregation unconstitutional, Justice Frankfurter addressed himself, in a memorandum for his associates, to the questions of *how* and *when*. He explained, in a covering note, that he was thinking out loud and that "sometimes one's thinking, whether good or bad, may stimulate good thoughts in others." He added parenthetically that "the typewriting was done under conditions of strictest security."

Whether the court was already thinking in terms of two decisions rather than one and had reached unanimity is not known. The memorandum's cautious restraint seems to indicate, however, that Frankfurter, in an attempt to achieve unanimity, was articulating the concerns of whatever recalcitrant justices remained, and perhaps trying to point out that implementation, while it had major difficulties, was not impossible. Because it introduces the concept of "with all deliberate speed," it is one of the most important pieces of writing on the segregation cases prior to their being decided.

Although, Frankfurter told his brethren, the court had before it only five individual cases, "we are asked in effect to transform state-wide school systems in nearly a score of states," and it was not going to be easy. First the court must define, Frankfurter wrote, exactly what the required result was. For the first time in the written discussions, the word *integration* was used; it has since become the heart of much of the controversy surrounding school racial problems. "Integration," Frankfurter said, "that is, 'equal protection,' can readily be achieved by lowering the standards of those who at the start are, in the phrase of George Orwell, 'more equal'. . . . It would indeed make a mockery of the Constitutional adjudication designed to vindicate a claim to equal treatment, to achieve 'integrated' but lower educational standards."

As to the time factor, the court does its duty, he explained, "if it gets effectively under way the righting of a wrong. When the wrong is a deeply rooted state policy the court does its duty if it decrees measures that reverse the direction of the unconstitutional policy so as to uproot it 'with all deliberate speed.' " This was a phrase Frankfurter had used previously in at least three decisions. Like *integration*, it became a controversial issue in the desegregation process.

Tentatively, Frankfurter preferred some gradual process of desegregation. "The Court does not know," he wrote, "that a simple scrambling of the two school systems may not work. It surely cannot assume that scrambling is all there is to it. . . . One is surely entitled to suspect that spreading the adjustment over time will more effectively accomplish the desired end. . . ."

However, he warned, before the court could fashion a decree, it faced an enormous and complex fact-finding task, made more difficult by the various interpretations that could be applied to facts "different in kind than courts usually consider" and "embedded in deep feeling."

"Physical, educational, budgetary, and time factors" must be considered; there would be problems for both teachers and students, and "problems caused by shifts in population which these readjustments may well induce." All these must be ascertained in a complex framework where "the spread of differences in the ratios of white to colored population among the various counties in different States is very considerable."

Awareness of these difficulties accounts for the fact that a remedy for segregated schools did not appear in the May 17, 1954, decision. The justices simply declared racially segregated schools unconstitutional, and the last paragraph of the unanimous opinion read:

> Because these are class actions, because of the wide applicability of this decision, and because of the great variety of local conditions, the formulation of decrees in these cases presents problems of considerable complexity. We have now announced that such segregation is a denial of the equal protection of the laws. In order that we may have the full assistance of the parties in formulating decrees, the cases will be restored to the docket, and the parties are requested to present further argument on questions 4 and 5 [the questions of *how*] previously propounded by the Court for the reargument this Term.

The Attorney General of the United States as well as the attorneys general of the states requiring or permitting segregation in public education were invited to participate as amici curiae. Undoubtedly the court hoped that by inviting participation of the states—most of them southern—that permitted or required segregation, the South itself, at least on an official level, would accept the inevitability of change and join in devising an acceptable remedy.

The justices knew they had touched sensitive nerves, but they were probably not prepared for the widespread resistance their decision drew, largely in the South. Emotion outran reason; invective submerged valid legal debate. Deep South prosegregationist states such as Alabama, Georgia, and Mississippi did not accept the court's invita-

In December, 1953, the Supreme Court posed for this official photograph. Seated, left to right: Felix Frankfurter, Hugo L. Black, Chief Justice Earl Warren, Stanley F. Reed, William O. Douglas; standing: Tom C. Clark, Robert H. Jackson, Harold H. Burton, Sherman Minton.

tion to participate in reargument lest they endow the May 17, 1954, decision with recognition. Vacationing in Massachusetts, Frankfurter mused on the problem and, in a letter to Warren, recommended that the court gather data on what "administrative, financial, commonsensical and other considerations legitimately enter" the normal school-districting process so as to have some frame of reference in dealing with southern redistricting. "The Southern States are fever patients. Let us find out, if we can, what healthy bodies do about such things in order to guard against attributing to the fever conduct and consequences that are not fairly attributable to fever. . . ."

Following Frankfurter's suggestion, Chief Justice Warren circulated among the justices in November, 1954, a seventy-nine-page Segregation Research Report containing background information to be referred to by the justices in thinking about implementing their decision of the past May. It included a survey of normal school-districting practices, a summary of southern reaction to the May 17 decision, analyses of previously desegregated schools, proposed plans to abolish public schools, discussion of court jurisdiction over school districting, and maps of school districts showing distribution of white and Negro students. The report pointed up the complexity of the *how* problem facing the Supreme Court: How could nine justices, sitting in their marble palace in Washington, with their limited knowledge of local problems, devise a formula that could be applied to such a diversified collection of school districts? The *when* was equally a problem:

" 'Forthwith' would either be given a meaning short of immediacy or introduce a range of leeway to render it imprecise," Frankfurter said in a memorandum of February 10, 1955. "And it would most certainly provoke resentment. Yet any limitation allowing a specific number of years in which to achieve compliance could well be treated as a grace period during which nothing need be done."

The segregation cases were reargued from April 11 to 14, 1955. On the last of those days, Frankfurter wrote to his colleagues: "Hamilton Basso is, as I dare say you know, a very perceptive Southern writer, and carries weight, I believe, both North and South. A letter of his in last Sunday's New York Times has for me the persuasiveness not of novelty but of emphasis."

Basso's letter, which Frankfurter reproduced, was an urgent *cri de coeur* for understanding of the South's present defiant temper. Segregation, it said, like slavery the century before, "was the foremost preoccupation of the Southern mind" in the press and in conversation. Out of a confusion of opinion, ranging from "logical argument to irrational bitterness," Basso wrote, "that which most clearly emerges is a feeling of deep resentment over what is looked upon as outside pressure. . . . It [the South] has gone far toward convincing itself that it is going to be 'pressured' in a quick reorganization of its whole society . . . and that the rest of the country is almost callously indifferent to the difficulties implicit in such a course."

Two days later, on April 16, 1955, the justices met in conference, still searching—against the background of angry resistance—for answers to the questions they had asked in court. Chief Justice Warren opened the discussion with his admission that he himself had not reached a fixed opinion; perhaps the brethren could talk it over, as they had the original desegregation decision.

There were, Warren began, some things the court should not do. The Supreme Court ought not to tell the lower courts what to do; it should not fix a definite date for completion of desegregation nor even suggest to a lower court that that court should set a date, nor should the Supreme Court dictate any procedural requirement. Clearly, Their Honors were not going to sit as a "super school board."

What appealed to Warren at the time, rather than a formal decree, was an opinion citing factors for the lower courts to consider, with some Supreme Court guidance; it would, he explained, be rather cruel to shift back and let them flounder. There were two ground rules to be observed: (1) these were class actions—that is, as the May 17, 1954, decision had declared, they affected everyone similarly situated, not only the plaintiffs—and (2) the lower courts should be entitled to consider physical factors but not psychological attitudes.

Adhering to conference protocol, the other justices spoke in turn, from the most senior (Black) to the most junior (John Marshall Harlan, who had replaced Robert Jackson on Jackson's death). There was little agreement among them except as to the fact that the final opinion should be unanimous. Justice Black expressed the feeling when he declared that if a unanimous opinion were humanly possible, he would do everything he could to achieve it. Nonetheless, the Alabaman differed with Chief Justice Warren. He knew, he said, every southern district judge on anyone's list, and not one of them was going to be for desegregation. Black advised saying and doing as little as possible; nothing was more important than that the Supreme Court should not issue what it could not enforce. He advised reiterating the unconstitutionality of racial segregation in public schools, formulating a decree affecting only the five cases before the court, and enjoining school boards from refusing to admit these specific Negro students.

Perhaps no one except the justices themselves will ever know exactly how the Warren-Black points of view were reconciled. However, the unanimity so necessary to this kind of decision was in some way achieved, and six weeks after the April 16 conference, on May 31, 1955, Chief Justice Earl Warren read the Supreme Court's unanimous opinion, outlining that court's plan for desegregating the nation's schools. It was very much a Warren opinion, conforming to the points he had made in the April 16 conference.

The court showed that *it* was not "callously indifferent" to the difficulties of reorganizing southern society, as Hamilton Basso had said the South believed most of the nation was. The decision in fact gave every opportunity to the South to itself solve whatever problems accompanied desegregation—and in its own good time.

As the 1954 decision had been clearly for the Negro plaintiffs, this 1955 decision was clearly for the defendant school boards. Together, the two decisions were an attempt to balance the claims of the two parties, to reconcile "public and private needs."

The court solved the *how* of desegregation by attempting to be neither so vague as to invite "confusion and evasion" nor so specific that the court would become the nation's school board. The burden of desegregating was placed on the local school boards, with the lower courts required to consider "whether the action of school authorities constitutes good faith implementation of the governing constitutional principles."

But the lower courts were not left to flounder. As Warren had suggested in the April 16 conference, they were given general guidelines: they were to adjust and reconcile "public and private needs";

they could consider "problems related to administration, arising from the physical conditions of the school plant, transportation system, personnel, revision of school districts and attendance areas into compact units to achieve a system of determining admission to the public schools on a non-racial basis"; and there was to be no gerrymandering. However, as Chief Justice Warren had also said in the April 16 conference, psychological factors were to be disallowed, and the opinion reaffirmed it: "the vitality of these constitutional principles cannot be allowed to yield simply because of disagreement with them."

The crucial question of *when* was reserved until the last paragraph. It was not going to be the beginning of the next school term, as NAACP lawyers had urged. Frankfurter had warned the court in a memorandum against requiring a deadline, because, he said, it would have to be an arbitrary deadline and would be considered "an imposition of our will without the ascertainment . . . of the local situation. And it would tend to alienate instead of enlist favorable or educable local sentiment." Instead, the phrase in Frankfurter's January, 1954, memorandum appeared in the final decision: "the cases are remanded to the District Courts to take such proceedings and enter such orders and decrees consistent with this opinion as are necessary and proper to admit to public schools on a racially nondiscriminatory basis with all deliberate speed the parties to these cases. . . ."

In the years since the desegregation decisions most observers have credited Chief Justice Warren with welding the various individuals together to achieve unanimity. Warren modestly denies it: "It was the most self-effacing job ever written there. . . . Everyone there was so cooperative and so helpful," he has said, going on to give credit to the three Southerners on the court—Clark, Reed, and Black—"not because they developed the legal philosophy of it, but because they had the courage to do what was done." It was, Warren points out, "tough for them to go home" for a time.

Justice Frankfurter had made the same observation, but with an added dimension, in a note he wrote to Justice Reed three days after the 1954 decision. It read:

> History does not record dangers averted. I have no doubt that if the *Segregation* cases had reached decision last Term there would have been four dissenters—Vinson, Reed, Jackson and Clark—and certainly several opinions for the majority view. That would have been catastrophic. And if we had not had unanimity now inevitably there would have been more than one opinion for the majority. That would have been disastrous.
>
> It ought to give you much satisfaction to be able to say, as you have every right to say, "I have done the State some service." I am inclined to think, indeed I believe, in no single act since you have been on this Court

have you done the Republic a more lasting service. I am not unaware of the hard struggle this involved in the conscience of your mind and in the mind of your conscience. I am not unaware, because all I have to do is look within.

As a citizen of the Republic, even more than as a colleague, I feel deep gratitude for your share in what I believe to be a great good for our nation.

Eisenhower as President

STEVE NEAL

The reputations of statesmen, like the reputations of artists, writers, and composers, tend to fluctuate over time. However, at least where statesmen are concerned, no mere shift in taste or fashion accounts for the changes that occur. In the first place, the passage of time can actually alter the significance of past events and thus change historians' judgments about the actors who shaped these events. Then too, new facts and new documents continually come to light, frequently suggesting more convincing explanations of what people did and why they behaved as they did, and thus causing historians to change their minds.

No better recent example of the ups and downs of a major figure's reputation exists than that provided by the case of President Dwight D. Eisenhower. In the following essay Steve Neal, the chief political correspondent of the Chicago Tribune, *traces the way historians have viewed the Eisenhower presidency. Neal explains why most historians took a dim view of "Ike" in the late 1950s and early 1960s, a time when the public admired him extravagantly, and why the historians' opinion of him has changed so much in recent years. Neal is the author of* The Eisenhowers, *a kind of history of the Eisenhower family, of* Dark Horse: A Biography of Wendell Willkie, *and other books.* ∎

Early in 1952, Gen. Dwight David Eisenhower confided to a friendly Republican politician why he was reluctant to seek the Presidency: "I think I pretty well hit my peak in history when I accepted the German surrender."

Emerging from World War II as the organizer of the Allied victory, Eisenhower was America's most celebrated hero. Both major political parties sought to nominate him for the Presidency. And when Ike decided to risk his historical reputation, he captured the 1952 Republican presidential nomination and ended twenty years of Democratic rule. Ronald Reagan was among the millions of Democrats who crossed party lines to support the Republican general. Afterward, the badly beaten Democratic candidate, Adlai E. Stevenson, asked his friend Alistair Cooke: "Who did I think I was, running against George Washington?"

Not only did Eisenhower win two terms by margins of historic proportions, but he maintained his popularity throughout his Presidency. He left office in 1961 still revered by two-thirds of his countrymen, and the American public never stopped liking Ike.

But until recently it seemed that Eisenhower had lost his gamble with history. Like Ulysses S. Grant and Zachary Taylor, Eisenhower was frequently portrayed by historians and political scholars as a mediocre Chief Executive. Soon after Ike left the White House, a poll of leading scholars ranked him among the nation's ten worst Presidents.

Since then, however, Eisenhower's historical image has been dramatically rehabilitated. In 1982 a similar poll of prominent historians and political scholars rated him near the top of the list of Presidents. Eisenhower is gaining recognition as one of the large figures of the twentieth century, not just for his role as Supreme Allied Commander in World War II, but also for his eight years as President of the United States.

One of the reasons for Eisenhower's comeback is nostalgia for an enormously popular President after an era of assassinations, political scandals, military defeat, and economic turmoil. Another factor in the reassessment is Eisenhower's record of eight years of peace and prosperity, which is unique among twentieth-century Presidents.

Eisenhower, a man of war, conducted his foreign policy with restraint and moderation. During the most turbulent era of the Cold War, he ended the Korean War, blocked British and French efforts to crush Arab nationalism, opposed military intervention in Southeast Asia, opened a new dialogue with the Soviet Union, and alerted the nation to the dangers of the expanding military-industrial complex. He was criticized for being too passive by the Cold Warriors Henry Kissinger and Gen. Maxwell Taylor, and the same critics berated him for a missile gap that turned out to be nonexistent. In retirement, Eisenhower said his most notable presidential achievement was that "the United States never lost a soldier or a foot of ground in my administration. We kept the peace."

In domestic affairs, Eisenhower also strove to maintain a peaceful equilibrium in handling such explosive issues as McCarthyism and segregation. While critics charged that Ike was spineless in his refusal to openly fight Sen. Joseph McCarthy, the President worked behind the scenes to reduce McCarthy's influence. Despite private doubts about a Supreme Court decision that outlawed segregation, he sent the 101st Airborne into Little Rock, Arkansas, when the state's governor defied the law. He also pushed through the first federal civil rights law since Reconstruction and established the United States Commission on Civil Rights.

Although Eisenhower's memoir of his first term was entitled *Mandate for Change,* his most notable achievement in domestic policy was the continuance of New Deal reforms initiated under President Roosevelt. For nearly a generation, congressional Republicans had been pledging to dismantle FDR's social programs. But Eisenhower had other ideas. "Should any political party attempt to abolish Social Security, unemployment insurance, and eliminate labor laws and farm programs, you would not hear of that party again in our political history," he wrote to his brother Edgar, an outspoken conservative. During the Eisenhower era the number of Americans covered by Social Security doubled, and benefits were increased. The Department of Health, Education, and Welfare was established as a domestic Pentagon. Eisenhower also launched the largest public-works project in American history by building the federal highway system, which turned out to be almost as important as the transcontinental railroad. Barry Goldwater denounced the Eisenhower administration as a "dime-store New Deal," and another conservative critic, William F. Buckley, Jr., characterized Eisenhower's record as "measured socialism." But the Republican President's acceptance of the Roosevelt legacy effectively ended debate over the New Deal and meant that the reforms would endure.

The prosperity of the Eisenhower years was no accident. He produced three balanced budgets; the gross national product grew by over 25 percent; and inflation averaged 1.4 percent. To hold the line on inflation, Eisenhower made the tough choice to accept three recessions. The AFL-CIO president George Meany, who often criticized Ike's policies, nonetheless said that the American worker had "never had it so good."

Although he continued Roosevelt's social programs, Eisenhower's concept of presidential leadership was very different from FDR's. Ike's style was managerial with an orderly staff system and a strong cabinet. FDR was an activist who encouraged chaos and creative tension among

*Eisenhower met with his cabinet and official family for the
last time on January 13, 1961. In the years since, ratings
of his ability as an administrator have improved a great
deal.*

his hyperactive staff and cabinet. Most political scholars shared Roosevelt's philosophy of government and viewed Eisenhower as an ineffectual board chairman. There were jokes about the Eisenhower doll; you
wound it up and it did nothing for eight years. A memorable Herblock
cartoon showed Ike asking his cabinet, "What shall we refrain from
doing now?"

The early Eisenhower literature consisted of affectionate memoirs
by World War II associates and adoring biographies by war correspondents. But as Chief Executive, Ike suddenly found a more independent panel of observers judging him by new and different standards.

Many of Ike's critics were Democratic partisans. A large factor in
his low rating among scholars and liberal commentators was the extraordinary popularity among intellectuals of his major political rival,
Adlai Stevenson. Stevenson's admirers were bitter that Eisenhower
had twice routed their champion. In *Anti-Intellectualism in American Life*,
the historian Richard Hofstadter described Stevenson as a "politician
of uncommon mind and style" and Eisenhower as "conventional in
mind, relatively inarticulate."

Arthur Larson, the University of Pittsburgh law dean who became
an Eisenhower speech writer, recalled: "It was one of the paradoxes
of my position in those days that the people I was most at home with,
intellectually and ideologically, were more often than not bitterly critical of Eisenhower, if not downright contemptuous of him." Eisenhower did not improve his image in the academic community by flip-
pantly remarking that an intellectual was someone "who takes more
words than are necessary to tell more than he knows." As for the

syndicated columnists, he declared that "anyone who has time to listen to commentators or read columnists obviously doesn't have enough work to do."

Eisenhower's poor showing in the poll taken shortly after he left office in which Arthur M. Schlesinger, Jr., got seventy-five historians to rate Ike's Presidency should not have been surprising: the participants included two of Stevenson's speech writers, a leader of the 1952 "Draft Stevenson" movement, and other Democratic partisans. Malcolm Moos, a political scholar and former Eisenhower speech writer, declined to participate in the survey, which he believed was stacked against Ike.

In the poll, Eisenhower finished twenty-second out of thirty-one Presidents, which placed him just between the White House mediocrities Chester Alan Arthur and Andrew Johnson. John F. Kennedy reportedly chuckled over Ike's low score in the Schlesinger survey. Eisenhower's associates were concerned that the negative rating might have staying power. "I'm very distressed at this tendency of academics to look down their noses at the Eisenhower administration," the former White House chief of staff Sherman Adams acknowledged years later. "It's a common sort of thing with the intelligentsia. It's just typical. Look at Mr. Roosevelt. He's a great favorite with the academics, and he's probably a great man. But he lost a lot of battles, didn't he? . . . Well, we may not have done as much, may not have been as spectacular in terms of our willingness to break with the past, but we didn't lose a lot of battles either. A lot of our most important accomplishments were negative—things we avoided. We maintained a peaceful front and adjudicated a lot of issues that seemed ominous and threatening at the time."

Had Eisenhower served just one term, it is unlikely that his historical stock would have dropped so much. Near the end of his first term, his reputation looked fairly secure. A respected journalist, Robert J. Donovan, had written an authoritative history of Eisenhower's first term, which in many ways remains the best study of a sitting President, and which showed Ike firmly in charge. The Pulitzer Prize-winning historian Merlo Pusey had written a friendly treatment of the Eisenhower administration and predicted that Ike would be remembered as a great President, while the political scholar Clinton Rossiter wrote in *The American Presidency* (1956) that Eisenhower "already stands above Polk and Cleveland, and he has a reasonable chance to move up to Jefferson and Theodore Roosevelt."

But like most second terms, Eisenhower's last four years were less productive than his first. The nation was jolted when the Soviet Union launched Sputnik in 1957, and it took months to rebuild American confidence. The recession of 1958 marked the worst economic slide

since the Great Depression; more than five million workers were job-
less before the recovery began. Ike's 1957 stroke, his third major
illness in three years, reinforced doubts about his health and capability
to govern. His chief aide, Sherman Adams, became entwined in a
political scandal and was forced to resign in 1958.

Eisenhower's 1960 Paris summit with Soviet premier Nikita
Khrushchev and leaders of the Western alliance was ruined when an
American reconnaissance aircraft, the U-2, was shot down over Central
Russia and the pilot, Francis Gary Powers, was captured. Khrushchev
stormed out of the summit, withdrawing his invitation for the President's scheduled June visit to the Soviet Union. Had Eisenhower followed his instincts, the U-2 fiasco might have been avoided. A year
earlier, he had suggested that the spy flights be halted, but he relented
when his National Security Council advisers objected. Later he personally approved Powers's flight. In suggesting that Eisenhower might not
have known of the secret mission over the Soviet Union, Khrushchev
provided Ike with an alibi that might have salvaged the summit. Indeed, Sen. J. William Fulbright had urged Ike to disclaim responsibility. But Eisenhower told associates that denials would have been
ineffectual because of the overpowering evidence. Furthermore, Eisenhower did not want to give credibility to the charge made by his
detractors that he was not in control of his own administration.

In his critical 1958 portrait, *Eisenhower: Captive Hero*, the journalist
Marquis Childs suggested that Ike was in the wrong job. "If his public
record had ended with his military career, it seems safe to assume that
a high place would be secure for him," Childs wrote. "But Eisenhower's performance in the presidency will count much more heavily
in the final summing up." Childs offered the interpretation that Eisenhower had been a weak and ineffective President, "a prisoner of his
office, a captive of his own indecisiveness," another James Buchanan.

Striking a similar theme, the Harvard political scholar Richard
Neustadt depicted Eisenhower as a passive, detached Chief Executive
in his 1960 study, *Presidential Power*. According to Neustadt, Eisenhower became too isolated from his staff and should have been more
involved in discussing policy options. "The less he was bothered,"
Neustadt quoted a White House observer, "the less he knew, and the
less he knew, the less confidence he felt in his own judgment. He let
himself grow stale."

In a revised 1960 edition of *The American Presidency*, Rossiter concluded that Eisenhower had been a disappointment. "He will be
remembered, I fear, as the unadventurous president who held on one
term too long in the new age of adventure." Without directly attacking
Eisenhower, Kennedy suggested in his 1960 presidential campaign
that the Republican incumbent was a tired old man, whose lack of

leadership had weakened America's prestige in the world. Following his election, Kennedy privately acknowledged that he was struck by Eisenhower's vitality and ruddy health.

Eisenhower's own history of his Presidency was more authoritative but less provocative than those written by his critics, and it had little immediate impact on his reputation. The first volume, *Mandate for Change,* was published in late 1963, and *Waging Peace,* the second installment, came out two years later.

The former President's refusal to disclose his unvarnished opinions of political contemporaries or admit mistakes helped set a bland tone for both volumes. In *Mandate,* Eisenhower described a secret meeting at the Pentagon with a prominent Republican senator in the winter of 1951, without revealing the other man's identity. At the meeting Ike offered to renounce all political ambitions if the senator would make a public commitment to economic and military aid to Western Europe and American participation in the North Atlantic Treaty Organization. When the senator declined, Eisenhower began thinking much more seriously about running for the Presidency.

This meeting had been a turning point in modern American history because the senator Eisenhower neglected to identify in his memoirs was Robert A. Taft, the leading conservative contender for the 1952 Republican presidential nomination. Ike's memoirs would have been much more compelling reading if he had written what he told associates—that in the wake of their meeting he considered Taft a very stupid man. Had the Ohio senator accepted Eisenhower's offer at the Pentagon, it is more than likely that he would have been nominated for the Presidency and Eisenhower would have remained a soldier.

When Johns Hopkins University Press issued the first five volumes of Ike's papers in 1970, the former President's historical image received a boost almost overnight. John Kenneth Galbraith, who had been Stevenson's adviser and had once described the Eisenhower administration as "the bland leading the bland," wrote in *The Washington Post* that Ike's private writings demonstrated that he had been an "exceedingly vigorous, articulate, and clearheaded administrator, who shows himself throughout to have been also a very conscientious and sensible man."

With the opening of Eisenhower's private correspondence and other key documents of his administration to scholars in the seventies, experts were soon focusing attention on the primary source material, and a major reassessment of the Eisenhower Presidency was inevitable. Herbert S. Parmet, one of the first historians to make extensive use of newly declassified papers, made the argument in *Eisenhower and the American Crusades* (1972) that those who rated presidential greatness had overlooked Ike's importance in restoring confidence and building

Ike (second from left) conferred in Geneva in 1955 with Nikolai Bulganin of Russia, Edgar Faure of France, and Anthony Eden of Great Britain. They were trying to promote détente by pushing for open exchange of military plans and aerial inspection of military bases.

a national consensus in postwar America. To many erstwhile critics, Eisenhower's restrained style of leadership looked better in retrospect during the Vietnam War. At a time when thousands of Americans were dying in a long, bloody, fruitless struggle in Southeast Asia, there were new interpretations of the Eisenhower foreign policy. Murray Kempton's "The Underestimation of Dwight D. Eisenhower," which appeared in the September 1967 issue of *Esquire,* described how Ike had rejected the advice of Cold Warriors to seek military adventure in Vietnam. "He is revealed best, if only occasionally, in the vast and dreary acreage of his memoirs of the White House years," wrote Kempton. "The Eisenhower who emerges here . . . is the President most superbly equipped for truly consequential decision we may ever have had, a mind neither rash nor hesitant, free of the slightest concern for how things might look, indifferent to any sentiment, as calm when he was demonstrating the wisdom of leaving a bad situation alone as when he was moving to meet it on those occasions when he absolutely had to."

Other influential political analysts later expanded the same theme. On the left, I. F. Stone noted that Eisenhower, because of his confidence in his own military judgment, was not intimidated into rash action by the Pentagon.

Eisenhower's most enduring and prescient speech was his 1961 farewell address warning of the potential dangers of the military-industrial complex. "In the councils of government," he declared, "we must guard against the acquisition of unwarranted influence, whether sought or unsought, by the military-industrial complex. The potential for the disastrous rise of misplaced power exists and will persist."

Eisenhower's correspondence effectively demonstrates that his farewell address was an accurate reflection of his political philosophy. In an October 1951 letter to the General Motors executive Charles E. Wilson, Eisenhower wrote: "Any person who doesn't clearly understand that national security and national solvency are mutually dependent, and that permanent maintenance of a crushing weight of military power would eventually produce dictatorship, should not be entrusted with any kind of responsibility in our country." The White House press secretary James Hagerty wrote in his diary that Ike had confided, "You know, if you're in the military and you know about these terrible destructive weapons, it tends to make you more pacifistic than you normally have been."

Stephen E. Ambrose, a former editor of the Eisenhower papers and author of the most comprehensive Eisenhower biography, shows how Ike slowed the arms race and exerted firm leadership in rejecting the Gaither Commission's call for sharp increases in defense spending. "Eisenhower's calm, common-sense, deliberate response to [the Soviets launching of Sputnik] may have been his finest gift to the nation," wrote Ambrose, "if only because he was the only man who could have given it." Because of his military background, Eisenhower spoke with more authority about the arms race than his critics. In a 1956 letter to Richard L. Simon, president of Simon & Schuster, who had written him and enclosed a column urging a crash program for nuclear missiles, Eisenhower replied, "When we get to the point, as we one day will, that both sides know that in any outbreak of general hostilities, regardless of the element of surprise, destruction will be both reciprocal and complete, possibly we will have sense enough to meet at the conference table with the understanding that the era of armaments has ended and the human race must conform its actions to this truth or die."

But while many recent historians have portrayed Eisenhower as a dove, a pioneer of détente, there are dissenters. Peter Lyon argued in his 1974 Eisenhower biography that the President's 1953 inaugural address was a "clarion" that "called to war," and that the general was a hawkish militarist. In her 1981 study *The Declassified Eisenhower*, Blanche Wiesen Cook says that Eisenhower used the CIA to launch a "thorough and ambitious anti-Communist crusade" that toppled governments on three continents.

Arthur Schlesinger, Jr., who had previously described Eisenhower as a weak, passive, and politically naïve executive, asserted in his 1973 book *The Imperial Presidency* that Ike went overboard in his use of presidential powers by introducing claims for "executive privilege" in denying government documents to Sen. Joseph McCarthy and by also approving the buildup of the CIA. Even so, Schlesinger now ranks Eisenhower with Truman and his former White House boss, John F. Kennedy, as the successful Presidents of the postwar era.

Another Eisenhower critic, William Leuchtenburg, insists that Ike was not so different from his more obviously hawkish successors. He points to Eisenhower's covert intervention in Iran and Guatemala, his threats to use nuclear weapons in Korea, and his war of words with China over the islands of Quemoy and Ma-tsu. Leuchtenburg also blames Eisenhower for neglecting major public issues, especially in the field of civil rights, "at a considerable cost." Even so, Schlesinger and Leuchtenburg both concede that Eisenhower was much more of a hands-on executive than was realized during his administration.

The records of the Eisenhower administration have ended the myth that the old soldier left foreign policy to his influential secretary of state, John Foster Dulles. A leading Eisenhower revisionist, Fred I. Greenstein, reported in his 1982 study *The Hidden-Hand Presidency* that Ike made the decisions and Dulles carried them out. Greenstein said that it was Eisenhower's international political strategy to be the champion of peace in his public statements, while his secretary of state acted as a Cold Warrior. Dulles once claimed that he, as secretary of state, had ended the Korean War by threatening the use of atomic weapons. But the diplomatic historian Robert A. Divine wrote in *Eisenhower and the Cold War* (1981) that Dulles had exaggerated his role. "It was Eisenhower, in his own characteristically quiet and effective way, who had used the threat of American nuclear power to compel China to end its intervention in the Korean conflict. . . ."

Eisenhower's decision not to intervene militarily in Vietnam is described by some revisionists as his finest hour. Nine years later Eisenhower explained in a private memorandum that he had not wanted to tarnish the image of the United States as the world's foremost anticolonial power. "It is essential to our position of leadership in a world wherein the majority of the nations have at some time or another felt the yoke of colonialism. Thus it is that the moral position of the United States was more to be guarded than the Tonkin Delta, indeed than all of Indochina."

Largely because of his White House staff structure and the authority that he delegated to ranking subordinates, Eisenhower was often characterized as a disengaged President. His chief of staff, Sherman Adams, wielded more power than any White House adviser since FDR's Harry Hopkins, and a popular joke of the fifties had the punch line: "What if Sherman Adams died and Ike became President?" But the memoirs of Adams, Richard M. Nixon, Henry Cabot Lodge, Hagerty, Emmet John Hughes, Milton and John Eisenhower have shown a President firmly in command.

Eisenhower's uneasy relationship with Nixon has also been distorted by some revisionist scholars. While Ike and Nixon were never close, some historians have demonstrated political naïveté in accepting Eisenhower's private criticism of his Vice-President at face value. If Eisenhower held such strong reservations about Nixon as they have suggested, it is unlikely that he would have retained him on the ticket in 1956 and supported him for the Presidency in 1960 and 1968. Eisenhower did not share Nixon's zest for Republican partisanship, but he considered him a loyal and capable Vice-President. Had one of Ike's personal favorites, such as his brother Milton or Treasury Secretary Robert Anderson, emerged as a potential heir, there is evidence that Eisenhower might have supported them over Nixon. But Ike definitely preferred his Vice-President over Nelson Rockefeller and Barry Goldwater.

Nothing damaged Eisenhower's standing with intellectuals more than his vague position on McCarthyism. Eisenhower historians are sharply divided over the President's role in ending the Wisconsin senator's reign of fear. Ambrose criticizes Eisenhower's "muddled leadership" and unwillingness to publicly condemn McCarthy and his abusive tactics. But Greenstein and William Bragg Ewald have made a strong argument that Eisenhower's behind-the-scenes efforts set the stage for McCarthy's censure by the Senate and destroyed his political influence. Eisenhower loathed McCarthy but believed that a direct presidential attack on him would enhance the senator's credibility among his right-wing followers. "I just won't get into a pissing contest with that skunk," Eisenhower told his brother Milton. The President's papers indicate that he never doubted his strategy against McCarthy, and in the end he felt vindicated.

Eisenhower is also still criticized for not showing sufficient boldness in the field of civil rights. The President was not pleased with the 1954 Supreme Court decision that overturned the "separate but equal" doctrine in public education, and he privately observed that the firestorm touched off by the *Brown* v. *Board of Education* decision had set back racial progress fifteen years. Despite his misgivings, Eisenhower never considered defying the Court, as his successors Gerald Ford and Ronald Reagan would do, over the volatile issue of school desegregation. Eisenhower enforced the Court's decision in sending federal troops into Little Rock, and he went on to establish a civil rights division in the Justice Department in 1957 that committed the federal government to defend the rights of minorities and provided momentum to the civil rights movement.

A Herblock cartoon reflects the concern of many that Eisenhower was not equipped to handle the confident, unscrupulous McCarthy.

As a national hero, Eisenhower's popular appeal transcended his political party. According to a 1955 Gallup Poll, 57 percent of the nation's voters considered Eisenhower a political independent, which may have been why Eisenhower was unable to transfer his enormous popularity to the Republican party. Between 1932 and 1968, he was the only Republican elected to the White House. Ironically the GOP-controlled Eightieth Congress may have shortened the Eisenhower era five years before it began by adopting the Twenty-second Amendment, prohibiting any future President from serving more than two terms. Without the constitutional limit, John Eisenhower said his father would have run for a third term in 1960. Even Truman acknowledged that Eisenhower would have been reelected in another landslide.

Eisenhower restored confidence in the Presidency as an institution and set the agenda for the economic growth of the next decade. He understood public opinion as well as Roosevelt had, and he had a keener sense of military problems than any President since George Washington. As the failings of his successors became apparent, Eisenhower's Presidency grew in historical stature. A 1982 Chicago *Tribune* survey of forty-nine scholars ranked him as the ninth best President in history, just behind Truman and ahead of James K. Polk.

With the renewed appreciation of Eisenhower's achievements, Ambrose predicts that Ike may eventually be ranked ahead of Truman and Theodore Roosevelt, and just behind Washington, Jefferson, Jackson, Lincoln, Wilson, and FDR. "I'd put Ike rather high," the historian Robert Ferrell says, "because when he came into office at the head of an only superficially united party . . . he had to organize that heterogeneous group, and get it to cooperate, which he did admirably with all those keen political instincts of his."

"Whatever his failings," Robert J. Donovan wrote of Eisenhower in 1984, "he was a sensible, outstanding American, determined to do what he believed was right. He was a dedicated peacemaker, a president beloved by millions of people . . . and, clearly, a good man to depend on in a crisis. Of his high rank on the list of presidents there can be little doubt."

Henry Steele Commager, who was among Eisenhower's most thoughtful critics during his Presidency, said recently that he would now rank him about tenth from the top. Though Commager faults Eisenhower for not showing leadership against McCarthyism and on behalf of civil rights, he gives Ike high marks in foreign policy for not intervening in Vietnam and "having the sense to say 'no' to the Joint Chiefs of Staff."

Commager says that Eisenhower's election was the decisive factor in ending the Korean War. "Only a general with enormous prestige could have made peace in Korea. An outsider couldn't have done it."

Even Adlai Stevenson told a reporter that the election of Eisenhower in 1952 had been good for the country. (He did not, however, feel the same way about Ike's second term.)

William Appleman Williams, the dean of revisionist historians, says that Eisenhower was far more perceptive in international politics than his predecessor or those who followed him. "He clearly understood that crusading imperial police actions were extremely dangerous," Williams notes, and he was determined to avoid World War III.

In the final months of his Presidency, Eisenhower made this private assessment of his managerial style: "In war and in peace I've had no respect for the desk-pounder, and have despised the loud and slick talker. If my own ideas and practices in this matter have sprung from weakness, I do not know. But they were and are deliberate or, rather, natural to me. They are not accidental."

Lyndon B. Johnson and Vietnam

LARRY L. KING

President Lyndon B. Johnson was the kind of politician people tend to tell tall stories about. He always had a strong—some would say an overpowering—personality. When he was placed by fate and an assassin's bullet in a position of enormous power, he came to project a larger-than-life image, to seem a kind of elemental, irresistible force that no mere mortal could successfully resist. He swiftly pushed through economic and social reforms that had appeared to paralyze his predecessor in the White House, the popular John F. Kennedy.

Although he could certainly be devious, Johnson was not a very subtle person and when, during the Vietnam war, he decided that the national honor and the safety of what he called the free world required that the United States pursue the conflict to victory, he devoted all his energies to the task. Of course he failed. Why he failed and how he reacted to failure is the subject of this article by Larry L. King. The account is one of the most graphic and tragic portraits we have of Johnson, or for that matter of any president. King is the author of a number of novels and also of Confessions of a White Racist. *He was active in the 1960 and 1964 presidential campaigns and is currently working on a biography of President Johnson.* ∎

He was an old-fashioned man by the purest definition. Forget that he was enamored of twentieth-century artifacts—the telephone, television, supersonic airplanes, spacecraft—to which he adapted with a child's wondering glee. His values were the relics of an earlier time; he had been shaped by an America both rawer and more confident than it later would become; his generation may have been the last to believe that for every problem there existed a workable solution: that the ultimate answer, as in old-time mathematics texts, always reposed in the back of the book. He bought the prevailing American myths without closely inspecting the merchandise for rips or snares. He often said that Americans inherently were "can-do" people capable of accomplishing anything they willed; it was part of his creed that Americans were God's chosen: why otherwise would they have become the richest, the strongest, the freest people in the history of man? His was a God, perhaps, who was a first cousin to Darwin: Lyndon B. Johnson believed in survival of the fittest, that the strong would conquer the weak, that almost always the big 'uns ate the little 'uns.

There was a certain pragmatism in his beliefs, a touch of fatalism, even a measure of common sense. Yet, too, he could be wildly romantic. Johnson truly believed that any boy could rise to become President, though only thirty-five had. Hadn't he—a shirt-tailed kid from the dusty hard-scrabble precincts of the Texas outback—walked with kings and pharaohs while reigning over what he called, without blushing, the Free World? In his last days, though bitter and withering in retirement at his rural Elba, he astonished and puzzled a young black teen-ager by waving his arms in windmill motions and telling the youngster, during a random encounter, "Well, maybe someday all of us will be visiting *your* house in Waco, because you'll be President and your home will be a national museum just as mine is. It'll take a while, but it'll happen, you'll see. . . ." Then he turned to the black teenager's startled mother: "Now, you better get that home of yours cleaned up spick-and-span. There'll be hundreds of thousands coming through it, you know, wanting to see the bedroom and the kitchen and the living room. Now, I hope you get that dust rag of yours out the minute you get home."

Doris Kearns, the Harvard professor and latter-day L.B.J. confidante, who witnessed the performance, thought it to be a mock show: "almost a vaudeville act." Dr. Johnson peddling the same old snake oil. Perhaps. Whatever his motives that day, Lyndon Johnson chose his sermon from that text he most fervently believed throughout a lifetime; his catechism spoke to his heart of American opportunity, American responsibility, American good intentions, American superiority, American destiny, American infallibility. Despite a sly personal cynicism—a suspicion of others, the keen, cold eye of a man determined not to be victimized at the gaming tables—he was, in his institutional instincts, something of a Pollyanna. There *was* such a thing as a free lunch; there *was* a Santa Claus; there *was,* somewhere, a Good Fairy, and probably it was made up of the component parts of Franklin Roosevelt, Saint Francis, and Uncle Sam.

These thoroughly American traits—as L.B.J. saw them—comprised the foundation stone upon which he built his dream castle; he found it impossible to abandon them even as the sands shifted and bogged him in the quagmire of Vietnam. If America was so wonderful (and it *was;* he had the evidence of himself to prove it), then he had the obligation to export its goodness and greatness to the less fortunate. This he would accomplish at any cost, even if forced to "nail the coonskin to the wall." For if Lyndon B. Johnson believed in God and greatness and goodness, he also believed in guts and gunpowder.

All the history he had read, and all he had personally witnessed, convinced him that the United States of America—if determined enough, if productive enough, if patriotic enough—simply could not lose a war. As a boy his favorite stories had been of the minutemen at Lexington and Concord, of the heroic defenders of the Alamo, of rugged frontiersmen who'd at once tamed the wild land and marauding Indians. He had a special affinity for a schoolboy poem proclaiming that the most beautiful sight his eyes had beheld was "the flag of my country in a foreign land." He so admired war heroes that he claimed to have been fired on "by a Japanese ace," though no evidence supported it; he invented an ancestor he carelessly claimed had been martyred at the Alamo; at the Democratic National Convention in 1956 he had cast his state's delegate votes for the Vice-Presidential ambitions of young John F. Kennedy, "that fighting sailor who bears the scars of battle."

On a slow Saturday afternoon in the 1950's, expansive and garrulous in his posh Senate majority-leader quarters, Johnson discoursed to a half dozen young Texas staffers in the patois of their shared native place. Why—he said—you take that ragtag bunch at Valley Forge, who'd have given them a cut dog's chance? There they were, barefoot in the snow and their asses hanging out, nothing to eat but moss and dead leaves and snakes, not half enough bullets for their guns, and facing the soldiers of the most powerful king of his time. Yet they sucked it up, wouldn't quit, lived to fight another day—and won. Or you take the Civil War, now: it had been so exceptionally bloody because you had aroused Americans fighting on *both* sides; it had been something like rock against rock, or like two mean ol' pit bull-dogs going at each other with neither of them willing to be chewed up and both of 'em thinking only of taking hunks out of the other. He again invoked the Alamo: a mere handful of freedom-loving men standing against the Mexican hordes, knowing they faced certain death, but they'd carved their names in history for all time, and before they got through with ol' General Santa Anna he thought he'd stumbled into a nest of stinging scorpions or bumble-bees.

Fifteen years later Johnson would show irritation when Clark Clifford suggested that victory in Vietnam might require a sustaining commitment of twenty to thirty years. No—L.B.J. said—no, no, the thing to do was get in and out quickly, pour everything you had into the fight, land the knockout blow: hell, the North Vietnamese *had* to see the futility of facing all that American muscle. If you really poured it on 'em, you could clean up that mess within six months. We had the troops, the firepower, the bombs, the sophisticated weaponry, the oil—everything we needed to win. Did we have the resolve? Well, the Texas Rangers had a saying that you couldn't stop a man who just kept on a-coming. And that's what we'd do in Vietnam, Clark, just keep on a-coming . . .

Always he talked of the necessity to be strong; he invoked his father's standing up to the Ku Klux Klan in the 1920's, Teddy Roosevelt's carrying that big stick, F.D.R.'s mobilizing the country to beat Hitler and Tojo. He liked ol' Harry Truman—tough little bastard and his own man—but, listen, Harry and Dean Acheson had lost control when they failed to properly prosecute the Korean War. They lost the public's respect, lost control of General MacArthur, lost the backing of Congress, lost the *war* or the next thing to it. Next thing you know, they got blamed for losing China and then there was Joe McCarthy accusing them of being soft on communism and everybody believed it. Well, it wouldn't happen to him, nosir. *He* hadn't started the Vietnam war—Jack Kennedy had made the first commitment of out-and-out combat troops, don't forget—but *he* wouldn't bug out no matter how much the Nervous Nellies brayed. Kennedy had proved during the Cuban missile crisis that if you stood firm then the Reds would back down. They were playground bullies, and he didn't intend to be pushed around any more than Jack Kennedy had. When a bully ragged you, you didn't go whining to the teacher but gave him some of his own medicine.

Only later, in exile, when he spoke with unusual candor of his darker parts, did it become clear how obsessed with failure Lyndon Johnson always had been. As a preschool youngster he walked a country lane to visit a grandfather, his head stuffed with answers he knew would be required ("How many head of cattle you got, Lyndon? How much do they eat? How many head can you graze to the acre?") and fearing he might forget them. If he forgot them, he got no bright-red apple but received, instead, a stern and disapproving gaze. L.B.J.'s

mother, who smothered him with affection and praise should he perform to her pleasure, refused to acknowledge his presence should he
somehow displease or disappoint her. His father accused him of being
a sleepyhead, a slow starter, and sometimes said every boy in town had
a two-hour head start on him. Had we known these things from
scratch, we might not have wondered why Lyndon Johnson seemed so
blind for so long to the Asian realities. His personal history simply
permitted him no retreats or failures in testings.

From childhood L.B.J. experienced bad dreams. As with much else,
they would stay with him to the grave. His nightmares were of being
paralyzed and unable to act, of being chained inside a cage or to his
desk, of being pursued by hostile forces. These and other disturbing
dreams haunted his White House years; he could see himself stricken
and ill on a cot, unable even to speak—like Woodrow Wilson—while,
in an adjoining room, his trusted aides squabbled and quarreled in
dividing his power. He translated the dreams to mean that should he
for a moment show weakness, be indecisive, then history might judge
him as the first American President who had failed to stand up and be
counted.

These deep-rooted insecurities prompted Lyndon Johnson always
to assert himself, to abuse staff members simply to prove that he held
the upper hand, to test his power in small or mean ways. Sometimes,
in sending Vice President Hubert Humphrey off on missions or er-
rands with exhortations to "get going," he literally kicked him in the
shins. "Hard," Humphrey later recalled, pulling up his trouser leg to
exhibit the scars to columnist Robert Allen. Especially when drinking
did he swagger and strut. Riding high as Senate majority leader, Johnson one night after a Texas State Society function, at the National
Press Club in Washington—in the spring of 1958—repaired to a
nearby bar with Texas Congressmen Homer Thornberry and Jack
Brooks. "I'm a powerful sumbitch, you know that?" he repeatedly said.
"You boys realize how goddamn *powerful* I am?" Yes, Lyndon, his
companions uneasily chorused. Johnson pounded the table as if attempting to crack stout oak: "Do you know Ike couldn't pass the Lord's
Prayer in Congress without me? You understand that? Hah?" Yes,
Lyndon. "Hah? Do you? Hah?" An observer thought he never had
seen a man more desperate for affirmations of himself.

Johnson always was an enthusiastic Cold Warrior. He was not made
uncomfortable by John Foster Dulles' brinkmanship rhetoric about
"rolling back" communism or of "unleashing" Chiang Kai-shek to free
the Chinese mainland. He was, indeed, one of the original soldiers of
the Cold War, a volunteer rather than a draftee, just as he had been
the first member of Congress to rush to the recruiting station following
Pearl Harbor. Immediately after World War II he so bedeviled House

Speaker Sam Rayburn about his fears of America dismantling its military machine that Rayburn appointed him to the postwar Military Policy Committee and to the Joint Committee on Atomic Energy. L.B.J. early had a preference for military assignments in Congress; he successfully campaigned for a seat on the House Naval Affairs Committee in the 1930's and, a decade later, the Senate Armed Services Committee. He eventually chaired the Senate Preparedness Committee and the Senate Space Committee. Perhaps others saw the exploration of outer space in scientific or peaceful terms. Johnson, however, told Senate Democrats that outer space offered "the ultimate position from which total control of the earth may be exercised. Whoever gains that ultimate position gains control, total control, over the earth."

Lyndon Johnson was a nagger, a complainer, a man not always patient with those of lesser gifts or with those who somehow inconvenienced him in the moment. Sometimes he complained that the generals knew nothing but "spend and bomb"; almost always, however, he went along with bigger military spending and, in most cases, with more bombing or whatever other military action the brass proposed. This was his consistent record in Congress, and he generally affirmed it as President.

On November 12, 1951, Senator Johnson rattled his saber at the Russians:

> We are tired of fighting your stooges. We will no longer sacrifice our young men on the altar of your conspiracies. The next aggression will be the last. . . . We will strike back, not just at your satellites, but at you. We will strike back with all the dreaded might that is within our control, and it will be a crushing blow.

Even allowing for those rhetorical excesses peculiar to senatorial oratory, those were not the words of a man preoccupied with the doctrine of peaceful coexistence. Nor were they inconsistent with Johnson's mind-set when he made a public demand—at the outbreak of the Korean War, in June, 1950—that President Truman order an all-out mobilization of all military reserve troops, national guard units, draftees, and even civilian manpower and industry. In a Senate debate shortly thereafter Senator Johnson scolded colleagues questioning the Pentagon's request for new and supplementary emergency billions: "Is this the hour of our nation's twilight, the last fading hour of light before an endless night shall envelop us and all the Western world?"

His ties with Texas—with its indigenous xenophobic instincts and general proclivities toward a raw yahooism—haunted him and, in a sense, may have made him a prisoner of grim political realities during the witch-hunting McCarthy era. "I'm damn tired," he said, "of being

*An unusual wall arrangement in the Johnson home; an
example of L.B.J.'s unembarrassed style.*

called a Dixiecrat in Washington and a Communist in Texas"; it perfectly summed up those schizophrenic divisions uneasily compartmen-
talizing his national political life and the more restrictive parochial role
dictated by conditions back home. He lived daily with a damned-if-I-
do-and-damned-if-I-don't situation. Texas was a particularly happy
hunting ground for Senator Joe McCarthy, whose self-proclaimed an-
ticommunist crusade brought him invitation after invitation to speak
there; the Texas legislature, in the 1950's controlled beyond belief by
vested interests and showing the ideological instincts of the early pri-
mates, whooped through a resolution demanding that Senator
McCarthy address it despite the suggestion of State Representative
Maury Maverick, Jr., that the resolution be expanded to invite Mickey
Mouse. Both Johnson's powerful rightist adversaries and many of his

wealthy Texas benefactors were enthusiastic contributors to the McCarthy cause.

Privately Johnson groused to intimates of McCarthy's reckless showboat tactics and particularly of the Texas-directed pressures they brought down on him: why, Joe McCarthy was just a damn drunk, a blowhard, an incompetent who couldn't tie his own shoelaces, probably the biggest joke in the Senate. But—L.B.J. reminded those counseling him to attack McCarthy—people believed him, they were so afraid of the Communists they would believe anything. McCarthy was as strong as horseradish. There would come a time when the hysteria died down, and then McCarthy would be vulnerable; such a fellow was certain to hang himself in time. But right now anybody openly challenging McCarthy would come away with dirty hands and with his heart broken. "Touch pitch," he paraphrased the Bible, "and you'll be defiled." By temperament a man who coveted the limelight and never was bashful about claiming credit for popular actions, Johnson uncharacteristically remained in the background when the U.S. Senate voted to censure McCarthy in late 1954. Though he was instrumental in selecting senators he believed would be effective and creditable members in leading the censure effort, Johnson's fine hand was visible only to insiders.

Johnson believed, however—and probably more deeply than Joe McCarthy—in a worldwide, monolithic Communist conspiracy. He believed it was directed from Moscow and that it was ready to blast America, or subvert it, at the drop of a fur hat. L.B.J. never surrendered that view. In retirement he suggested that the Communists were everywhere, honeycombing the government, and he told surprised visitors that sometimes he hadn't known whether he could trust even his own staff. The Communists (it had been his first thought on hearing the gunshots in Dallas, and he never changed his mind) had killed Jack Kennedy; it had been their influence that turned people against the Vietnam war. One of L.B.J.'s former aides, having been treated to that angry lecture, came away from the Texas ranch with the sad and reluctant conclusion that "the Old Man's absolutely paranoid on the Communist thing."

In May, 1961, President Kennedy dispatched his Vice President to Asia on a "fact-finding" diplomatic trip. Johnson, who believed it his duty to be a team player, to reinforce the prevailing wisdom, bought without qualification the optimistic briefings of military brass with their charts and slides "proving" the inevitable American victory. "I was sent out here to report the *progress* of the war," he told an aide, as if daring anyone to give him anything other than good news. Carried away, he publicly endowed South Vietnam's President Ngo Dinh Diem with the qualities of Winston Churchill, George Washington, Andrew

Jackson, and F.D.R. Visiting refugee camps, he grew angry at Communist aggressions "against decent people" and concluded: "There is no alternative to United States leadership in Southeast Asia. . . . We must decide whether to help to the best of our ability or throw in the towel . . . [and] . . . pull back 'our defenses to San Francisco and a 'Fortress America' concept." He believed then—and always would—in the "domino theory" first stated by President Eisenhower. Even after announcing his abdication, he continued to sing the tired litany: if Vietnam fell then the rest of Asia might go, and then Africa, and then the Philippines . . .

When Lyndon Johnson suddenly ascended to the Presidency, however, he did not enter the Oval Office eager to immediately take the measure of Ho Chi Minh. Although he told Ambassador Henry Cabot Lodge that "I am not going to be the President who saw Southeast Asia go the way China went," he wanted, for the moment, to keep the war —and, indeed, all foreign entanglements—at arm's length. His preoccupation was with his domestic program; here, he was confident, he knew what he was doing. He would emulate F.D.R. in making people's lives a little brighter. To aides he eagerly talked of building schools and houses, of fighting poverty and attaining full employment, of heating the economy to record prosperity. The honeymoon with Congress—he said—couldn't last; he had seen Congress grow balky and obstinate, take its measure of many Presidents, and he had to assume it would happen again. Then he would lean forward, tapping a forefinger against someone's chest or squeezing a neighboring knee, and say: "I'm like a sweetheart to Congress right now. They love me because I'm new and courting 'em and it's kinda exciting, like that first kiss. But after a while the new will wear off. Then Congress will complain that I don't bring enough roses or candy and will accuse me of seeing other girls." The need was to push forward quickly: pass the Civil Rights bill in the name of the martyred John F. Kennedy, then hit Capitol Hill with a blizzard of domestic proposals and dazzle it before sentiment and enthusiasms cooled. Foreign affairs could wait.

Lyndon Johnson at that point had little experience in foreign affairs. Except for showcase missions accomplished as Vice President, he had not traveled outside the United States save for excursions to Mexico and his brief World War II peregrinations. He probably had little confidence in himself in foreign affairs; neither did he have an excessive interest in the field. "Foreigners are not like the folks I am used to," he sometimes said—and though it passed as a joke, his intimates felt he might be kidding on the level.

Ambassadors waiting to present their credentials to the new President were miffed by repeated delays—and then angrily astonished when L.B.J. received them in groups and clumps, seemingly paying

only perfunctory attention, squirming in his chair, scowling or muttering during the traditional ceremonies. He appeared oblivious to their
feelings, to their offended senses of dignity. "Why do *I* have to see
them?" the President demanded. "They're Dean Rusk's clients, not
mine."

Defense Secretary Robert McNamara was selected to focus on Vietnam while L.B.J. concocted his Great Society. McNamara should send
South Vietnam equipment and money as needed, a few more men,
issue the necessary pronouncements. But don't splash it all over the
front pages, don't let it get out of hand, don't give Barry Goldwater
Vietnam as an issue for the 1964 campaign. Barry, hell, he was a hip
shooter; he'd fight Canada or Mexico—or, at least, give that impression—so the thing to do was sit tight, keep the lid on, keep all Vietnam
options open. Above all, "Don't let it turn into a Bay of Pigs." Hunker
down; don't gamble.

The trouble—Johnson said to advisers—was that foreign nations
didn't understand Americans or the American way; they saw us as "fat
and fifty, like the country-club set"; they didn't think we had the steel
in our souls to act when the going got rough. Well, in time they'd find
out differently. They'd learn that Lyndon Johnson was not about to
abandon what other Presidents had started; he wouldn't permit history
to write that he'd been the only American President to cut and run; he
wouldn't sponsor any damn Munichs. But for right now—cool it. Put
Vietnam on the back burner and let it simmer.

But the Communists—he later would say—wouldn't permit him to
cool it. There had been that Gulf of Tonkin attack on the United States
destroyer *Maddox*, in August of 19-and-64, and if he hadn't convinced
Congress to get on record as backing him up in Vietnam, why, then,
the Reds would have interpreted it as a sign of weakness and Barry
Goldwater would have cut his heart out. And in February of 19-and-65,
don't forget, the Vietcong had made that attack on the American
garrison at Pleiku, and how could he be expected to ignore that? There
they came, thousands of 'em, barefoot and howling in their black
pajamas and throwing homemade bombs: it had been a damned insult,
a calculated show of contempt. L.B.J. told the National Security Council: "The worst thing we could do would be to let this [Pleiku] thing
go by. It would be a big mistake. It would open the door to a major
misunderstanding." Twelve hours later American aircraft—for the
first time—bombed in North Vietnam; three weeks later L.B.J. ordered
continuing bombing raids in the north to "force the North Vietnamese
into negotiations"; only a hundred and twenty days after Pleiku,
American forces were involved in a full-scale war and seeking new ways
to take the offensive. Eight Americans died at Pleiku. Eight. Eventually
fifty thousand plus would die in Asia.

President Johnson with Defense Secretary McNamara at the White House after one of McNamara's inspection trips to Vietnam.

Pleiku was the second major testing of American will within a few months, in L.B.J.'s view. Then in the spring of 1965 rebels had attacked the ruling military junta in the Dominican Republic. Lives and property of U.S. citizens were endangered, as Johnson saw it, but—more—this might be a special tactic by the Reds, a dry run for bigger mischief later on in Vietnam. The world was watching to see how America would react. "It's just like the Alamo," he lectured the National Security Council. "Hell, it's like you were down at that gate, and you were surrounded, and you damn well needed somebody. Well, by God, I'm going to *go*—and I thank the Lord that I've got men who want to go with me, from McNamara right down to the littlest private who's carrying a gun."

Somewhat to his puzzlement, and certainly to his great vexation, Lyndon Johnson would learn that not everybody approved of his rushing the Marines into the Dominican Republic, and within days building up a twenty-one-thousand-man force. Attempting to answer criticism, he would claim thousands of patriots "bleeding in the streets and with their heads cut off," paint a false picture of the United States ambassador cringing under his desk "while bullets whizzed over his head," speak of howling Red hordes descending on American citizens and American holdings, and, generally, open what later became known as the Credibility Gap.

By now he had given up on his original notion of walking easy in Vietnam until he could put the Great Society across. Even before the three major testings of Tonkin Gulf, the Dominican Republic, and Pleiku, he had said—almost idly—"Well, I guess we have to touch up those North Vietnamese a little bit." By December, 1964, he had reversed earlier priorities: "We'll beat the Communists first, then we can look around and maybe give something to the poor." Guns now ranked ahead of butter.

Not that he was happy about it. Though telling Congress "This nation is mighty enough, its society is healthy enough, its people are strong enough to pursue our goals in the rest of the world while still building a Great Society here at home," he knew, in his bones, that this was much too optimistic an outlook. He privately fretted that his domestic program would be victimized. He became touchy, irritable, impatient with those who even timorously questioned America's increasing commitment to the war. Why should *I* be blamed—he snapped—when the Communists are the aggressors, when President Eisenhower committed us in Asia in 1954, when Kennedy beefed up Ike's efforts? If he didn't prosecute the Vietnam war now, then later Congress would sour and want to hang him because he hadn't—and would gut his domestic programs in retaliation. He claimed to have "pounded President Eisenhower's desk" in opposing Ike's sending two hundred Air Force "technicians" to assist the French in Indochina (though those who were present recalled that only Senators Russell of Georgia and Stennis of Mississippi had raised major objections). Well, he'd been unable to stop Ike that time, though he *had* helped persuade him against dropping paratroopers into Dien Bien Phu to aid the doomed French garrison there. And after all that, everybody now called Vietnam Lyndon Johnson's war. It was unfair. "The only difference between the Kennedy assassination and mine is that I am alive and it [is] more torturous."

Very well; if it was his war in the public mind, then he would personally oversee its planning. "Never move up your artillery until you move up your ammunition," he told his generals—a thing he'd said as Senate majority leader when impatient liberals urged him to call for votes on issues he felt not yet ripe. Often he quizzed the military brass, sounding almost like a dove, in a way to resemble courtroom cross-examinations. He forced the admirals and generals to affirm and reaffirm their recommendations as vital to victory. Reading selected transcripts, one might make the judgment that Lyndon Johnson was a most reluctant warrior, one more cautious than not. The evidence of Johnson's deeds, however, suggests that he was being a crafty politician—making a record so that later he couldn't be made the sole scapegoat. He trusted McNamara's computers, perhaps more than he trusted men, and took satisfaction when their print-outs predicted that X amount of bombing would damage the Vietcong by Y, or that X number of troops would be required to capture Z. Planning was the key. You figured what you had to do, you did it, and eventually you'd nail the coonskin to the wall.

He devoutly believed that all problems had solutions: in his lifetime alone we'd beaten the Great Depression, won two world wars, hacked away at racial discrimination, made an industrial giant and world power of a former agrarian society, explored outer space. This belief in available solutions led him, time and again, to change tactics in Vietnam and discover fresh enthusiasm for each new move; he did not pause, apparently, to reflect upon why given tactics, themselves once heralded as practical solutions, had failed and had been abandoned. If counterinsurgency failed, you bombed. If bombing wasn't wholly effective, then you tried the enclave theory. If *that* proved disappointing, you sent your ground troops on search-and-destroy missions. If, somehow, the troops couldn't find the phantom Vietcong in large numbers (and therefore couldn't destroy them), you began pacification programs in the areas you'd newly occupied. And if *this* bogged down, you beefed up your firepower and sent in enough troops to simply outmuscle the rice-paddy ragtags: napalm 'em, bomb 'em, shoot 'em. Sure it would work. It always had. Yes, surely the answer was there somewhere in the back of the book, if only you looked long enough . . .

He sought, and found, assurances. Maybe he had only a "cow-college" education, perhaps he'd not attended West Point, he might not have excessive experience in foreign affairs. But he was surrounded by good men, what David Halberstam later would label "the best and the brightest," and certainly these were unanimous in their supportive conclusions. "He would look around him," Tom Wicker later said, "and see in Bob McNamara that [the war] was technologically feasible, in McGeorge Bundy that it was intellectually respectable, and in Dean Rusk that it was historically necessary." It was especially easy to trust expertise when the experts in their calculations bolstered your own gut feelings—when their computers and high-minded statements and mighty hardware all boiled down to reinforce your belief in American efficiency, American responsibility, American destiny. If so many good men agreed with him, then what might be wrong with those who didn't?

He considered the sources of dissatisfaction and dissent: the liberals—the "red-hots," he'd often sneeringly called them, the "pepper pots"—who were impractical dreamers, self-winding kamikazes intent on self-destruction. He often quoted an aphorism to put such people in perspective: "Any jackass can kick down a barn, but it takes a carpenter to build one." He fancied, however, that he knew all about these queer fellows. For years, down home, Ronnie Dugger and his *Texas Observer* crowd, in L.B.J.'s opinion, had urged him to put his head in the noose by fighting impossible, profitless fights. They wanted him to take on Joe McCarthy, slap the oil powers down, kick Ike's rear end, tell everybody who wasn't a red-hot to go to hell. Well, he'd learned a long time ago that just because you told a fellow to go to hell, he didn't necessarily have to go. The liberals didn't understand the Communists. Bill Fulbright and his bunch—the striped-pants boys over at the State Department and assorted outside pepper pots—thought you could *trust* the Communists; they made the mistake of believing the Reds would deal with you honorably when—in truth—the Communists didn't respect anything but force. You had to fight fire with fire; let them know who had the biggest guns and the toughest heart.

Where once he had argued the injustice of Vietnam being viewed as "his" war, Lyndon Johnson now brought to it a proprietary attitude. This should have been among the early warnings that L.B.J. would increasingly resist less than victory, no matter his periodic bombing halts or conciliatory statements inviting peace, because once he took a thing personally, his pride and vanity and ego knew no bounds. Always a man to put his brand on everything (he wore monogrammed shirts, boots, cuff links; flew his private L.B.J. flag when in residence at the L.B.J. ranch; saw to it that the names of Lynda Bird Johnson and Luci Baines Johnson and Lady Bird Johnson—not Claudia, as she had been named—had the magic initials L.B.J.), he now personalized and internalized the war. Troops became "my" boys, those were "my" helicopters, it was "my" pilots he prayed might return from their bombing missions as he paid nocturnal calls to the White House situation room to learn the latest from the battlefields; Walt Rostow became "my" intellectual because he was hawkish on L.B.J.'s war. His machismo was mixed up in it now, his manhood. After a cabinet meeting in 1967 several staff aides and at least one cabinet member—Stewart Udall, Secretary of the Interior—remained behind for informal discussions; soon L.B.J. was waving his arms and fulminating about his war. Who the hell was Ho Chi Minh, anyway, that he thought he could push America around? Then the President did an astonishing thing: he unzipped his trousers, dangled a given appendage, and asked his shocked associates: "Has Ho Chi Minh got anything like that?"

By mid-1966 he had cooled toward many of his experts: not because they'd been wrong in their original optimistic calculations so much as that some of them had recanted and now rejected *his* war. This Lyndon Johnson could not forgive: they'd cut and run on him. Nobody had deserted Roosevelt, he gloomed, when he'd been fighting Hitler. McGeorge Bundy, deserting to head the Ford Foundation, was no longer the brilliant statesman but merely "a smart kid, that's all." Bill Moyers, quitting to become editor of *Newsday,* and once almost a surrogate son to the President, suddenly became "a little puppy I rescued from sacking groceries"—a reference to a part-time job Moyers held while a high-school student. George Ball, too, was leaving? Well, he'd always been a chronic beller-acher. When Defense Secretary McNamara doubted too openly (stories of his anguish leaked to the newspapers), he found it difficult to claim the President's time; ultimately he rudely was shuttled to the World Bank. Vice President Hubert Humphrey, privately having second thoughts, was not welcomed back to high councils until he'd muffled his dissent and shamelessly flattered L.B.J. Even then Johnson didn't wholly accept his Vice President; Hubert, he said, wasn't a real man, he cried as easily as a woman, he didn't have the weight. When Lady Bird Johnson voiced doubts about the war, her husband grumbled that *of course* she had doubts; it was *like* a woman to be uncertain. *Has Ho Chi Minh got anything like that?*

Shortly after the Tet offensive began—during which Americans would be shocked by the Vietcong temporarily capturing a wing of the American embassy in Saigon—the President, at his press conference of February 2, 1968, made such patently false statements that even his most loyal friends and supporters were troubled. The sudden Tet offensive had been traumatic, convincing many Americans that our condition was desperate, if not doomed. For years the official line ran that the Vietcong could not hang on: would shrink by the attritions of battle and an ebbing of confidence in a hopeless cause; stories were handed out that captured documents showed the enemy to be of low morale, underfed, ill-armed. The Vietcong could not survive superior American firepower; the kill ratio favored our side by 7-to-1, 8-to-1, more. These and other optimisms were repeated by the President, by General Westmoreland, by this ambassador or that fact-finding team. Now, however, it became apparent that the Vietcong had the capability to challenge even our main lair in Asia—and there to inflict serious damage as well as major embarrassments.

It was a time demanding utmost candor, and L.B.J. blew it. He took the ludicrous position that the Tet offensive (which would be felt for weeks to come) had abysmally failed. Why, we'd known about it all along—had, indeed, been in possession of Hanoi's order of battle. Incredible. To believe the President one had also to believe that

In the aftermath of the Vietcong's temporary capture of a part of the Saigon embassy compound, U.S. officials and military police inspect the body of a Vietcong soldier.

American authorities had simply failed to act on this vital intelligence, had wittingly and willingly invited disaster. The President was scoffed at and ridiculed; perhaps the thoughtful got goose bumps in realizing how far Lyndon Johnson now lived from reality. If there was a beginning of the end—of Johnson, of hopes of anything remotely resembling victory, of a general public innocence of official razzmatazz— then Tet, and that press conference, had to be it.

Even the stubborn President knew it. His Presidency was shot, his party ruined and in tatters; his credibility was gone; he could speak only at military bases, where security guaranteed his safety against the possibility of mobs pursuing him through the streets as he had often dreamed. The nightmare was real now. Street dissidents long had been chanting their cruel "Hey, Hey, L.B.J. / How Many Kids Did You Kill Today"; Senator Eugene McCarthy soon would capture almost half the vote in the New Hampshire primary against the unpopular President. There was nothing to do but what he'd always sworn he would

President Johnson during television speech in which he announced that he would not seek reelection.

not do: quit. On March 31, 1968, at the end of a televised speech ordering the end of attacks on North Vietnam in the hope of getting the enemy to the negotiation table, Johnson startled the nation by announcing: "... I do not believe that I should devote an hour or a day of my time to any personal partisan causes or to any duties other than the awesome duties of this office—the Presidency of your country. Accordingly, I shall not seek, and I will not accept, the nomination of my party for another term ..."

"In the final months of his Presidency," former White House aide Eric Goldman wrote, "Lyndon Johnson kept shifting in mood. At times he was bitter and petulant at his repudiation by the nation; at times philosophical, almost serene, confidently awaiting the verdict of the future." The serenity always was temporary; he grew angry with Hubert Humphrey for attempting to disengage himself from the Johnson war policy and, consequently, refused to make more than a token show of support for him. He saw Richard Nixon win on a pledge of having "a secret plan" to end the war—which, it developed, he did not have.

In his final White House thrashings—and in retirement—Lyndon Johnson complained of unfinished business: he had wanted to complete Vietnam peace talks, free the crew of the *Pueblo,* begin talks with the Russians on halting the arms race, send a man to the moon. But the war—he would say in irritation—the war had ruined all that; the people hadn't rallied around him as they had around F.D.R. and Woodrow Wilson and other wartime Presidents; he had been abandoned—by Congress, by cabinet members, by old friends; no other President had tried so hard or suffered so much. He had a great capacity for self-pity and often indulged it, becoming reclusive and rarely issuing a public statement or making public appearances. Doris Kearns has said that she and others helping L.B.J. write his memoirs, *The Vantage Point,* would draft chapters and lay out the documentation—but even then Lyndon Johnson would say no, no, it wasn't like that, it was like *this;* and he would rattle on, waving his arms and attempting to justify himself, invoking the old absolutes, calling up memories of the Alamo, the Texas Rangers, the myths and the legends. He never seemed to understand where or how he had gone wrong.

Watergate

WALTER KARP

In 1984, ten years after the resignation of President Richard M. Nixon, the editors of American Heritage *asked the journalist Walter Karp and the novelist Vance Bourjaily to look back at the events that followed the "third-rate burglary" that we know of as "Watergate" and to write articles describing and explaining those events. Both produced fascinating accounts. Bourjaily's is primarily personal; Karp's is in the form of a narrative account of events and is better suited to the purposes of this volume. Karp takes a dim view of the courage and moral character not merely of the chief culprits and the other main characters in the drama he describes, but also of most of the members of Congress who, he argues, put off doing what in their hearts they knew they had to do for far too long. Whether or not one agrees with this judgment, Karp's account is both good history and eventually heartening, for it is a tale in which justice, after many trials and tribulations, finally triumphs.*

■

Exactly ten years ago this August, the thirty-seventh President of the United States, facing imminent impeachment, resigned his high office and passed out of our lives. "The system worked," the nation exclaimed, heaving a sigh of relief. What had brought that relief was the happy extinction of the prolonged fear that the "system" might not work at all. But what was it that had inspired such fears? When I asked myself that question recently, I found I could scarcely remember. Although I had followed the Watergate crisis with minute attention, it had grown vague and formless in my mind, like a nightmare recollected in sunshine. It was not until I began working my way through back copies of *The New York Times* that I was able to remember clearly why I used to read my morning paper with forebodings for the country's future.

The Watergate crisis had begun in June 1972 as a "third-rate burglary" of the Democratic National Committee headquarters in Washington's Watergate building complex. By late March 1973 the burglary and subsequent efforts to obstruct its investigation had been laid at the door of the White House. By late June, Americans were asking themselves whether their President had or had not ordered the payment of "hush money" to silence a Watergate burglar. Investigated by a special Senate committee headed by Sam Ervin of North Carolina, the scandal continued to deepen and ramify during the summer of 1973. By March 1974 the third-rate burglary of 1972 had grown into an unprecedented constitutional crisis.

By then it was clear beyond doubt that President Richard M. Nixon stood at the center of a junto of henchmen without parallel in our history. One of Nixon's attorneys general, John Mitchell, was indicted for obstructing justice in Washington and for impeding a Securities and Exchange Commission investigation in New York. Another, Richard Kleindienst, had criminally misled the Senate Judiciary Committee in the President's interest. The acting director of the Federal Bureau of Investigation, L. Patrick Gray, had burned incriminating White House documents at the behest of a presidential aide. Bob Haldeman, the President's chief of staff, John Ehrlichman, the President's chief domestic adviser, and Charles Colson, the President's special counsel, all had been indicted for obstructing justice in the investigation of the Watergate burglary. John Dean, the President's legal counsel and chief accuser, had already pleaded guilty to the same charge. Dwight Chapin, the President's appointments secretary, faced trial for lying to a grand jury about political sabotage carried out during the 1972 elections. Ehrlichman and two other White House aides were under indictment for conspiring to break into a psychiatrist's office and steal confidential information about one of his former patients, Daniel Ellsberg. By March 1974 some twenty-eight presidential aides or election offi-

cials had been indicted for crimes carried out in the President's interest. Never before in American history had a President so signally failed
to fulfill his constitutional duty to "take care that the laws be faithfully
executed."

It also had been clear for many months that the thirty-seventh
President of the United States did not feel bound by his constitutional
duties. He insisted that the requirements of national security, as he and
he alone saw fit to define it, released him from the most fundamental
legal and constitutional constraints. In the name of "national security," the President had created a secret band of private detectives,
paid with private funds, to carry out political espionage at the urging
of the White House. In the name of "national security," the President
had approved the warrantless wiretapping of news reporters. In the
name of "national security," he had approved a secret plan for massive, illegal surveillance of American citizens. He had encouraged his
aides' efforts to use the Internal Revenue Service to harass political
"enemies"—prominent Americans who endangered "national security" by publicly criticizing the President's Vietnam War policies.

The framers of the Constitution had provided one and only one
remedy for such lawless abuse of power: impeachment in the House
of Representatives and trial in the Senate for "high Crimes and Misdemeanors." There was absolutely no alternative. If Congress had not
held President Nixon accountable for lawless conduct of his office,
then Congress would have condoned a lawless Presidency. If Congress
had not struck from the President's hands the despot's cudgel of "national security," then Congress would have condoned a despotic Presidency.

Looking through the back issues of *The New York Times,* I recollected
in a flood of ten-year-old memories what it was that had filled me with
such foreboding. It was the reluctance of Congress to act. I felt anew
my fury when members of Congress pretended that nobody really
cared about Watergate except the "media" and the "Nixon-haters."
The real folks "back home," they said, cared only about inflation and
the gasoline shortage. I remembered the exasperating actions of leading Democrats, such as a certain Senate leader who went around telling
the country that President Nixon could not be impeached because in
America a person was presumed innocent until proven guilty. Surely
the senator knew that impeachment was not a verdict of guilt but a
formal accusation made in the House leading to trial in the Senate.
Why was he muddying the waters, I wondered, if not to protect the
President?

It had taken one of the most outrageous episodes in the history of
the Presidency to compel Congress to make even a pretense of action.
Back on July 16, 1973, a former White House aide named Alexan-

der Butterfield had told the Ervin committee that President Nixon secretly tape-recorded his most intimate political conversations. On two solemn occasions that spring the President had sworn to the American people that he knew nothing of the Watergate cover-up until his counsel John Dean had told him about it on March 21, 1973. From that day forward, Nixon had said, "I began intensive new inquiries into this whole matter." Now we learned that the President had kept evidence secret that would exonerate him completely—if he were telling the truth. Worse yet, he wanted it kept secret. Before Butterfield had revealed the existence of the tapes, the President had grandly announced that "executive privilege will not be invoked as to any testimony [by my aides] concerning possible criminal conduct, in the matters under investigation. I want the public to learn the truth about Watergate. . . ." After the existence of the tapes was revealed, however, the President showed the most ferocious resistance to disclosing the "truth about Watergate." He now claimed that executive privilege—hitherto a somewhat shadowy presidential prerogative—gave a President "absolute power" to withhold any taped conversation he chose, even those urgently needed in the ongoing criminal investigation then being conducted by a special Watergate prosecutor. Nixon even claimed, through his lawyers, that the judicial branch of the federal government was "absolutely without power to reweigh that choice or to make a different resolution of it."

In the U.S. Court of Appeals the special prosecutor, a Harvard Law School professor named Archibald Cox, called the President's claim "intolerable." Millions of Americans found it infuriating. The court found it groundless. On October 12, 1973, it ordered the President to surrender nine taped conversations that Cox had been fighting to obtain for nearly three months.

Determined to evade the court order, the President on October 19 announced that he had devised a "compromise." Instead of handing over the recorded conversations to the court, he would submit only edited summaries. To verify their truthfulness, the President would allow Sen. John Stennis of Mississippi to listen to the tapes. As an independent verifier, the elderly senator was distinguished by his devotion to the President's own overblown conception of a "strong" Presidency. When Nixon had ordered the secret bombing of Cambodia, he had vouchsafed the fact to Senator Stennis, who thought that concealing the President's secret war from his fellow senators was a higher duty than preserving the Senate's constitutional role in the formation of United States foreign policy.

On Saturday afternoon, October 20, I and millions of other Americans sat by our television sets while the special prosecutor explained why he could not accept "what seems to me to be non-compliance with

*John Dean, White House counsel, testified during the Senate
hearings in the summer of 1973. Directly in back of him
was his much-photographed wife Mo.*

the court's order." Then the President flashed the dagger sheathed
within his "compromise." At 8:31 P.M. television viewers across the
country learned that he had fired the special prosecutor; that attorney
general Elliot Richardson had resigned rather than issue that order to
Cox; that the deputy attorney general, William Ruckelshaus, also had
refused to do so and had been fired for refusing; that it was a third
acting attorney general who had finally issued the order. With trembling voices, television newscasters reported that the President had
abolished the office of special prosecutor and that the FBI was standing
guard over its files. Never before in our history had a President, setting
law at defiance, made our government seem so tawdry and gimcrack.
"It's like living in a banana republic," a friend of mine remarked.

Now the question before the country was clear. "Whether ours
shall continue to be a government of laws and not of men," the ex-
special prosecutor said that evening, "is now for the Congress and
ultimately the American people to decide."

Another witness at the Senate hearings was H. R.
Haldeman, White House chief of staff.

Within ten days of the "Saturday night massacre," one million
letters and telegrams rained down on Congress, almost every one of
them demanding the President's impeachment. But congressional
leaders dragged their feet. The House Judiciary Committee would
begin an inquiry into *whether* to begin an inquiry into possible
grounds for recommending impeachment to the House. With the obvious intent, it seemed to me, of waiting until the impeachment fervor had abated, the Democratic-controlled committee would consider whether to consider making a recommendation about making
an accusation.

Republicans hoped to avoid upholding the rule of law by persuad-
ing the President to resign. This attempt to supply a lawless remedy
for lawless power earned Republicans a memorable rebuke from one
of the most venerated members of their party: eighty-one-year-old
Sen. George Aiken of Vermont. The demand for Nixon's resignation,
he said, "suggests that many prominent Americans, who ought to
know better, find the task of holding a President accountable as just

*Jeb Stuart Magruder, deputy director of CREEP, also
testified at the hearings.*

too difficult. . . . To ask the President now to resign and thus relieve
Congress of its clear congressional duty amounts to a declaration of
incompetence on the part of Congress."

The system was manifestly not working. But neither was the President's defense. On national television Nixon bitterly assailed the press
for its "outrageous, vicious, distorted" reporting, but the popular
outrage convinced him, nonetheless, to surrender the nine tapes to the
court. Almost at once the White House tapes began their singular
career of encompassing the President's ruin. On October 31 the White
House disclosed that two of the taped conversations were missing,

including one between the President and his campaign manager, John Mitchell, which had taken place the day after Nixon returned from a Florida vacation and three days after the Watergate break-in. Three weeks later the tapes dealt Nixon a more potent blow. There was an eighteen-and-a-half-minute gap, the White House announced, in a taped conversation between the President and Haldeman, which had also taken place the day after he returned from Florida. The White House suggested first that the President's secretary, Rose Mary Woods, had accidentally erased part of the tape while transcribing it. When the loyal Miss Woods could not demonstrate in court how she could have pressed the "erase" button unwittingly for eighteen straight minutes, the White House attributed the gap to "some sinister force." On January 15, 1974, court-appointed experts provided a more humdrum explanation. The gap had been produced by at least five manual erasures. Someone in the White House had deliberately destroyed evidence that might have proved that President Nixon knew of the Watergate cover-up from the start.

At this point the Judiciary Committee was in its third month of considering whether to consider. But by now there was scarcely an American who did not think the President guilty, and on February 6, 1974, the House voted 410 to 4 to authorize the Judiciary Committee to begin investigating possible grounds for impeaching the President of the United States. It had taken ten consecutive months of the most damning revelations of criminal misconduct, a titanic outburst of public indignation, and an unbroken record of presidential deceit, defiance, and evasion in order to compel Congress to take its first real step. That long record of immobility and feigned indifference boded ill for the future.

The White House knew how to exploit congressional reluctance. One tactic involved a highly technical but momentous question: What constituted an impeachable offense? On February 21 the staff of the Judiciary Committee had issued a report. Led by two distinguished attorneys, John Doar, a fifty-two-year-old Wisconsin Independent, and Albert Jenner, a sixty-seven-year-old Chicago Republican, the staff had taken the broad view of impeachment for which Hamilton and Madison had contended in the *Federalist* papers. Despite the constitutional phrase "high Crimes and Misdemeanors," the staff report had argued that an impeachable offense did not have to be a crime. "Some of the most grievous offenses against our Constitutional form of government may not entail violations of the criminal law."

The White House launched a powerful counterattack. At a news conference on February 25, the President contended that only proven criminal misconduct supplied grounds for impeachment. On February 28, the White House drove home his point with a tightly argued legal paper: If a President could be impeached for anything other than a crime of "a very serious nature," it would expose the Presidency to "political impeachments."

The argument was plausible. But if Congress accepted it, the Watergate crisis could only end in disaster. Men of great power do not commit crimes. They procure crimes without having to issue incriminating orders. A word to the servile suffices. "Who will free me from this turbulent priest," asked Henry II, and four of his barons bashed in the skull of Thomas à Becket. The ease with which the powerful can arrange "deniability," to use the Watergate catchword, was one reason the criminal standard was so dangerous to liberty. Instead of having to take care that the laws be faithfully executed, a President, under that standard, would only have to take care to insulate himself from the criminal activities of his agents. Moreover, the standard could not reach the most dangerous offenses. There is no crime in the statute books called "attempted tyranny."

Yet the White House campaign to narrow the definition of impeachment met with immediate success. In March one of the members of the House of Representatives said that before voting to impeach Nixon, he would "want to know beyond a reasonable doubt that he was directly involved in the commission of a crime." To impeach the President for the grave abuse of his powers, lawmakers said, would be politically impossible. On the Judiciary Committee itself the senior Republican, Edward Hutchinson of Michigan, disavowed the staff's view of impeachment and adopted the President's. Until the final days of the crisis, the criminal definition of impeachment was to hang over the country's fate like the sword of Damocles.

The criminal standard buttressed the President's larger thesis: In defending himself he was fighting to protect the "Presidency" from sinister forces trying to "weaken" it. On March 12 the President's lawyer, James D. St. Clair, sounded this theme when he declared that he did not represent the President "individually" but rather the "office of the Presidency." There was even a National Citizens Committee for Fairness to the Presidency. It was America's global leadership, Nixon insisted, that made a "strong" Presidency so essential. Regardless of the opinion of some members of the Judiciary Committee, Nixon told a joint session of Congress, he would do nothing that "impairs the ability of the Presidents of the future to make the great decisions that are so essential to this nation and the world."

I used to listen to statements such as those with deep exasperation. Here was a President daring to tell Congress, in effect, that a lawless Presidency was necessary to America's safety, while a congressional attempt to reassert the rule of law undermined the nation's security.

Fortunately for constitutional government, however, Nixon's conception of a strong Presidency included one prerogative whose exercise was in itself an impeachable offense. Throughout the month of March the President insisted that the need for "confidentiality" allowed him to withhold forty-two tapes that the Judiciary Committee had asked of him. Nixon was claiming the right to limit the constitutional power of Congress to inquire into his impeachment. This was more than Republicans on the committee could afford to tolerate.

"Ambition must be made to counteract ambition," Madison had written in *The Federalist.* On April 11 the Judiciary Committee voted 33 to 3 to subpoena the forty-two tapes, the first subpoena ever issued to a President by a committee of the House. Ambition, at last, was counteracting ambition. This set the stage for one of the most lurid moments in the entire Watergate crisis.

As the deadline for compliance drew near, tension began mounting in the country. Comply or defy? Which would the President do? Open defiance was plainly impeachable. Frank compliance was presumably ruinous. On Monday, April 29, the President went on television to give the American people his answer. Seated in the Oval Office with the American flag behind him, President Nixon calmly announced that he was going to make over to the Judiciary Committee—and the public—"edited transcripts" of the subpoenaed tapes. These transcripts "will tell it all," said the President; there was nothing more that would need to be known for an impeachment inquiry about his conduct. To sharpen the public impression of presidential candor, the transcripts had been distributed among forty-two thick, loose-leaf binders, which were stacked in two-foot-high piles by the President's desk. As if to warn the public not to trust what the newspapers would say about the transcripts, Nixon accused the media of concocting the Watergate crisis out of "rumor, gossip, innuendo," of creating a "vague, general impression of massive wrongdoing, implicating everybody, gaining credibility by its endless repetition."

The next day's *New York Times* pronounced the President's speech "his most powerful Watergate defense since the scandal broke." By May 1 James Reston, the newspaper's most eminent columnist, thought the President had "probably gained considerable support in the country." For a few days it seemed as though the President had pulled off a coup. Republicans on the Judiciary Committee acted accordingly. On the first of May, 16 of the 17 committee Republicans voted against sending the President a note advising him that self-edited transcripts punctured by hundreds upon hundreds of suspicious "inaudibles" and "unintelligibles" were not in compliance with the committee's subpoena. The President, it was said, had succeeded in making impeachment look "partisan" and consequently discreditable.

Nixon with the transcripts of the Watergate tapes, in their forty-two loose-leaf binders.

Not even bowdlerized transcripts, however, could nullify the destructive power of those tapes. They revealed a White House steeped in more sordid conniving than Nixon's worst enemies had imagined. They showed a President advising his aides on how to "stonewall" a grand jury without committing perjury: "You can say, 'I don't remember.' You can say, 'I can't recall. I can't give any answer to that, that I can recall.' " They showed a President urging his counsel to make a "complete report" about Watergate but to "make it very incomplete." They showed a President eager for vengeance against ordinary election opponents. "I want the most comprehensive notes on all those who tried to do us in. . . . They are asking for it and they are going to get it." It showed a President discussing how "national security grounds" might be invoked to justify the Ellsberg burglary should the secret ever come out. "I think we could get by on that," replies Nixon's counsel.

On May 7 Pennsylvania's Hugh Scott, Senate Republican Minority Leader, pronounced the revelations in the transcript "disgusting, shabby, immoral performances." Joseph Alsop, who had long been friendly toward the President in his column, compared the atmosphere in the Oval Office to the "back room of a second-rate advertising agency in a suburb of hell." A week after Nixon's seeming coup Republicans were once again vainly urging him to resign. On May 9 the House Judiciary Committee staff began presenting to the members its massive accumulation of Watergate material. Since the presentation was made behind closed doors, a suspenseful lull fell over the Watergate battleground.

Over the next two months it was obvious that the Judiciary Committee was growing increasingly impatient with the President, who continued to insist that, even in an impeachment proceeding, the "executive must remain the final arbiter of demands on its confidentiality." When Nixon refused to comply in any way with a second committee subpoena, the members voted 28 to 10 to warn him that "your refusals in and of themselves might constitute a ground for impeachment." The "partisanship" of May 1 had faded by May 30.

Undermining these signs of decisiveness was the continued insistence that only direct presidential involvement in a crime would be regarded as an impeachable offense in the House. Congressmen demanded to see the "smoking gun." They wanted to be shown the "hand in the cookie jar." Alexander Hamilton had called impeachment a "National Inquest." Congress seemed bent on restricting it to the purview of a local courthouse. Nobody spoke of the larger issues. As James Reston noted on May 26, one of the most disturbing aspects of Watergate was the silence of the prominent. Where, Reston asked, were the educators, the business leaders, and the elder statesmen to delineate and define the great constitutional issues at stake? When the White House began denouncing the Judiciary Committee as a "lynch mob," virtually nobody rose to the committee's defense.

On July 7 the Sunday edition of the *New York Times* made doleful reading. "The official investigations seem beset by semitropical torpor," the newspaper reported in its weekly news summary. White House attacks on the committee, said the *Times*, were proving effective in the country. In March, 60 percent of those polled by Gallup wanted the President tried in the Senate for his misdeeds. By June the figure had fallen to 50 percent. The movement for impeachment, said the *Times*, was losing its momentum. Nixon, it seemed, had worn out the public capacity for righteous indignation.

Then, on July 19, John Doar, the Democrats' counsel, did what nobody had done before with the enormous, confusing mass of interconnected misdeeds that we labeled "Watergate" for sheer convenience. At a meeting of the Judiciary Committee he compressed the endlessly ramified scandal into a grave and compelling case for impeaching the thirty-seventh President of the United States. He spoke of the President's "enormous crimes." He warned the committee that it dare not look indifferently upon the "terrible deed of subverting the Constitution." He urged the members to consider with favor five broad articles of impeachment, "charges with a grave historic ring," as the *Times* said of them.

In a brief statement, Albert Jenner, the Republicans' counsel, strongly endorsed Doar's recommendations. The Founding Fathers, he reminded committee members, had established a free country and a free Constitution. It was now the committee's momentous duty to determine "whether that country and that Constitution are to be preserved."

How I had yearned for those words during the long, arid months of the "smoking gun" and the "hand in the cookie jar." Members of the committee must have felt the same way, too, for Jenner's words were to leave a profound mark on their final deliberations. That I did not know yet, but what I did know was heartening. The grave maxims of liberty, once invoked, instantly took the measure of meanness and effrontery. When the President's press spokesman, Ron Ziegler, denounced the committee's proceedings as a "kangaroo court," a wave of disgust coursed through Congress. The hour of the Founders had arrived.

The final deliberations of the House Judiciary Committee began on the evening of July 24, when Chairman Peter Rodino gaveled the committee to order before some forty-five million television viewers. The committee made a curious spectacle: thirty-eight strangers strung out on a two-tiered dais, a huge piece of furniture as unfamiliar as the faces of its occupants.

Chairman Rodino made the first opening remarks. His public career had been long, unblemished, and thoroughly undistinguished. Now the representative from Newark, New Jersey, linked hands with the Founding Fathers of our government. "For more than two years, there have been serious allegations, by people of good faith and sound intelligence, that the President, Richard M. Nixon, has committed grave and systematic violations of the Constitution." The framers of our Constitution, said Rodino, had provided an exact measure of a President's responsibilities. It was by the terms of the President's oath of office, prescribed in the Constitution, that the framers intended to hold Presidents "accountable and lawful."

That was to prove the keynote. That evening and over the following days, as each committee member delivered a statement, it became increasingly clear that the broad maxims of constitutional supremacy had taken command of the impeachment inquiry. "We will by this impeachment proceeding be establishing a standard of conduct for the President of the United States which will for all time be a matter of public record," Caldwell Butler, a conservative Virginia Republican, reminded his conservative constituents. "If we fail to impeach . . . we will have left condoned and unpunished an abuse of power totally without justification."

There were still White House loyalists of course; men who kept demanding to see a presidential directive ordering a crime and a documented "tie-in" between Nixon and his henchmen. Set against the great principle of constitutional supremacy, however, this common view was now exposed for what it was: reckless trifling with our ancient liberties. Can the United States permit a President "to escape accountability because he may choose to deal behind closed doors," asked James Mann, a South Carolina conservative. "Can anyone argue," asked George Danielson, a California liberal, "that if a President breaches his oath of office, he should not be removed?" In a voice of unforgettable power and richness, Barbara Jordan, a black legislator from Texas, sounded the grand theme of the committee with particular depth of feeling. Once, she said, the Constitution had excluded people of her race, but that evil had been remedied. "My faith in the Constitution is whole, it is complete, it is total and I am not going to sit here and be an idle spectator to the diminution, the subversion, the destruction of the Constitution."

On July 27 the Judiciary Committee voted 27 to 11 (six Republicans joining all twenty-one Democrats) to impeach Richard Nixon on the grounds that he and his agents had "prevented, obstructed, and impeded the administration of justice" in "violation of his constitutional oath faithfully to execute the office of President of the United States and, to the best of his ability, preserve, protect, and defend the Constitution of the United States, and in violation of his constitutional duty to take care that the laws be faithfully executed."

On July 29 the Judiciary Committee voted 28 to 10 to impeach

Richard Nixon for "violating the constitutional rights of citizens, impairing the due and proper administration of justice and the conduct of lawful inquiries, or contravening the laws governing agencies of the executive branch. . . ." Thus, the illegal wiretaps, the sinister White House spies, the attempted use of the IRS to punish political opponents, the abuse of the CIA, and the break-in at Ellsberg's psychiatrist's office—misconduct hitherto deemed too "vague" for impeachment—now became part of a President's impeachable failure to abide by his constitutional oath to carry out his constitutional duty.

Lastly, on July 30 the Judiciary Committee, hoping to protect some future impeachment inquiry from a repetition of Nixon's defiance, voted 21 to 17 to impeach him for refusing to comply with the committee's subpoenas. "This concludes the work of the committee," Rodino announced at eleven o'clock that night. Armed with the wisdom of the Founders and the authority of America's republican principles, the committee had cut through the smoke screens, the lies, and the pettifogging that had muddled the Watergate crisis for so many months. It had subjected an imperious Presidency to the rule of fundamental law. It had demonstrated by resounding majorities that holding a President accountable is neither "liberal" nor "conservative," neither "Democratic" nor "Republican," but something far more basic to the American republic.

For months the forces of evasion had claimed that impeachment would "tear the country apart." But now the country was more united than it had been in years. The impeachment inquiry had sounded the chords of deepest patriotism, and Americans responded, it seemed to me, with quiet pride in their country and themselves. On Capitol Hill, congressional leaders reported that Nixon's impeachment would command three hundred votes at a minimum. The Senate began preparing for the President's trial. Then, as countless wits remarked, a funny thing happened on the way to the forum.

Back on July 24, the day the Judiciary Committee began its televised deliberations, the Supreme Court had ordered the President to surrender sixty-four taped conversations subpoenaed by the Watergate prosecutor. At the time I had regarded the decision chiefly as an auspicious omen for the evening's proceedings. Only Richard Nixon knew that the Court had signed his death warrant. On August 5 the President announced that he was making public three tapes that "may further damage my case." In fact they destroyed what little was left of it. Recorded six days after the Watergate break-in, they showed the President discussing detailed preparations for the cover-up with his chief of staff, Bob Haldeman. They showed the President and his henchman discussing how to use the CIA to block the FBI, which was coming dangerously close to the White House. "You call them in," says the President. "Good deal," says his aide. In short, the three tapes proved that the President had told nothing but lies about Watergate for twenty-six months. Every one of Nixon's ten Judiciary Committee defenders now announced that he favored Nixon's impeachment.

The President still had one last evasion: on the evening of August 8 he appeared on television to make his last important announcement. "I no longer have a strong enough political base in Congress," said Nixon, doing his best to imply that the resolution of a great constitutional crisis was mere maneuvering for political advantage. "Therefore, I shall resign the Presidency effective at noon tomorrow." He admitted to no wrongdoing. If he had made mistakes of judgment, "they were made in what I believed at the time to be in the best interests of the nation."

On the morning of August 9 the first President ever to resign from office boarded Air Force One and left town. The "system" had worked. But in the watches of the night, who has not asked himself now and then: How would it all have turned out had there been no White House tapes?

Epcot: Walt Disney's World's Fair

ELTING E. MORISON

This essay by Professor Elting E. Morison of the Massachusetts Institute of Technology is both an analysis of the functions performed by world's fairs since the first huge Crystal Palace Exposition of 1851 in London, and a commentary on contemporary American society. These fairs, he notes, have been both summaries of human achievement, particularly in the fields of science and technology, and glimpses into the future. His description of the great Chicago World's Fair of 1893, which he considers a kind of ideal of the form, is particularly interesting. That fair was visited by 14 million people, roughly a quarter of the population of the United States at that time. Clearly, it must have had something to offer everyone, without regard for the individual's interests, education, or social background.

Epcot, the "permanent world's fair," a Walt Disney creation in Florida, strikes Professor Morison differently, despite its evident popularity. He considers it an imitation of reality rather than a display of human ingenuity. In describing why this is so and what it can tell us about the dominant attitudes of our society, Morison makes some extremely sharp criticisms of contemporary values. In addition to his interest in the history of technology, Morison has written Turmoil and Tradition, *a biography of Henry L. Stimson, and edited eight volumes of the letters of Theodore Roosevelt.* ∎

Most of the world must know by now that Epcot is a place built in north-central Florida by the followers of Walt Disney to explain how science and technology fit into the human scheme of things. . . .

. . . Walt Disney was a very interesting man. Except in his view of what the Middle West was like when he was growing up there, he tended to look upon the received tradition or the authorized version of anything as suspect. Whether it was rodents or Snow White, roller coasters or Beethoven, he sought offbeat forms of expression and novel interpretations. Those who have followed him are trained to his perceptions, very sophisticated in their own right as engineers, and almost equally shrewd in their calculation of certain aspects of the American temperament. What they have found to say about the place and meaning of science and technology in this society would certainly be interesting, especially at a time when no one is quite sure in such matters. . . .

. . . Epcot is said to be a kind of world's fair, part of the long history of great expositions that began with the Crystal Palace. It would be interesting, I thought, to see how Epcot fits within this larger story of technological display, and so that is where I'll begin.

In 1912 a convention of nations defined a universal exhibition— what is now called a world's fair—as "embracing the majority of products of human activity." From 1851, the year of the Crystal Palace, to 1904 there were twelve gatherings that seem to fall within this general definition. They took place in London, Paris, Melbourne, Vienna, Philadelphia, Chicago, Buffalo, and St. Louis.

In these cities collections of infinite variety were brought together to reveal what men and women were doing in all fields from art to zoology. But the center of interest increasingly as time went by was what they were doing in industry.

These fairs were summarizing statements, clarifying expressions of what was happening in the industrial civilization that, in the last half of the last century, was developing unevenly around the world. As such they began to serve an unexpected purpose. In the opinion of Sir Henry Cole, who studied the phenomenon, they exerted "a greater influence on the development of tastes, habits and activities of the civilized peoples than the less direct, slower process of natural development of needs following in the train of modern scientific and mechanical progress." In other words these fairs, which brought many products together, suggested new kinds of relationships among disparate parts and brought the whole into clearer focus.

The exposition at Chicago in 1893 is a case in point. It stood on 586 acres spread out along the lake shore. In accordance with suggestions by Frederick Law Olmsted, the plot was formed into a gracious

*The interior of the electrical building at the World's
Columbian Exposition in Chicago, 1893.*

arrangement of land and water. The design and distribution of the
structures set on this ground were determined by a body of architects
that included Daniel Burnham, Stanford White, Richard Hunt, Henry
Van Brunt, and Louis Sullivan. The result of their labors was the White
City. There it stood amid flowering shrubs and blue lagoons, a harmonious composition of great buildings, glittering by day, magical when
illuminated at night. "A great milestone," it was said, "a turning point
in our national life."

What went on in and around these buildings was at least as significant. There was, in fact, something for everybody. Dominating the
Midway Plaisance was the imposing wheel that had been built by
George Washington Ferris to put the Eiffel Tower—the wonder of the
Paris Exposition four years earlier—into satisfying eclipse. Beneath it
lay a diversity of distractions—a Hawaiian volcano in canvas, a squadron of Bedouins, a captive balloon, and a "real Dahomey village of
genuine savages."

In other parts of the grounds there was a massive display of foodstuffs that was later believed to have modified somewhat the dietary

habits of Americans. Nearby was a large exhibition of furniture, which, it was also later said, altered the interior arrangements of American homes for a generation. Elsewhere, in the pavilion for anthropology and ethnology, where the long course of human evolution and the gradual development of regional difference was painstakingly set forth, one could look upon a display of tribal dwellings in which some-one had thought to introduce a full-scale house of a factory worker in upper New York State. And spotted about the grounds were such working enterprises as a logging camp, a weather bureau, an Indian school, a filtration plant, a military hospital, and a Japanese teahouse.

Within this various collectivity the center of gravity was to be found in the buildings devoted to transportation, manufacture, and electric-ity. Here, among the Corliss engines, the dynamos, the machine tools, the locomotives, and turret lathes, one would come in time upon all the instrumentation of the industrial process—much of it doing actual work.

And here also were many indications of how the process itself worked. There were the stages of development in the locomotive from the Stourbridge Lion in 1829 to the newest engine on the New York Central. Along one wall was laid out the linear progression of materials and ideas that Alexander Graham Bell had followed until he arrived at that first telephone he had used to inform Watson he needed him.

The current American performance was therefore ordinarily pre-sented within the context of past activity. It was also put up against what other industrial nations were doing at the time. So there was an opportunity to make comparisons among other processes, procedures, and artifacts. The British, for instance, had an elaborate demonstra-tion of the advances that had been made in ocean liners driven by steam propulsion and the Germans revealed their steady progress in ballistics in their exhibit of rifled cannon—one of which Mr. Krupp thoughtfully offered to Chicago "to protect the port."

And the current American performance was set within yet another and larger context by a series of week-long colloquiums. The authors Hamlin Garland, Charles Dudley Warner, and Thomas Lounsbury, the leading Chaucerian, argued about the role of literary criticism; the philosopher Josiah Royce discussed Kant; and Frederick Jackson Turner revealed for the first time his concept of the significance of the Frontier in American history. Nikola Tesla lectured on induction mo-tors, and when the great physicist Baron Hermann von Helmholtz appeared at one of the sessions, he received the loudest and longest acclamation given to anyone who attended the exposition.

The fair lasted for six months, and one out of every four Americans came to see it. And what did these fourteen million make of it all? The vast installation had been put together by so many different heads and hands representing so many different skills and attitudes that the range for exploration was almost endless and there were, of course, marked divisions of interest among the multitudes. Farmers tended to look at livestock, housewives to study textiles and dining room suites, factory workers to examine machinery, and small boys to stare at genuine savages.

But there was at the time, and has been ever since, a conviction that the whole added up to a good deal more than, something quite different from, the sum of the parts. It was not so much a fair as a kind of clearinghouse for the study of present attainments and future possibilities where you could reach your own conclusions. As such it was a powerful instrument of public instruction. As one shrewd observer said, "Educational game started like rabbits from every building."

The lessons were of various kinds. One had to do with aesthetics—those buildings that Theodore Roosevelt said "make the most beautiful architectural exhibit the world has ever seen." Not everybody thought so, and as in any sound pedagogy, there was a debate that has continued ever since. The prevailing style of the White City was called "freely classical," which left a good deal of room for what one critic called a "duplication of other modes." Lewis Mumford argued it was "a retrogression" from the daring work that John Root and Louis Sullivan had been doing in that same city of Chicago.

But such views, however wise and perceptive, were held by a very small minority. Just by its presence, it was said again and again, the White City excited the "forces making for aesthetic appreciation in America." It awakened the sense of the possibility of beauty—from wherever derived—in one's own surroundings. Quite possibly both sides were right, and no one denied the continuing influence of these remarkable structures on the American consciousness.

And there were the lessons in the nature of the physical plant, the state of the country's industrial development. Father Day sent his son Clarence off to the fair because "it is a great educational opportunity." The boy should spend time, particularly, in the Transport Pavilion, where he would learn the things he needed to know when, at some future time, he took his father's place on the boards of several railroads. More generally, it was said that "by daily practical demonstrations it became apparent even to the minds of very ordinary people" how electricity, "the new force," had been "applied to human service," how steam machines worked, and how the machines that manufactured things operated.

And then there was at least the opening chapter in the harder lesson of what to do with all the new power available, what kind of larger life to build upon the extraordinary mechanical foundations. In this area Oswald Garrison Villard found that the fair "as an educational institution was a tremendous success." "Every kind of civic and social endeavor was stimulated by that exhibition," he concluded.

Henry Adams carried the point somewhat further. He was roused from twenty years of torpor by the "education" that "ran riot in Chicago." Men who had never laid a hand on a lever, who had never touched a battery, who could not tell an erg from an ampere, after studying the exhibits "had no choice but to sit down on the steps beneath Richard Hunt's dome and brood as they had never brooded before." And on those steps Adams started his remarkable fifteen-year search for those principles by which the extraordinary forces in science and engineering could be wisely organized in the interests of human society.

So it was quite a fair. Since that time it has been followed by others at such places as London, St. Louis, Brussels, Chicago again, San Francisco, and New York. And now in Florida there is being created an arresting mutation in the long sequence: something thought of by its creators as a continuing or permanent world's fair.

It didn't start out that way. In the early sixties Walt Disney, impressed by the success of his Disneyland in California, decided to build a similar installation in Florida that would be called the Walt Disney Magic Kingdom.

He intended to surround it with Epcot, an unwieldy acronym for Experimental Prototype Community of Tomorrow. This scheme was the product of his conviction that American cities were going to pieces under the pressure of modern conditions. Disney was determined to make Epcot a demonstration of how an urban community of twenty thousand permanent residents—a clean, organized, efficient, and satisfying community—could be built on the foundation of modern technology. Since, as he well knew, the technology was always changing, Epcot itself would always be "in a state of becoming, a living blueprint of the future." In the planning and construction of this small city, he intended to engage "the best thinking" of American industry.

It was his most ambitious, serious, and interesting enterprise. As a beginning he bought 27,400 acres (43 square miles) in the dull landscape near Orlando. Then, in 1966, suddenly and unexpectedly, he died. One of the things he left behind him was W(alter) E(lias) D(isney) Enterprises, an organization that through the years had learned to give very precise expression to the perceptions, ideas, prejudices, insights, and aesthetic judgments of Walt Disney. WED Enterprises proceeded in the course of the last decade to build on the site the Walt Disney Magic Kingdom. It then turned its attention to Epcot.

As it stands today, Epcot is a modification of the original intent. If not exactly a universal exhibition, it does look a good deal like the more recent versions of a world's fair. In an area called Future World,

The Spaceship Earth dome at Epcot looms above an artful re-creation of an eighteenth-century French chateau.

constituent elements of industry—transport, communications, energy, agriculture—are displayed in pavilions shaped in geometric forms: spheres, circles, pyramids, and rectangles. They are built of glass, metal, and plastic, and they glisten in the sun.

In a second area, World Showcase, there is a kind of architectural counterpoint. Here, in careful replication, are streets, squares, piazzas, lanes, and platzes derived from other countries in other times. Here also are distinguishing landmarks—Eiffel Tower, Temple of Heaven, campanile, pagoda. These provide an engaging surround for a Georgian edifice, which, in a kind of structural bloat, appears to include embellishments taken from Independence Hall, Williamsburg, Mount Vernon, and the Harvard House Plan. In this area the nations purvey in pub, bierstube, café, ristorante, and numerous small shops their identifying food, drink, and consumer goods.

The whole—Future World and World Showcase—is organized within an attractive scheme of promenades, paths, waterways, and plantings. All elements are brought together in a limited space by a masterly manipulation of scale and proportion that produces a sense of magnificent sizes and distances. It is quite an emplacement.

It is also, from top to bottom and from edge to edge, absolutely clean. Every Disney land and world is built on the cultural premise that a decent community abhors even one used plastic cup or a single cigarette butt. At Epcot the premise has the force of natural law. People don't drop things or throw them away and leave them lying there. They dispose of them in the available, appropriate containers.

There are at any given time a great many of these people or, in the local idiom, guests. In continuing streams they are processed through channels by computer-controlled devices—an elevated monorail, groups of theater seats that convert into vehicles holding ninety-seven passengers, a "linear induction-powered" people mover, and countless small cars that transport observers past the intricately contrived exhibits.

If not all is as new as it is made to seem (there were six miles of electric-powered elevated railway at Chicago in 1893 and also a moving sidewalk), it is still an impressive demonstration of how to produce a carefully ordered and directed flow out of what Herbert Hoover called the "fluidity of the human particle." And when the machinery does not serve, the continuing streams are ingeniously reduced to carefully controlled, slowly moving, short, pedestrian segments that damp down the sensation of standing in line. In part this is because of the system and in part also because the human particle, as in the matter of cleanliness, accepts the system as something imposed by the nature of that world. Even at a popcorn cart, six people wait in a quiet line.

The continuing crowds are drawn to Epcot, in the words of the Disney group, by a "unique" conception in which "entertainment will be a highly visible attraction," but the "underlying educational value of Future World is its important contribution." In earlier Disney installations there had always been some sort of intent to educate, if not so deep as a well, at least as broad as a barn door. Amid the gnomes, the tree houses, the shop for Disney merchandise, and the runaway train ride, one finds the detailed and faithful reconstruction of Main Street as it was a hundred years ago or the demonstration (if one knew enough to separate the mermaid from the algae and the fish) of what life beneath the surface of the sea was like.

But at Epcot the intent to educate is more consciously assumed. The pedagogical object, broadly stated, is "to create a gala atmosphere that transforms formidable technology into something we can understand and look forward to enjoying."

The principal tool of instruction is the ride. Using the means previously developed in earlier lands, worlds, and kingdoms, trips are taken through several areas of technology—transport, energy, communications, agriculture, and within the next year "The Living Seas," and "Horizons," or the shape of things to come. These rides have certain common characteristics. There is the movement by vehicles through tunnels that at intervals open out to reveal striking scenes that are carefully contrived in background and are populated by Audio-Animatronics. This last is an art form, refined over the years, in which plastic, wire, paint, and electronic devices are brought together into a system that looks and acts and sounds as much like a living thing as a living thing does. Indeed, these artifacts disturbingly seem, in the words of Lewis Carroll, "as large as life" and within the limits of their programs, "twice as natural."

In the literature the rides are variously described as dazzling, wacky, psychedelic, and refreshingly zany. In their multiplying scenes, sharply framed by enclosed space, vividly rendered in precise detail, set on beds of flowering prose, wrapped in music, laced with light, and, when appropriate, penetrated by supporting smells, they are designed to "engulf us in the wonders of modern science and technology."

The principle of engulfment has been applied in different ways in the Disney universe for many years. It puts the pressure into the obligation to keep the place clean. It is the primary means through which the Magic Kingdom brings off its enchantments. Given its demonstrated power to drench, condition, and excite in gala atmospheres, what can it do to educate, to transform formidable technology into something understood?

In any engulfment there is an overwhelming gross effect. Here the sum of the rides and their supporting exhibitions put several points within the reach of even the laggard schoolboy: Men for a long time have made machines to extend their competence and improve their lot; as a result the world today is filled with machines that determine many of the conditions within which we live; in the future (which is just around the next corner in any ride you take), there will be many more machines widening the range of what can be done, adding far more excitement and increasing the choices of what to do.

That these points can be variously interpreted is one of the inevitable complications of pedagogy. As realized at Epcot, they have been said by some recent observers to constitute a "tribute to human ingenuity" or an "extraordinary encomium to a capitalist future" or something "to help make possible the survival of civilization." Whatever the angle of observation, however interpreted, the desired points have been put across.

But, as in any engulfment, the gross impression is attended by subsidiary responses, side effects, secondary sensations, and loose ends. It is difficult to sort them out and identify them even after the event. They appear in no natural order, and they can be arranged in no reasonable progression of significance. What follows, therefore, is not a sequential narrative, but simply a set of notes and various reflections.

The rides, taken all together, are designed to give some feeling for the process of technological development from the start into the probable future. They present some telling and instructive occasions: a brief, quite straightforward, illustrated statement on the nature of energy in its various forms; a demonstration of the way farming has changed through the mechanization of agriculture; a vivid description of how oil is brought from its far-flung sources to the consumer.

But the conditions work against converting these episodes or any of the others into a sense of developing process or consistent narrative. For one thing, there is the rate of transit—the diverse scenes keep coming at you or sliding by—and it's hard to take it all in. For another thing, there is the size of the subject matter—four hundred centuries in one case, a billion years in another—to get exposed to in fifteen minutes. These may be thought of as practical limitations imposed on the pedagogical exercise.

The instruction is further complicated by the views of those who put the rides together. The passage of time is subject to varying shifts of mood. What happened in the past is understood to be fairly funny—or in the words of one admiring commentator, "charmingly droll." The present is earnest and quite remarkable. And the future is exhilarating—singularly free of irregular or imperfect forms in its conjugation. Such varying perspectives alter the significance—indeed the very nature—of the several stages of the developing process.

And then there is the question of what's put in and what's left out—always a problem in any general survey and especially difficult when the line of sight extends across an aeon. Here the age of flight begins with Mona Lisa stamping her foot as Leonardo turns from his easel to look at a primitive mock-up of a flying machine and continues with an eighteenth-century balloon filled with a cargo of pigs and goats. But there is no attempt to represent the more powerful agencies at work in the development of such aircraft as the DC-3 or 707.

Given the present state of things, it is useful to consider fossil fuels at some length, starting from an extended view of dinosaurs at work and play in former times. But in any study of energy it would also be useful to give more than the most casual mention of the energy in the atom.

And more generally, in the sum of all the rides from which one is supposed to derive some sense of technological development, where is steam? It appears when bandits hold up a train in the Old West but never as the prime mover that laid the foundation for all industrial advance and for many technological systems.

These lapses may suggest the difficulty of establishing a reasonable balance in any large-scale presentation. They may also suggest the special interest of WED Enterprises and those corporations that joined it in this exercise. They may further suggest the difficulty in establishing the sense of causality and process in any extended progression by presenting, however selected, a few isolated occasions.

Those who made Epcot are skilled in modern instrumentation and comfortable with its amazing potential. If they have not yet found a *deus ex machina,* they have already extracted a Thomas Jefferson and a Mark Twain from the Audio-Animatronics. And through the years they have developed sophisticated technical surroundings that have operated with benign effect on the multitudes that entered them. They would like to make other people feel equally "at home with the wonders of technology." As one means to this end they have surrounded the machines at Epcot with a festival mood.

There is the breathtaking—a simulated pell-mell descent in a snowmobile. There is the folksy—an articulate robot, a graduate of Solid State, who kids the customers. There is the astounding—a three-dimensional movie in which, if memory serves, a horse seems to reach out of the screen to crop your hair. And there is the soothing, jejune, if not really apposite message, such as the voice that affirms and reaffirms throughout the passage through the World of Motion that "it's fun to be free."

The aim to make people feel comfortable with the kind of world they have to live in is certainly commendable. The occasional penultimate assertion that people in the technological future must understand, choose, and wisely manage is certainly to the point. And the reminder that machinery has done a good deal to improve the lot of us on Spaceship Earth is well taken.

Still, even the wonders of technology are, like everything else,

An Audio-Animatronic figure of a violinist, one of many such figures appearing in the exhibits at Epcot.

subject to the claims of reality. And it turns out to be very difficult to make that hard point by the means that have served so well in the Magic Kingdom, where not only disbelief but the laws of nature and the facts of life are momentarily suspended.

For instance, there is a robot who has been doing time on an assembly line. With the assistance of a bird, he gets into show business and, having learned to claim his just desserts, winds up conducting a symphony orchestra. This is about as close as one gets to life on the shop floor, job retraining, or the technological unemployment of the non-Audio-Animatronic worker.

One gets no closer to the neutralizing of acid rain, the disposal of toxic waste, the changing character of work, the calculation of acceptable risk in the building of power plants, the question of how and why the Japanese make more efficient use of some of their industrial installations than the United States does, the question of how to understand and choose whether to put an MX in a silo or on a freight car or in a dense pack or to build it at all. Or the larger, longer question of how far human responses can be trimmed and fitted into the rigidities of technical systems before there is not as much fun as there used to be.

As an educational device the gala atmosphere is a good deal like those temporary villages Potemkin built to persuade the empress, on her progress through the south, that things were going her way.

Throughout the grounds there are displays of one kind or another that, if not coigns of silence fit for brooding, are places where customers are on their own and can do whatever they want to. There are a good many things to do: look at an attractive collection of windmills; press a button on a scaffolding of wire and glass that will reveal by the extent of its illumination the amount of fossil fuel still available in the various deposits around the world; turn a crank that will excite a light bulb and explain how many hours of cranking would produce a dollar's worth of electricity. Over in the World Showcase there is a handsome collection of Chinese art and in the same building an absolutely stunning movie, spread around a 360-degree screen, of the landscape of China. Farther on, in the German quarter, there are porcelain wares and stuffed animals for sale, and in the English shops Pringle sweaters and Royal Doulton chinaware.

There are computer terminals everywhere, usually in the form of television screens on which there are illuminated spots that can be touched with a finger to produce messages containing a great many different kinds of information. One is programed with material from the 1980 census; another with data on cities and vacation spots around the world; a third with the availability of reservations at the restaurants in World Showcase, and so on and so on. Then there are numbers games and problem-solving exercises. Anyone can play, and everyone is continually encouraged to have this "hands-on" experience. Those who do so seem, more often than not, to be the young, in spite of all the obvious effort to make the programs, as they say in the trade, "user friendly" for those of every age.

It may be true, as my wife says, that the only piece of knowledge every man, woman, and child in this country now hold in common is Mickey Mouse. It is at least arguable that the art form Walt Disney developed gets through in some way to more Americans than any other that has been devised. And he may have taken us about as far along the road to some sort of wonderment as we are prepared to go.

The content of Disney's art form was shaped, of course, by a well-defined and particular view of things, but its structure was determined by a deep intuitive feeling for engineering and by the kind of resourcefulness and precision required to make engineering constructions serve the end in view. It seems at least probable, therefore, that Walt Disney first thought of Epcot as an actual experiment in the interactions between men and machines because he knew he could not teach people to understand technology (and how to handle it) by the spectacular means he had devised to divert them.

For instance, those early animations that became a universal model derived primarily from his long, hard, painstaking work. As did all his later constructions. Though not much of an inventor, he understood and shrewdly used the system of research and development that invention has become. The point of that system is to get the intuitive perception of the possible new connections among things within the firmer discipline of logical progression. There is a good deal of trial and error in it, but it makes for a more orderly and predictable course, a more organized momentum toward novelty. By this process the imaginative impulse is informed, steadied, and directed by the workings of the mind. This system is now the intellectual mainspring in technological movement.

Explaining this process, getting across its place in technological advance, is hard enough to do by any means, even if life depends upon it. Some companies, to be sure, have understood research and development well enough to make millions; but a good many others have failed or gotten lost in conglomeration because they failed to understand. At Epcot the subject is dealt with only through the stimulation of the imaginative impulse.

There is a ride, not available when I was there, but sufficiently described in the literature, which passes through a curiosity shop that contains things like a box of childish delight, a diving bell for deep thoughts, and an Imaginometer. In such surroundings a man named Dreamfinder and a dragon called Figment take sounds, "glows," shapes, and colors out of the atmosphere and mix them into new combinations. From there one moves to the Image Works, already in operation during my trip, where visitors can mix their own colors, shapes, and sounds by touch of finger, tone of voice, and tread of foot. It is said to be a "fun-house experience," and it is to invention, research, and development as any fun house is to Bell Laboratories.

If it is hard to explain how an idea in science is taken up and applied through engineering to come out at the other end as a plastic cup or a communications satellite, it is at least as hard to explain how the machinery works. All you had to do to understand a waterwheel was to look at it. A steam engine exposed, quite dramatically, its *modus operandi* and how it distributed its energy through belts and shafting to do work. But as Henry Adams discovered in the Gallery of Machines at Paris in 1900, a dynamo is an "occult mechanism." Ever since that time things have moved through the servomechanism, reactor, and computer to the increasingly occult. And the technical systems developed to organize the workings of the machinery have become steadily more abstract and arcane.

This tends to put increased distance between people and their machines and the work machines do. Henry Adams in the presence of the dynamo decided that the best way to deal with it was to pray to it. At Epcot the solution is to dramatize, and the means of dramatization—the vivid constructs of wire, paint, and plastic; the garish orchestrations in sound and color; the absolutely exact personification of Audio-Animatronics—produce such effective translations from the real that they acquire their own actuality.

There is more here than the entertaining prestidigitation of a wonderland or magic kingdom. It becomes a question of figuring out which side of the looking glass one is on. Three days of careful observation, for instance, were required to determine that the wading birds across the lagoon were living birds. Coming upon an actual gray iron bucket of a steam shovel amid the simulacra of an energy exhibit was like finding a live foal in a mare's nest. And there was the shock of nonrecognition at the end of the ride through the fabrications of The Land when growing vegetables appeared, which, it was said, one could "see, touch, feel, and even *eat.*"

Such confusion between the real and the apparent is imposing testimony to the skills of WED Enterprises. It also suggests what can happen when the circumstances of experience are set not so much by natural conditions as by the expanding energy in technology. One may wonder, amid the dazzling demonstrations, about what things may become if the machinery gets so far out ahead that it can impose the logic of its structure, the explicitness of its organization, and the uniformity of its operations on the ordinary course of human events.

On so large a speculation as this, as on so limited a consideration as what to do with acid rain, the message from Epcot is: Not to worry. The record as presented shows that machinery always does good (even the first traffic jam is blamed on a horse) and indicates that it will soon do better—if you can make the moon shot, you will certainly soon colonize outer space.

But anyone looking around today has to do some worrying and must come to recognize that the understanding and good sense required to manage the marvelous powers of technology wisely cannot be obtained solely by prayer or dramatic productions. That is why one may regret that Epcot did not develop in accordance with its original intent. The real problem is not to find out what the machinery can do—it can do almost anything; it is what we will do with the machinery.

An experimental prototype community could serve as a vocational school in this subject, a place where the potential in the technology could be investigated and learned about through trial and error. In such a place Walt Disney thought it would be possible to discover what given quantities and what unknowns had to be worked into the equation for future successful community living—what it might take, through the proper integration of technical efficiencies, social concern, and emotional satisfaction, to build a new sort of city on a hill.

It would have been very hard to do. There might not have been much money in it. He would have found it almost impossible to keep his hands off it. And it might have been useful and, even, very important.

Epilogue

America: Experiment or Destiny?

ARTHUR M. SCHLESINGER, JR.

It is fitting that we end this excursion through American history with a question. History leads to a present we can never wholly understand and points to a future we can discern only in barest outline. Serious historians, however, never attempt to predict the future and deal with contemporary affairs rarely and usually very tentatively. Therefore, although Professor Arthur M. Schlesinger, Jr., of the City University of New York, has been a maker of history as a close adviser to President John F. Kennedy and a recorder of very recent events—as in his book A Thousand Days—*he has in this article asked a question about the past—about "the meaning of the American experience." Such broadgauged, interpretive works as this are the most difficult historians can attempt, and it takes one of Schlesinger's intellectual powers to carry off the task successfully. Readers of such efforts, however, need not possess the depth of knowledge that goes into writing them in order to appreciate and profit from them. Ask yourself after reading the following essay and thinking about its relation to the other essays in the collection: "What is the meaning of the American experience?"*

Nearly two centuries after Crèvecoeur propounded his notorious question—"What then is the American, this new man?"—Vine Deloria, Jr., an American Indian writing in the Bicentennial year on the subject "The North Americans" for *Crisis,* a magazine directed to American blacks, concluded: "No one really knows at the present time what America really is." Surely few observers were more entitled to wonder at the continuing mystery than those who could accurately claim the designation Original American. Surely no audience had more right to share the bafflement than one made up of descendants of slaves.

But we are all baffled by the meaning of the American experience. All any of us can do is descry a figure in the carpet—realizing as we do that contemporary preoccupations define our own definitions. My effort here will be to suggest two themes that seem to me to have subsisted in subtle counterpoint since the time when English-speaking white men first began the invasion of America. Both have dwelt within the American mind and struggled for its possession through the course of our history. Their competition will doubtless continue for the rest of the life of the nation. This essay aims to present these rival themes and to propose some points about the relationship between the divergent outlooks and the health of the republic.

I will call one theme the tradition and the other the countertradition, thereby betraying at once my own bias. The tradition, as I prefer to style it, sprang initially from historic Christianity as mediated by Augustine and Calvin. The Calvinist ethos was suffused with convictions of the depravity of man, of the awful precariousness of human existence, of the vanity of mortals under the judgment of a pitiless and wrathful deity. Harriet Beecher Stowe recalled the atmosphere in *Oldtown Folks:* "The underlying foundation of life . . . in New England, was one of profound, unutterable, and therefore unuttered, melancholy, which regarded human existence itself as a ghastly risk, and, in the case of the vast majority of human beings, an inconceivable misfortune."

So terrible a sense of the nakedness of the human condition turned all of life into an unending and implacable process of testing. "We must look upon our selves," said William Stoughton, the chief justice of the court that condemned the Salem witches, "as under a *solemn divine Probation;* it hath been and it is a Probation-time, even to this whole People. . . ." So had it been at all times for all people. Most had failed the test. Were the American colonists immune to the universal law?

In the Calvinist view, all secular communities were finite and problematic; all flourished and all decayed; all had a beginning and an end. For Christians this idea had its *locus classicus* in the attempt to solve the problem of the decline and fall of Rome—a problem that transfixed the

serious historical minds of the West. . . . By the time the revolutionaries
came to Philadelphia in 1776, the flames of Calvinism were already
burning low. Hell was dwindling into an epithet. Still, for the fathers
of the republic as for the fathers of the church, the history of Rome
remained the example from which they thought to learn the most
about human possibilities.

From different premises, Calvinists and classicists reached the same
conclusion about the fragility of human striving. Antiquity haunted the
Federal imagination. The Founding Fathers had embarked on a singular adventure—the adventure of a *republic*. "The Roman republic,"
Alexander Hamilton wrote in the *Federalist*, "attained to the pinnacle
of human greatness." In this conviction the first generation of the
American republic designed its buildings, wrote its epics, named the
upper chamber of its legislature, signed its greatest political treatise
"Publius," sculpted its heroes in togas, organized the Society of the
Cincinnati, and instructed the young. There was plausibility in the
parallel. There was also warning. For the grandeur that was Rome had
come to an inglorious end. Could the United States of America hope
to do better?

The Founding Fathers passionately ransacked the classical historians for ways to escape the classical fate. But the classical indoctrination
reinforced the Calvinist judgment that this was probation-time for
America. For the history of antiquity did not teach the inevitability of
progress. It proved rather the perishability of republics, the subversion
of virtue by power and luxury, the transience of glory, the mutability
of human affairs. The apprehension of the mortality of states was a
vital element in the sensibility of Philadelphia in 1787. Not only was
man vulnerable through his propensity to sin, but republics were vulnerable through their propensity to corruption. The dread of corruption, as Professor Bernard Bailyn has demonstrated, was readily imported from England to the colonies. History showed that, in the
unceasing contest between corruption and virtue, corruption had always—at least up to 1776—triumphed.

The Founding Fathers had an intense conviction of the improbabil-
ity of their undertaking. Such assets as they possessed came in their
view from geographical and demographic advantage, not from divine
intercession. Benjamin Franklin ascribed the inevitability of American
independence to such mundane factors as population increase and
vacant lands, not to providential design. But even these assets could
not be counted on to prevail against history and human nature.

Hamilton said in the New York ratifying convention, "The tendency of things will be to depart from the republican standard. This
is the real disposition of human nature." If Hamilton be discounted as
a temperamental pessimist or a disaffected adventurer, his great adver-

saries were not always more sanguine about the republic's future. "Commerce, luxury, and avarice have destroyed every republican government," Adams wrote Benjamin Rush in 1808. ". . . We mortals cannot work miracles; we struggle in vain against the constitution and course of nature." "I tremble for my country," Jefferson had said in the 1780's, "when I reflect that God is just." Though he was trembling at this point—rightly and presciently—over the problem of slavery, he also trembled chronically in the nineties over the unlikely prospect of "monarchy." In 1798 he saw the Alien and Sedition Acts as tending to drive the states "into revolution and blood, and [to] furnish new calumnies against republican government, and new pretexts for those who wish it to be believed, that man cannot be governed but by a rod of iron."

This pervasive self-doubt, this urgent sense of the precariousness of the national existence, was no doubt nourished by European assessments of the American prospect. For eminent and influential Europeans regarded the New World, not as an idyl of Lockean felicity—"in the beginning, all the world was America"—but as a disgusting scene of degeneracy and impotence.

In the middle of the eighteenth century, the famous Buffon lent the weight of scientific authority to the proposition that life in the Western Hemisphere was consigned to biological inferiority. American animals were smaller and weaker; European animals shrank when transported across the Atlantic, except, Buffon specified, for the fortunate pig. As for the natives of the fallen continent, they too were small and weak, passive and backward.

No one made this case more irritatingly and perseveringly than Abbé Raynal in France. His much-reprinted work, *Philosophical and Political History of the Settlements and of the Commerce of Europeans in the Two Indies,* first published in 1770, explained how European innocence was under siege by American depravity. America, Raynal wrote, had "poured all the sources of corruption on Europe." The search for American riches brutalized the European intruder. The climate and soil of America caused the European species, human as well as animal, to deteriorate. "The men have less strength and less courage . . . and are but little susceptible of the lively and powerful sentiment of love"—a comment that perhaps revealed Raynal in the end more as a Frenchman than as an abbé.

The Founding Fathers were highly sensitive to the proposition that America was a mistake. Franklin, who thought Raynal an "ill-informed and evil-minded Writer," once endured a monologue by the diminutive abbé on the inferiority of the Americans at his own dinner table in Paris. "Let us try this question by the fact before us," said Franklin, calling on his guests to stand up and measure themselves back to back.

"There was not one American present," wrote Jefferson, who was also there, "who could not have tost out of the Windows any one or two of the rest of the Company."

Though the Founders were both indignant and effective in their rebuttal, the nature of the attack could hardly have increased their confidence in the future of their adventure. The European doubt, along with the Calvinist judgment and the classical pessimism, made them acutely aware of the chanciness of an extraordinary enterprise. From the fate of the Greek city-states and the fall of the Roman Empire, they drew somber conclusions about the prospects of the American republic. They had no illusions about the inviolability of America to history, nor about the perfectibility of man, Americans or others. The Constitution, James Bryce has well said, was "the work of men who believed in original sin, and were resolved to leave open for transgressors no door which they could possibly shut."

We have all applied the phrase "end of innocence" to one or another stage of American history. This is surely an amiable flourish—or a pernicious delusion. No people who systematically enslaved black men and killed red men could be innocent. No people reared on Calvin and Tacitus, on Jonathan Edwards and the *Federalist,* could be innocent. No nation founded on invasion, conquest, and slaughter could be innocent. No state established by revolution and thereafter rent by civil war could be innocent. The Constitution was hardly the product of immaculate conception. The Founding Fathers were not a band of saints. They were brave and imperturbable realists who committed themselves, in defiance of the available lessons of history and theology, to a monumental gamble.

This is why Hamilton, in the third sentence of the first *Federalist,* formulated the issue as he did. The American people, he wrote, had the opportunity "by their conduct and example, to decide the important question, whether societies of men are really capable or not of establishing good government from reflection and choice, or whether they are forever destined to depend for their political constitutions on accident and force." So Washington defined it in his first Inaugural Address: "The preservation of the sacred fire of liberty and the destiny of the republican model of government are justly considered, perhaps, as *deeply,* as *finally,* staked on the experiment intrusted to the hands of the American people." The Founding Fathers saw the American republic not as a consecration but as the test against history of a hypothesis.

Washington's early successors, with mingled anxiety and hope, reported on the experiment's fortunes. In his last message to Congress, James Madison permitted himself "the proud reflection that the American people have reached in safety and success their fortieth year as an independent nation." "Our institutions," said James Monroe in his last message, "form an important epoch in the history of the civilized world. On their preservation and in their utmost purity everything will depend." Washington, said Andrew Jackson in his own Farewell Address, regarded the Constitution "as an experiment" and "was prepared to lay down his life, if necessary, to secure to it a full and a fair trial. The trial has been made. It has succeeded beyond the proudest hopes of those who framed it." "The present year," Martin Van Buren said in 1838, "closes the first half century of our Federal institutions. . . . It was reserved for the American Union to test the advantages of a government entirely dependent on the continual exercise of the popular will." "After an existence of near three-fourths of a century as a free and independent Republic," said Polk in the next decade, "the problem no longer remains to be solved whether man is capable of self-government." Sixty years after the Constitution, Zachary Taylor pronounced the United States of America "the most stable and permanent Government on earth."

How is one to account for this rising optimism? It was partly a tribute, reasonable enough, to survival. It was partly the spread-eagleism and vainglory congenial to a youthful nationalism. It was no doubt also in part admonitory exhortation, for the Presidents of the middle period must have known in their bones that the American experiment was confronting its fiercest internal trial. No one understood more profoundly the chanciness of the adventure than the young man who spoke in 1838 on "The Perpetuation of our Political Institutions" before the Young Men's Lyceum of Springfield, Illinois. Over most of the first half century, Abraham Lincoln said, America had been felt "to be an undecided experiment; now, it is understood to be a successful one." But success contained its own perils; "with the catching, end the pleasures of the chase." As the memory of the Revolution receded, the pillars of the temple of liberty were crumbling away. "That temple must fall, unless we . . . supply their places with other pillars, hewn from the solid quarry of sober reason." The conviction of the incertitude of life informed his Presidency—and explained its greatness. His first message to Congress asked whether all republics had an "inherent and fatal weakness." At the Gettysburg cemetery he described the great civil war as "testing" whether any nation conceived in liberty and dedicated to the proposition that all men are created equal "can long endure."

This was, then, a dominant theme of the early republic—the idea of America as an experiment, undertaken in defiance of history, fraught with risk, problematic in outcome. But a countertradition was also emerging—and, as the mounting presidential optimism suggests, with accumulating momentum. The countertradition, too, had its roots in the Calvinist ethos.

Historic Christianity embraced two divergent thoughts: that all people were immediate unto God; and that some were more immediate than others. At first, Calvin had written in the *Institutes,* God "chose the Jews as his very own flock." Then, with what Edwards called "the abolishing of the *Jewish dispensation,*" the wall was "broken down to make way for the more extensive success of the gospel." The chosen people thereafter were the elect as against the reprobate. The age that sent the Calvinists to New England also saw a revival of the primitive millennialism of the first century. The New Englanders felt they had been called from hearth and home to endure unimaginable rigor and ordeal in a dangerous land; so they supposed someone of importance had called them, and for important reasons. "God hath convenanted with his people," said Increase Mather, "that sanctified afflictions shall be their portion. . . . *Without doubt, the Lord Jesus hath a peculiar respect unto this place, and for this people.*"

It was not only that they were, in Winthrop's words, as a City upon a Hill, with the eyes of all people upon them. It was that they had been despatched to New England, as Edward Johnson said, by a Wonder-working Providence because "this is the place where the Lord will create a new Heaven, and a new Earth." The "Lord Christ" intended "to make his *New England* Souldiers the very wonder of this Age." The fact that God had withheld America so long—until the Reformation purified the church, until the invention of printing spread the Bible among the people—argued that He had been preparing it for some ultimate manifestation of His grace. God, said Winthrop, having "smitten all the other Churches before our eyes," had reserved America for those whom He meant *"to save out of this generall callamitie,"* as he had once sent the ark to save Noah. The new land was certainly a part, perhaps the climax, of redemptive history; America was divine prophecy fulfilled.

The achievement of independence gave new status to this theory. The Reverend Timothy Dwight, Jonathan Edwards' grandson, called Americans "this chosen race." "God's mercies to New England," wrote Harriet Beecher Stowe, daughter of one minister, wife of another, foreshadowed "the glorious future of the United States . . . commissioned to bear the light of liberty and religion through all the earth and to bring in the great milliennial day, when wars should cease and the whole world, released from the thralldom of evil, should rejoice in the light of the Lord." "We Americans," wrote the youthful Herman Melville, "are the peculiar, chosen people—the Israel of our time; we bear the ark of the liberties of the world. . . . Long enough have we been skeptics with regard to ourselves, and doubted whether, indeed, the political Messiah had come. But he has come in *us.*"

The belief that Americans were a chosen people did not imply a sure and tranquil journey to salvation. As the Bible made amply clear, chosen people underwent the harshest trials and assumed the most grievous burdens. The rival propositions—America as experiment, America as destiny—thus shared a belief in the process of testing. But one proposition tested works; the other, faith. So Lincoln and Mrs. Stowe agreed from different standpoints in seeing the Civil War as the climactic test. Northern victory, however, strengthened the conviction of providential appointment. "Now that God has smitten slavery unto death," Mrs. Stowe's brother Edward wrote in 1865, "he has opened the way for the redemption and sanctification of our whole social system."

It was a short step from the Social Gospel at home to Americans carrying the Social Gospel to the world. In 1898 the Reverend Alexander Blackburn, who had been wounded at Chickamauga, spoke of "the imperialism of righteousness"; and from Blackburn to the messianic demagoguery of Albert J. Beveridge was only another short step: "God has not been preparing the English-speaking and Teutonic peoples for a thousand years for nothing but vain and idle self-contemplation. . . . And of all our race He has marked the American people as His chosen nation to finally lead in the regeneration of the world."

So the impression developed that in the United States of America the Almighty had contrived a nation unique in its virtue and magnanimity, exempt from the motives that governed all other states. "America is the only idealistic nation in the world," said Woodrow Wilson on his pilgrimage to the West in 1919. ". . . The heart of this people is pure. The heart of this people is true. . . . It is the great idealistic force of history. . . . I, for one, believe more profoundly than in anything else human in the destiny of the United States. I believe that she has a spiritual energy in her which no other nation can contribute to the liberation of mankind. . . ."

In another forty years the theory of America as the savior of the world received the furious imprimature of John Foster Dulles, another Presbyterian elder, and from there roared on to the horrors of Vietnam. So the hallucination brought the republic from the original idea of America as exemplary experiment to the recent idea of America as mankind's designated judge, jury, and executioner. Nor are we yet absolutely clear that the victor in the Bicentennial election may not believe that nations, like Presidents, may be born again.

Why did the conviction of the corruptibility of men and the vulnerability of states—and the consequent idea of America as experiment —give way to the myth of innocence and the delusion of a sacred mission and a sanctified destiny? The original conviction was rooted in realistic conceptions of history and of human nature—conceptions that waned as the republic prospered. The intense historical-mindedness of the first generation did not endure. "The Past," Melville said in *White Jacket,* "is dead, and has no resurrection; but the Future is endowed with such a life that it lives to us even in anticipation." The new nation was largely populated by people torn from, fleeing from, or in revolt against their own histories. "Probably no other civilised nation," said the *Democratic Review* in 1842, "has . . . so completely thrown off its allegiance to the past as the American."

We find ourselves now, for all the show-business clatter of the Bicentennial celebrations, an essentially historyless people. Businessmen agree with the elder Henry Ford that history is bunk. The young no longer study history. Intellectuals turn their backs on history in the enthusiasm for the ahistorical behavioral "sciences." As the American historical consciousness has thinned out, the messianic hope has flowed into the vacuum. Experiment has given ground to destiny as the premise of national life.

So the theory of the elect nation, the redeemer nation, the happy empire of perfect wisdom and perfect virtue, almost became the official creed. Yet, while the countertradition prospered, the tradition did not quite expire. Some continued to regard it all as the deceitful dream of a golden age, wondering perhaps why the Almighty should have chosen the Americans. "The Almighty," Lincoln insisted at his second Inaugural, "has His own purposes." He clearly knew what he was saying, because he wrote soon thereafter to a fellow ironist, Thurlow Weed: "Men are not flattered by being shown that there has been a difference of purpose between the Almighty and them. To deny it, however . . . is to deny that there is a God governing the world."

After the war, Walt Whitman, once the supreme poet of democratic faith, suddenly perceived a dark and threatening future. The experiment was in jeopardy. These States no longer a sure thing, were caught up in a "battle advancing, retreating, between democracy's convictions, aspirations, and the people's crudeness, vice, caprices." America, Whitman apprehended, might well "prove the most tremendous failure of time." " 'Tis a wild democracy," Emerson said in his last public address; "the riot of mediocrities and dishonesties and fudges." A fourth generation of Adamses raised particularly keen doubts whether Providence in settling America had after all opened a grand design to emancipate mankind. Henry Adams began as a connoisseur of political ironies; later he became a sort of reverse millennialist, convinced that science and technology were rushing the planet toward an apocalypse unredeemed by a Day of Judgment. "At the rate of increase of speed and momentum, as calculated on the last fifty years," he wrote in 1901, "the present society must break its damn neck in a definite, but remote, time, not exceeding fifty years more." The United States, like everything else, was finished. In the end Adams too aban-

doned experiment for destiny; but destiny for him was not only manifest but malign. "No one anywhere," he wrote a few weeks before the
outbreak of the First World War, ". . . expects a future."

William James, the philosopher, retained the experimental faith,
abhorring the fatalisms and absolutes implied by "the idol of a national
destiny . . . which for some inscrutable reason it has become infamous
to disbelieve in or refuse." We are instructed, James said, "to be
missionaries of civilization. . . . We must sow our ideals, plant our
order, impose our God. The individual lives are nothing. Our duty and
our destiny call, and civilization must go on. Could there be a more
damning indictment of that whole bloated idol termed 'modern civilization'?" All this had come about too fast "for the older American
nature not to feel the shock." One cannot know what James meant by
"the older American nature"; but he plainly rejected the supposition
that American motives were, by definition, pure; and that the United
States enjoyed a divine immunity to temptation and corruption. Like
the authors of the *Federalist*, James was a realist. "Angelic impulses and
predatory lusts," he precisely wrote, "divide our heart exactly as they
divide the heart of other countries."

So the warfare between realism and messianism, between experiment and destiny, continued to our own day. If some political leaders
were messianists, the perception of America as an experiment conducted by mortals of limited wisdom and power without divine guarantee informed the practical intelligence of others. The second Roosevelt saw life as uncertain and the national destiny as problematic. The
republic was still an experiment and "demands bold, persistent ex-
perimentation. It is common sense to take a method and try it: If it fails,
admit it frankly and try another. But above all, try something." Roosevelt's realism kept American participation in the Second World War
closer to a sense of national interest than of world mission. In a later
time John Kennedy argued that antimessianic case: "We must face the
fact that the United States is neither omnipotent nor omniscient—that
we are only 6 per cent of the world's population—that we cannot
impose our will upon the other 94 per cent of mankind—that we
cannot right every wrong or reverse each adversity—and that therefore
there cannot be an American solution to every world problem." "Before my term has ended," he said in his first annual message, "we shall
have to test anew whether a nation organized and governed such as
ours can endure. The outcome is by no means certain."

This evoked the mood of the Founding Fathers. But the belief in
national righteousness and providential destiny remains strong—a
splendid triumph of dogma over experience. One cannot but feel that
this belief has encouraged our recent excesses in the world and that
the republic has lost much by forgetting what James called "the older

American nature." For messianism is an illusion. No nation is sacred and unique, the United States or any other. All nations are immediate unto God. America, like every country, has interests, real and fictitious; concerns, generous and selfish; motives, honorable and squalid. Providence has not set Americans apart from lesser breeds. We too are part of history's seamless web.

Yet we retain one signal and extraordinary advantage over most nations—an entirely secular advantage, conferred upon us by those quite astonishing Founding Fathers. For they bequeathed us standards by which to set our course and judge our performance—and, since they were exceptional men, the standards have not been rendered obsolete even by the second law of thermodynamics. The Declaration of Independence and the Constitution establish goals, imply commitments, and measure failures. The men who signed the Declaration, said Lincoln, "meant to set up a standard maxim for a free society, which should be familiar to all, and revered by all; constantly looked to, constantly labored for, and even though never perfectly attained, constantly approximated, and thereby constantly spreading and deepening its influence, and augmenting the happiness and value of life to all people of all colors everywhere."

We can take pride in our nation, not as we pretend to a commission from God and a sacred destiny, but as we struggle to fulfill our deepest values in an inscrutable world. As we begin our third century, we may well be entering our golden age. But we would be ill advised to reject the apprehensions of the Founding Fathers. Indeed, a due heed to those ancient anxieties may alone save us in the future. For America remains an experiment. The outcome is by no means certain. Only at our peril can we forget the possibility that the republic will end like Gatsby in Scott Fitzgerald's emblematic fable—Gatsby who had come so long a way and whose "dream must have seemed so close that he could hardly fail to grasp it. He did not know that it was already behind him, somewhere back in that vast obscurity beyond the city, where the dark fields of the republic rolled on under the night.

"Gatsby believed in the green light, the orgastic future that year by year recedes before us. It eluded us then, but that's no matter—tomorrow we will run faster, stretch out our arms farther. . . . And one fine morning—

"So we beat on, boats against the current, borne back ceaselessly into the past."

Acknowledgments: Articles

Acknowledgments: Illustrations

1   Library of Congress
7   Library of Congress
9   Free Library of Philadelphia
18 Library of Congress
19 *Harper's Weekly,* April 17, 1875
21 Culver Pictures, Inc.
24 Library of Congress
34 Mississippi Department of Archives and History
38 By permission of the Houghton Library, Harvard University
49 THE GRANGER COLLECTION, New York
50 THE GRANGER COLLECTION, New York
52 THE GRANGER COLLECTION, New York
55 THE GRANGER COLLECTION, New York
59 Brown Brothers
63 (top) Brown Brothers; (bottom, both) UPI/Bettmann Newsphotos
68 Brown Brothers
75 THE GRANGER COLLECTION, New York
85 The Phillips Collection, Washington, D.C.
86 UPI/Bettmann Newsphotos
94 Culver Pictures, Inc.
96 Culver Pictures, Inc.
98 Brown Brothers
101 Library of Congress
110 Photo by Margaret Bourke-White, *Life* Magazine, © Time Inc.
111 1958 Time Inc.
114 Culver Pictures, Inc.
115 Drawn by Michael Ramus for *American Heritage*
120 New-York Historical Society, Abbot-Lennox Fund, 1972
122 New-York Historical Society
126 UPI/Bettmann Newsphotos
134 Library of Congress
139 Library of Congress
146 THE GRANGER COLLECTION, New York
150 THE GRANGER COLLECTION, New York
153 THE GRANGER COLLECTION, New York
155 THE GRANGER COLLECTION, New York

160   THE GRANGER COLLECTION, New York
164   Jane Addams Memorial Collection. Special Collections, The University
      Library. University of Illinois at Chicago. Photographer: Wallace Kirk-
      land
165   Chicago Historical Society
169   (top and middle) Jane Addams Memorial Collection. Special Collec-
      tions, The University Library. University of Illinois at Chicago. Photog-
      rapher: Wallace Kirkland; (bottom) Chicago *Tribune* Library
175   Chicago Historical Society
183   Daniel Kramer
195   Brown Brothers
203   Official U.S. Navy Photograph
207   Culver Pictures, Inc.
209   New York *Journal*
213   Chicago Historical Society
220   State of Vermont
226   *Leslie's Official History of the Spanish-American War*
231   *Puck,* March 22, 1899
237   Library of Congress
240   Garraty, *Henry Cabot Lodge*
242   Library of Congress
244   The San Francisco *Chronicle*
249   UPI/Bettmann Newsphotos
262   Culver Pictures, Inc.
270   THE GRANGER COLLECTION, New York
276   THE GRANGER COLLECTION, New York
284   UPI/Bettmann Newsphotos
287   THE GRANGER COLLECTION, New York
290   UPI/Bettmann Newsphotos
295   AP/Wide World Photos
302   *Judge,* November, 1929
305   AP/Wide World Photos
306   Culver Pictures, Inc.
308   Collection of Rita and Daniel Fraad
315   Brown Brothers
318   Culver Pictures, Inc.
325   Culver Pictures, Inc.
333   UPI/Bettmann Newsphotos
337   Brown Brothers
340   Evans, in the Columbus *Dispatch,* November, 1938
347   AP/Wide World Photos
358   Memphis Room, Memphis-Shelby County Public Library and Informa-
      tion Center
363   *Progressive Grocer*
367   Judy Sloan/Gamma Liaison
371   Carl Iwaski, *Life* Magazine, © Time, Inc.

376 UPI/Bettmann Newsphotos
379 AP/Wide World Photos
387 UPI/Bettmann Newsphotos
391 Erich Leasing/Magnum
395 from *Herblock's Here and Now* (Simon & Schuster, 1955)
404 The Lyndon Baines Johnson Library, GSA
408 UPI/Bettmann Newsphotos
413 Dick Swanson, *Life* Magazine, © Time, Inc., 1968
414 UPI/Bettmann Newsphotos
420 Marc Riboud/Magnum
421 UPI/Bettmann Newsphotos
422 UPI/Bettmann Newsphotos
426 © Wally McNamee 1986/Woodfin Camp
434 Chicago Historical Society
438 © The Walt Disney Company
443 © The Walt Disney Company

Note: An attempt has been made to obtain permission from all suppliers of
photographs used in this edition. Some sources have not been located,
but permission will be requested from them upon notification to Harper
& Row of their ownership of the material.